FIELDS OF VICTORY

Vijayanagara and the Course of Intensification

Kathleen D. Morrison

Number 53
Contributions of the University of California
Archaeological Research Facility
Berkeley

Library of Congress Catolog Card Number 95-78982
ISBN 1-882744-04-7
© 1995 by the Regents of the University of California
Archaeological Research Facility
University of California at Berkeley

Printed in the United States of America.

All rights reserved. No part of this publication may be reproduced or transmitted in any form or by any means, electronic or mechanical, including photocopy, recording, or any information storage or retrieval system, without written permission from the publisher.

Contents

List of Figures v

List of Tables vi

Acknowledgements vii

Introduction 1

1 Agricultural Intensification 3
    Intensification of Production: Definitions 6
    The Boserup Model: Do We Know the Course of Intensification? 6
    Beyond Boserup: Causes of intensification in Complex Urban Societies 8
    The Process: Diversity and the Courses of Intensification 10
    Vijayanagara as a Case Study 13

2 Agricultural Production in the Vijayanagara Region 14
    Agriculture and the Archaeological Record 14
    The Vijayanagara Region: Climate, Soils, and Topography 15
    Agricultural Production: Categories 21
    Agricultural Facilities 24
    Wet, Dry, and Wet-cum-Dry 30

3 Vijayanagara Agriculture in Context 31
    South India: Language and Religion 31
    Pre-Vijayanagara Settlements 32
    Polity and Economy: Models 40
    Agriculture in the Vijayanagara Period: Background 46
    The Vijayanagara Metropolitan Region 51
    Previous Archaeological Research at Vijayanagara 52

4 The Vijayanagara Metropolitan Survey 55
    Methodological Issues 55
    The Vijayanagara Metropolitan Survey 57
    Surveyed Areas and the Layout of the City 60
    Fortification 63
    Settlement 66
    Roadways 71
    Religious Architecture 79
    Wells and Cisterns 82
    Nonagricultural Production 85
    Agricultural Features 87

5 Archaeological Patterns of Land Use 98
    Agricultural Land Use 100

6 The Historical Record 110

    Literary Sources 110
    Foreign Accounts 111
    Inscriptions 116
    Analysis 120
    Qualitative Analysis 128
    Discussion 133

7 Identifying Land Use: Pollen and Charcoal 135
    Pollen Analysis 135
    Pollen Analysis and Agriculture 138
    Pollen Analysis from the Vijayanagara Region 139
    Charcoal Analysis 152
    Charcoal Analysis from the Vijayanagara Region 154
    Discussion 157

8 Conclusion: Intensification at Vijayanagara 159
    Intensity 159
    The Course of Intensification 161
    Discussion: Independent Lines of Evidence 166
    Discussion: Boserup and the Course of Vijayanagara Intensification 166
    Conclusion: The Study 167

Appendix 1 List of Recorded Sites in Blocks O, S, and T **169**

Appendix 2 Vegetation **173**

References Cited **183**

List of Figures

2.1 Topographic zones of southern India..16
2.2 Average annual rainfall, southern India..16
2.3 Mean daily minimum and maximum temperatures by month, Bellary District...................................20
2.4 Monthly rainfall AD 1850-1870, Bellary District..20
2.5 Annual rainfall: variation about the mean between AD 1850 and 1870, Bellary District...................21
2.6 Cross section of reservoir embankment..27
2.7 Four Vijayanagara-period sluice gates 28
3.1 Southern India in the Vijayanagara period, with locations of major settlements and rivers...............39
3.2 The region around the city of Vijayanagara 52
4.1 The Vijayanagara Metropolitan Region..58
4.2 Blocks N, O, S, and T with locations of recorded sites..61
4.3 "Horse Stones," (VMS-158) lying outside city walls, Block S 65
4.4 Heavily disturbed Vijayanagara-period settlement (Venkatapuram), VMS-2, Block O 68
4.5 Northern gateway complex of the Kamalapuram fort (VMS-256) and associated temple (VMS-257)...........70
4.6 Distribution of Vijayanagara-period settlements around the city of Vijayanagara..............................72
4.7 Columned structure under construction located along canal roadway (VMS-79), Block O 73
4.8 Road segment leading to Nageshwara temple, VMS-82 (VMS-81), Block O 74
4.9 Roadway complex with cobbled surface flanked by walls and platforms and a small temple (VMS-183), Block S 76
4.10 Two-level platform associated with roadway VMS-183 (VMS-186), Block S 77
4.11 Opening in the city wall north of VMS-183. The cobbled pathway is lined with boulders, walls, and sculptures (VMS-182), Block S..78
4.12 Hill complex containing terraces, temple, and gateway (VMS-83) above large walled spring (VMS-84), Block O...81
4.13 Late Vijayanagara *Vaisnavite* temple complex (VMS-142), Block S 82
4.14 Temple complex with formal shrine, gate platforms, and mandapa surrounded by informal structures (VMS-164), Block S 83
4.15 Temple located along roadway (VMS-173), Block S 84
4.16 Islamic-style tomb, (VMS-297), Block T 85
4.17 Elaborate step well with carved *Nandi* figures located along roadway (VMS-112), Block O 86
4.18 Small well with stepped masonry sides (VMS-175), Block S 86
4.19 Step well built into natural rock outcrop (VMS-210), Block S 87
4.20 Masonry-lined spring (VMS-136), Block S 88
4.21 Furnace/working platform with kiln debris and superimposed shrine (VMS-121), Block S 89
4.22 Scatter of iron slag, iron, and overfired brick (VMS-179), Block S 90
4.23 Heavily disturbed reservoir embankment (VMS-72) Block O 91
4.24 Masonry-edged earthen embankment (VMS-108), Block O 92
4.25 Check-dams and channel (VMS-100), Block O..93
4.26 Spring with masonry edges (VMS-99), Block O 92
4.27 Small embankment without outlets (VMS-138), Block S 95
4.28 Integrated system containing terraces (VMS-131) and a small reservoir (VMS-226), Block S..........96
5.1 The Vijayanagara Metropolitan Region: zones of land use 101
5.2 Selected reservoirs from the Daroji Valley 105
6.1 Districts of the state of Karnataka 121
6.2 Major categories of first gift noted in inscriptions, all districts 122
6.3 Inscription subject: both gifts (all districts)..122

6.4 Number of inscriptions by year, all districts...123
6.5 Number of inscriptions by year for each district..124
6.6 Temporal distribution of inscriptions by donor..125
6.7 Temporal distribution of inscriptions by donee..126
6.8 Temporal distribution of inscriptions by first gift..127
6.9 Temporal distribution of land grants by district..129
6.10 Temporal distribution of irrigated land grants by district 130
6.11 Provenience of coded inscriptions...131
6.12 Canal construction and maintenance, all districts..132
6.13 Reservoir construction, all districts..133
6.14 Temporal distribution of reservoir construction by district...138
7.1 VMS-231, the Kamalapuram Kere. Map of water depths and core locations................................140
7.2 Kamalapuram Kere, cores 1-3 stratigraphy..143
7.3 Vegetation groups: percentage...145
7.4 Vegetation groups: concentration...145
7.5 Grasses, aquatic, and herbaceous plants: percentage...148
7.6 Grasses, aquatic, and herbaceous plants: concentration 149
7.7 Aquatic plants: concentration 149
7.8 Trees: percentage 150
7.9 Trees: concentration 150
7.10 Non-grass cultivated plants: percentage..151
7.11 Non-grass cultivated plants: concentration 151
7.12 Charcoal concentrations by count and area...157
8.1 Temporal distribution of the construction of agricultural facilities, all districts 163
8.2 Temporal distribution of the construction and maintenance of agricultural facilities recorded in published inscriptions, Bellary District 163

List of Tables

2.1 Dominant tree species in the *Albizia-amara-Acacia* series..18
2.2 Dominant shrub species in the *Albizia-amara-Acacia* series..18
2.3 Dominant herb species in the *Albizia-amara-Acacia* series..19
2.4 Dominant species associated with reservoirs...19
3.1 Dynastic list of Vijayanagara rulers...38
5.1 Agricultural features of surveyed blocks O, S, T, and from Block N, by type 102
6.1 Plants identified by Paes and Nuniz in the vicinity of Vijayanagara 116
6.2 Inscriptional data base reference codes 117
7.1 Radiocarbon dates from Kamalapuram core 1. Dates are uncalibrated..143
7.2 Charcoal in 1KP: Level, number of charcoal particles, minimum, maximum, mean, and standard deviation of area. 156

Acknowledgements

So many people have contributed to this work that it is not possible to adequately convey my appreciation or to thank them all. However, I would like to thank the Government of India and the Archaeological Survey of India for granting research permission, and the American Institute of Indian Studies (AIIS) for facilitating this research and for their continuing efforts on my behalf. Dr. Pradeep R. Mehendiratta, the director of the AIIS, has provided invaluable help through the years I worked in India as an AIIS fellow and during my tenure as a Junior Fellow. I thank also Mr. M. D. Bhandare, director of the Poona AIIS office, and Mr. L. S. Suri, Mrs. Soundara Raghavan, and all the other staff of the AIIS. My work in Karnataka would not have been possible without the generous assistance of the Directorate of Archaeology and Museums, Government of Karnataka. The current director, Dr. D. V. Devaraj, and the former director, Dr. M. S. Nagaraja Rao, both extended the hospitality of the department. Special thanks to Dr. C. S. Patil and to Balasubramanya. I would like to thank both the former and current directors of Deccan College, Drs. Dhavalikar and Misra, and Drs. Kajale, Paddayya, Deotare, and the rest of the archaeology faculty and students for extending the hospitality of the college in 1990. At the French Institute, Pondicherry, invaluable assistance was given by Drs. Caratini, Tissot, and George, and Ms. K. Anupama. Other assistance in India was provided by the Department of Instrumentation Science, Poona University, as well as Irrigation Department officials from the Kamalapuram and Kampli offices, Karnataka.

I would also like to acknowledge financial support from a National Science Foundation Graduate Fellowship (1984-1988), an American Institute of Indian Studies Junior Research fellowship (1989-1990), a Society for Women Geographers Fellowship (1991-1992), and grants from the Lowie Fund of the University of California, Berkeley. The Vijayanagara Metropolitan Survey was supported by several agencies, including the National Geographic Society, the Wenner-Gren Foundation, the Smithsonian Foreign Currency Program, and by a grant from the Research and Training Revolving Fund, University of Hawai'i. Additional support from the Social Science Research Institute, University of Hawai'i allowed time for manuscript revisions.

I extend my thanks to members of the survey team: Shinu Abraham, Rob Brubaker, Meenakshi Chellam, Mark Lycett, Girish M., Bernard Means, Rukshana Nandi, Somphong Rattanaphan, Carla Sinopoli, Richa Thaladiyal, Nilam Thatte, and all the others who joined us on the outcrops and in the banana fields. Thanks also to John Fritz, George Michell, Anna Dallapiccola, Richard Blurton, Phil

Wagoner, Ben Marsh, Anila Verghese, Sughanda, Asim Krishna Das, and Sriniwas.

Special thanks to my friend and collaborator, Carla Sinopoli, co-director of the Vijayanagara Metropolitan Survey. I am also grateful to Ruth Tringham, Pat Kirch, Roger Byrne, the late George Dales, Meg Conkey, Les Rowntree, Alison Wylie, and Eric Edlund. Finally, I acknowledge the constant inspiration of my family, most especially of my husband, Mark Lycett, who has contributed greatly to this work at every stage, from the field to the final product.

Introduction

> Production is the totality of operations aimed at procuring for a society the material means of existence...In the end we see that all production is a twofold act subject to the technical norms of a certain relationship between men and nature and to the social norms governing the relations between men in their use of the factors of production. (Godelier 1978a:71)

VIJAYANAGARA, THE "CITY OF VICTORY," was the capital city of an expansive empire which lay claim to large tracts of land in southern India between the fourteenth and seventeenth centuries A.D. For the approximately two hundred years of its existence, Vijayanagara was not merely a political center, it was also a population center and a locus of production, trade, and consumption. Today this great city lies abandoned and although there has been a continuous record of human settlement in the region, it was not until the twentieth century that large settlements again developed in this area. The dry interior districts of northern Karnataka present special challenges to agricultural production, including shallow soils, rocky slopes, and a low and highly variable rainfall regime. The success of the city depended on meeting these challenges. There would be no city, then, and perhaps no empire without the diverse repertoire of agricultural strategies practiced by Vijayanagara food producers, without "fields of victory."

Agricultural production is, however, not just a base upon which political and social structures are built. The organization of agricultural production is itself integrally connected to demography, ecology, and culture. This organization is flexible, and the courses and causes of its change are a fundamental analytical concern of this work. Agricultural production provides an excellent example of what Godelier refers to as a "twofold act," lying as it does at an intersection between ecological and social forces, broadly conceived.

Chapter 1 reviews the concept of productive intensification, with particular focus on the roles accorded to intensification in archaeological research and on the overall perspectives by which such discussions of economic processes are structured. The process of intensification itself is considered next, suggesting that an understanding of the course of change is an essential prerequisite for coming to terms with competing models of cause. The remainder of the book is devoted to the examination of one such study—the path of agricultural change in and around the city of Vijayanagara.

The second chapter introduces the agricultural landscape of the study area. This landscape consists both of physical features of the environment and of a repertoire of crops, facilities, and techniques of production.

Chapter 3 presents geographical, archaeological, and historical background on the southern Deccan and Karnatak Plateau regions. This chapter reviews the major themes in Vijayanagara historiography and their implications for the definition of archaeological research problems and for archaeological analysis. The sociopolitical context of

Vijayanagara agricultural production, particularly the important mechanism of temple investment in agriculture, is introduced.

The fourth chapter introduces the Vijayanagara Metropolitan Survey, a program of systematic regional survey in the hinterland of the city of Vijayanagara. The aims of the survey, sampling strategies, recording procedures, and its relationship to archaeological and architectural research in the city itself are discussed. This chapter also summarizes some of the results of the survey, with special emphasis on the content and distribution of settlement, transportation, and agricultural facilities.

Chapter 5 discusses general patterns of land use, settlement, and transport identified through survey. Some preliminary interpretations relating to zonation, patterns of growth and decline, and scalar and typological variation in land use are suggested.

A review of the corpus of contemporary texts relating to Vijayanagara opens the sixth chapter. The brief descriptive accounts of the city and region presented by European and Islamic travellers, traders, and ambassadors are discussed in light of what they reveal about land use, labor, and political control. Stone and copper inscriptions, usually associated with temples, constitute the other major corpus of historical material, essential to understanding the nature of agricultural investment. A quantitative study of published inscriptions is presented in order to document the early sixteenth-century expansion of reservoir and canal construction.

Chapter 7 presents the results of analyses of Vijayanagara vegetation. After a brief introduction to some methodological issues in pollen and charcoal analysis from lacustrine sediments, the sampling program from the Kamalapuram Kere, a Vijayanagara-period reservoir, is described. The results of pollen and charcoal analysis are discussed in terms of vegetation and fire history and the hydraulic regime of the reservoir.

The final chapter returns to the issue of productive intensification, drawing together the evidence from chapters 4 through 7. The overall course of Vijayanagara agricultural intensification is charted, and discussed in view of more general models of change.

1

Agricultural Intensification

AGRICULTURAL LANDSCAPES represent significantly new forms of environments, environments that are both natural and artifactual, that result from both the noncultural elements of the landscape and the intended and unintended consequences of human action. If then, we consider agricultural systems as ecosystems (Grigg 1982:68), they are ecosystems with a difference. Human agricultural strategies lie at an intersection between the ecological constraints of soil, climate, crop requirements, and other "natural" forces and such cultural demands as the structure of domestic life, social obligations, political coercion, and transportation.

In the following study it is argued that in order to understand the organization of agricultural economies and the nature of agricultural change, it is necessary to situate agricultural production within this intersection. This study traces the path or course of productive intensification in one specific region over time. Archaeological conceptions of productive intensification underlie much debate about subsistence change and about the development of surplus production and social complexity. Whether intensification of production is viewed as a response to environmental, demographic, social, or political forces, or as a natural and inevitable outcome of the human condition, archaeologists and others have recognized the importance of intensification for understanding change in productive systems. Many arguments regarding the causes and consequences of productive intensification among agriculturalists focus exclusively on either social or environmental factors, the result of a ping-pong history of reaction against existing scholarship. However, I examine here not so much the causes of agricultural intensification in the study area as the route or path of that change and its implications for the material record.

The following chapters describe the agricultural landscape and its changing structure and content in the region surrounding the large pre-Colonial city of Vijayanagara in southern India. Vijayanagara was the political capital of an empire that controlled much of southern India between approximately A.D. 1330 and 1650. An influx of population in the early fourteenth century dramatically modified the region around the city, transforming it from a sparsely settled and politically peripheral area into one of the largest cities in South Asia. Around the beginning of the sixteenth century, major population movements appear to have occurred throughout southern India (discussed below, see also Breckenridge 1985; Stein 1980, 1989) with concomitant expansions in Vijayanagara militarism, agricultural investment, and construction of monumental architecture. The shift of the capital to the south after a military defeat in A.D. 1565 entailed an equally dramatic population shift away from the Vijayanagara region, a trend that was not reversed until the construction of a major dam in the 1950s. This history makes the Vijayanagara region an excellent setting for investigating proposals regarding the causes, courses, and archaeological consequences of agricultural intensification.

Methodological issues are fundamental in any analysis of past intensification. How can intensification be recognized? Assigning meaning to patterns evident in the archaeological record is a problem of all archaeological studies, but studies of past agriculture can be particularly difficult, given its broad spatial extent and often ephemeral material remains. My approach in this work is to employ multiple independent lines of evidence that inform on agricultural organization and practice across a large scale. These three lines of evidence can be broadly classified as archaeological, historical, and botanical. Each source of information presents its own methodological challenges and interpretive potentials and is discussed separately below.

AGRICULTURAL INTENSIFICATION AND CHANGING SUBSISTENCE

Production—the making, constructing, or creating actions of human beings—is a major focus of investigation of the archaeological record, with subsistence production among its most basic forms. Anthropologists have long been intrigued by the causes and consequences of subsistence change, focussing on the more dramatic transformations such as the shift from one "mode" of subsistence to another, as in the change from hunting and gathering to farming. This typological focus may be misplaced, however, in its implication that forms of subsistence can be characterized by a single strategy. The category of farming, for instance, contains a great deal of variability, and the transition by farmers from one set of productive strategies to another may also constitute a dramatic change in subsistence. One such transition is the process known as agricultural intensification. While the debate on the causes of intensification is well developed (Morrison 1994), relatively little attention has been paid to the process or course of change itself. In this study, I examine the courses of agricultural intensification and the relationships of this process of change in productive strategies to ecological, ritual, and socio-political constraints on producers.

CONCEIVING ECONOMY AND PRODUCTION

In anthropological analysis, productive activities are usually classified under the heading of economy, and, as such, much of the debate on the causes and nature of change in production stems from varying conceptions of the economic. These conceptions range from universalistic ones that argue for the existence of cross-culturally valid principles of economic behavior to particularistic ones, in which the unity of cultural practice is stressed as is the "embeddedness" (Polanyi 1957) of economic activities in other cultural arenas. This debate becomes more concrete when considering Vijayanagara agricultural production. Can agriculture be considered separately from political organization, from settlement, transportation, or social organization? Clearly it cannot. Are processes such as intensification implicated in changing forms of Vijayanagara agriculture analytically isolable? I think they are. We are confronted, then, with the problem of defining, recognizing, isolating, and understanding a process on the basis of an archaeological sequence. This is the central problem of this book, and in order to begin we need to first consider the definition of intensification and its place in production.

Studying Production: Substantivist-Formalist Legacies

One legacy of the substantivist position in economic anthropology (e.g. Bohannon and Dalton 1962; Dalton 1961, 1969; Firth 1956; Godelier 1978a; Herskovits 1952; Polanyi 1957), which stressed the nonexistence of a discrete economic sphere in societies outside the modern world (in either time or space), is the existence of an implicit divide between the study of the industrial west and the remainder of the world. Thus, advocates of the substantive position create a divide between different forms (types, modes) of society (or production), with "modern" or "western" societies composed of economically motivated, independent, and rational individuals, and "premodern" or "nonwestern" societies as constituting integral, communal, and religiously or ideologically motivated corporate groups (cf. Kohl 1987:5).

Within India, orientalist discourse (Said 1979) has stressed this distinction as essentially "Indian," ascribing deviations from this ideal as the consequence of outside influences (Inden 1990). Louis Dumont, influential scholar of the caste system, writes of Indian village society:

> One can say that just as religion in a way encompasses politics, so politics encompasses economics with itself. The difference is that the politico-economic domain is separated, named, in a subordinate position as against religion, while economics remains undifferentiated within politics. (Dumont 1980:165)

Inden comments (1990:153) on this statement that "when some sort of autonomous economic activity is uncovered at the ideological 'level,' it is off-loaded, following Weber, on to the religions such as Jainism that are, in Dumont's consideration, not essentially Indian, that is, Hindu (1980:166)." As we shall see in chapter 3, the Vijayanagara empire has often been exemplified by scholars as quintessentially Hindu (e.g. Saletore 1982), an expression of Indian (Hindu) nationalism against the Muslim invaders of the north (Krishnaswami Ayyangar 1991 [1921]). Even where this notion has been submerged, the wholeness or integration of ideology, politics, and economics into a traditional sphere has remained as a guiding assumption of historical scholarship.

Lansing (1991) makes a similar point in his analysis of Balinese water temples. Bali has been taken as an example of "Oriental Despotism" (Geertz 1980:45; Marx 1969; Wittfogel 1957) in which strong centralized control over irrigation networks was exercised. Geertz (1980) effectively challenged the Oriental Despotism model, showing that kings had virtually no effective managerial control over irrigation. Lansing has demonstrated that, in fact, some supralocal coordination of irrigation does take place, with religious institutions (water temples) playing an important role in decision making with regard to the timing and allocation of water. He suggests that contemporary social theory, which is based on the premise of a fundamental distinction between "modernism" and its opposite, finds no place for such a "nonmodern" system, in which control over certain economic forces are *not* "embedded" in society as a whole (1991). This point is extremely important for the following consideration of Vijayanagara agricultural production, where agricultural decision making appears to have been carried out by a variety of institutions, groups, and individuals, but not (directly) by political leaders (Morrison and Sinopoli 1992, and below). Certainly classifying Vijayanagara agricultural production as "premodern" provides little illumination into its structure and change.

In contrast to such integral (Morrison 1994) approaches, which view economic activities as epiphenomena of some overarching cultural structure, formal economic analyses (cf. Earle and Christiansen 1980; Smith and Winterhalder 1992; Winterhalder and Smith 1981; see also Martin 1983), linked to a definition of economies as "rational" in terms derived from studies of modern market economies, posit an analytical isolation between economic and other (political, social, ecological) aspects of society. Thus, in such analyses economic strategies can be clearly differentiated from political and social concerns, and further, their logic can be assumed a priori to relate to the maximal, minimal, or optimal use of effort and calories (for a fuller discussion see Keene 1983; Martin 1983; D. Clarke 1972; and Morrison 1994). The use of formal models may not strictly require adherence to an economic model of communities as diversified firms (Earle 1980:14) rationally selecting the optimal mix of subsistence options (Green 1980), but it does promote a segmented and static conception of subsistence strategies and economic organization. Models such as Brookfield's (1972) and others that employ production functions as graphical devices (Friedman 1979; Renfrew 1982; Sachs 1966) imply that technological change occurs primarily because of input-output balances and that intensification is primarily a technological change (see also Glassow 1978:40). Organizational changes are rather difficult to graph, and thus have low visibility in the "well-structured" solution (Johnson 1980:20) to the problem of intensification. This perspective has had a great influence on the study of intensification and lies behind most of the explicit definitional discussion of intensification. However, as discussed below, in their quest for analytical rigor (cf. Johnson 1980:20) formalist analyses of intensification have promoted such simplified pictures of agricultural production that they have little credibility when dealing with the complex problems and opportunities facing agriculturalists and other producers in the context of highly differentiated urban societies (see also Kohl 1987:5).

Intensification of Production: Definitions

The concept of intensification requires reference to a constant. That is, the difference between intensification and simple increase involves the introduction of a second variable; the difference is analogous to the difference between *concentration* and *amount*. Intensification of production refers to an increase in productive output per unit of land or labor (or some other fixed quantity) (Boserup 1965:43-44; Kaiser and Voytek 1983:329; Tringham and Krstic 1990). This increase may be achieved in a number of ways. In the archaeological literature, the variable held constant almost always refers to land in reference to agriculture (getting more out of a given area) and to labor in studies of craft production (increasing efficiency of production). Alternate situations, such as technological intensification in which both land and labor are held constant while capital inputs are increased, as in industrialized agriculture, are rarely discussed (but see Brookfield 1984). Thus, what we term intensification may be quite different, depending on whether the variable held constant is space, labor, or technology.

The multivariate nature of intensification is of considerable importance, serving to distinguish it from "mere" expansion or increase. A temporal dimension is generally also implicit in conceptions of intensification. Productive activities take place within definite temporal parameters such as a growing season, and archaeologists may examine long-term temporal trends in strategies of intensification. Thus, we can also speak of courses or paths of intensification. Intensification, then, must be viewed as a process, consisting of multiple potential strategies, rather than as an event. A consequence of this view, discussed below, is that there may also be multiple paths or courses of intensification rather than a single route from long to short fallows.

There has been surprisingly little attention paid to definition, given the voluminous literature on intensification (but see Netting 1993:271). The seminal definition of Brookfield is worth citing at length, given his influence on later work (e.g., Kirch 1994; Renfrew 1982:265). He writes (1972:31):

> Strictly defined, intensification of production describes the addition of inputs up to the economic margin, and is logically linked to the concept of efficiency through consideration of marginal and average productivity obtained by such additional inputs. In regard to land, or to any natural resource complex, intensification must be measured by inputs only of capital, labor, and skills against constant land. The primary purpose of intensification is the substitution of these inputs for land, so as to gain more production from a given area, use it more frequently, and hence make possible a greater concentration of production.

The Boserup Model: Do We Know the Course of Intensification?

The model of population growth and agricultural intensification set forth by the Danish economist Ester Boserup (1965, 1981, 1990) has been the most influential formulation of the problem in this century. Her model has both the appeal and limitations associated with parsimonious, general, and comprehensive views of structure and of change (cf. Netting 1977:72). Boserup's vision of intensification engendered fierce debate in anthropology during the 1960s and 1970s (Morrison 1994), centered around the cause or causes of intensification. The debate has largely come to an end although, as in many anthropological battles, no clear resolution was ever achieved. I believe that one of the reasons theoretical ferment surrounding the concept of intensification has died down considerably in recent years is that while perspectives on cause have become polarized, other aspects of the Boserup model have become archaeological dogma. These unexamined aspects include assumptions about the unilinear course of intensification and about the utility of cropping frequency as an adequate measure of intensification. It is my contention that the debates about cause are stalled precisely because of these unexamined assumptions about the nature and course of intensification. I suggest that it is necessary to come to an adequate understanding of the process of intensification in order to understand the multiplicity of causes and the conditions under which they operate.

Ironically, although Boserup's focus on population has engendered the fiercest attacks, this aspect of the model has the most empirical support. Although I have argued (Morrison 1994) that in this view of change, population is too simply conceived as a proximate cause of economic change, it is clear that demography is important in the structure of and changes in agricultural production. Other aspects of Boserup's model—its technological associations and its unilineal sequence of cropping intensity—have been subject to much less criticism, even though they are actually based on much shakier empirical ground. I suggest that uncritical acceptance of these aspects has hindered archaeological studies of intensification.

Boserup and Intensification: An Overview

Boserup's model of population as an *independent* variable driving intensification of agricultural production turned the earlier Malthusian formulation "on its head" (Rubin 1972:36). While Malthus saw land, and particularly arable soils, as limiting factors to increases in production (production that eventually would be outstripped by a growing population) (Malthus 1872; Rubin 1972:36), Boserup turned the production-population pair around. She asserted that the role of an increasing population was as a sort of "motor" driving technological (in a broad sense) changes in land use along an extensive-intensive continuum. Population is assumed to be an independent variable (Boserup 1965:11; Grigg 1982:37), not a consequence of food supply, an assertion that drew heavy criticism from a number of different perspectives (Cowgill 1975a; Brown and Podolefsky 1976:212; Sanders 1972:147; Bender 1978, 1981, 1985; Friedman and Rowlands 1978; Blanton 1975; Kowalewski 1980; and see Turner, Hanham, and Portararo 1977). By population, Boserup apparently refers to sheer numbers of people, though in her second book (198:66, see also Boserup 1990) she does consider the issue of population distribution (Carneiro 1970; Binford 1968; Flannery 1969; see also Von Thunen 1966; Sanders and Santley 1983). Just what aspect of population constitutes an independent variable in intensification? Both advocates and detractors of a Boserupian approach seem to refer either to population size or to density when speaking of population when, in fact, in age-structured populations such as human beings (Charlesworth 1980), the distributions of various age groups and the nature of the domestic cycle (Netting, Wilk, and Arnould 1984; Wilk 1989) impinge directly on the organization of labor in production. Thus, population dynamics cannot be considered to be independent of the organization of labor and consumption.

By far the most contested aspect of Boserup's model of intensification is that of the causal efficacy of population in driving the process. The view of population as a causal agent rests on a number of related assumptions. First, producers are assumed to exert the minimum effort possible to meet their needs—the Law of Least Effort (Boserup 1965; Zipf 1949). Thus, the most labor extensive regime possible will always be employed. Second, there are diminishing returns to labor (declining efficiency) with increasingly intensive modes of agricultural production (Boserup 1965:28-34). The disadvantages, then, of intensive agriculture—increased labor inputs and declining efficiency of that labor—ensure in this formulation that such modes of production will be adopted only when strictly necessary.

There are a number of difficulties with the Law of Least Effort. It assumes that producers will universally maximize leisure rather than labor (Grigg 1982:37), presupposing the existence of a valid cross-cultural definition of effort (Bronson 1972:199), and of a tradeoff between labor and leisure (de Vries 1972:47). Bender (1978:218) notes the essential ethnocentrism of the Law of Least Effort, based as it is on western notions of labor and work as belonging to a discrete and uniquely "economic" sphere. Work expended in agricultural production cannot always be neatly divided up into subsistence and social components, or production for use as entirely distinct from social or other production (Brookfield 1972:37-38; see also Godelier 1978a; Ruyle 1987). The Law of Least Effort is also explicitly ahistorical. That is, the amount and forms of labor inputs involved in different agricultural strategies may be directly contingent on past efforts. Production of crops on terraced hillsides involves differing degrees of effort depending on whether terrace walls need to be built, already exist, or are in need of repair. Decisions regarding work take place within a historically and situationally specific context. Thus, Lansing refers to the highly modified Balinese agricultural landscape as the product of "congealed labor" of cultivators' forbears (1991:12, after Marx). Decisions about labor, then, can be transformative, creating new contexts which must thereafter be taken into account. In the case of Vijayanagara, landscape modification was extensive and included both intentional and unintentional changes in vegetation, the distribution, structure, and fertility of soil, and water runoff. The construction of agricultural facilities, burning, clearing of vegetation, livestock grazing, quarrying, and construction all served to create through time new landscapes and new contexts for production.

The assumption that increasingly intensive agricultural production necessarily leads to declining marginal returns has been empirically challenged. This issue cannot be completely separated from a consideration of Boserup's operationalization of agricultural intensity in terms of cropping frequency (1965:15-18; 1981:23), since the empirical support marshalled by Boserup (1965:43-48) is intended to demonstrate the labor-efficiency of long fallow swidden over shorter fallow systems. Boserup's contention of declining marginal returns seems to hold for many regions and many crops, but the specific conditions of wet rice (paddy) cultivation appear to violate the assumed inverse relationship between intensity and efficiency (Conelley 1992:205; Hanks 1972:64-66; Nakana 1980:61; W. Clarke 1985:868) up to a certain point (Geertz 1963; see also Waddell 1972). Additional empirical studies of labor efficiency will eventually make it clear if wet rice is simply an energetic anomaly or if the widely accepted view that intensive agriculture promotes declining marginal returns (a fundamental assumption for all formal models of intensification, Morrison 1994a) must be reevaluated. In the Vijayanagara region, sorghum and other millets were among the major food crops, but rice was also important and was highly valued. Thus, the relative efficiency and security (see below) of wet rice must be weighed against its labor demands, and the possibility that a course of intensification incorporating paddy rice might be quite distinctive must be carefully considered.

Boserup also discusses the association of classes of agricultural tools with cropping regimes (1965:23-27). In general, she contends that tool types, if not specific forms, are determined by the prevailing agricultural practice and that technological change is thus also tied to population growth. For example, short fallow farming creates a "compelling" need for plows, while forest fallow requires only digging sticks and axes (Boserup 1965:24-25). Thus, Boserup posits a course of technological progress along a path of increased complexity (e.g. Sherratt 1973:427), counterbalancing (but only temporarily) diminishing returns. Bray (1986), among others (e.g. Bronson 1975:25-26), has challenged this unilineal view of technological change, noting that in fact the most intensive and organizationally complex agricultural systems (such as paddy rice cultivation) may use very simple tools. Further, a single tool assemblage can be used in the context of many different forms of production. Consideration of technology in intensification is of particular importance to archaeologists, who often make inferences about productive strategies based on the material evidence of tools.

Both the unilineal and monolithic character of Boserup's model are evident in her operational definition of intensification in terms of frequency of cropping (1965:15-18; 1981:23). This definition has much to recommend it over the more usual models of land use set forth by economists in that it embraces such disparate agricultural practices as swidden and multicropping into a single analytic model, but the definition tends to gloss over the considerable diversity apparent in productive strategies, both synchronically and diachronically, and in strategies of intensification. The frequency of cropping becomes a *de facto* measure of progress along a single route of intensification. Although Boserup does discuss the coexistence of different cultivation systems (1965:56-64), this coexistence is seen as reflecting a sort of evolutionary lag. That is, the diversity is said to be more apparent than real, not reflecting differing adaptations or adjustments but only the misleading result of considering an artificial slice of time along the route of increased cropping frequency (1965:56-59). In this volume, I directly challenge this view that diversity in agricultural strategies is somehow only a shadow of an evolutionary process. Instead, following Colson (1979), I argue that agriculturalists may actively seek to maintain diversity in productive strategies and that diversification may itself be an aspect of the course of intensification (cf. Kaiser and Voytek 1983).

BEYOND BOSERUP: CAUSES OF INTENSIFICATION IN COMPLEX URBAN SOCIETIES

Cities, with their dense and clustered concentrations of people, present special challenges for agriculture and animal husbandry. Given the prior existence of constraints on mobility that keep people in or near cities, such population aggregations almost by definition require intensive forms of agricultural production. More than this, however, expanding urban populations have to be considered in the same context as any expanding population facing severe mobility constraints largely structured by the costs of transportation (see below). Nonetheless, the causes of intensification in urban contexts need not be viewed in a simplistic way, as direct pressures and responses. We must examine the possibility that different variables may come into play in the process of intensification at different times. Further, while demographic factors may represent an ultimate (and partial) cause of intensification, they may be mediated by a number of more proximate variables.

Two such mediating factors may be broadly classified into the categories of mobility constraints and sociopolitical structure. The first extends consideration of population density (cf. Boserup 1981) to include more specific geographic constraints and attractions. Carneiro's circumscription model (1970) postulates that intensification takes place due to mobility constraints and resultant population pressure on a restricted land base. What Zvelebil (1986:9) refers to as the second generation population models (Binford 1983; Newell 1984; Wobst 1974) incorporate similar notions of population packing, and of "pseudo-density" (Bronson 1975:40-41) caused by small- or medium-scale locational constraints, irrespective of larger-scale population levels. Such models take a step away from the "naive demographic" (Bronson 1975:33) model in recognizing the importance of mobility and transport costs (Sanders and Santley 1983; Sutton 1985); the existence of multiple productive options, including abandonment (Stone 1993b); the implications of unequal access to resources and production opportunities; and the impact of productive strategies themselves in shaping responses to changing conditions. Von Thunen's model of the "isolated state" (1966) stressed the importance of proximity to markets, transport costs, and perishability in influencing intensity of cultivation and choice of crops in an urban landscape (see also Chisholm 1968; Rawski 1972). Bronson (1975:43) adds land values and produce prices to the equation.

Clearly, the structure of cities as clustered aggregations of food consumers (some of whom are also producers) presents an extreme form of locational constraint. Transportation, perishability, the distribution of land of different productive potentials, the size and structure of the consuming population, the organization of markets, fairs, taxes, and other forms of produce disposition, and the structure of access to land and other resources all create special constraints on, and opportunities for, agriculturalists. It would be a mistake, however, to simply view cities as unchanging points on a landscape, since they are themselves partly structured by the organization of food production and can change in response to changes in productive forms and strategies.

Spatial concerns must be balanced by a consideration of social and political forces. For example, in addition to the obvious locational constraints presented by island settings, Kirch's discussion (1984, 1985) of agricultural intensification in Polynesia incorporates demographic, political, and social dynamics. Contrary to both the single-factor Boserupian and "political economy" models (Kirch 1985:449, discussed below), Kirch (1984:164) describes a multicausal, hierarchical relation (see also Earle 1978, 1980; Kirch 1977, 1992) in which chiefly demands for surplus are seen as the proximate and population growth as the ultimate cause of intensification (see also Brumfiel and Earle 1987). Others would prefer to dispense with demographic variables altogether, giving elite demands for produce causal priority in promoting intensification (see discussion in Morrison 1994). Netting (1993:283), on the other hand, has questioned whether or not coercion has ever been an effective cause of agricultural intensification. This debate may best be settled empirically through careful case studies. As discussed below, Vijayanagara political elites appear to have employed both coercion and incentives in order to expand production, with scattered references in the historical literature to enforced cultivation (e.g. Karashima 1992:46) and many more to tax incentives (chapter 6) for clearing new land, establishing agricultural settlements, and constructing agricultural facilities.

Cities and towns are excellent examples of loci in which political and economic elites and competing and cooperating groups of producers and consumers may actively seek to structure agricultural activities (cf. Grigg 1982:41-42). Indeed, urban and periurban areas merit special consideration as loci of intensification, for the demands of cities have been integral in shaping the structure of agriculture in the contemporary world (but cf. Williams 1989). Urban societies are marked by inequities in social and political status and in access to resources. Such inequities have profound consequences for the organization of food production. Thus, descriptions of the intensification of food production in urban settings must include not only its component strategies, but also their relative proportions (W. Clarke 1985:867; Netting 1974:39) as well as the role of producers in the larger economic and political setting.

One additional mediating factor may be the mechanism of price in market economies (de Vries 1972, 1974; Hassig 1985; Slicher van Bath 1963). Boserup has been criticized for ignoring the role of markets in mediating productive and consumptive demands (see discussion in Netting 1993:288-94 and Stone, Netting, and Stone 1990). This is an important topic, and one that may be significant in the case of the Vijayanagara period during which historians (e.g. Palat 1987:22) suggest there was a growing degree of monetization of the economy. More important may be asymmetrical power relations and extractive demands on production. Taxes or customary shares of produce (Breckenridge 1985:51) were collected in kind only for rice (which stores well), while shares of dry crops and garden crops were assessed in cash. Thus, subsistence producers may have been forced to participate to some extent in a market system. In the case of Vijayanagara, it is also necessary to consider the structure of agricultural investment and opportunity in order to adequately understand the course of intensification. In complex urban economies, population clearly must be considered a mediated variable, and not a simple and proximate cause for change.

THE PROCESS: DIVERSITY AND THE COURSES OF INTENSIFICATION

Boserup and the Unilinear Path of Intensification

Part of the great appeal of Boserup's (1965) model has been its simplicity and comprehensiveness. Patterns of land use, demography, and technology all follow a unitary course, and relevant variables are easily charted as matched sets of fallowing systems, population density groups, agricultural tasks, and agricultural tools (Boserup 1981:table 3.7, table 5.1). Comprehensive, multi-component developmental schemes (such as those of Fried 1967; Service 1963; Sahlins 1972) hold a perennial appeal for archaeologists, perhaps because these allow the construction of an integrated picture of the past from the recovery of a single element of the model. Intensification, in Boserup's scheme, is also assumed to be a steady and gradual process (1981:46), with labor inputs added continuously through time (cf. Bronson 1972:206). The notion of gradual addition of inputs can realistically be sustained only for certain activities—perhaps manuring can be gradually increased, but irrigation networks, for example, represent more discrete "packages" of labor and capital outlay, as discussed in the following chapters.

Boserup's operational definition of intensification as cropping frequency also reflects her focus on continuous variability and gradual change. Technological change is allowed to be more discontinuous but is ultimately a reflection of fallowing length. The adequacy of cropping frequency as a measure of the actual course of intensification (cf. Boserup 1965:18) in specific areas has been questioned (W. Clarke 1985:867; Morrison 1989), and several alternate, more complex classifications of land use (Conklin 1957; Denevan 1980; Brookfield and Brown 1963) have been devised.

Fallow lengths may indeed provide a useful measure of production intensity in some areas and at some times. The problem with fallow length as a proxy measure of intensification lies in the fact that fallow length is a univariate measure of a multivariate phenomenon and thus can only provide a partial index at best. Actual systems of production are internally complex and organizationally flexible. Different strategies may be open to different groups of producers, and even a single household may simultaneously practice multiple strategies of production. Diversity can also be seen in the purposes of production (after Brookfield 1972), with what Brush and Turner (1987:33) call the "dual farmer" producing for both subsistence and exchange. Collapsing this variability and flexibility into a single measure forces us to ignore the richness of the archaeological record and, ironically, to seek a measure that we may never be able to reconstruct. The following study responds to precisely this point—can a simple index of intensification be devised? What was the course of intensification at Vijayanagara? How can we recognize it, and what form or forms did it take?

The diversity of agricultural (and other) production strategies evident in the Vijayanagara archaeological record is itself of interest, and suggests that we might also be alert for diversity in the process of intensification itself, as people seek to adjust productive strategies in accord with complex and changing sets of demands, constraints, and opportunities. These conditions are themselves historically contingent, depending on past histories of decisions and actions. Thus, I propose that there may in fact be multiple paths of intensification and that the process of intensification may incorporate a much greater degree of variability than allowed for in the Boserup model. Kaiser and Voytek (1983:329-30) divide the process into three components: specialization, diversification, and intensification proper (see also Tringham and Krstic 1990). These aspects of intensification involve changes in the amount and organization of labor and in its application through technology (Kaiser and Voytek 1983:330), and cannot be measured simply in terms of a single variable such as cropping frequency. As part of larger economic and political systems, agricultural production also has to be considered in light of overall strategies of production, distribution, and consumption. These three categories are not intended as rigid types or forms of intensification, but instead have been selected to highlight the potential diversity and multiplicity of routes of change. I fully expect that not all strategies would have been equally available to all groups of Vijayanagara producers at all times. Context matters.

Intensification Proper

Intensification proper involves increased labor and/or capital inputs to a plot of land. These additions constitute what is commonly considered to *be* intensification and can include changes in both the quantity, type, and organization of labor and other resources. Intensification proper may take the form of increased investments in practices such as plowing, seed bed preparation, weeding, transplanting, manuring, or watering. Many of these practices have low archaeological visibility but may be amenable to careful study (e.g. Wilkinson 1989). The construction of soil and water control facilities, both permanent and temporary, is also included in this category. Enduring facilities such as canals, stone walls, and other structures generally constitute the primary archaeological evidence for intensification, but more ephemeral features such as brush dams, earthen field borders, and biodegradable mulch are also important.

A temporal dimension is implicit in this view of intensification proper. Many of the activities identified as increased labor take place in the context of a single growing season; decisions to transplant rice seedlings, manure a cotton field, or weed a garden plot can be made each season. The nature of the growing season itself may constitute an aspect of intensification proper, so that an increased frequency of cropping (cf. Boserup 1965), possibly facilitated by improved control over conditions of plant growth, is one strategy of intensification proper. In what may be a larger temporal context are decisions about the construction of soil and water control facilities. Agricultural facilities may allow double-cropping or the extension of the growing season. They may simply make production more secure or reliable; they may allow the production of specialized cultigens or a greater range of cultigens (see below). As noted, the creation of permanent facilities changes a landscape in a rather dramatic way, just as other choices (direction of plowing, method of vegetation clearance, etc.) also continuously recreate the physical landscape.

What Kaiser and Voytek (1983) have termed intensification proper is a large category but one which has a certain coherence in terms of standard views of intensification strategies. Of the various forms of intensification proper noted above, some require large outlays of capital or access to specific resources, such as water, tools, draft animals, or building material, while others primarily involve labor. Thus, within this conceptual category, some strategies will be possible only where producers have access to non-labor resources, and the adoption of these strategies can be expected to be tied to the economic and sociopolitical opportunities of producers. Certainly labor itself constitutes a resource that is not uniformly distributed (cf. Patir 1987).

Kirch (1994) distinguishes between what he terms "landesque capital intensification" (after Blaike and Brookfield 1987) in which primary labor investment results in a permanent modification of the landscape, and other forms of labor intensification which do not create permanent facilities (landscape modifications such as canals or terraces). The construction of facilities may, he notes, actually reduce labor demands for subsequent producers. It is necessary to disaggregate the labor organization involved in constructing facilities from the subsequent demands of maintenance and production. As Lansing (1991) has noted, the process of landscape transformation is historically contingent, so that decisions about productive strategies, decisions which may involve the construction of facilities, have consequences for all future producers. The history of past decisions is represented in the "congealed labor" (Lansing 1991, and see above) of past activities, features which have themselves become part of the productive landscape (see also Netting 1993:267). For producers at a given point in time, however, the potential permanence of their works may not be the primary concern. Perhaps it may be most useful to consider the diverse strategies of intensification proper in terms of the "raw materials" required: labor, water, land, stone, draft animals, tools, manure, seeds.

Specialization

Specialization, the reduction of diversity or the channeling of production into restricted ends, is another potential strategy of intensification. Specialization may occur at a number of different scales. Farmers may seek to increase profits in market gardening by specializing in a high value crop; villages or regions may specialize in produce well adapted to local environmental conditions. Thus, crop species and varieties or specific conditions or locations of production may be differentially deployed in strategies of specialization. Costin (1991:4) defines specialization in terms of entire societies as "... a differentiated, regularized, permanent, and perhaps institutionalized production system in which producers depend on extra-household exchange relationships" (see also Muller 1984). Specialization in craft production is generally viewed as promoting efficiency, while intensified agriculture has often been depicted as necessarily inefficient (producing declining returns).

An important form of specialized agricultural production is wet rice agriculture, which, as noted above, appears to violate the assumption of declining returns. Wet rice entails very specific and labor-intensive techniques of field preparation, irrigation, and drainage, and promotes major modification of soil structure. Rice paddies require standing water at certain points in the cropping cycle, and dry land at others. The standing water is never stagnant, however, and a constant flow-through must be maintained. The labor and scheduling demands of paddy rice, then, may interfere with the production of other crops, and fields subjected to the careful levelling and water control of rice paddies may or may not be allowed to revert to a less-productive crop. Specialization may not refer simply to crop species or production strategy, however. Crop varieties may themselves be developed as specialized responses to local environments (e.g., Gallagher 1989; Kirkby 1973), and most "traditional" agriculturalists employ a number of different locally adapted varieties.

Specialization in agriculture implies exchange. As such, it is not intelligible outside the context of the entire economic and social system and must be considered in concert with the structure of productive diversity. In urban societies, specialization in agricultural production may be related to production for markets and non-agriculturalists may have various degrees of involvement in agricultural decision-making. At Vijayanagara, the demands of a monetizing economy may have driven producers to participate in urban markets. As with other aspects of productive intensification in complex societies, specialization might most profitably be considered as a strategy of intensification, and possibly as a strategy differentially available to and differentially employed by different groups of producers.

Diversification

The difference between specialization and diversification may at times be primarily a matter of scale, since at least some minimum level of system-wide diversity in food production is required to maintain adequate nutritional levels. Considerable latitude exists, however, in the degree of diversity in crop species, varieties, production strategies, and locations. Diversification is probably the least obvious aspect of productive intensification, in that it may involve the addition or elaboration of productive strategies which seem to be *extensive* rather than *intensive* of land or labor. Diversification relates to an increase in the number of components of a productive system (diversity), as well as to changes in the organization of that diversity. Temporal dimensions of diversification might include strategies such as staggered planting and harvesting times which, as Mencher (1978) has pointed out, make more efficient use of limited labor forces during periods of labor bottlenecks (and see Stone, Netting, and Stone 1990). Spatial diversity includes dispersed landholdings and the cultivation of crop mixes and of multiple crop varieties, each with different growth characteristics. In considering strategies of diversification, it is necessary to look beyond agriculture itself, as households, individuals, and groups may seek to diversify not only in terms of plot sizes and locations, types of crops, and forms of soil and water control facilities, but also in terms of other productive activities (craft production, animal husbandry, wage labor, etc.). Nonagricultural strategies of diversification include the forging of social or other ties and the creation of entitlements across regions. Changes in labor organization might also be considered under the rubric of diversity. For example, in South India both contemporary and historical studies have noted that dependent low-status landless laborers (but not slaves; Netting 1993:283) are differentially concentrated in areas of intensive wet rice production (Mencher 1978; Ludden 1985), and indeed, a greater diversity of occupations and statuses is seen in these areas.

It is useful to recall the distinction between intensification and expansion, where intensification involves some fixed quantity, most often land. Clearly, mobility constraints and mobility options, which are entailed in structures of access to land, are relevant to both expansion and intensification, either of which may be employed in response to similar imperatives. In fact, agricultural change may involve both expansion and intensification, and expansion may be considered in some contexts a form of spatial diversification or a component strategy of intensification. In the context of Vijayanagara, the expansion of cultivation into new areas was an explicit political strategy connected to the extension of revenues and political control. Moreover, settlers were also a part of the empire, participating in its economy and reducing demographic and political pressure in more densely settled areas. Thus, expansion must be considered in tandem with intensification.

The Course of Intensification: Discussion

In Boserup's (1965) scheme, the intensity of any land use system can be measured by the single variable of fallow time, leaving no room for multiple strategies within a single system of land use or for a multivariate process of change. I argue instead that the course of agricultural change during the Vijayanagara period was complex, involving both expansion and intensification, and further that the path of intensification was not uniform, moving from longer to shorter fallow periods, or from simpler to more complex systems, but was internally diverse, involving intensification proper, specialization, and diversification. The process of agricultural change, then, involved the transformation—or creation—of an entire agricultural landscape, structured and defined as much by settlements, agricultural facilities, temples, and roadways as by productive potential.

Vijayanagara as a Case Study

Both the land use history of the region in and around the city of Vijayanagara as well as the diversity of potential sources of information about Vijayanagara production make this an excellent case study. Because this large fourteenth century city was established in a region that had never been densely occupied, its material remains are relatively easy to identify. The city grew rapidly and had a considerable impact on the surrounding landscape. By the late sixteenth century, the city was virtually abandoned, although many of the most productive agricultural facilities have remained in use until the present. Large-scale reoccupation of the area did not take place until the middle of the twentieth century. This sharply defined occupational history makes the Vijayanagara region a good candidate for archaeological survey work and for the study of intensification.

Vijayanagara archaeology is facilitated by this land use history, but regional scale studies are also possible because of the semi-arid environment of northern Karnataka. Surface visibility is excellent and the denuded natural vegetation cover sparse. Abundant surface and subsurface archaeological remains of the Vijayanagara period attest to the intensity and complexity of land use in the region. Archaeological data on Vijayanagara production are abundant, and they can be supplemented by a corpus of contemporary documents. These texts serve as an additional source of information on production and also provide a rich social and political context. Finally, the natural environment itself bears the scars of Vijayanagara economic activity. Landscape modifications have left their mark in the botanical and sedimentary records. The analysis of pollen, spores, charcoal, and sediments constitutes the third form of information used in this study to trace the course of change in Vijayanagara agricultural systems.

2

Agricultural Production in the Vijayanagara Region

THE INCREASING demands on agricultural production prompted by growing populations, by increased demands for surplus production, and particularly by dense population concentrations such as cities, have historically resulted in transformations in productive strategies designed to extract a greater amount of produce from a given quantity of land and/or labor. These strategies of intensification take place within specific ecological, political, and historical contexts. The constraints and possibilities of agricultural production in the Bellary and southern Raichur districts of South India, briefly outlined below, provide a partial context for consideration of agricultural structure and change in the Vijayanagara region.

AGRICULTURE AND THE ARCHAEOLOGICAL RECORD

The investigation of past agriculture poses a particular problem to archaeologists because of the large spatial scale of agricultural activities, and the often ephemeral material remains they produce. For this reason, it may be necessary to consider a constellation of direct and indirect indicators of past land use at a number of spatial scales. Such indicators may include artifacts, historical documents, settlement distributions, agricultural features, and botanical remains.

Because excavation generally is focused at the scale of the site, recovery of nonbotanical material related to agriculture is limited primarily to artifacts. Some organizational information can be derived from agricultural artifacts (e.g. Barker 1985; Dimbleby 1967; McAnany 1992; Sherratt 1981). However, some tools may be so generalized that the same implement may play an entirely different role in different contexts (Bray 1986; Rowly-Conwy 1984a).

Written documents provide information on agricultural practices and strategies for some places and time periods (e.g. Hall 1982; Hall 1983; Postgate 1992; Slicher Van Bath 1963). These materials cannot provide all the answers, however. Written materials typically record only the components of the agricultural economy of interest to the literate elite, and often omit reference to small-scale or marginally productive strategies (chapter 6). Attempts to trace the antiquity of names for crops, agricultural implements, or practices via linguistic analysis have also been made (Ehret 1984; see also Stahl 1984). This procedure, however, requires the questionable assumption of stability in meaning through time.

Systematic archaeological surveys and regional-scale remote sensing allow patterning at a scale larger than that of the individual site to be discerned. The development of regional or landscape approaches in archaeology has revitalized studies of past agriculture. Human land use patterns are complex and variable, and agricultural strategies may relate to disparate spatial scales. Residents of a single village, for example, may plant intensively manured and irrigated "kitchen gardens" (Killion 1992; and see Turner 1992) near individual households, have wet rice fields in a valley bottom, have extensive rainfed fields on a terraced hillside, and perhaps also manage stands of certain useful wild species. Such an internally differentiated system might be expected to leave a complex archaeological and archaeobotanical record, and one that looks different in different locations. A research strategy for investigating this case would require multiple lines of inquiry at several spatial scales. This study of Vijayanagara agriculture represents an initial attempt at such an analysis, but inevitably represents only a partial view. Only a portion of the agricultural landscape is examined here, and agricultural production within the city walls (Paes in Sewell 1900) and at long distances from the city (Morrison and Sinopoli 1992; Subrahmanyam 1990) is not explicitly considered here.

On a regional or sub-regional scale, archaeological evidence of past land use includes the location, content, and temporal placement of settlement and various special-purpose sites and features along with geological, geochemical, and botanical profiles. In settlement pattern studies, the locations of archaeological sites and features in relation to one another and to the structure of resources are related to their economic, social, and political context. The material record of past agriculture may also include the physical remains of agricultural features and facilities, and their distribution across the landscape. Soil ridges and plow marks (Bradley 1978; Butzer 1982; Fowler and Evans 1967; Hall 1983; O'Connell 1986), bordered and raised fields (Denevan and Turner 1974; Matheny 1978; Siemens and Puleston 1972; Turner 1974), gravel-mulched fields (Buge 1984; Maxwell and Anschuetz 1992; Vivian 1974), terraces (Donkin 1979; Fowler and Evans 1967; Spencer and Hall 1961; Wheatley 1965), and canals and reservoirs (Farrington and Park 1978; Matheny 1978; Maxwell and Anschuetz 1992; Mosley and Deeds 1982; Seneviratna 1989) all present direct indications of agricultural practice.

THE VIJAYANAGARA REGION: CLIMATE, SOIL, AND TOPOGRAPHY

A visitor to the Bellary District today might well imagine that this agricultural landscape has remained unchanged for thousands of years. Nearly every level piece of ground is covered with fields of all sizes, shapes, and descriptions, from vast green oceans of sugarcane to small straggly patches of millet or brilliant expanses of sunflowers. Groups of cows wander down well-worn paths, small children herd flocks of sheep and goats, and film songs blare from movie houses in nucleated villages. However, thislandscape is a recent product, planted with many introduced New World cultigens, drawing water from a modern dam project, and serving the needs of cities and towns far from the district.

During the Vijayanagara period, the capital city was located near the northern frontier of the empire, in what was also, in a sense, an agricultural frontier. Vijayanagara was as populous or more populous than any modern town in the area today, all of which rely to a greater or lesser extent on rail and road transportation of foodstuffs. In contrast to rich alluvial deltas that had supported earlier South Indian capitals, the semi-arid Karnatak Plateau lies well within the rain shadow of the Sahyadris and receives a low and temporally variable rainfall of less than 500 millimeters per year (Johnson 1969; Spate 1954). For this reason, and because almost all of the rain falls within three months of the year, productive agriculture in this region requires the use of fairly specialized agricultural strategies, mostly having to do with the control and storage of water.

Topography and Geology

The major mountain chain of the Indian peninsula south of the Vindhyas is the Sahyadri, or Western Ghat chain, which runs along the western coast of India (figure 2.1). These mountains act as an orographic barrier to rainfall, so that the narrow west coastal strip and the western side of the Ghats receive proportionately more rainfall than the inland plateaus to the east (figure 2.2). These plateaus include the Deccan Plateau to the north, and the smaller Karnatak Plateau to the south. Both slope downward to the east, so that the major rivers of southern India, most of which originate in the Ghats, run from west to east. A minor mountain chain (the Eastern Ghats) extends down the eastern coast of India, but this chain is

16   *Fields of Victory*

FIGURE 2.1
Topographic zones of southern India

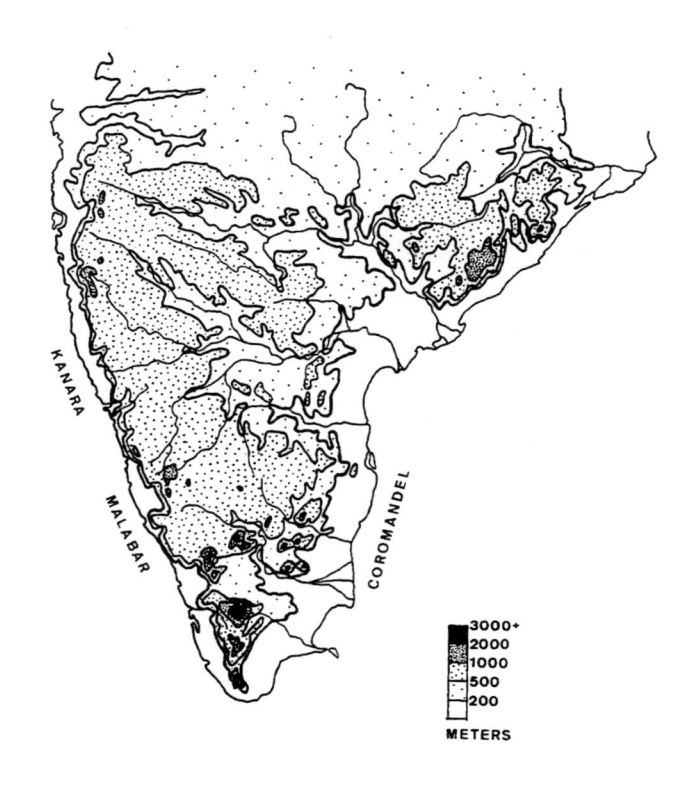

FIGURE 2.2
Average annual rainfall, southern India

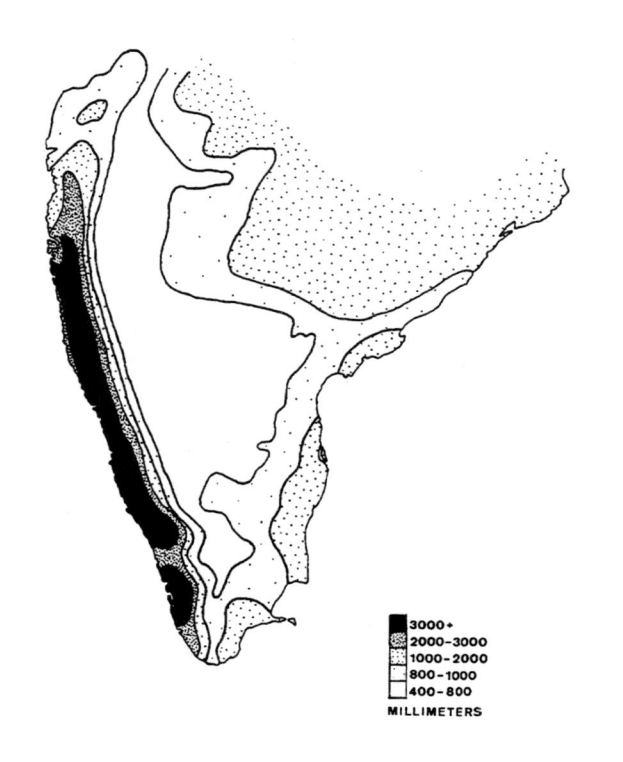

low and discontinuous, and does not have the strong effect on climate that the western mountains do. The Western Ghats also partially isolate the west coast from the rest of the peninsula, an isolation that has been consistently reflected in political boundaries.

The Deccan Plateau consists of a great shield of basalt formed during the Late Cretaceous to Early Tertiary (Naqvi and Rogers 1987). The Deccan Plateau ends at the Tungabhadra River, so that the study area, which spans the Tungabhadra but is mostly to the south of it, is contained largely within the Karnatak Plateau. The study area is located in the Bellary and Raichur districts of Karnataka state, at approximately 15 degrees north latitude and 76 degrees east longitude.

The base geologic formation of the area is a gneissic complex (Krishnamurthy 1978), or what Naqvi and Rogers (1987) term undifferentiated gneiss. In the study area, however, unlike much of South India, igneous rocks overlie gneiss. The Hampi-Daroji Hills are a series of roughly parallel northwest-southeast trending ridges of grey granodiorite that have weathered into froms that appear as immense piles of boulders of various shapes. The study area is sandwiched between two narrow bands of metamorphic rocks known as the Dharwar chlorite schists (Gaussen et al. 1966; Krishnamurthy 1978). One of these bands runs along the southern edge of the study area, forming the high east-west trending Sandur Hills. The Tungabhadra basin lies at an elevation of between 300 and 600 meters, while the Sandur Hills rise to between 600 and 900 meters.

The principal river in the area is the Tungabhadra, a tributary of the Krishna. The Tungabhadra originates in the Western Ghats and is not deeply entrenched. Its winding and sometimes shallow and rocky course prevents navigation. Until the construction of the Tungabhadra dam in the 1940s and 1950s, the river often overflowed its banks in the rainy season. An important feature of the Vijayanagara agricultural landscape, the Tungabhadra both provides a narrow alluvial strip and is the primary supply for perennial irrigation.

Vegetation

The western slopes of the Ghats support a lush lowland tropical evergreen forest dominated by vegetation of the *Dipterocarpus-Mesua-Palaquium* series and the *Machilus-Holigarna-Diospyros* series (Gaussen et al. 1966). The land to the east of the Ghats is divided into two zones, the *malnad* and the *maidan*. Although these zones are topographic, they also have a strong association with vegetation. The *malnad* consists of the rolling hills to the east of the Ghats and has a relatively higher rainfall and more luxuriant vegetation than the *maidan*. The *malnad* contains tropical dry deciduous forests, which give way to dry mixed deciduous forests on the east (Champion 1936). The *maidan*, or tableland, consists of dry plains dominated by vegetation belonging to the southern thorn forests and southern thorn scrub (Champion 1936).

The vegetation of the study area has been greatly modified by human use of the landscape, which has included agriculture, grazing, burning, and settlement. Vegetation on the Sandur Hills belongs to the *Anogeissus-Terminalia-Tectona* series, with vegetation of the *Hardwickia-Anogeissus* series on the lower slopes (see chapter 7). These vegetation series, particularly the *Anogeissus-Terminalia-Tectona* series, are also found on the Ghat foothills in the *malnad* and do not occur throughout dry eastern Karnataka (N. P. Singh 1988). Thus, the Sandur Hills, with their well-developed forests, presented a rather sharp contrast to the sparse scrub vegetation below, and the Sandur forests undoubtedly represented an important resource for inhabitants of the Vijayanagara area.

The dominant vegetation association in the survey area is the *Albizia amara-Acacia* series, which is characterized by narrow-leafed, thorny trees and scrub adapted to dry conditions. Characteristic species of this series are *Albizia amara* and *Chloroxylon swietenia* (Gaussen et al. 1966). The principal tree species of this series are listed in table 2.1, shrub species in table 2.2, and herbaceous species in table 2.3. A number of distinctive plant microenvironments have been created by agricultural activity. These include cultivated fields and bodies of water (canals, ponds, reservoirs). Plant species associated with reservoirs are listed in table 2.4.

TABLE 2.1 Dominant tree species in the *Albizia amara-Acacia* series.

Family	Genus	Species
LEGUMINOSAE	*Albizia*	*amara*
LEGUMINOSAE	*Acacia*	*sundara*
LEGUMINOSAE	*Acacia*	*latronum*
LEGUMINOSAE	*Dichrostachys*	*cinerea*
FLINDERSACEAE	*Chloroxylon*	*swietenia*
APOCYNACEAE	*Holarrhena*	*antidysenterica*
ULMACEAE	*Holoptelea*	*integrifolia*
MELIACEAE	*Azadirachta*	*indica*
SALVADORACEAE	*Salvadora*	*persica*
VERBENACEAE	*Gmelina*	*asiatica*
CELASTRACEAE	*Gymnosporia*	*spinosa*
BIGNONIACEAE	*Dolichandrone*	*falcata*
RHAMNACEAE	*Zizyphus*	*xylopyrus*
RHAMNACEAE	*Zizyphus*	*mauritiana*

TABLE 2.2 Dominant shrub species in the *Albizia amara-Acacia* series.

Family	Genus	Species
RUBIACEAE	*Randia*	*dumetorum*
RUBIACEAE	*Terenna*	*asiatica*
RUBIACEAE	*Canthium*	*dicoccum*
APOCYNACEAE	*Carissa*	*spinarum*
CAPPARIDACAEAE	*Capparis*	*aphylla*
EUPHORBIACEAE	*Euphorbia*	*antiquorum*
EUPHORBIACEAE	*Euphorbia*	*caducifolia*
EUPHORBIACEAE	*Securinega*	*leucopyrus*
LEGUMINOSAE	*Cassia*	*auriculata*
LEGUMINOSAE	*Mundelia*	*serica*
ANACARDIACEAE	*Dodonaea*	*viscosa*
ERYTHROXYLACEAE	*Erthyroxylum*	*monogynum*
CELASTRACEAE	*Maytenus*	*emerginata*

Climate

The temperature of the study area is characterized by a moderate degree of diurnal and a low degree of annual variability. Figure 2.3 indicates the mean daily temperature minima and maxima by month for the Bellary District. The high temperatures of the study area contribute to a high rate of evaporation, but in themselves are not limiting to plant growth.

The tropical monsoon system consists of two seasonal patterns of rain-bearing monsoonal winds, the southwest monsoon and the retreating, or northeast monsoon (Rawson 1963:34-35). The former bout of rainfall occurs between June and October, and constitutes the principal rainy season on the Karnatak Plateau. Rains of the northeast monsoon fall between late October and early January, and are of lesser importance in the study

TABLE 2.3 Dominant herb species in the *Albizia amara-Acacia* series.

Family	Genus	Species
GRAMINEAE	*Aristida*	*adscensionis*
GRAMINEAE	*Aristida*	*funiculata*
GRAMINEAE	*Aristida*	*hystrix*
GRAMINEAE	*Chrysopogon*	*fulvis*
GRAMINEAE	*Heteropogon*	*contortis*
GRAMINEAE	*Apluda*	*varia*
GRAMINEAE	*Cymbopogon*	*martinii*
COMPOSITAE/ASTERACEAE	*Tridax*	*procumbens*

TABLE 2.4 Dominant species associated with reservoirs.

Family	Genus	Species
ACANTHACEAE	*Hygrophilia*	*longifolia*
LYTHRACEAE	*Ammannia*	*baccifera*
SCROPHULARIACEAE	*Bacopa*	*monneiri*
GRAMINEAE	*Echinocloa*	*colonum*
PONTEDERIACEAE	*Eichornia*	*crassipes*
HYDROPHYLLACEAE	*Hydrolaea*	*zeylanica*
ONAGRACEAE	*Ludwigia*	*suffruticosa*
NELUMBONACEAE	*Nelumbo*	*nucifera*
CYPERACEAE	*Scirpus*	*articulatus*
POTAMOGETONACEAE	*Potamogeton*	*indicus*
ARACEAE	*Pistia*	*stratiotes*
VERBENACAEA	*Phyla*	*nodiflora*

area (figure 2.4, and see Kanitkar 1960). A marked orographic barrier to the winds of the southwest monsoon is presented by the Western Ghat mountain chain, the western slopes of which capture the bulk of the moisture-bearing winds before they can reach the eastern plateaus (figure 2.2).

The Bellary District receives a relatively low annual rainfall which is also characterized by annual and inter-annual variability. The annual distribution of rainfall between the years A.D. 1850 and 1870 is illustrated in figure 2.4, which shows the typical bimodal distribution of seasonal rainfall in the area. However, the amounts and distributions of rainfall are not consistent from year to year, so that, for example, the spring or even the fall rains may altogether fail to arrive. Figure 2.5 shows yearly variation about the mean for the same twenty-year period. Given the generally low and often variable rainfall of the study area, it is not difficult to see why it is classified by Kanitkar (1960:1) as falling within the "scarcity tract."

Soils

Soils of the study area consist of tropical red sandy loams (Gaussen et al. 1966), generally classified as red (*masab*) and mixed black and red soils (N. P. Singh 1988:22). A more extensive zone of tropical black clays surrounds the

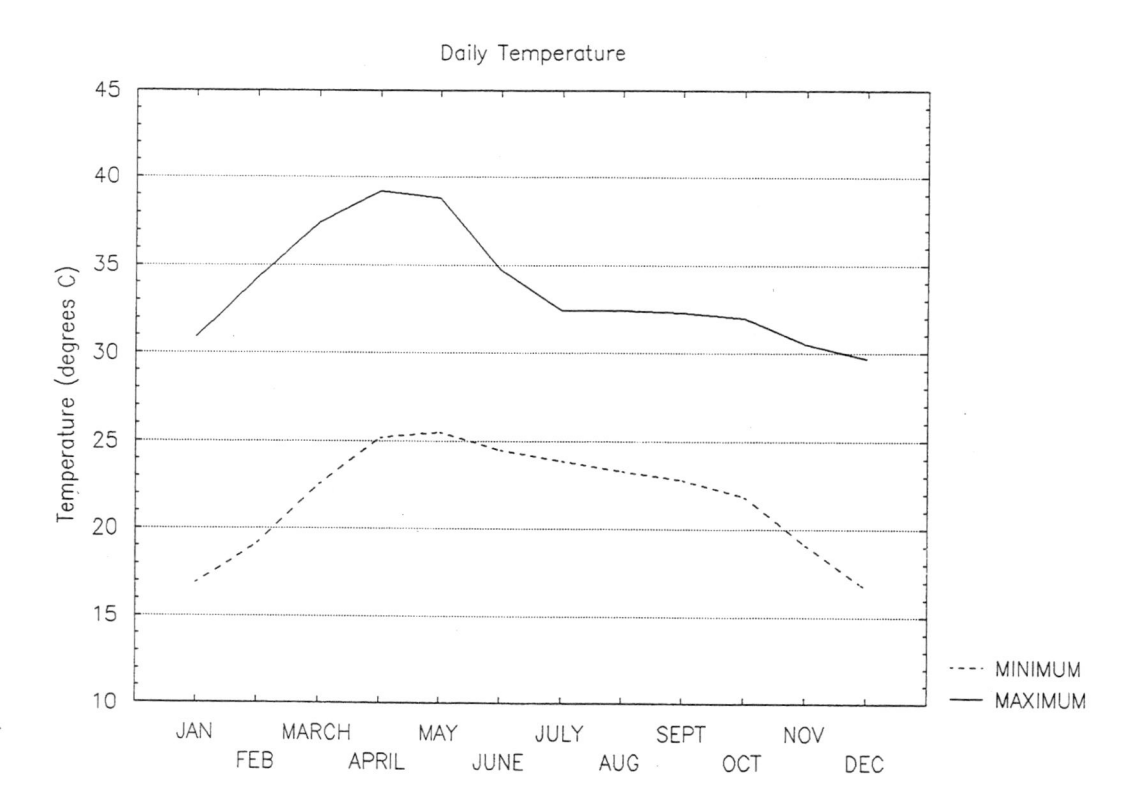

FIGURE 2.3 Mean daily minimum and maximum temperatures by month, Bellary District (data from N. P. Singh 1988:30).

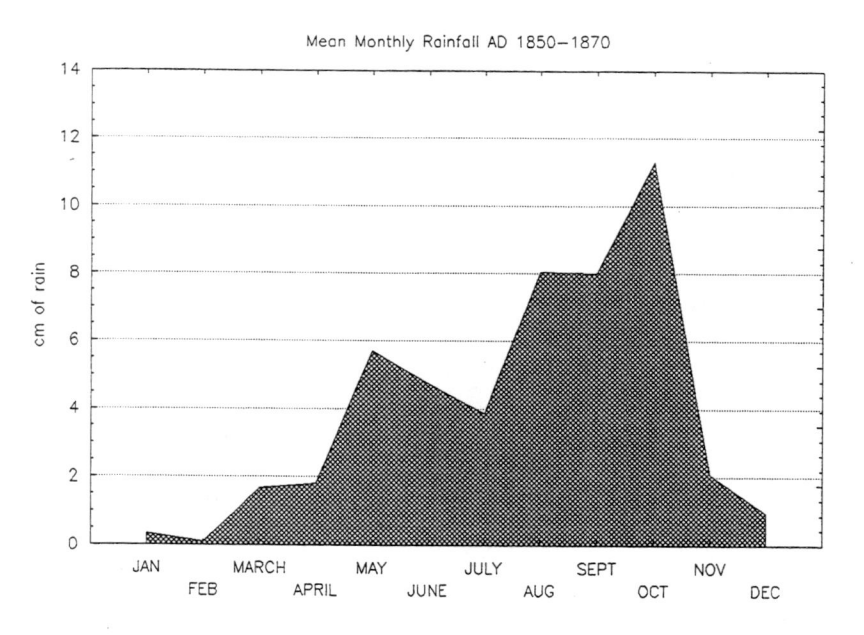

FIGURE 2.4 Monthly rainfall A.D. 1850-1870, Bellary District (data from Kelsall 1872).

Vijayanagara region. The most well known of these black clays is regur (or *regada*, Kelsall 1872:1), or black cotton soil, which covers the extensive plains to the east and south of the study area. In general, soils in the study area are thin and poorly developed, with a high sand and low silt and clay content. A small but agriculturally important zone of alluvial soils is found adjacent to the Tungabhadra River. The city of Vijayanagara is situated near a bend in the river where this alluvial soil strip is slightly wider.

AGRICULTURAL PRODUCTION: CATEGORIES

In discussing South Indian agriculture, it is customary to draw a distinction between "wet" and "dry" cultivation, differentiated on the basis of the water availability. Thus, "wet" agriculture is based on perennial supplies of water, while "dry" agriculture consists primarily of rainfall-dependent production. There is also a third form of production, what has been termed "wet-cum-dry" cultivation, in which the water supply is seasonal but some form of water collection and storage facility is involved. Water supply significantly influences not only the type of crop grown but also the potential number of crops grown per year, the relative security of obtaining an adequate harvest, and the degree of long-term fluctuation in yields. Scales of production, the degree of investment and control exercised by non-cultivators, and the labor organization of the cultivators are also related to these categories. This section briefly reviews these categories in terms of water requirements, the types of crop grown, and their potential productivity, reliability, and storability. The following section describes the types of agricultural facilities associated with each category in the Vijayanagara period.

This tripartite classification is derived from local classification systems, and differs slightly from that employed in British revenue documents. In Tamil, *nanjai* refers to wet land, *punjai* to dry land, while the term *nanjai-mel-punjai* translates as "dry crops on wet lands" (Ludden 1985:57; in Kannada *gadde* means wet land and *beddalu* dry land). Thus, for example, in a bad year sorghum (a

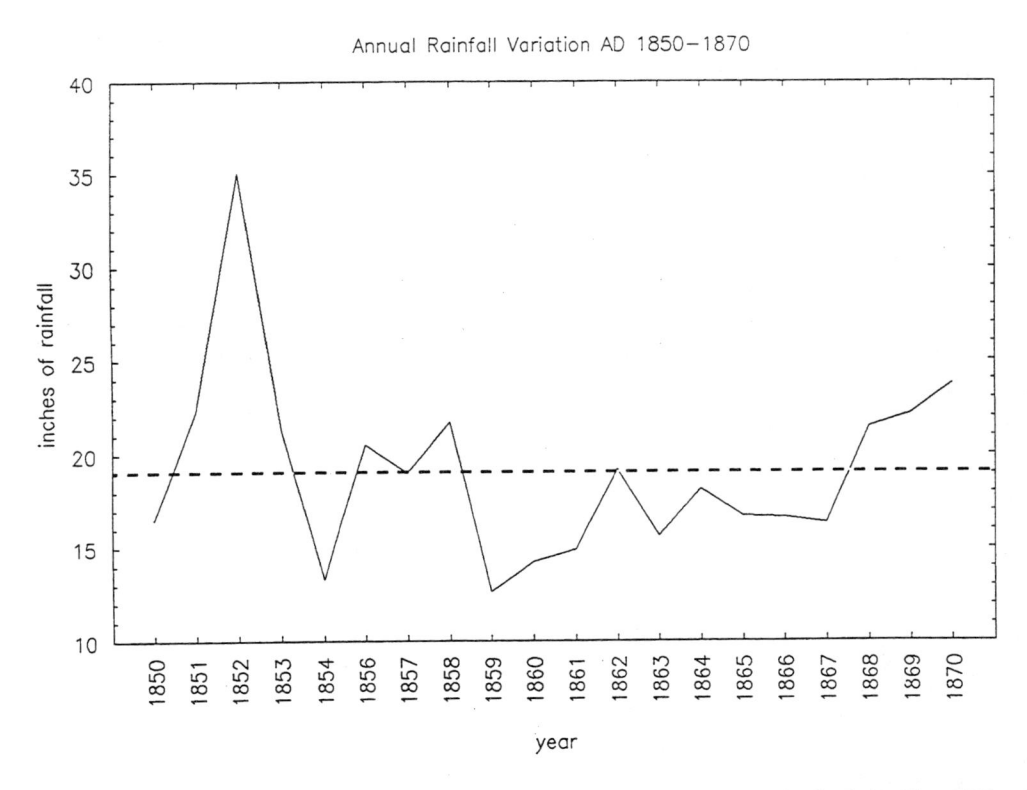

FIGURE 2.5 Annual rainfall: variation about the mean between A.D. 1850 and 1870, Bellary District (data from Kelsall 1872)

dry crop) might be grown on land otherwise planted with rice (a wet crop). Mencher (1978:61) describes wet-cum-dry cultivation (she uses the term *manavari*) as being "midway" between wet and dry. The British did use the term *nanjai-melpunjai* (which they modified to *nunjah-melpunjah*). However, for revenue purposes, land was classified as wet, dry, or garden land (Maclean 1877). In this scheme, garden land is a special category of wet land that is intensively farmed (often with well water) and may be planted with cash crops. This distinction within the general category of wet land is potentially very useful, but one which is difficult, if not impossible, to make archaeologically. Instead, I employ the three-part classification since each category is generally associated with a particular set of agricultural facilities, features visible in the archaeological record. In Vijayanagara-period inscriptions garden land is sometimes referred to, but the categories wet and dry appear to be more consistently employed. Land beneath reservoirs (tanks) is also often mentioned as a category; I take this to be wet-cum-dry land since the vast majority of reservoirs in the survey area are fed by seasonal runoff, as discussed below.

Wet Agriculture

Wet agriculture and wet crops play an important role in South Indian structures of power, status, and wealth. Rice was (and is) the preferred grain of the elite, while sorghum and millets make the breads of the poor. Wet crops include such species as paddy rice (*Oryza sativa*), sugarcane (*Saccharum officinarum*), vegetables, and tree crops. Vegetables include, for example, turmeric (*Curcuma domestica*), onions (*Allium cepa*), garlic (*A. sativum*), mustard (*Brassica*), and various squashes. Tree crops include, but are not limited to, tamarind (*Tamarindus indicus*), coconuts (*Cocos nucifera*), mangos (*Mangifera indica*), jackfruit (*Artocarpus heterophyllus*), Areca nut (*Areca catechu*), *ber* (*Zizyphus jubjuba*), and dates (*Phoenix sylvestris*) which also grow wild in the area. These crops require a secure and abundant source of water, but with such a supply, it is possible to obtain two crops per year from the annuals. Further, yields from irrigated fields are much more consistent than those dependent upon sometimes-erratic rainfall. There is a price to pay for this high level of production. Wet agriculture in the Vijayanagara region is only possible with the aid of labor and capital intensive facilities requiring extensive landscape modification such as canals, canal-fed reservoirs, and wells. The initial construction of such facilities involved considerable labor and organization. However, these initial costs must be considered independently from routine requirements for maintenance, scheduling, and operation of the facility.

The labor demands and scheduling constraints of wet agriculture are significant. For rice in particular (Grist 1954; Hanks 1972), paddy cultivation requires a great deal of field preparation and constant monitoring of water levels in addition to other chores such as planting, weeding, transplanting, and harvesting. Mencher (1978:21) has suggested that a "sizeable" landless population of agricultural laborers may have existed in Tamil Nadu for the last thousand years, based on the labor requirements of wet rice. She comments (1978:146), "An economy based on rice cultivation needs to have either a very efficient system of cooperative production or a high labor force of agricultural workers since even those who own as little as one hectare cannot manage without some outside help." In the study area rice can be grown at any time of year as long as there is sufficient water, and today one sees rice paddies in all stages of growth throughout the year. During the Vijayanagara period, seasonal fluctuations in river levels and runoff must have constituted the major physical impediment to continuous rice cultivation making paddy cycles more seasonal than they are today.

Scheduling demands of labor in wet rice production are also significant, however, since planting, harvesting, and other operations on more seasonally determined dry crops may have conflicted with the more constant labor demands of rice production. In the Philippines, with a roughly similar rainfall distribution, Conelley (1992) notes that among the Napsaan farmers the timing of labor demands of wet rice are compatible with the (dry) swidden cycle. He observes that while operations of the two forms of production do overlap, the periods of peak labor demands are not simultaneous (1992:215). This could also have been the case for dry and wet agriculture at Vijayanagara if planting, transplanting, and harvesting were carefully orchestrated, but even so it would have been necessary for most wet rice producers to mobilize suprahousehold labor at certain times of year.

In addition to the high potential productivity of irrigated crops, wet cultivation in the semi-arid

Vijayanagara region permitted the production of many crops which could not otherwise have survived this dry environment. Among these are many arboreal crops, including coconut. Sugarcane, which is commercially important in the region today, has a maturation period of approximately eleven months, during which it requires a consistent supply of water. Thus, the presence of plant taxa such as these in the botanical record indicates some human involvement in their maintenance.

Dry Agriculture

Until very recently, dry crops constituted the staple food grains for most of the population in the Vijayanagara region. Dry crops include sorghum (*Jowar* or *Cholum*, *Sorghum bicolor*) and various other grains classified as millets: *bajra* (*Pennisetum typhoides*); *ragi* (*Elusine coracana*); and others (*Panicum sumatrense*, *Setarica italica*, *Paspalum scrobiculatum*, *Echinochloa colonum*, *Panicum miliare*, and *Panicum miliaceum*). Other dry crops include oilseeds such as sesame and castor (*Sesamum indicum* and *Ricinus communis*), legumes (e.g. *Lens esculenta*, *L. culinaris*, *Vigna sp.*, *Dolichos sp.*, *Phaseolus sp.*, *Lathyrus sativus*, and *Pisum sp.*), and cotton (*Gossypium*). Although most dry fields appear to have been relatively small affairs, cotton was grown on a large scale in the Vijayanagara period. A visiting Portuguese horse-trader remarked on the "infinity of cotton" (Sewell 1900:237; see chapter 6) that he saw growing. It is possible to raise dry crops using only rainfall, and in fact cotton was almost certainly raised this way, but the high degree of annual variability in precipitation and the sometimes erratic distribution of rainfall makes this form of production very risky (cf. Yegna Narayan Aiyer 1980).

In general, production levels from dry agriculture are low, and yields are highly variable, depending on weather conditions. Many dry crops, such as the millets, have the advantage of producing both grain for human consumption and fodder for animal consumption. Today, the leaves of sugarcane are a widely used fodder source. The provision of fodder for domestic animals is a critical issue. The expansion of dry cultivation can entail a direct competition with grazing land, as the same agriculturally marginal areas are used for both purposes. Indeed, dry agricultural practices are closely connected with strategies of animal husbandry, as the manure of livestock grazing on dry field stubble constitutes a major nutritional input to dry soils. Dry agriculture in the study area is a strictly seasonal enterprise, being restricted to the period during and immediately after the monsoon (Kanitkar 1960). Thus, the tempo of labor demands in dry farming is quite different from that of wet cultivation, where many perennial crops are grown, and multicropping may be practiced. Dry fields in the area today are often fallowed, although wet fields rarely are. Vijayanagara-period fields of various sorts were undoubtedly also allowed to lie fallow periodically, but this has proved difficult to determine.

A wide range of agricultural facilities are associated with dry farming, such as check dams, gravel-mulched fields, and terraces. These facilities also require labor investments for initial construction and for maintenance but generally not on the scale of wet facilities. There are many dry agricultural features in the Vijayanagara region; unfortunately, these are often difficult to date precisely. It is important to note here, however, that there is a much greater scalar range in dry facilities than in wet facilities and that dry agriculture covered a much larger area than did wet agriculture (see chapter 5). The relatively small scale of dry facilities, their lack of inscriptional notice, and the scheduling demands of dry farming suggest that the organization of production of dry-farmed crops was quite different from that of irrigated crops.

Wet-cum-Dry Agriculture

The third category, wet-cum-dry cultivation, is dependent upon seasonal sources of water, of which the most important are runoff-fed reservoirs, or tanks. Wells are also an important component of wet-cum-dry farming systems. With wet-cum-dry cultivation, it may be possible in a good year to obtain one wet and one dry crop, but more often only one crop is attempted, either wet or dry, depending on the generosity of the monsoon. Reservoirs were an extremely important component of the Vijayanagara agricultural landscape, and although they have been built in South Asia for perhaps as much as two thousand years (Sankalia 1962:103), and thus were not a new invention in the Vijayanagara period, they constituted an important form of intensification of regional agriculture.

As noted, the term wet-cum-dry is derived from an expression meaning "dry crops on wet lands" (Ludden 1985:57). If this meaning is taken literally, then it would seem that a major concern of wet-cum-dry agriculture had to do with security or risk reduction. Given the low and uncertain rainfall regime of northern interior Karnataka, the potential low production or even failure of dry crops can leave farmers without sufficient seed for the following year (cf. Conelley 1992). Irrigated "dry" crops have a higher and more secure yield (Kanitkar 1960). In practice, however, actual production strategies on wet-cum-dry plots seem to be quite variable. The great variability in the amount and reliability of water supplied by different reservoirs and wells makes it difficult to generalize about cultivation practices. Crops grown under reservoirs might consist of traditionally dry cultigens such as sorghum, millets, or cotton, or wet crops such as vegetables or rice. The extension of reservoirs would have had the effect, not only of making the production of dry crops more secure, but also of expanding the area in which other, more water-intensive (and productive) cultigens could have been grown.

Agricultural Facilities

In the following sections, I briefly review the major types of agricultural facility associated with each category of agricultural production. For the most part, the associations are made on the basis of contemporary and historically documented agricultural practice, but the facilities I describe are those of the pre-Colonial period. Some facilities, such as reservoirs, may crosscut categories (cf. Morrison 1993) as do some of the systems of interconnected features found in the Vijayanagara region.

Wet Facilities

Many different types of facilities are associated with wet agriculture. Of these, the most important are canals, fed by water from the perennial Tungabhadra River. Diversion weirs or *anicuts* were strategically placed across channels of this braided watercourse, directing a portion of the river flow into the extensive Vijayanagara canal network. Other facilities associated with canals include canal-fed reservoirs and aqueducts. Wells also supported intensive wet cultivation on a small scale, generally in the context of household gardens. As discussed below, wells are also often associated with reservoirs and may have supported very small-scale wet cultivation far from the river in what were otherwise dry and wet-cum-dry production areas.

The Vijayanagara canal network consists of sixteen major canals and numerous smaller ones. The *ayacut*, or area watered by these canals, in the Bellary District was estimated in 1872 at 11,010 acres (Kelsall 1872:16). However, Kelsall's estimate did not include the channels on the left bank of the Tungabhadra River in Raichur District. Sivamohan (1991:55) reports that the Vijayanagara channels on both sides of the river now water an area of 29,000 acres (11,736 hectares or 117 square kilometers), although post-Vijayanagara extensions of the Basavanna channels have increased this area slightly (Davison-Jenkins 1988). In its present configuration the canal network appears as a maze of channels, some cut through bedrock and others running in raised beds created by earthen embankments, often with masonry facing. For the most part, canals are open earth channels, and thus experience a high degree of water loss to seepage and evaporation (Sharma and Sharma 1990).

The canals generally follow the natural contours of the countryside, winding their way across the alluvial plain of the Tungabhadra, combining with and splitting from other channels, and eventually emptying back into the river. The careful contouring belies the massive investment represented by these canals. Very few canals were simply excavated out of an earthen substrate; almost every one required either some cutting or moving of granite boulders and the construction of substantial raised earthen and masonry embankments and beds. A more extensive description of the canal network can be found in Davison-Jenkins (1988). One of the canals, the Hiriya Kaluve, or "main canal" (Filliozat and Filliozat 1988; now known as the Turtha, or "swift" canal), ran through the Urban Core (Fritz, Michell, and Nagaraja Rao 1985, and see chapter 3) walls near the eastern end of town, watering an area of gardens and orchards. Domestic water supply must also have been a consideration in the routing of the canal, but travellers' accounts from the period make it clear that some food production took place within the city walls.

Because the Vijayanagara channels have been continuously maintained, it is not possible to be certain of the antiquity of sluice arrangements nor indeed to disentangle the construction history of the canals using physical evidence alone. The major sluices and outlets have been replaced by the irrigation authorities with modern devices, but smaller outlets leading into individual fields are generally quite simple, some consisting of little more than a board or stone slab stuck into an earthen channel. Small feeder canals into individual fields are created on an *ad hoc* basis, and are recreated each growing season. Drainage may have presented some problems, and many canals are equipped with escape channels to redirect excess flow back into the river.

The Tungabhadra River contains tens of thousands of large granitic boulders within and between its braided courses. Even though water flow is now regulated by a modern dam, there is still considerable seasonal variation in river levels. During the drought of the early 1980s, many smaller channels were completely dry but during the wet conditions in the early 1990s, many structures along the riverbanks were submerged and smaller channels were no longer even visible. Rivers levels were even more variable prior to construction of the dam, and headworks of the Vijayanagara canal system would have been subject to damage in the summer rainy season. Similarly, some canals probably did not flow consistently every winter dry season.

Anicuts were opportunistically placed between boulders in order to divert water into the headworks of a canal. Anicuts, or *bandharas* (Sharma and Sharma 1990:18-19), are designed as low diversion works over which excess water can flow. The upstream faces are usually vertical, while the downstream faces have a slight batter. Anicuts were constructed of masonry, with brick and plaster, often using iron hooks to anchor masonry to the boulders or to tie several boulders together. The anicuts of many of the canals have been submerged by the waters of the modern dam (Kotraiah 1959), and many other have been repaired with concrete, but several apparently unmodified Vijayanagara-period anicuts are still operative. Anicuts and less formal canal take-offs from the river were situated in order to avoid the primary channel with its rapid flow of water and heavy silt load.

With the exception of small-scale wet cultivation supported by wells, all other wet agricultural facilities were associated with the canal network. These include the Kamalapuram *Kere*, or reservoir, which is fed by the Turtha Canal, an unnamed canal-fed reservoir north of the river (which no longer operates as a reservoir), and the Bhupati Kere, a reservoir fed by the Turtha Canal in the "irrigated valley" (Fritz, Michell, and Nagaraja Rao 1985) between the city and the Tungabhadra River. Canal-fed reservoirs are more common in areas of southern India with longer histories of intensive agriculture, such as parts of the southern state of Tamil Nadu (Ludden 1985; Mencher 1978).

A massive aqueduct (VMS-3) is also associated with the Anegundi Channel, which runs along the north side of the river. This aqueduct, essentially a raised channel carried on massive stone piers, carried water from a canal across the river to irrigate a large island. The aqueduct channel is lined with concrete (of a type seen in other Vijayanagara-period structures), and the masonry piers are constructed of closely fitted blocks of dry-laid granite, much like fortification walls surrounding the city. Elaborate brackets similar to those used in temple architecture span the piers. Unfortunately, the connections between the Anegundi Channel and the aqueduct on the north and the aqueduct and the island on the south have been obliterated by the partial collapse of the feature. However, a massive bastion on the island near the offtake of the aqueduct attests to the degree of seriousness with which this small area of wet agriculture was guarded.

Dry Facilities

The range of features associated with dry farming includes walls, check dams, terraces, and gravel-mulched fields. The most common type of dryland feature is simply a small wall or barrier designed to control surface runoff and erosion. Such walls are generally of masonry or rubble (though they may consist simply of mounded earth) and are rarely more than a single course high or wide (see chapter 4). Erosion control walls are placed perpendicular to the direction of surface runoff, and occur on slopes throughout the study area. Series of soil and water control walls in a single drainage channel are referred to as check dams, and connected the networks of walls across sloping fields that formed terraces. Soil commonly builds up behind the wall, particularly on steeper slopes. Thus, walls, check dams, and terraces may all be considered as serving similar functions; they slow down and spread out runoff, prevent soil erosion, and encourage soil build-up. In some cases, boundary demarcation is clearly also an important consideration. Several examples of double-walled terraces are found in the study area.

Dry facilities are also sometimes physically linked to other kinds of features (see chapter 5). For example, many terrace systems are integrated with runoff-fed reservoirs. Terraced hillsides may also cover large portions of the watersheds of large reservoirs and thus have important roles in preventing erosion and silt deposition into the reservoir. Terraces, then, may operate at a larger scale than that of the area contained within them. Small, isolated walls are also often found on the rocky slopes around the edges of Vijayanagara reservoirs, walls which apparently served no local agricultural purpose other than as reservoir erosion-control features. In spite of this effort, siltation was evidently a serious problem. Many Vijayanagara reservoirs have become completely silted in, and additions to the embankments of others are evidence of usually futile attempts to overcome the growing base of silt in the reservoir bed.

Several extensive gravel-mulched fields have been located in the study area. Although the natural soil of much of the area is already quite rocky, in gravel-mulched fields, small quartzite pebbles are intentionally applied to the surface of the field. The gravel is often carefully size-sorted, with graded piles of gravel lying on the edges of the field. Gravel-mulched fields are known prehistorically in the North American Southwest (Buge 1984; Maxwell and Anscheutz 1992), but in the Vijayanagara region they are in current use. In the case of Vijayanagara, it is clear that soil temperature conservation is not an issue, and the mulching effects of the gravel undoubtedly relate to water, the limiting factor in local agricultural production (see Vivian 1974:100-101 for a discussion of gravel function in prehistoric North American gravel-mulched fields). Webster and Wilson (1966) have discussed the potentially devastating effects of runoff caused by high intensity rainfall, indicating that mulch may protect soils from the erosional effects of runoff almost as well as does vegetation cover. The mulch breaks up the impact of the raindrops, and slows the movement of water over the soil surface, promoting greater absorption (Webster and Wilson 1966:18). Gravel is a locally abundant and inexpensive mulch, and gravel-mulching would have been an important strategy in the region since the natural vegetation cover had already been greatly modified by the Vijayanagara period (chapter 7). Gravel-mulched fields are located only in areas of dry cropping, and some are part of terrace systems.

The dating of gravel-mulched fields is problematic. Gravel-mulching is neither intrinsically temporally diagnostic, nor are the fields usually associated with diagnostic artifacts. Some gravel-mulched fields observed are in use today; however, many are not. In one case, gravel-mulched fields are found within a terrace system which has been cut by a modern canal, in an area not currently in use for agriculture. Adjacent to the gravel-mulched terrace system is another system which incorporates a Vijayanagara reservoir. Thus, it seems likely that at least some of the gravel-mulched fields, or at least the technique of gravel mulching, were used in the Vijayanagara period.

Wet-cum-Dry Facilities

The two major categories of facility associated with wet-cum-dry cultivation are runoff-fed reservoirs and wells. Wells, as noted, are often spatially associated with reservoirs, and worked to supplement or safeguard crops grown under reservoirs. Wells may also have been important for watering livestock. Although canals have been extensively discussed in considerations of South Indian agriculture (Ludden 1985; Mahalingam 1951; Randhawa 1980), reservoirs have received comparatively less attention (Leach 1971; Morrison 1993; Seneviratne 1989). Reservoirs are usually referred to as "tanks," an English-language term dating back to the Colonial period. However, stepwells, pools, and just about every type of water-holding structure is also referred to as a tank (e.g. temple tanks for bathing), a practice which ignores important differences in operation and morphology of the different facilities.

Reservoirs consist of a water-holding basin and a dam or embankment. The basin is generally situated in a natural hollow or erosion channel; it may also be excavated. Water is retained by an earthen embankment. Embankments located and described in the survey varied from 2 meters to more than 3 kilometers long; the highest was 28 meters high. Embankments use to good advantage the rocky hills of the region, often damming up valleys between ridges or capturing the runoff from high granitic outcrops. Earthen embankment sections consist of hundreds or thousands of soil lenses; presumably the result of innumerable head-loads of soil laid down by large groups of laborers, as described in travellers' accounts of the period (chapter 6). Most earthen embankments are faced with stepped masonry on the upstream side, and occasionally on both sides. Small reservoirs may have no masonry, or a few rows of roughly coursed boulders, while large reservoirs may have fifteen or more courses of cut stone blocks. In many instances, projecting steps and staircases are built into the masonry face. A more extensive discussion of reservoir morphology can be found in Morrison (1993); figure 2.6 illustrates a hypothetical reservoir in cross section. Land in the *ayacut*, or area watered by a reservoir, is described as lying "below" the reservoir, while the higher land constituting the watershed of the reservoir is described as lying "above" the reservoir.

The great majority of Vijayanagara reservoirs are filled by seasonal runoff and fall in the wet-cum-dry category. Such reservoirs usually contain water only during the monsoon and for a few months afterwards, although some retain small permanent pools. Runoff-fed reservoirs vary greatly in size and in water-holding capacity, depending on the size and nature of their catchments. The Daroji Kere, for example, is the largest reservoir in the entire district but is supplied entirely by runoff, partly from fairly reliable streams originating in the Sandur Hills.

The Daroji Kere is also the lowest reservoir in a system of connected or grouped reservoirs. Sharma and Sharma (1990:20) classify reservoirs into three categories: (1) *system reservoirs*, which are fed by canals or rivers and thus may have little or no runoff catchment in the immediate area; (2) *nonsystem reservoirs*, or isolated runoff-fed reservoirs; and (3) *grouped reservoirs*, or series of interconnected reservoirs in which the excess flow from one is channeled to another downstream. Grouped reservoirs may be system or nonsystem reservoirs, but in the study area all grouped reservoirs are runoff fed. As discussed in chapter 5, several large systems of grouped reservoirs are found in the study area.

Some runoff-fed reservoirs belong in the category of dry cultivation, since they rarely collect any surface water and have no outlets. In all respects these small reservoirs, or embankments (Morrison 1991b), operate like terraces or check-dams, but their morphology is similar to that of larger reservoirs. Of course, during dry years cultivation may also take place in the beds of reservoirs fitted with sluices.

Permanent and seasonal reservoirs evince great variability in water collection, but methods of water distribution are similar. Water is released from the reservoirs to the fields below by means of tunnels which are constructed under the embankment. The tunnels are generally rectangular or square in cross section, and are lined with stone slabs on all sides. The slabs are then encased in a brick-and-plaster sheath (e.g. Morrison 1993:figure 5). On the upstream side of the embankment, the tunnel outlet is usually under water, and the flow of water is regulated by sluices.

Vijayanagara sluices are highly distinctive, and serve as one of the best indicators of chronology and degree of elaboration of a reservoir. A typical sluice consists of two stone uprights joined by two or three cross-pieces (figure 2.7). The tunnel outlet is located between the uprights, and all the cross pieces are perforated by round openings above the outlet. The tunnel can be blocked by lowering a wooden plug attached to a bar or rope into the opening. The end of the bar or rope may be secured to one of the cross-pieces, depending

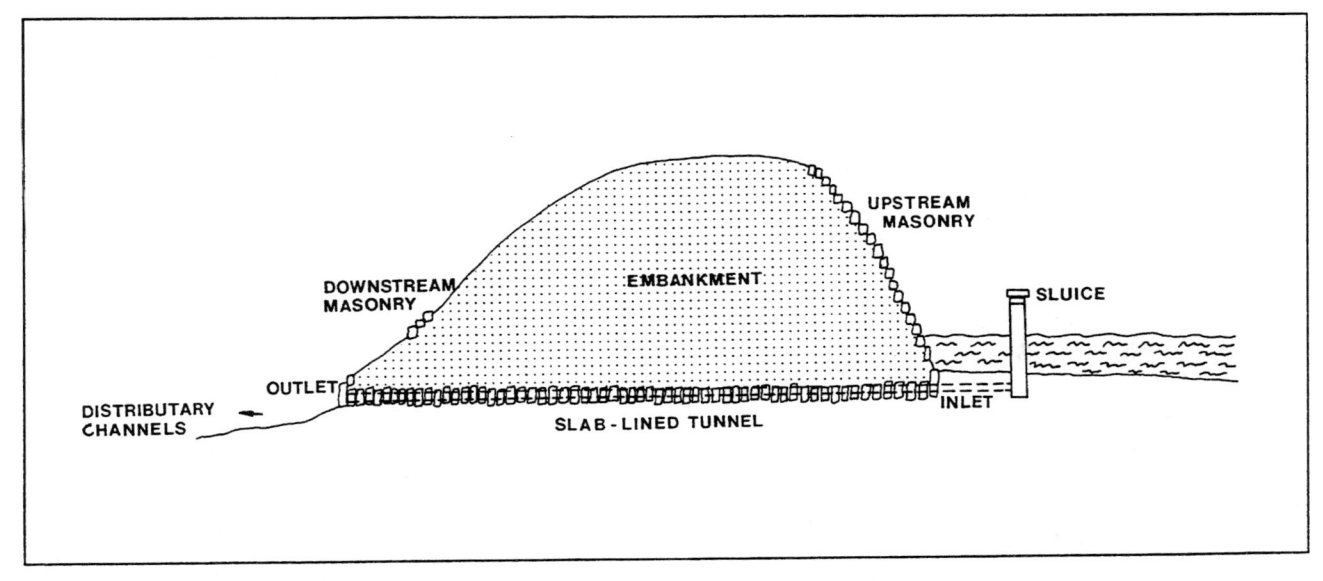

FIGURE 2.6 Cross section of reservoir embankment

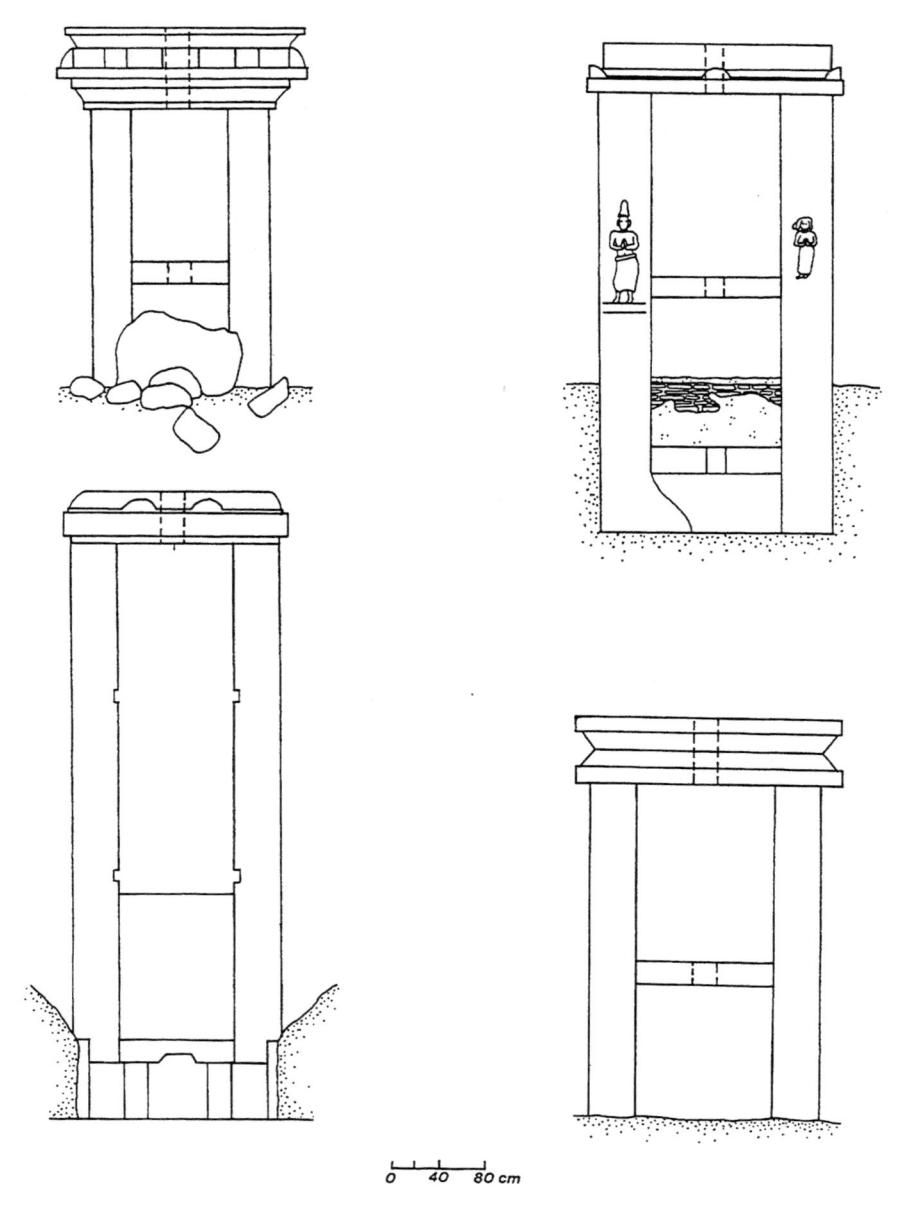

FIGURE 2.7 Four Vijayanagara-period sluice gates. Note donor portraits on upper right sluice gate, VMS-4.

on the level of the water. The upper cross-piece commonly consists of a three-part moulding sequence, similar to those seen in formal architecture of the period (Fritz, Michell, and Nagaraja Rao 1985). Sculptures of deities are also common, and at least two reservoirs south of the city, one a moderately sized, runoff-fed reservoir near the village of Malapannagudi (VMS-4), contains sculptures of the sort termed "donor portraits" in temple architecture. In most cases, sculpted figures are those commonly associated with doorways (Lakshmi and Ganesha being the most common) in temples and the overall form of the sluice itself mimics that of a temple doorway. These architectural forms thus create a deliberate formal link with Hindu temples.

Water can also be released from the reservoir by spillways, or waste weirs. These "overflow sluices" may consist of very closely fitted stone aprons and low walls or, more commonly, appear to be a jumble of boulders and cobbles. The rocky landscape, the sparse vegetation, and the seasonality of precipitation virtually ensure that the velocity of runoff in the rainy season can be sufficient to breach even the largest reservoir. Spillways allow the excess water to flow out of the reservoir with the minimum impact on the embankment. Some very small reservoirs do not have tunnels, but only spillways, and could have been used for only a very limited period of time each year.

On the downstream side of the embankment, water either flowed out of the tunnel directly into the fields, or it flowed into a small basin (or both). These basins were made either of stone or of brick and plaster, and contain outlets for water to flow into earthen ditches to the fields. Only two of the hundreds of Vijayanagara reservoirs I have observed contain basins (for a description of the brick basin associated with the reservoir VMS-4, see Morrison 1991a). The primary function of these basins may have been for domestic use, but they may also have allowed silt to settle.

Anantarajasagar and Reservoir Construction

The Anantarajasagar reservoir, located in Cuddapah District of the modern state of Andhra Pradesh (approximately 250 km east of Vijayanagara), is associated with an unusually detailed inscription regarding its construction. Even though it lies outside the metropolitan region, it is worth considering in more detail. This reservoir was constructed in A.D. 1369, during the reign of Bukka I (A.D. 1335-1377), the first Vijayanagara king. The water-spread of this large reservoir covers an area of approximately 41.4 square kilometers. Fed by the Maldev River, this reservoir was fitted with four sluices, and has a masonry-edged earthen embankment 1,372 meters long, 45.7 meters wide, and 10 meters high (Randhawa 1980). What is unusual about the inscription associated with this reservoir is its enumeration of the labor involved in its construction: one thousand laborers were employed over a period of two years. One hundred carts were employed in carrying stone to the construction site (Randhawa 1980). If one assumes a five-day work week as a first guess, this comes to 520,000 person-days of labor (perhaps excluding the cart drivers?). The size of the Anantarajasagar reservoir is comparable to that of the larger reservoirs in the survey area but is smaller than the largest of the Vijayanagara-area reservoirs. Thus, it is clear that a large amount of labor was invested in reservoirs; this is discussed in more detail in chapter 5.

The Anantarajasagar inscription is also important in that it provides a sort of prescriptive litany of desirable and undesirable factors in reservoir location, construction, and sociopolitical context:

1. A righteous king, wealthy, happy, and desirous of acquiring fame.
2. A person well-versed in patha*s shastra* (texts on hydrology).
3. Hard soil in the bed of the tank.
4. A river with sweet water with a course of about 38.6 km [3 *yojanas*]
5. Two projecting portions of hills
6. Between these projecting portions of hills a dam built of compact stone, not too long, but firm.
7. Two extremities of hills should be devoid of fruit-bearing trees.
8. Bed of tank extensive and deep.
9. A quarry nearby, with long and straight stones.
10. Fertile, low and level land in neighborhood to be irrigated.
11. A watercourse with strong eddies in the mountain region.
12. Masons skilled in the art of tank construction. (Randhawa 1980:99)

The inscription also lists six faults to be avoided in the placement and construction of a reservoir:

1. Oozing of water from the dam.
2. Saline soil.
3. Location of the site at a boundary of two kingdoms.
4. High ground in the middle of the tank.
5. Scanty water supply and too extensive an area to be irrigated.
6. Too little land to be irrigated and excessive supply of water. (Randhawa 1980:99)

What we know about the organization of reservoir construction is primarily derived from the stone and copper inscriptions of the period, most of which are associated with temples. Information is available only for the larger reservoirs, however; the thousands of smaller ones are ignored in the historical record. It may be that individual households or other groups were responsible for the construction and maintenance of the small reservoirs. Agricultural production under even large reservoirs, however, did not appear to have been centrally controlled (Morrison 1993, and below). The discussion in the following chapters will explain why facility size can not be used as a simple indicator of the degree of elite involvement in the construction or operation of that facility (and see Morrison and Lycett 1994).

Wells are often associated with Vijayanagara reservoirs, and almost every large reservoir has one or more deep wells lying in the field immediately below it. Reservoirs raise the water table in their immediate area, and wells were constructed to take advantage of this fact. Wells may be used for supplemental watering of fields, though not as the primary water source. The major problem of well irrigation consists, of course, of lifting water out of the well. In southern India, one way of accomplishing this was to harness the energy of cattle. A type of facility I have informally named "cows go up, cows go down" was constructed adjacent to certain wells. The structure consists of a large ramp that leads to a point directly above the well. Cattle were backed up the ramp, and then harnessed to containers of water down in the well. As the cattle walk forward down the ramp, they lift the containers of water (via ropes and pulleys), which then flows down special channels or chutes in or adjacent to the ramp and from there into fields around the well. The high ramp not only gives the cattle a runway, but it also raises the water high enough that it will flow quickly down the chutes and further into fields around the well. These rather elaborate wells are rare in the Vijayanagara region. A solitary example from the survey area is associated with a spring-fed well; other wells may have been too variable in supply to merit such elaborate construction.

Interconnected Facilities

Vijayanagara agricultural facilities were often only components of large-scale systems of features. The canals, for example, now form a connected network, albeit one which emerged over a period of time. Many reservoirs also did not operate in isolation, but were physically linked with other agricultural facilities such as canals, as in the case of the Kamalapuram reservoir. One of the most dramatic examples of interlinked facilities is that of the multiple-reservoir systems (grouped reservoirs). In this arrangement, reservoirs are arranged along the length of a valley or sloping plain such that the irrigation channels below one reservoir flow into and help supply the reservoir or reservoirs downstream. There are several of these integrated systems in the area around Vijayanagara; one in the Daroji Valley contains at least fourteen reservoirs. The Daroji system is located in a long valley surrounded by hills on three sides, and opens into a wide plain. The valley slopes gently down to the east, so that reservoirs are situated to collect runoff from the west, south, and north. Almost all of the reservoirs in this system have been breached and are out of use; even so, it is still possible to trace connections between reservoirs. The lowest reservoir in this system is the Daroji Kere which today is permanently full of water. Its huge double sluices date to the late or immediately post-Vijayanagara period, suggesting that the pre-Colonial capacity of this reservoir must also have been substantial (see also Morrison 1993; Morrison and Sinopoli 1992).

Several other integrated systems of reservoirs are found in the region around the city, particularly in the area to the west and south of Hospet. Among these is the Dhanayakanakere system as well as several others now partially submerged by the waters of the Tungabhadra reservoir. Many reservoirs in the Dhanayakanakere area date to the sixteenth century, and at least one contains large double sluices of a type seen on a reservoir (z/1) in the Daroji Valley. However, systematic study of this area has not been completed.

In the driest upland areas, reservoirs sometimes occur in linked systems with agricultural terraces. The reservoir is usually located at the head of the system, releasing water to terraced areas below. Terraces, as noted above, are also important in protecting the watershed of reservoirs from erosion. Wells may also be associated with terraces and with reservoirs.

WET, DRY, AND WET-CUM-DRY

The three-part classification of South Indian agriculture constitutes one way of partitioning the diversity of strategies employed by producers in the region. It has the great advantage, from the perspective of the material record, of being associated with specific and recognizable forms of agricultural facilities. However, the degree of facility interconnection and of linkage across the landscape, even between ostensibly different types of features, makes it imperative that this classification be viewed as merely a descriptive device. The agricultural landscape of the Vijayanagara period described in chapter 4 and discussed in chapter 5 was, in a real sense, a whole. That is, the landscapes of production, of settlement, of transportation, and of meaning, were connected. Movements of soil and of water and changes in vegetation could have a significant impact on the region as a whole. Even more than this, the establishment of settlements and the construction of agricultural features and of roads both built upon the existing landscape and created new landscapes that provided frameworks for subsequent actions.

3

Vijayanagara Agriculture in Context

THE CITY OF VIJAYANAGARA was located in a sparsely populated area that had been integrated into several South Indian states prior to the fourteenth century but had never itself been politically central. Within a short time, possibly less than fifty years, the city grew to contain a population of at least 100,000, perhaps as much as 500,000 (Stein 1989; and see below), and came to be considered the political and ritual center of the empire. This chapter considers political and economic strategies and institutions in the Vijayanagara region and empire, which, combined with the ecological constraints on agricultural production discussed in chapter 2, defined the changing course of agricultural production.

This chapter consists of wo distinct parts. The first is chronological, focussing on the nature of pre-Vijayanagara settlement in the study area, setting the stage for consideration of the Vijayanagara material record in chapters 4 and 5. The second part considers the Vijayanagara period, but moves beyond the Vijayanagara region, in order to situate local economic and political concerns within their imperial context. I discuss several structuring models of Vijayanagara political and economic organization and introduce the events of the sixteenth century leading to agricultural intensification in the Vijayanagara metropolitan region.

SOUTH INDIA: LANGUAGE AND RELIGION

South India, that portion of peninsular India south of the Vindhya mountains (Saletore 1973:1), is divided into several linguistic regions. Although numerous languages and dialects are spoken, the principal languages in southern India are Kannada, Telugu, Tamil, and Malayalam. These four languages all belong to the Dravidian language family. The linguistic divide between the "Dravidian" south and the "Aryan" (Indo-European) north has been emphasized by historians and anthropologists to such an extent that it has almost attained the status of an impenetrable barrier that, together with the Vindhyas, creates a great divide between north and south. In actuality, of course, the distinction is not so clear-cut. Several polities, based both in the north and the south, have spanned the divide. Further integration in language is manifest in the widespread use of Sanskrit in religious ritual and as a scholarly language.

South India in the Vijayanagara period

contained adherents of numerous religious traditions, including Muslims, Jews, Christians, Jains, and Hindus. Within Hinduism, major distinctions exist between different religious sects or orders (cf. Inden 1990) such as Vaisnavism and Shaivism. Both linguistic and religious traditions and their working and reworking by participants in the Vijayanagara polity are important for understanding its political and economic dynamics. Agricultural production was closely tied to temples (discussed below), and association with temples provided a variety of groups and individuals with ways of structuring production, forming alliances, and obtaining access to agricultural produce.

Pre-Vijayanagara Settlements

The pioneering geological and archaeological explorations of Robert Bruce Foote (1914, 1916) in the late nineteenth and early twentieth centuries remain among the most thorough studies of the early prehistory of the Bellary District. Foote noted the existence of seventy-seven archaeological localities within the Bellary District containing a variety of stone implements, which he identified as belonging to the Palaeolithic, Neolithic, and Iron ages. Further, he noted the existence of Neolithic ashmounds, or "cinder camps" (see below), correctly attributing them to dung burning (1916). He was the first to map the geology of the region, and paid particular attention to varying uses of lithic raw materials in different periods, a focus which has continued in Indian archaeology to the extent that material type is often used as chronological marker.

Palaeolithic

Palaeolithic sites are well represented in peninsular India, but they often suffer from poor stratigraphic context. Notable research into the Lower Palaeolithic of Karnataka includes that of Paddayya (1982, 1985) at Hunsgi in Raichur District (see also B. Allchin 1959; Allchin and Allchin 1982). Palaeolithic materials are not well represented in the Vijayanagara survey area, although Foote (1916:78) noted the presence of a "chopper-shaped Palaeolith" of quartzite-hematite from Daroji, just southeast of the survey area, and Ansari has noted the presence of "Soan" pebble tools from an unspecified location on the bank of the Tungabhadra in Bellary District (1985). In the 1994 season, a possible Palaeolithic site was located in Block R to the southwest of Mallapannagudi; it is currently undergoing analysis (Morrison and Sinopoli in press).

Neolithic/Chalcolithic

Not until the Neolithic period (ca. 2300 B.C. to 1000 B.C.) does dated archaeological material reappear in the area (Allchin 1969; Paddayya 1973). South-central India contains a type of Neolithic site not found elsewhere in South Asia, the ashmound. Neolithic ashmounds, also referred to as "cinder camps," are large (up to about 8 meters high and 50 meters in diameter) accumulations of a vitrified, slaggy material identified as the remains of fired cattle dung (Allchin 1963; Zeuner 1960). These mounds are often, though not always, associated with artifact scatters and settlements and thus far have been found only in the Bellary and Raichur districts of Karnataka. They were first described by the British Captain Newbold in a short report to the *Madras Journal of Literature and Science* in 1838. Both Newbold and later, the British civil servant, antiquarian, and historian of Vijayanagara, Robert Sewell, accepted traditional accounts that the mounds were funeral pyres of giants, demons, and other mythic and heroic figures or that they represented the remains of "enormous human or animal sacrifices performed by holy *Rishis* [sages]" (cited in Foote 1916:92; see also Longhurst 1916). Foote (1916:92) noted, however, that the mounds he examined contained no bone at all, with the exception of a single bovine horn core. He also noticed straw impressions from *Sorghum* (*Jowar* or *Cholum*) in the slaggy material and remarked on the overall scarcity of artifacts from within the mounded deposits. Foote distinguished two types of sites: the cinder camp, which he took to be a vallated settlement, and the cinder mound, without evidence of settlement. In fact, although this distinction does appear to usefully highlight some of the variation in Neolithic sites in the area, personal observations suggest that some "cinder mounds" contain abundant evidence of artifactual material and may have been the locations of seasonal settlement or at least of ephemeral structures. Six of each type of mound were noted to occur in Bellary District (Foote 1916; and see Foote 1887).

Excavated ashmound sites close to the study area include Budihal (Paddayya 1992), Kupgal (Majumdar and Rajaguru 1966), Piklihal (Allchin 1960), and Utnur (Allchin 1961). A small ashmound (VMS-26) was located during the

Vijayanagara survey (Sinopoli and Morrison 1991). This low mound, situated near the south bank of the Tungabhadra River, has been diminished by the plowing, irrigating, and movement of soil associated with the expansion of intensive agriculture in the Vijayanagara period, but was at least 30 by 20 meters in extent. Unpublished surface collections from the site have been made by the Directorate of Archaeology and Museums, Karnataka. Additional collections were made in 1988 and are reported on by Lycett (1991a), Morrison and Lycett (1989), and Sinopoli and Morrison (1991). Locally known as "Walighat" (Valighat), this site has made its way into the sacred geography of the region. Vali, a demon associated with the epic of the Ramayana, is believed to have been incinerated on this spot (for other examples of Ramayana associations, see Fritz, Michell, and Nagaraja Rao 1985; Dallapiccola et al. 1992). Foote described this site as "the great mound at Nimbapur, a little to the east of the ruins of Vijayanagar" (1916:90). Nimbapur can be found on nearly all maps of the area before about A.D. 1960 but is consistently located several kilometers to the north and west of VMS-26. However, there is no doubt that Foote's mound is the same as VMS-26:

> The third [mound] in point of size, the Nimbapur mound, a little east of the ruins of Vijayanagar (Hampi) I notice next because it was described by Captain Newbold who mentioned the native legend that it was the ashes of the giant Bali. The dimensions of the mound given by Newbold are: length 45 yards [41 meters], width 18 yards [16 meters], and height 10 to 14 feet [3.4 to 4.2 meters]. They appeared to me to be correct. I examined the mound very carefully but found nothing whatever to assist in determining its age which may be and very probably is, post-Neolithic. (Foote 1916:93-94)

We have now no more chronological information on this site than did Foote, but no post-Neolithic ashmounds have yet been identified.

Iron Age

Iron Age (ca. 1000 B.C. to 300-200 B.C.) sites include both megaliths, some with burials and some without, and settlements (Leshnik 1974). Hence, this period is often termed "Megalithic" (Deo 1973). A large Megalithic site, Hire-Benkal, is reported in southern Raichur District (Ray 1986:66). No sites within the survey area could be assigned to this time period.

Early Historic

In the Early Historic period, as its name implies, the first few traces of writing are found. This period dates from about 300-200 B.C. to A.D. 400 (Begley 1986). By the fourth century B.C., a supra-regional polity known as the Mauryan empire had formed in northern India (Kosambi 1956; Kulke and Rothermund 1986; Thapar 1966) at Pataliputra (Patna). Little is known about the actual organization and administration of the Mauryan empire (Mookerji 1960; Nilakanta Sastri 1966), but it seems to have been linked to east coast trade networks as far south as Tamil Nadu by the third century B.C. (Begley 1983:469). The boundaries of the empire are assumed to coincide with the area in which inscriptions of its most famous ruler, Ashoka, are found (Nilakanta Sastri 1966). Several of these inscriptions, or rock-cut edicts, are located quite close to Vijayanagara, at Koppal, Maski, Nittur, Udegolam, Siddapur Jatingarameswara, and Brahmagiri (Sircar 1975:110-19; Kotraiah 1983:381). Thus, the study area has been suggested to be a Mauryan border zone (Davies 1959). The Mauryan period also provides a convenient marker for the spread of Buddhism throughout India, as signified by the well-known account of the conversion of Ashoka.

Between the Early Historic and the Early Medieval periods (see below), the political history of southern India was very complex and changeable, with numerous small polities competing for power, and shifting alliances and territories. The Kadamba polity ruled the western Kanara coast of India between about the fourth and fourteenth centuries A.D. (Kulke and Rothermund 1986; Mores 1931); the Chalukyas of Badami were tributary princes under the Kadambas before asserting their independence in the seventh century and taking control over the Deccan.

The Medieval Periods

The seventh century A.D. ushers in the period known in South Asian history as the *Early Medieval* period, followed by the *Medieval* period in the thirteenth century. A great deal of debate has centered around both the use of this term, which implies developmental parallels to European history, and around characterizations of Medieval society as "feudal," in analogy with western Europe (Sircar 1969; Venkataramanayya 1935; Krishnswami Pillai 1964; Stein 1980; Kulke and Rothermund 1986). Further, since the Medieval periods are generally held to continue until the onset of European dominance in the Colonial period, there exists a temporal lag between the European and the South Asian "Medieval" periods, reinforcing the impression of retarded cultural development. I do not use the term "Medieval" here, but instead refer either to specific polities (Chola, Hoysala, Chalukya, Vijayanagara) or call the time between the seventh and seventeenth centuries A.D., "precolonial."

This periodization (Prehistoric, Ancient or Early Historic, and Medieval), like archaeological attempts to impose European developmental terminology on the prehistoric record, has significant implications beyond the ordering of time. The European model embodies certain fundamental assumptions about the nature and course of change (development). These include an assumption of progressive, linear evolution of social and material life which can be captured in a terminology of "stages." The terminology may vary: bands, tribes, chiefdoms, states (Service 1962); archaic, feudal, capitalist (Marx 1859; cited in Krader 1975), but the essential attempt to structure and order a perceived unilinear process of change is common to all of these. In India, as in other countries subjected to European colonialism, this mania for evolutionary classification was allied with a perception of difference between the prehistory of Europeans and the (presumably inferior) prehistory of others, an aspect of what Said (1979) has termed "Orientalism." In Vijayanagara historiography, the evolutionary/Orientalist tension is most clearly manifest in two debates over the concepts of feudalism and the Asiatic Mode of Production. These two topics will be discussed below in the context of the Vijayanagara period.

The precolonial political history of southern India is extremely complex, involving periods of supra-regional unification followed by "balkanization" into smaller, competing polities. To further complicate the picture, polities were spread out across the peninsula, so that from the perspective of the study area, the political "center" was located in different directions at different times, and control over the study area (which had never been near the core of any pre-Vijayanagara power) shifted fairly rapidly. In the following sections, I present an extremely simplified framework of political history for the Vijayanagara region. In this discussion, I have tried to relate the locations of pre-Vijayanagara places to the position of the city of Vijayanagara. In doing so, I have not taken great pains to point out that when I mention "Vijayanagara" in a period before the mid-fourteenth century, I am referring to the location in which the city would eventually be placed (since it did not yet exist). This point should be kept in mind.

Chalukyas (A.D. 624-1061)

The two major imperial powers in southern India before the Vijayanagara empire were the Cholas in the south and the Chalukyas in the north. Both of these large polities broke up into smaller states prior to the establishment of Vijayanagara in the fourteenth century. The Eastern Chalukyan polity controlled the area around Vijayanagara between the seventh and eleventh centuries A.D. With their capital at Badami (Vatapi), in present-day Andhra Pradesh, the Eastern Chalukyas must be distinguished from the Western Chalukyas of Kalyani (A.D. 973-1200). Further south, the Chola empire (A.D. 849-1279; Heitzman 1987; Nilakanta Sastri 1966; Stein 1980) ruled what is now Tamil Nadu and the southern part of Karnataka at the same time as the Chalukyas were extending their control over the Deccan Plateau. In A.D. 1071, Kulottunga of Vengi, a member of the Eastern Chalukyan ruling family, took over the Chola throne, with which he was affinally associated (Kulke and Rothermund 1986). This resulted in the nominal unification of the entire southeastern coastal region of India under one house, called by Chopra, Ravindran, and Subrahmanian (1979) the Chalukya-Cholas. The borders of the Chalukyan polity were not entirely stable during this long period, however, and the Rashtrakutas of the northern and western Deccan must also be counted as significant political players on the Karnatak Plateau (Inden 1990; Nilakanta Sastri 1966).

The Vijayanagara region contains several indications of small-scale Chalukya-period occupation. Just east of the modern town of Hospet, near Muniribad, two Chalukyan temples are situated on the southern bank of the Tungabhadra River. In one of these small temples a large inscription, known as the Muniribad Vikramaditya inscription, dates to A.D. 1088 (Davison-Jenkins 1988:135). This inscription mentions the construction of a channel, almost certainly the Premogal Channel, a short, pre-modern irrigation canal which runs for approximately eight kilometers from the north bank of the river. This channel is still used and maintained but is not linked to any of the Vijayanagara-period channels. That irrigated agriculture was carried out in the eleventh century seems certain; what is not known is the scale of that production or of associated settlement. There is no known Chalukyan settlement in the area around the two temples and the canal, but that area has never been systematically studied. Later intensive agriculture and urban growth have undoubtedly caused a great deal of disturbance in the area, but it may be possible to isolate areas of settlement.

Further east, within the area now covered by the city of Vijayanagara, there are several Chalukya-period religious structures, probably indicating the presence of a small settlement, perhaps important primarily as a holy place. These temples are clustered on Hemakuta Hill, a low rocky outcrop near the south bank of the river. Subsequent construction has obscured pre-Vijayanagara non-religious architecture and other material, if indeed substantial settlement in this area did occur.

Michell (1991) describes several Chalukyan temples located on the low hill near the village of Hampi (in the "Sacred Center" using the terminology of Fritz, Michell, and Nagaraja Rao 1985). These temples are situated within a cluster of pre-Vijayanagara and early Vijayanagara temples (see also Wagoner 1991) in a walled area of approximately 300 by 150 meters. The cluster of Hemakuta temples has been overshadowed by the imposing Virupaksha temple and its long bazaar street, which form the focal point of the village of Hampi. The Virupaksha temple itself was built around a ninth to tenth century "core," although its present form is primarily structured by sixteenth-century additions (Michell 1991:38). On Hemakuta Hill itself, Michell notes the presence of an eighth- to ninth-century Rashtrakuta-period temple; a similar temple is located to the north of Hemakuta Hill near the large temple tank (Manmatha tank) associated with the Virupaksha temple. Next to the latter stands a Hoysala-period temple, containing an inscription that refers to a gift to the Virupaksha sanctuary in A.D. 1199 (Michell 1991:42). Michell describes eight temples on Hemakuta Hill that date to the fourteenth century, of which three, he believes, are pre-Vijayanagara. One of the latter contains an inscription referring to a fourteenth-century chieftain of Kampli, the small kingdom which ruled this area immediately prior to the founding of Vijayanagara (see below). Several thirteenth- and fourteenth-century temples are also located near the Manmatha tank, and with the establishment of the Vijayanagara polity in the mid-fourteenth century, the area became densely built up and settled. Thus, it is clear that the area around Hemakuta Hill and the Virupaksha temple was more or less continuously maintained as a religious area, if not as a settlement, from the ninth or tenth century up to the present. Years of concerted effort and archaeological excavation in the built-up core of the city of Vijayanagara (to the south of Hampi and the Hemakuta Hill area) by both federal and state archaeological agencies have failed to reveal any more substantial evidence of pre-Vijayanagara settlement than some reused architectural elements, including several Buddhist-period (Early Historic) carved slabs, which were probably not in their original context.

The British gazetteer-writer Francis suggested (1904:29) that the minor Chalukyan capital of Pottalakere was located on the site of Dhanayakanakere (Davison-Jenkins 1988:19) to the south of Hospet. It is not clear, however, on what evidence this suggestion is based. The modern settlement of Dhanayakanakere is on the edge of a very large Vijayanagara-period reservoir, and I have not located any pre-Vijayanagara architecture or artifacts near this reservoir.

Hoysalas (A.D.1006-1346)

The Hoysalas were a small imperial power centered to the south of the study area in the Mysore region, with their capital at Dvarasamudra. Kulke and Rothermund note:

> Several local tributary princes [under the Cholas] emerged as independent kings, among them the Pandyas of Madurai, the Hoysalas of the southern mountains, and the Kakatiyas of Warrangal. But in due course they fell to the superior military strategy of the Delhi Sultanate in the early fourteenth century A.D. (1986:116)

The study area lay within the zone of Hoysala control in the period before the establishment of the Vijayanagara state, and as I discuss below, the debate concerning the nature of the transition from the Hoysalas to Vijayanagara's Sangam dynasty is important for understanding historical characterizations of Vijayanagara polity and economy.

The Hoysala period is known for a distinctive architectural style involving elaborate and finely detailed stone carving. A cluster of Hoysala-period temples, presumably also the location of a Hoysala settlement, is found at Lakkundi, 70 kilometers north of Vijayanagara. Within the study area, several thirteenth- and fourteenth-century temples are located on Hemakuta Hill and near the Virupaksha temple, as discussed above. Undoubtedly the locus of some small-scale settlement in the Hoysala period, the area contains little direct evidence beyond that of the temples themselves, as noted. Other Hoysala-period settlements in the region around Vijayanagara are better known. These include the fortified town of Anegundi (Purandare 1986), located on the north bank of the Tungabhadra River opposite Vijayanagara city. Both Kampli (Venkata Ramanayya 1929) and Kummata Durga (Patil 1991c) were fortified settlements occupied in the centuries before the founding of Vijayanagara. While earlier scholars felt that Kampli was the capital of the small Kampli kingdom, from which the first Vijayanagara rulers seized control of the region, C. S. Patil has argued that Kummata Durga was the seat of the Kampli chieftains (Patil 1991b). Further, he has suggested (1991b:196) that the Kampli chieftains were, in fact, powerful kings who successfully resisted incursions into the area by leaders of "Muslim" polities to the north.

The Delhi Sultanate and the South

The spread of Islam throughout the Mediterranean area and Western Asia first made an impact on South Asia in the eighth century A.D. It was not until the twelfth century, however, that the Delhi Sultanate, headed by Muslim rulers and a Muslim ruling elite, established itself in northern India. South Asian archaeologists and historians often label different polities as "Hindu" or "Muslim," depending on the creed of their rulers. This somewhat misleading practice in no way necessarily implies anything about the religious composition of the population under that government, and what were economic and political conflicts much more than ritual/religious disagreements are all too easily cast in the terms of ideological struggle (see discussion in Wagoner 1993:51).

Around A.D. 1300, the Delhi Sultan Alaud-din launched a campaign of conquest and plunder against the territories to the south. He captured the "impregnable" fortress of Devagiri (later renamed Dalautabad) ruled by the Yadava kings, successors of the Chalukyas in the northwest portions of their empire. After demanding tribute payments from the Yadavas, Alaud-din sent his general Malik Kafur, a converted Hindu slave, to capture and plunder the fortress of Warrangal (Kulke and Rothermund 1986:170). This accomplished, Dvarasamudra was captured from the Hoysalas while their king, Ballala III, was away attacking the Pandyan capital of Madurai. After Ballala agreed to pay tribute to Delhi, as had the Yadava and Warrangal rulers, Malik Kafur burned and looted Madurai, returning to Delhi with the riches of southern Indian cities and temples. This expedition lasted no more than eleven months (Kulke and Rothermund 1986) but has loomed large in the minds of historians as establishing a threat to the Hindu cultures of the south from the Muslim north. In part, this emphasis is well founded, since the expansionist plans of the Delhi Sultanate did indeed constitute a threat to southern kingdoms. Moreover, the medium of Islam proved a powerful social and ideological instrument in political alliance formation, trading, and in many other contexts. According to many historians (e.g. Saletore 1982; Nilakanta Sastri 1966), however, the establishment of the Vijayanagara state was a direct response to the religious and cultural threat posed by the military activities of the Delhi Sultanate, and this interpretation certainly overstates the impact of the "threat" of Islam on the south.

The Delhi Sultanate established territories in the Deccan and in the far south, near Madurai, all of which promptly declared their independence. The Sultanate of Ma'bar was established in 1333 (Nilakanta Sastri 1966:53), and in the Deccan, the Bahmani Sultanate was founded in A.D. 1346, ten years after the traditional founding date of Vijayanagara. In 1482, the Bahmani Sultanate disintegrated into the five independent kingdoms of Bijapur, Bidar, Berar, Golconda, and Ahmednagar (the Deccani Sultanates).

The Vijayanagara Period (A.D.1336-1650)

The remainder of this chapter will outline several of the major areas of debate regarding the structure and operation of the Vijayanagara polity, as these issues are inseparably connected to considerations of agricultural production and distribution. The nature of Vijayanagara control over outlying areas of the empire has engendered a substantial debate (e.g. Palat 1987; Stein 1980, 1989; Morrison and Sinopoli 1992; Sinopoli 1988; Sinopoli and Morrison 1995). This debate has significant implications for understanding the nature of production and distribution in and around the city itself. Finally, the Vijayanagara region is itself discussed in terms of its relationship to the larger polity.

The political history of Vijayanagara has been exhaustively covered elsewhere (Appadorai 1936; Appadurai 1978; Heras 1927; Krishnaswami Pillai 1964; Nagaraju 1991; Nilakanta Sastri 1966; Nilakanta Sastri and Venkata Ramanayya 1946; Saletore 1934; Sewell 1900; Stein 1980, 1989; Venkata Ramanayya 1929, 1935), and will only be broadly sketched here. The numerous treatments of Vijayanagara economic history (Breckenridge 1985; Karashima 1984, 1992; Mahalingam 1940, 1951; Palat 1987; Ramaswamy 1985a, 1985b, 1985c; Stein 1979, 1980, 1982; Subrahmanyam 1984, 1990) also provide valuable information about institutional arrangements in agricultural production.

The Founding of Vijayanagara

The Vijayanagara polity seems to have taken over the sovereignty of northern Karnataka from the Hoysalas by the beginning of the fourteenth century, establishing their dynasty, as Stein has put it, "upon the foundation of the failing Hoysala house under Ballala II" (1980:381). Kulke and Rothermund (1986:189) mention an inscription of A.D. 1320 recording the founding of a town called Vijayavirupaska Hoshapattana (meaning roughly: victory to the god Virupaksha, new town). The son of the Hoysala king, Ballala III, was named Virupaksha by his father on the spot that was later to become the city of Vijayanagara. In fact, this inscription probably referred to an area near the Virupaksha temple, in the present-day village of Hampi. As noted, Hemakuta Hill in this area contains numerous pre-Vijayanagara and early Vijayanagara temples (Michell 1991; Wagoner 1991). The widow of Ballala II was apparently present at the coronation of Harihara, king of Vijayanagara, in A.D. 1346 (Kulke and Rothermund 1986:189). In an inscription of A.D. 1349 her name is mentioned before that of Harihara, indicating, as Kulke and Rothermund (1986:189) suggest, that Harihara derived his legitimation from being "a kind of devoted heir to the Hoysalas."

In A.D. 1336, the traditional founding date of the city of Vijayanagara, Harihara constructed a fort at Barakur (Bankapur; figure 3.1) to the west of Vijayanagara in an area claimed by the Hoysalas. Desai, Ritti, and Gopal (1981:332) argue that Ballala III sanctioned this construction, since he visited the fort in 1338. Furthermore, as many historians have pointed out, the first Vijayanagara kings did not assume royal titles, and thus might be more accurately considered subject rulers or "little kings" (Dirks 1987; Inden 1990) under the titular control of the Hoysalas or some other dynasty.

There exist several different "founding myths" of the city, accounts that perhaps reveal more about Vijayanagara historiography than about the early Vijayanagara period. Structural similarities can be seen between the Vijayanagara accounts and other founding myths in South Asia (Sewell 1900:19). These accounts stress the sacredness of the founding location, the religious experience or revelation of the founder(s), and their political legitimacy in terms of previous polities (Kulke 1985). Much of the debate about the founding of Vijayanagara, both as a city and as a polity, revolves around the identity of the two sons of Sangama and the first Vijayanagara kings, Hakka (or Harihara) and Bukka. Historians have argued about whether Hakka and Bukka were Telugu speakers (Nilakanta Sastri 1966; Venkata Ramanayya 1933, 1935) or Kannada speakers (Saletore 1934; Heras 1927; Krishnaswami Ayyangar 1919; Kulke and Rothermund 1986). Themes that run through the founding stories include political legitimation through links to previous dynasties (e.g. Stein 1989:1), stress on associations with particular religious orders (religious institutions were powerful political and economic agents, as discussed below), and focus on the supposed founding ideology of Vijayanagara as a regeneration of Hindu *dharma* (law, proper behavior) in response to the threat of Islam (discussed in Filliozat and Filliozat 1988; Kulke 1985; Stein 1980; Wagoner 1993).

Scholars of Vijayanagara have seemed to feel that if only the "mystery" of the foundation of Vijayanagara could be resolved then its operation would also be made clear. Its origins are thus conceived of as containing the "essence" of the Vijayanagara polity, and these "essences" or themes, whether Hindu *dharma* or linguistic nationalism, can be employed as the "substantialized agents" (after Inden 1990) of Vijayanagara history. Thus, the political, economic, and religious stratagems of participants in the empire are reduced to mechanical expressions of some ideal theme or goal of Vijayanagara history.

The Vijayanagara Empire

The Vijayanagara rulers are conventionally divided into four dynasties, three of which ruled from the city of Vijayanagara (Sangamas, Saluvas,

Tuluvas). Historians have reconstructed lists of Vijayanagara kings from contemporary inscriptions (see chapter 6). Not all of these lists agree; table 3.1 presents two of these schemes.

The area claimed by Vijayanagara grew very quickly, so that the overall outlines of the imperial territory were established already by the late fourteenth century (Desai, Ritti, and Gopal 1981) although certain areas passed in and out of Vijayanagara control. Stein (1989:2) estimates the

TABLE 3.1 Dynastic list of Vijayanagara kings

Sangam Dynasty			
Harihara I	1336-1357	Harihara I	1336-1343
Bukka I	1344-1377	Bukka I	1343-1379
Harihara II	1377-1404	Harihara II	1379-1399
Virupaksha I	1404-1405		
Bukka II	1405-1406	Bukka II	1399-1406
Devaraya I	1406-1422	Devaraya I	1406-1412/13
Ramachandraraya	1422		
Vijaya Raya I	1422-1426 (?)	Vira Vijaya	1412/13-1419
Devaraya II	1422-1446	Deva Raya II	1419-1444
Vijayaraya II	1446-1447	?	1444-1449
Mallikarjuna	1447-1465	Mallikarjuna	1452-53, 1464-65
Rajashekhara	1466	Rajasekhara	1468-1469
Virupaksha II	1465-1485	Virupaksha I	1470-1471
Praudharaya	1485	Praudha Deva	1476-1477 (?)
		Rajasekhara	1479-1480
		Virupaksha II	1483-1484
		Rajasekhara	1486-1487
Saluva Dynasty			
Saluva	1486-1491	Narasimha	?1490-?
Immadi	1491-1505		
Tuluva Dynasty			
Vira Narasimha	1505-1509	Vira Narasimha	? to 1509
Krishnadeva	1509-1529	Krishnadeva Raya	1509-1530
Achuyatadeva	1529-1542	Achutyadeva Raya	1530-1542
Venkata I	1542		
Sadashiva	1542-1576	Sadasiva	1542-1567
Nilakanta Sastri 1966		*Sewell 1900*	

maximum extent of the empire at 140,000 square miles (358,400 square kilometers), about the same area as the British-ruled Madras presidency. The empire, at its peak, controlled much of India south of the Tungabhadra River. Attempts to draw boundaries and define political control inevitably raise the issue of the nature and basis of this control (cf. Morrison and Lycett 1994). These issues are discussed in the following section. In the fourteenth century, Kumara Kampana, son of Bukka I, conquered Madurai and gained control over the Coromandel coast and much of the far south (Nilakanta Sastri 1966). The southern territories were expanded throughout the fourteenth century, and during the reign of Harihara II (A.D. 1377-1404) tribute was collected from as far south as Sri Lanka (Desai, Ritti, and Gopal 1981:368).

The Vijayanagara empire never directly controlled the Malabar coast (see figure 2.1), west of the Ghats. Honavar, on the Kanara coast, was conquered by A.D. 1342 (Desai, Ritti, and Gopal 1981:331; figure 3.1). Although the Vijayanagara rulers demanded and received tribute from several other small principalities on the Kanara coast, Subrahmanyam (1984) suggests that in the sixteenth century little direct political influence was

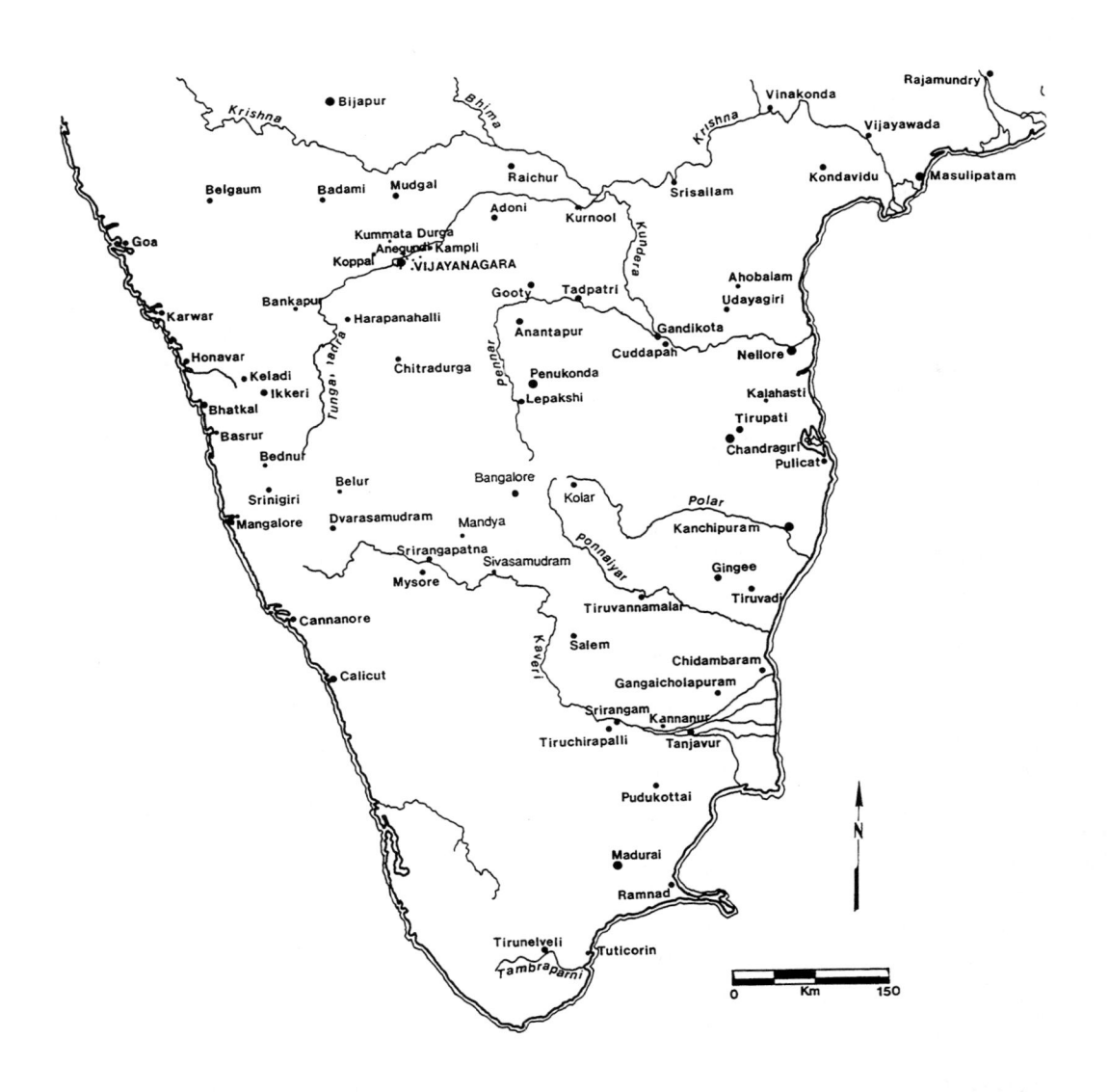

FIGURE 3.1 Southern India during the Vijayanagara period, with the locations of major settlements and rivers.

exerted over the economic operations of these polities. Vijayanagara held Goa, one of the major ports of the west coast and later the Portuguese base of operations in India, only briefly (1366-1470) before losing control of it to Bijapur, who in turn lost it to the Portuguese.

In the east, Vijayanagara waged constant territorial wars with the Hindu Gajapatis of Orissa, temporarily losing a large portion of the eastern coast, from about Kondavidu to Chidambaram, to the Orissa polity in A.D. 1463 (Kulke and Rothermund 1986:382). While this area was held by Orissa for only a short time, other areas further north are generally classified as "contested" since they passed back and forth so often (e.g. Schwartzberg 1992).

Vijayanagara territorial expansion to the south and west was held in check by the militarily powerful states to the north. These "Muslim" states initially had several military advantages over their southern neighbors, including a strong cavalry and, in the sixteenth century, a willingness to use new munitions technology such as cannons. These strategies were quickly adopted by the Vijayanagara rulers, however, who employed Muslim soldiers and generals. Horses and cavalry had long been important strategic and symbolic adjuncts of Indian kingship (e.g. Inden 1990). Because of the difficulty of successfully breeding war-horses in South India, it was necessary to constantly import horses from the Arabian Peninsula (Digby 1982:147). In fact, the horse trade seems to have been one of the only economic arenas in which Vijayanagara kings directly intervened (Nilakanta Sastri 1966:274; see also Stein 1980, 1989; Subrahmanyam 1984, 1990). Stein (1989) suggests that the military power of the Deccani Sultanates and the barrier they presented to Vijayanagara expansion in the north was actually responsible for the great economic success of the empire, forcing it to expand into the rich deltaic regions of the far south that had nurtured earlier South Indian empires.

The Raichur *doab*, or the region between the Tungabhadra and Krishna rivers, was another contested zone. The northern border of the Vijayanagara empire moved back and forth from the Krishna to the Tungabhadra, with the capital city perilously close to this battle zone. Thus, after the establishment of the empire in its first hundred years, the northern and eastern boundaries constituted the primary zones of territorial dispute, although rebellions and conflicts in the south also kept the army engaged throughout the Vijayanagara period.

Claims of territory and control were established and maintained in several ways. Chief among these seem to have been military raids and campaigns, many of which are commemorated in contemporary inscriptions and in monumental architecture. The sixteenth-century Krishna temple complex in the city of Vijayanagara, for example, is said to have been built in order to commemorate the success of Krishnadevaraya's (A.D. 1513-1514) military expedition to Orissa, in which he captured the god Balakrishna from the temple at Udayagiri (Kulke and Rothermund 1986; Stein 1980), an important fort. Thus, military successes could result in the appropriation of symbolic as well as material "goods" and territory (and see Morrison and Lycett 1994).

Claims of territorial control were made by Vijayanagara rulers and recognized (at least by historians) through the commissioning of structures and inscriptions. The location and content of these inscriptions constitute the primary historical data base for the period (see chapter 6). Buildings commissioned by Vijayanagara rulers consisted almost exclusively of fortifications and temples. The importance of military outposts for establishing and maintaining some form of imperial control is evident (cf. Morrison and Lycett 1994; Sinopoli and Morrison 1995). The right to construct temples and to make donations to them was, however, no less important in terms of the political and economic goals of the rulers.

The occupational history of the city came to an abrupt termination in the latter half of the sixteenth century although the empire continued to exist for several hundred years. In A.D. 1565, the Vijayanagara armies were decisively defeated at the battle of Talikota (or Rakshasa-Tangadi), and the city was occupied, sacked, and looted. The court (and hence the capital) fled south to Penukonda, making later moves south to Chandragiri and then Vellore. Although Tirumala attempted to recoccupy the city (Wagoner 1993:28), by the end of the sixteenth century the city itself was abandoned and only smaller agricultural communities persisted.

POLITY AND ECONOMY: MODELS

The Asiatic Mode of Production

In order to understand the nature of Vijayanagara productive systems and strategies, both on the local and regional scales, it is necessary to consider the nature of political power exerted by the Vijayanagara kings and by others and the extent to which they did or did not involve themselves in productive activities and decision making. It is possible to recognize several political models in Indian studies generally and in the Vijayanagara case in particular. More general conceptions which have structured historical scholarship include the formulations of the Asiatic Mode of Production and its associated constructs. Indian polities of the "Medieval" period have also often been described as feudal. This model and the terminology of feudalism have been widely employed in descriptions of Vijayanagara. Specific applications of the feudal model to Vijayanagara will be discussed below. Stein's (1980) segmentary state model, and finally, several recent reactions to Stein are also considered.

Marx's Asiatic Mode of Production represented an attempt to come to terms with the newly perceived differences between the European historical experience and those of other parts of the world (cf. Claessen and Skalnik 1978; Godelier 1978b), particularly the colonized countries of Asia. These many alternate histories were, however, homogenized and combined into a single model of political economy taken as characteristic of the "Orient." Historical and ethnographic sources used by Marx to construct the Asiatic mode were based entirely on colonial accounts of Asia (Krader 1975:7), particularly British colonial accounts of India. O'Leary (1989:263) notes that Marx in fact made rather selective use of his limited sources which included travellers' tales, the British Parliamentary reports, and historical works by British administrators Wilks and Campbell. Later Marx also consulted the historical works of the British officials Elphinstone and Sewell (O'Leary 1989:263). These colonial constructions of "traditional" Indian society were aimed at legitimating colonial rule and facilitating revenue collection. An extensive and important literature has grown up around this point, focussing on how the construction of power relations in the creation of "texts" about colonized peoples has shaped much that has been considered fundamental to anthropological thought (e.g. Breckenridge and van der Veer 1993; Cohen 1990; Dirks 1992; Inden 1990; Boon 1982). The colonial legacy of mythmaking with regard to the Indian past cannot be dissociated from the Asiatic Mode of Production. Pervasive myths about Indian society include that of the "village republic," a term coined by Mark Wilks, a British colonial officer stationed in South India. In his history of Mysore (later Karnataka), Wilks depicted Indian villages as self-sustaining, self-governing, isolated, stable, closed, and consisting of a traditional, passive populace (Krader 1975:62-67). This view, while not supported by archaeological, historical, or contemporary evidence, has proved to be both persistent and pervasive in discussions of Indian villages (see Ludden 1985 and O'Leary 1989 for more discussion).

Allied to the notion of the village republic is that of "Oriental Despotism." This construct, most extensively developed by Wittfogel in the 1950s (1955, 1957), was also largely fabricated out of the colonial experience in India. Krader writes:

> In the accounts of the European travellers to Asia in the seventeenth century, the Oriental peoples were represented as living either in utter want or luxury and the government of the Orient as despotic, the power of the autocrats who ruled the various countries of Asia being arbitrary, absolute and unbounded. (1975:19)

These accounts stressed the passivity of the ruled and the fundamental separation between agricultural communities and state organization (Claessen and Skalnik 1978:8). Asian rulers were conceived of as the sole proprietors of the land, with a concomitant absence of private property rights as were found in Europe (cf. O'Leary 1989). This debate regarding land ownership can also be seen in the context of Vijayanagara history, as I note below in discussions of the feudal model of Vijayanagara political economy.

Besides stressing the distance and inferiority of the "Oriental" in relation to the European, the assumption of Oriental Despotism served a dual purpose in facilitating and legitimating colonial rule (see Breckenridge and van der Veer 1993). British rule in India was seen as benign and humane, an improvement over the capriciousness of earlier despots. The British have been depicted as reluctant imperialists (e.g. Wolpert 1989), spreading the benefits of British law and civilization to the oppressed masses. Colonial depictions of earlier Indian rulers as sole proprietors over land represented a definite position in the contemporary debate regarding revenue collection. Were revenues "taxes" or "rent"? If the latter (where the state stands in the relation of landlord), then revenue extraction could "justifiably" be higher. The rent model was adopted, with recourse to the argument that this was the "traditional" arrangement in India. Thus, constructions of the past served very immediate political goals. As these contexts have disappeared, however, the models have not.

Oriental Despotism is often assumed to have an ecological determinant—dry climates and the consequent need for artificial irrigation. Indian history served as one source for Wittfogel's formulation of this relationship, although Wittfogel described places such as Bengal that were neither dry nor had extensive hydraulic works (O'Leary 1989:264, 270). Marx wrote (cited in Krader 1975:88) that irrigation was the work of the central government alone and that the "passive" peasantry had never formed voluntary organizations for community water control as existed in Europe. "Orientals" were viewed as backward and isolated pawns of the state without organizational or entrepreneurial abilities (cf. Ludden 1985; Said 1978). The irrigation link to despotism was, of course, most fully developed by Wittfogel (1957) and has been subjected to considerable criticism (e.g. Hunt 1989; Hunt and Hunt 1976). Like Marx, Wittfogel apparently also saw what he wanted in the sources available to him:

> The evidence of [the traveller] Bernier's texts is also at odds with Marx and Wittfogel's idea that the alleged centralized despotism of the Mughals was caused by (or associated with) the imperative of hydraulic agriculture in arid regions. Bernier's travelogue described the Indian monsoons, the humid fertility of Bengal, the lack of agriculture in arid regions and entirely localized methods of irrigation (ditches and channels). Marx's sources for his belief that the state played a key role in hydraulic agriculture in India thus remain obscure, and from wherever they were derived they directly contradicted Bernier's eyewitness account. (O'Leary 1989:264)

The Asiatic Mode of Production, then, is a stage in an alternate formulation of historical change. In Europe and the Mediterranean, modes of production moved from Primitive to Ancient to Feudal to Capitalist. In Asia, there were only the Primitive and the Asiatic modes. One of the major features of the Asiatic Mode of Production (following Krader 1975:120-22) was a low degree of urbanization. The Asiatic city was not thought to possess significant industries but instead existed only for military purposes as a sort of "armed camp" (Marx 1853, cited in Krader 1975:82 and see O'Leary 1989). There was no wage labor and no private ownership of land. In both the Ancient and the Asiatic modes, the production of commodities was not a significant aspect of the economic relations of society, and even within villages commodity exchange was not highly developed. Villages being independent "republics," of course there was no specialization between villages. Production was directed toward subsistence, with most of the surplus going to the state.

With the advent of colonialism, capitalism was brought to Asia, and only with this event, Marx asserted, did Asia enter history (Krader 1975:90-93; O'Leary 1989:267). This depiction of an almost monotonous continuity and of an absence of significant change in Indian society is much more than simply a historical curiosity. Indeed, it remains the orthodox perception of time and process in Indian prehistory and history (e.g. Allchin and Allchin 1982:352-54; and see Leach 1990), leading to, for example, a relatively uncritical use of the direct-historical approach in archaeological interpretation. Much more could be (and has been) written about the Asiatic Mode of Production and the way in which it has shaped perceptions of India's past. While the terminology of the Asiatic mode is long gone, the structuring concepts of the village republic and Oriental Despotism persist.

Vijayanagara as a Centralized Empire

Perspectives on the political and economic organization of the empire range from depictions of Vijayanagara as a powerful, centralized empire to a loose association of semi-autonomous localities. K. A. Nilakanta Sastri, perhaps the most well-known historian of South India, has discussed the Vijayanagara polity in terms which stress the importance of the military to state organization. Sastri's work was focussed primarily on the earlier Chola polity, and only secondarily on Vijayanagara. In his earlier work Nilakanta Sastri (Nilakanta Sastri and Venkata Ramanayya 1946:299) depicted Vijayanagara as a powerful, centralized, bureaucratic empire, at least according to Stein (1980:405). In his later, widely read survey of South Indian history (1966), however, Nilakanta Sastri's view might be characterized as a modified feudal perspective. The notion that Vijayanagara was essentially a strong centralized power despite its never quite achieving full centralization (cf. Stein 1989:10), in fact seems to owe more to an underlying desire to locate Oriental

Despotism than to anything else. Few explicit references to the powerful political and economic control exerted by Vijayanagara over its subjugated provinces actually exist in the historical literature (but see Krishnaswami Pillai 1964), a view which later historians such as Stein have asserted they are reacting against (Stein 1989:10).

Sastri's depiction of Vijayanagara is, however, certainly "hegemonic" (cf. Inden 1990), and as such merits further examination. Nilakanta Sastri can be placed together with those who feel that the guiding ideology of the empire was Hindu *dharma* and resistance to Islam (e.g. 1966:264). Nonetheless, he freely admits that Hindus served in the armies and courts of "Muslim" polities, that Muslims served in the Vijayanagara army, that Vijayanagara kings warred against Hindus and Muslims alike, and that Vijayanagara rulers forged political and even dynastic alliances with Muslim rulers (1966:271). In his influential *History of South India*, Nilakanta Sastri (1966) recounts the activities of each Vijayanagara ruler in turn, stressing their military expeditions to establish and maintain control over the empire. A theme that emerges from these discussions is one of constant rebellions and rejections of imperial authority by subject/subjugated leaders and consequent attempts on the part of the Vijayanagara kings to subdue them and receive their tribute and "fealty." Nilakanta Sastri writes that Vijayanagara was a "hereditary monarchy" (1966:305) in which kings were required to have "high attainments in diplomacy and war" (1966:306). The empire was divided into several districts, or *rajyas*, the boundaries of which changed through time with conquest and consolidation or rebellion and reduction of the realm. Nilakanta Sastri calls local leaders either "feudatories" or "provincial governors," according to whether or not they were appointed (imposed) by the center (and see Karashima 1992). Discussing the reign of Krishnadeva Raya, during which the power of the center was at its apogee:

> The empire, although under his [the king's] direct rule, was itself divided into a number of governorships under generals, each of whom enjoyed practical independence so long as he maintained a certain quota of horse, foot, and elephants in constant readiness for action and paid his annual contributions to the central treasury. (Nilakanta Sastri 1966:284)

Nilakanta Sastri writes of the capital city that a number of government "departments" existed, including a "well-organized" secretariat near the palace and two treasuries (1966:306). The revenue of the central government consisted, he said, of several sources:

> Crown lands, annual tribute from feudatories and provincial governors paid at the time of the *Mahanavami* festival [October, after the harvest], port and customs dues from commerce passing through the numerous ports of the empire, formed the chief sources of revenue which was collected both in cash and in kind. (Nilakanta Sastri 1966:306-307)

The military focus of Vijayanagara served, for Nilakanta Sastri, as its chief defining character. Vijayanagara, he noted, "was perhaps the nearest approach to a war-state ever made by a Hindu kingdom," (1966:307) and a large standing army was maintained in addition to the "feudal levies" required of the "provincial governors."

Nilakanta Sastri's view of the Vijayanagara polity is not dissimilar to that expressed by Stein (1980, discussed below). Unlike Stein, he did assign some role to the central government, particularly in the region around the capital (e.g. crown lands) and did stress the importance of the military and of military considerations in shaping policy and polity. However, he also noted the factiousness of local leaders, the ease with which they slipped free of the bonds of Vijayanagara hegemony, and the unstable state of internal and external borders.

Vijayanagara as a Feudal Polity

Given the general label of "Medieval" for the period from about the seventh to the seventeenth century A.D., it should come as no surprise that Indian polities of this period have often been described in terms of the categories of European feudalism (Karashima 1992; Krishnaswami Pillai 1964; Sharma 1965; Sircar 1966b; and refer to discussions in Byers and Mukhia 1985). Rulers of kingdoms and of empires have been depicted as *primus inter pares* in a group of petty kings and "chiefs." Such lesser kings or "feudatories" are said to hold "fiefs" given by the paramount king. Feudal models have been particularly popular in Vijayanagara historiography. This may be due to the great importance in the Vijayanagara period of local leaders or chiefs known as *nayakas* or *amaranayakas*. Although this term is known from earlier periods (e.g. Kulke and Rothermund 1986), *nayakas* became prominent only in the Vijayanagara period (Stein 1980). *Nayakas* held specified areas within the empire and enjoyed the land revenues from that area. In return they owed allegiance to the Vijayanagara rulers, and were required to maintain armies of a certain size and to contribute specified sums to the royal treasury each year (Mahalingam 1951; more detailed discussions of this relationship can be found in Karashima 1992; Stein 1980, 1989). This form of tenure was known as *amaram* tenure.

The structural similarities between *amaram* tenure and feudal obligation in Europe are certainly evident. However, important differences exist as well. The troops maintained by the *nayakas* were, apparently, conceived of as belonging to the king rather than to the *nayaka* (Paes in Sewell 1900:280-81), and the king (contrary to the Asiatic Mode of Production model) was never the actual owner of the land. Land was freely bought and sold, and agriculturalists were not "tied" to the land (cf. Stein 1980:374-79; O'Leary 1989:265-66). In general, historians who employ feudal terminology for southern India do not actually suggest that precolonial polities were "feudal" in the sense that they were variants of European political/economic forms (cf. Byers and Mukhia 1985; Venkata Ramanayya 1935; but see Sharma 1965). Instead, the terms are used as a convenient shorthand, and in order to avoid a heavy reliance on indigenous terms for the plethora of tax and tenure arrangements. More recent historical work does not generally employ European feudal terminology (e.g. Heitzman 1987; Ludden 1985; but see Kulke and Rothermund 1986), using instead an assortment of Tamil, Telugu, and Kannada words to describe land tenure, occupation, and taxation. There is certainly a gain in precision associated with the change, but perhaps also a loss in that non-specialists may no longer even attempt to come to terms with the Indian past (see also Subrahmanyam 1990).

The Segmentary State

In 1980, the historian Burton Stein introduced to scholars of South Asia his model of the segmentary state. Based on Aidan Southall's (1956) model of African political organization, Stein has proposed (1980) that both the Chola and the Vijayanagara empire were "segmentary" in character. Authority in the segmentary state is pyramidal, with higher level political units replicating the structure of lower levels. Sovereignty is ritual rather than material, and there is no significant control of material resources except in the ruler's core territory (Stein 1989). Except in terms of legitimation, the leader of the segmentary state is only the first among equals. The center of the segmentary state also fulfills a moral and ritual role. It is "exemplary" of structuring principles rather than a mundane seat of economic and coercive power. A parallel perspective can be seen in the work of Geertz on the "theater state" of Bali (1980). The work of Fritz (1986, 1987; Fritz, Michell, and Nagaraja Rao 1985) at Vijayanagara has built on both of these models.

In the segmentary state, the ruler's "power" is moral, "expressed in a ritual idiom" (Stein 1980:23) divorced from coercive control except in his or her own (small) domain, and yet he or she remains the analytical pivot in much scholarship that explicitly or implicitly accepts this model (e.g. Fritz, Michell, and Nagaraja Rao 1985). Stein explains:

> The theory of South Indian kingship as articulated in medieval law texts (*dharmasastra*) and other literary works as well as in the normative language of medieval inscriptions, especially the often lengthy inscriptional preambles, speak of sacred kingship, not of bureaucratic or constitutional monarchy as so often construed by South Indian historians. And, concrete historical evidence of the activities of royal figures—whether these are military (and the king is seen as a great conqueror), or religious (and the king is seen as the greatest of devotees of gods whom he protects and upon whom he confers rich gifts), or whether in the more rare royal intervention as the upholders of law or dharma—these are the activities of a sacral and incorporative kingship. (1980:23-24)

It is not entirely clear why the "sacral" and "incorporative" nature of kingship necessarily precludes kings from acting as bureaucratic or constitutional monarchs. The latter terms refer only to the action of the rulers or the operation of authority while the former refer to how they are perceived in a normative fashion.

The depiction of authority structures as "segmentary" places great emphasis on local institutions (although scholarship has remained focussed on elites). This focus echoes an ongoing interest of historians of South India with the local structures of governance, irrigation, and land control in Tamil country, *nadus* and their assemblies, *urs* (Nilakanta Sastri 1966; Ludden 1985; Mahalingam 1951; Stein 1980). Supraregional political authority is only uncomfortably perched atop this "basic" stratum of political and economic structure, able only to replicate its form and functioning on a larger scale. This view strangely echoes that of "Oriental society" in which the essential substratum of peasant agriculture persists unchanged in spite of the exigencies of political fortune. As Marx noted:

> India had no history in general, at least no written history: what we call the history of that country is external history, the succession of foreign conquerors who set up their kingdoms on the passive foundations of their societies, who offered no resistance to them, and who underwent no change. (1853, cited in Krader 1975:90)

Certainly, the segmentary state model would not go this far is depicting the "basic ethno-ecological unit" (Stein 1980:3) of peasant society (*nadus* or "peasant ecotypes;" Stein 1980:25) as eternal and unchanging (cf. Ludden 1985). Or would it? Stein writes (1980:24-25) that a constant factor in his analysis—which covers a five-hundred-year period—is technology. Stasis is not demonstrated in this model but simply assumed. During a period in which fundamental political and economic relationships were in a state of rapid change throughout the world (Chaudhuri 1985; Wallerstein 1974; Wolf 1982), such an assumption hardly seems supportable. Further, this view of technology is an extremely limited one that does not consider the organization of technology and the relationships between different strategies of production, distribution, and consumption.

The segmentary state model is fundamentally an idealist one, in which the coercive power of the state is either denied or minimized. In fact, the power of the Vijayanagara rulers *did* appear to have included coercive dimensions. As just one minor example, numerous people were reportedly sacrificed in the construction of a reservoir (Paes in Sewell 1900:245; see also Sinopoli and Morrison 1995). If power is "only" ritual, then religion, ideology, or "will" must explain the participation of lesser elites and non-elites in the dangerous and destructive activities of warfare, and the extraction of "surplus" production. In the segmentary state model, people are seen to participate in a supra-regional system which is often fundamentally opposed to their own material well-being because of an unchanging belief system, and there are few material considerations above the level of the locality (the fundamental unit of society).

Stein has backed away slightly (1985; but see Stein 1989:10) from this earlier extreme view of Vijayanagara political organization, suggesting instead that Vijayanagara be viewed as transitional between segmentary and patrimonial forms (1985), the latter term derived from Weber (and after Blake 1979). Patrimonial political economies are viewed as transitional between "traditional" (Stein-communal; Weber-patriarchal) modes of authority and "modern" bureaucratic capitalist forms. Patrimonial authority, as formulated by Blake (1979), includes:

> (1) a ruler claiming special, divine authority which was (2) highly personalistic and (3) enforced or rendered powerful, by a standing army (4) directed by an administration of royal household servants without (5) distinguishing between military and civil functions. (cited in Stein 1985:75)

Further, patrimonial political economies are said to be reliant for state income on commerce and leaders of mercantile groups (cf. Perlin 1983). Local chiefs, while they are subordinate to the central authority, have considerable autonomy (Stein 1985:76). The patrimonial model, though the label itself is somewhat disturbing, seems to "fit" the Vijayanagara data better than the more extreme segmentary model. However, this construction also seems to differ little from that of Nilakanta Sastri, except that the latter was conceived of as historically specific description and the former as a type or stage.

Dissenting Views: Palat

Stein's treatment of Vijayanagara has been subject to a considerable amount of criticism (e.g. Champakalakshmi 1981), but I will discuss only two of these critiques here. The first critique, that of Palat, is based on a "world systems" perspective of Vijayanagara economic relations. The second, that of Inden (1990), is not actually based on a consideration of the historical data but on a "textual" reading of Stein.

Palat (1987) discusses the growth in political authority during the Vijayanagara period and the increase in efficiency of surplus extraction, thus suggesting a basic empirical break with Stein's formulation. Palat finds that, in part, increased demands for cash, producing for markets, and the expansion of artisan production in the growing urban centers of the period led to "the greater concentration of political power and the resultant concentration of resources in the royal bureaucracy during the period of the Vijayanagara empire in comparison to the earlier epochs of agrarian integration in South India" (1987:170).

Importantly, Palat has focussed attention on the critical role of South Asian cities and of trading relationships in structuring the economic and political dynamics of the Vijayanagara period. The city of Vijayanagara (see figure 3.1 for other cities and towns of this period) was one of the largest cities of its day, and certainly represented an increase in scale over earlier South Indian cities (at least in surface area and probably also in population). Any model that ignores this phenomenon, or the rapidly expanding volume of international trade in the sixteenth century (Chaudhuri 1985; Mathew 1983; Subrahmanyam 1990), in order to stress the essential continuity and stasis of productive activities and organization can provide only a partial understanding at best. Thus, Palat's view is compelling in that it integrates both rural and urban production in a model of political economy.

Palat asserts (1987:175) that surplus appropriation of agricultural produce was made more efficient in the Vijayanagara period, and that the *melvaram*, or superior share of the produce went to the emperor, whose control over distant localities was enhanced (rather than reduced, as Stein would have it) by the *nayankara* system. Karashima (1992) also stresses the dependence of *nayakas* on the king. The inscriptional record is, I believe, equivocal at best about the actual volume and efficiency of resource flows, but the degree of fundamental disagreement between scholars suggests that a great deal more investigation is warranted.

Dissenting Views: Inden

Inden (1990) has criticized Stein's segmentary state model on the grounds that it merely replaces the enduring, self-governing "village republic" with the *nadu*, or "peasant state." Although Inden praises Stein's formulation for the role it accords peasants as active participants in their own history (1990:210), he suggests that Stein's reaction against the unitary models of postcolonial historiography has induced a certain "amnesia" (1990:207), in that it postulates kinship to be the unifying "essence" of the *nadu*, and indeed of the entire segmentary state, much as kinship (in its manifestation as caste) was viewed as the basis of Indian society in the Colonial period (Inden 1990:207; and see Dumont 1980). While Inden's contention that Stein's "peasant society" is little more than a throwback to colonial history may be overdrawn, his assertion that the ritual sovereignty of the segmentary state need not be dissociated from control over resource flows is more compelling. Inden notes that although authority is ritually constituted, this does not also mean that it is somehow immaterial:

> Equally serious is the dichotomy of the ritual and political in classifying actions. Stein's construct assumes that because it was 'ritual' in nature and did not entail the use of 'force,' royal sovereignty did not involve the transfer of substantial resources or the mobilization of large numbers of men at a royal or imperial centre. (Inden 1990:209)

AGRICULTURE IN THE VIJAYANAGARA PERIOD: BACKGROUND

Scholars of South Indian agriculture have been greatly concerned with issues of land tenure and land revenue (Karashima 1984, 1992; Mahalingam 1951; Stein 1982; Subrahmanyam 1990). In general, resource rights consisted both of rights related to "ownership" (land could be bought and sold) and to "shares." Without reviewing the debates regarding details of land control (cf. Frykenberg 1979), it seems that patterns of access to land, to water, and to shares of agricultural produce were structured at least partially by group membership. The disposition of agricultural produce was complex, but producers were compelled to part with some of their crop to holders of specific rights (shares or grants). These shares included, but were not limited to, service shares, which were paid to "village servants" (*ayagars*; Stein 1980; Subrahmanyam 1990). *Ayagars* included members of occupational groups such as barbers, smiths, potters, and accountants, as well as *niranikkar*, or "watermen," who were responsible for the distribution of irrigation water (Stein 1982:112). The "royal," "landlord's," or "superior" share (*melvaram*; Breckenridge 1985:50; Palat 1987:175, though these were not necessarily always the same; Subrahmanyam 1990) was mentioned in chapter 2. This share was paid to the king, *nayaka*, or other authority, and could be granted to Brahmins or temples. Finally, there also existed what I would term investment shares (such as *kattukodaga* rights). These are described below.

Temples, Power, and Production

Institutions relevant to understanding the nature of political and economic power in the Vijayanagara period are not limited to kings and *nayakas*. Hindu temples (and, earlier, Buddhist monasteries and Jain temples) operated as political actors, landlords, "development agencies," centers of religious/ritual life and scholarship, redistribution centers, and as institutions facilitating supraregional integration (Appadurai 1978; Breckenridge 1985; Heitzman 1987). Temples often controlled extensive landholdings, and maintained large numbers of residents and visitors. They were major employers, supporting tens or hundreds of specialists: priests, scholars, dancers, cooks, craft specialists, and sweepers, and periodically employing large labor forces in construction projects (Ismail 1984; Nagaswamy 1965). Temples contained huge kitchens, and produced feasts and regular meals for hundreds or even, on occasion, thousands of people.

Temples of all sizes were found in the Vijayanagara period, but large temples resembled nothing so much as cities. Like cities, they were often conceptually distinguished by specific names, so that within the greater area of the city of Vijayanagara, inscriptional evidence indicates that the larger temple complexes were known by their name with the suffix of *pura*, or town. Thus, the area around the Vithala temple was known as Vithalapura (Filliozat and Filliozat 1988), the area around the Krishna temple as Krishnapura, and so on.

As I have noted, temples controlled extensive landholdings as well as other forms of wealth: livestock, gold and silver, precious stones, and rights in produce. Much of their wealth was taken in the form of gifts. I discuss temple donation in more detail below, as it is a vital aspect of the operation of the agricultural economy. Several different forms of land tenure existed in the Vijayanagara period, including forms of tenancy, and temples were involved in tenant arrangements primarily as landlords.

Temples appear in the historical record primarily as the recipients of gifts. In the pre-Vijayanagara periods these were mostly gifts of cash or livestock, but increasingly in the Vijayanagara period gifts were of land or villages. Gifts of villages were made by kings or political leaders; what appear to have been given were rights in produce from that village. For other gifts, donors included not only kings and members of the royal family, but also local leaders, temple servants, merchant groups, and individuals (Breckenridge 1985; Morrison and Lycett 1994; Stein 1978).

Donation and Investment

The pivotal role of temples in agriculture stemmed not only from their status as landholders, but also from their investment in the construction and maintenance of agricultural facilities. Gifts to temples were not alienations (Breckenridge 1985:55) but investments. Temples took individual gifts or pooled smaller gifts and invested them in agricultural facilities, especially reservoirs. Land was often given with the express intent that it should be improved through the construction of irrigation facilities (Stein 1979:194). The temple was then entitled to a share in the increase in production of the lands watered by the new or newly repaired facility, rights called *kattu-kodage* rights (Stein 1982:114-15). These rights were shared with the original donor, who thus received a material benefit as well as religious merit for his or her gift. The donor's portion was given as raw or cooked food, *prasad*, offered to the god of the temple. This *prasad* could be consumed, or sold. In this way, complex networks of entitlements were set up which linked institutions and individuals with the agricultural landscape and its productivity.

While the construction of large canals was undertaken almost exclusively by kings, the financing of reservoir construction and, to a certain extent, maintenance, were matters of more general participation. Not only kings, queens, and members of elite households, but also groups of merchants or craft producers, villagers, and individual investors made grants of land or money (see chapter 6 for more details), many of which were invested in the construction of irrigation works, especially reservoirs. Investment in irrigation meant improved crop yields from the land watered by the reservoir, or made an extension of cultivation possible. In this way, small donations or investments were pooled to finance irrigation works requiring large capital outlays.

There were also important political implications of this network of temple investment. The overlordship of the Vijayanagara kings was expressed and recognized in their right to construct and endow temples in their territories, and in the expression of loyalty to them in the donative inscriptions of others. Regional leaders, including those appointed by the center, were also able to forge horizontal ritual and material ties with temples in their own areas, and thus subvert efforts at centralization (Appadurai 1978).

What may be particularly important for intensification, however, is the role temples played in instituting regional integration in production, facilitating a kind of regional agricultural diversification. Networks of donation, investment, and entitlement were large, stretching across ecological and agronomic boundaries. Donors could forge ties, for example, between wet and dry zones of production (Breckenridge 1985), enabling them to make claims on produce in non-local areas, thus evening out imbalances or differences in productivity or type of crop. Donors in dry areas such as the Vijayanagara region were able to create rights in produce from more productive zones such as the alluvial deltas of the east coast. Thus, temple investment was important in facilitating spatial diversity in agriculture which was both ritual/political and economic in character.

Temples must also be factored into the agricultural equation as consumers of agricultural goods. As noted, temples themselves were often population centers and contained large kitchens. They may have also required special produce, such as coconuts, for ritual use.

Knowledge, Control, and Technology

The critical role of temples in agricultural production may be contrasted with the minimal importance of institutions of government. Kings and political leaders were prominent as donors and as holders of rights in produce. Agricultural decision making and, in a larger sense, control over production seem to have been vested at a number of different levels, subject to numerous competing claims. Kings are presented in the historical record as investing, and not as directing. It is not clear, however, that temples actually directed agricultural practice except in situations in which they were the landholders, and even then tenants may have had some autonomy.

Temples were repositories of agricultural knowledge as well as of religious lore (Breckenridge 1985). Temple functionaries directed the ritual calendar of festivals and holy days, a temporally ordered system in tune with the agricultural cycle (cf. Condominas 1986). Temples also stored some agricultural produce, and Breckenridge (1985) has suggested that temples acted as seed banks and agricultural "development agencies." Thus, temples played an economic role in agriculture in that they were landlords and facilitators of construction of and investment in agricultural facilities. Their role was educational and organizational in that they provided technological information and temporal structure. It was social, political, and ritual in that they were nodes of integration between political authorities and agriculturalists, locations of record-keeping and assembly, and directors of the ritual/agronomic calendar.

The material record of agriculture reflects these critical roles of temples. Inscriptions recording donations and grants were sometimes associated with agricultural facilities. Some agricultural facilities themselves echoed the architectural forms of temples. Reservoir sluices, with their two uprights and a lintel bearing moldings (sometimes also finials and sculptures of gods or donors), are formally similar to the door motif common on the facades of temples in the Vijayanagara period and to actual temple doorways. Sluices often bear sculptures of the god Ganesha or the goddess Lakshmi, deities who are often carved over doorways in Vijayanagara temples (Morrison 1993).

Part of the significance of this system of investment and of rights in produce is that risks as well as rights and obligations of cultivators and investors were shared. For the investor, the mechanism of temple investment meant that he or she could have small-scale rights in produce from a number of different areas simultaneously, an important strategy in this agriculturally uncertain region. For the cultivator, outside capital made more productive agriculture possible; and although it increased the number of demands on their harvest, the cultivators' share also apparently increased (cf. Palat 1987).

The context of temple investment in agriculture is vital for understanding the course of Vijayanagara intensification. However, it is also important to consider what is left unsaid in the inscriptional record and to consider what roles those aspects and forms of production that are not part of the historical record may have played. As discussed in chapters 4 and 5, the material record of land use and of agricultural production in the Vijayanagara region indicates a much more diverse set of strategies and scales of production than we might otherwise expect, based solely on the historical record.

The Political Role of Temples

Temples played active political roles, with both elites and corporate groups gaining prestige and legitimation through their support of temples. As I have noted, rulers often expressed territorial claims in terms of rights to construct and endow temples. Patterns of investment in different temples through time surely reflect the changing political and economic fortunes of different temples and religious orders. Kings and other elites might favor particular religious orders or sects at different times, and differentially endow temples in certain key areas or dedicated to favored deities. These relationships between temple and donor were subject to a great deal of manipulation. Temples themselves had considerable material and social resources that could be employed in seeking out beneficial relationships. Temple priests could give out certain ritual symbols and privileges such as fly whisks and the right to commission and participate in certain rituals. These symbolic honors included very expensive items such as lamps and musical instruments (Appadurai 1978). Temples also employed numerous functionaries and employees, as noted, and temple management positions appear to have been given as political favors.

By far the most visible strategy of political manipulation and integration, however, was gift-giving. Gifting was not restricted to royalty, or to men, and constituted an economic, social, and ritual arena in which a fairly large number of people could participate. Donations to temples entailed certain benefits for the donors, benefits which were at once ritual, social, and material. Both the temple and the donor(s) were entitled to shares in produce from the land watered by newly constructed (or repaired) facilities financed by the temple, and the donors were publicly honored for his/her/their contributions in the form of stone inscriptions (and perhaps also some public function?). Temple investments could extend across long distances (e.g. Breckenridge 1985). Thus, gifting created links in the form of material entitlements between people of different professions and from different areas.

Temple investment could be used as a way of forging horizontal political links, thus subverting attempts at political centralization. In the early sixteenth century, Vijayanagara rulers, in an attempt to gain more secure control over outlying areas, began replacing local political leaders in the Tamil country of the far south with Telugu-speaking "warriors" who would be loyal to the emperor (Karashima 1992; Stein 1980). Appadurai (1978) has described how these Telugu *nayakas* used temple endowments to legitimate their rule and to create stable horizontal political-social links in their new territories. Telugu *nayakas* created strong local political and material ties through their association with particular sectarian leaders (*Sri Vaishnavas*) at local temples, eventually gaining complete independence from Vijayanagara control.

Temple construction and endowments, along with the more evidently authoritarian projects of military expeditions and the construction of forts, served as expressions of political authority and incorporation over subject peoples. Appadurai, in discussing the growing importance of temples in the early Vijayanagara period, comments:

> Royal endowments to temples became a major means for the redistributive activities of Vijayanagara sovereigns, which played an important role in agrarian development in this period. At the same time, temple endowment was a major technique for the extension of control into new areas, and transactions involving both material resources and temple 'honors,' permitted the absorption of new local constituencies into Vijayanagara rule. (1978:49)

Temples operated as agents of incorporation on a number of levels. Stein (1978) describes how local non-Vedic deities, primarily goddess or *Ammam* deities, were incorporated into large Shiva temples and thus into "national" scale religions. This incorporation, interestingly, was not a policy of the center or of the large temples, but was, according to Stein (1978:37), a consequence of attempts by locally dominant castes (who worshipped in the *Ammam* temples and shrines) to strengthen their local control through improved horizontal integration (shared ritual affiliation with other Shiva worshippers) and the establishment of vertical links with major Shaivite sects. The period between A.D. 1450 and 1750 has been identified by Stein (1978:38) as the period of the most rapid growth of *Amman* shrines.

The Sixteenth Century

The sixteenth century was a time of great importance for understanding the course of Vijayanagara intensification. The rapid growth of the city in the mid-fourteenth century is mirrored in a second, early sixteenth century expansion in settlement, construction, trade, political control, and possibly also population size.

The early sixteenth century saw the establishment of a new ruling dynasty, the Tuluva dynasty. One of its first kings produced thousands of inscriptions; built, repaired, and added on to hundreds of temples, forts, and other structures; and pursued several quite successful military campaigns. This king, Krishnadeva Raya (1509-1529), was succeeded by his brother, Achutya Raya (1529-1542), and by the time of Sadashiva Raya (thought to have been a mere figurehead, Sewell 1900), the number of inscriptions in the Vijayanagara region reached an all-time high (chapter 6). The Tuluva rulers presided over an expansionist period in the history of Vijayanagara which was marked by increased urbanism, commercialization, monetization, and attempts at political centralization (Palat 1987; Stein 1980, 1989). Historical accounts traditionally stress the personal characteristics of these rulers, especially Krishnadeva Raya, and their role in creating and directing the events of the early sixteenth century. However, it is not necessarily the case that events such as the large-scale population movements in southern India or the dramatic expansion of trade along the South Indian coasts were in any way planned or directed by Vijayanagara rulers. A variety of forces and processes seem to have been operative. I will briefly consider four of these: military expansion and attempts at political centralization; long distance and local trade relations; population movements; and monetization and commercialization.

The Empire and the Sixteenth Century

The territorial maximum of the empire was attained by the middle of the sixteenth century (Chopra, Ravindran, and Subrahmanian 1979; Desai, Ritti, and Gopal 1981). The southern provinces were brought under control (although this required repeated expeditions), and the provinces, or *rajyas*, were reorganized (Nilakanta Sastri 1966:278). Krishnadeva Raya and Achutya Raya both were involved in numerous campaigns in the Raichur *doab*, capturing key forts such as Raichur and Mudgal (figure 3.1). Successful wars against the Orissa kingdom were waged, and in 1513-1514 the Vijayanagara armies under Krishnadeva Raya captured the fort of Udayagiri, a victory commemorated by the construction of a major new temple in the city (Kulke and Rothermund 1986).

Producers, merchants, and rulers in southern India had long been involved in an extensive network of long-distance and local trade in both agricultural and forest products, as well as manufactured goods, but in the sixteenth century, the volume of this trade (Mathew 1983), particularly in spices such as the pepper grown on the Malabar and Kanara coasts, increased dramatically. In the early sixteenth century, the Portuguese began to establish a trade empire in South and Southeast Asia, participating both in the long-distance spice trade and the local "country" trade in provisions for the agriculturally dependent coastal trading cities. An extensive literature deals with sixteenth century trade in the Vijayanagara territories (e.g. Das Gupta and Pearson 1987; Digby 1982; Mathew 1983; Pearson 1981; Subrahmanyam 1984, 1990).

Population and the Sixteenth Century

Southern India in the sixteenth century was in a state of movement. Breckenridge (1985:43) notes that "although migration has a long history in South India, there is every reason to suppose that in the Vijayanagara period the scale, pace, and social depth of migration vastly increased." Whole communities migrated to new locations, as evident in the modern and Colonial period distributions of language communities, oral histories, and contemporary inscriptions and literature (Breckenridge 1985:43; Mahalingam 1940, 1951). This large-scale movement, particularly of Telugu-speakers into Tamil areas, but other moves as well mirrored, in some respects, earlier population movements of Tamil-speakers into southern Karnataka and Andhra Pradesh (Ludden 1985; Subrahmanyam 1990). Certainly, the sixteenth century did not see the beginning of this process.

It is not entirely clear what these large-scale population movements implied for the Vijayanagara region or for the city of Vijayanagara. I discuss this issue again in chapter 5, but I note here a dramatic expansion of settlement in the Vijayanagara region and a boom in construction within the city in the sixteenth century. The relationship of the increased scale and tempo of construction to regional population is, however, not necessarily straightforward. Within the empire as a whole, this construction boom can also be seen. Not only were many new temples and other structures built during the reign of the Tuluvas, but existing temples were added to and modified. One can have little confidence in inferences about population size based on construction of monumental architecture, however. Ample inscriptional evidence does exist regarding the expansion of cultivation into new areas and the clearing of forests (chapter 6). Concessional tax rates were offered for settlers of new lands, but it is not possible to assess how much this expansion reflected policy making, population redistributions, or actual pressure on land. Because no research on domestic contexts outside of the Vijayanagara region exists, estimates of population sizes or changes based on the archaeological record are simply not available (historians have hazarded guesses, however, cf. Moreland 1920; Stein 1989).

Money, Markets, and the Sixteenth Century

Monetization and commercialization in the sixteenth century helped structure changes in economic organization. Allied to these two processes was urbanization (see Ramaswamy 1985c; Stein 1982). Cities grew larger and more numerous during the Late Vijayanagara period (Palat 1987), with major temple towns (such as Tirupati) increasingly distinct from centers of administration and trade (such as Vijayanagara and the west coast emporia). Coined money had been employed in India for hundreds of years but became increasingly important in the sixteenth century (Breckenridge 1985; Palat 1987). This monetization may have been prompted by a desire on the part of elites for cash in order to be able to participate more effectively in the growing international trade, a trade that brought elite goods such as Chinese porcelain into the city. Elites who were able to make revenue demands on producers and others may have attempted to shift these obligations to cash demands. Certainly the historical record makes it very clear that tax obligations were increasingly cash obligations in the sixteenth century, a shift that would have forced agriculturalists to participate in the market economy, if they did not already do so.

Melvaram, or the "landlord's share" of produce, was paid differently for rice than for other crops (Breckenridge 1985:339). Assessments on paddy rice, which is highly storable, were in kind, while revenue demands for other crops were made in cash. The existence of large urban markets in Vijayanagara is well documented (e.g. Paes and Nuniz in Sewell 1900; Dames 1989); participation in these markets probably met the cash requirements of most Vijayanagara-area agriculturalists. Indeed, the needs for urban provisioning would seem to require some sort of mechanism for moving agricultural products to non-agriculturalists. There is no evidence for central control over the disposition of produce. Temples did serve important redistributive roles, but they also operated in conjunction with markets. Thus, they were just one part of the economic picture.

The structural changes of the sixteenth century surely had consequences for the material record of the Vijayanagara region. This work is largely an attempt to isolate and understand these changes and their consequences in the configuration of the archaeological landscape.

THE VIJAYANAGARA METROPOLITAN REGION

The city of Vijayanagara lies within several zones of fortified space. The immediate agricultural hinterland of the city is situated along the banks of the Tungabhadra River on an "island" of relative fertility surrounded by rocky and semi-arid uplands (figure 3.2). As noted, Vijayanagara was situated either on or very near the northern frontier of the empire. The military and territorial losses of A.D. 1565 did not lead to the end of the polity but certainly to the end of the city as a political and economic capital. What was the nature of rule in this core territory of the empire? Surprisingly, it is difficult to answer this question as the region immediately around the city has not been well studied by historians (but see Rajasekhara 1985a). South Indian historical scholarship has tended to focus on the Tamil regions to the exclusion of all other areas. This Tamil-centric view of the Vijayanagara empire has resulted in a perspective of Vijayanagara rule from the "provinces" of the empire; a view from the "outside in." Paradoxically, the city itself has received a great deal of attention, much of it archaeological, as discussed below, but the regional context of the city, as a province of the empire, is less well studied.

In recent work on Vijayanagara (1989), Stein has advanced the notion of an imperial "core" territory, directly ruled over by the Vijayanagara emperors. This is the personal domain of the paramount king, just as subordinate kings and chiefs also maintain control over their own domains. However, Stein does not develop this argument or suggest how such control might have been exercised or manifest. In part, the work of Sinopoli on ceramic production in the city has been directed toward establishing the presence or absence of control over the processes of ceramic production (1986). She has not found any evidence for control over this low-status commodity. This

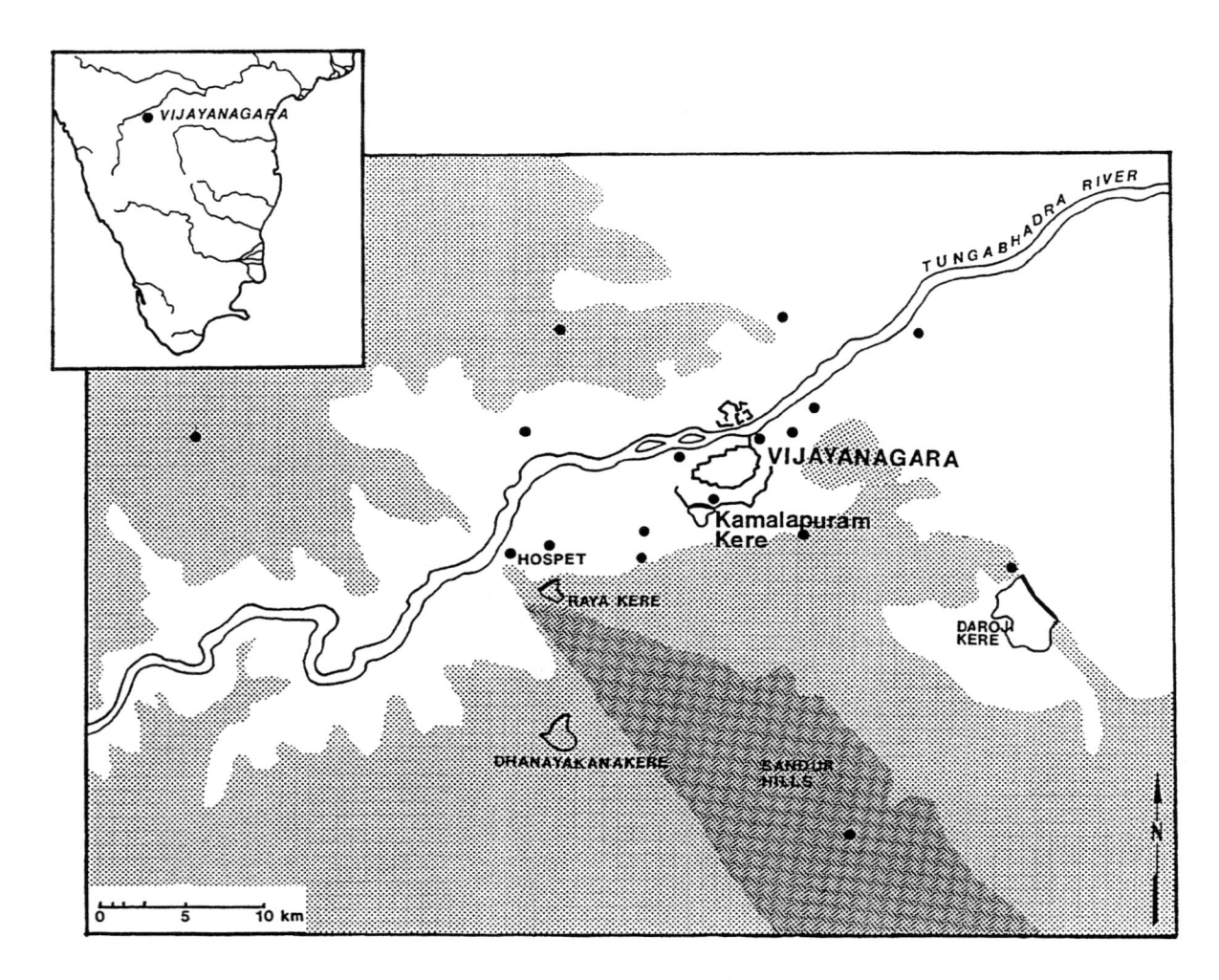

FIGURE 3.2   The region around the city of Vijayanagara. Light shading represents land over 500 m, darker shading, land over 700 m. Small circles are Vijayanagara-period settlements and fortifications. Selected reservoirs are shown.

finding, however, does not allow for generalizations to other forms of production (Morrison and Sinopoli 1992).

Very little is known about political processes in the "core" region, however, it is clear from inscriptions that there were *nayakas* even within the metropolitan region. It is not clear if these might have been less autonomous versions of more distant *nayakas*, royal functionaries, agents, or instruments of royal control, or if local leadership were also strong within the core.

Previous Archaeological Research at Vijayanagara

Early Research

In addition to the historical scholarship on the Vijayanagara empire (cf. Rajasekhara 1985b), a long tradition of research on the monuments and ruins of the city itself also exists. Until recently, such studies have focussed almost exclusively on monumental structures, particularly those within the city. An excellent account of the early history of archaeological and architectural studies at the city of Vijayanagara is provided by Michell (1985b).

The first survey of the ruins (and a collection of water colors) was made by the British surveyor Colin MacKenzie, who also collected an extraordinary corpus of ancient documents and oral histories. MacKenzie's map of the site is reproduced in Michell and Filliozat (1981). Later in the nineteenth century, about sixty waxed-paper negatives of various monuments in the city were exposed by

Alexander Greenlaw in 1856. These photographs indicate a certain amount of decay and destruction of architecture (though surprisingly little) on the site. Recently, a volume (Nagaraja Rao 1988) has been brought out which counterposes Greenlaw's photographs with a similar set taken by the photographer John Gollings in 1983. A comparison of these photographs shows that although the types of vegetation in the region do not appear to have changed significantly, the amount of vegetation on and around the structures was greater in the nineteenth century. In part this relates to archaeological clearing and conservation of monuments, but even where this is not relevant, the twentieth century vegetation has clearly been subject to much greater pressure from grazing animals and from humans.

In 1880, the Madras survey brought out a topographic map (incomplete) of the site, and several descriptions of the monuments also appeared at about this time (Kelsall 1872; Rea 1886, 1887; Francis 1904), with various structures and parts of the site acquiring the functional labels they still retain. In the first part of the twentieth century the fledgling Archaeological Survey of India (see Chakrabarti 1988 for a history of the early survey), Madras circle, began the work of conservation and vegetation clearance on the site (Michell 1985b). Collapsing structures were shored up with brick pillars (many of which are now being replaced by the Archaeological Survey), and roofs and foundations repaired. Michell notes, however, that vandalism was a constant problem, with copper pipes and teak beams in particular demand (1985b:200). The activities of the survey are reported in various *Annual Reports of the Archaeological Survey of India* (detailed in Dallapiccola 1985:5-7). In 1917, Longhurst brought out his celebrated guide to the site, *Hampi Ruins Described and Illustrated*. This guide continues to be widely read, although superseded in the tourist offices by Devakunjari (1970) and Fritz and Michell (1986).

Post-1970s

Although historical and epigraphical research on Vijayanagara continued, little archaeological work was carried out there until the 1970s. The site did come under the purview of the Public Works Department in the 1950s and 1960s, Michell notes (1985b:202), and they carried out conservation and clearing operations without, unfortunately, keeping any records of their projects. In the 1970s Filliozat and Filliozat began their research into architectural, art historical, and epigraphic issues in the city and in the surrounding region (1988; Filliozat 1973, 1984). Their research is important for many reasons, but a major one is their focus on understanding the layout of the entire city and not just of the larger structures. They also identified smaller settlements in the vicinity of the city (Filliozat and Filliozat 1988). Filliozat and Filliozat have employed a very productive approach in which inscriptional research is combined with architectural description, providing a more secure foundation for functional identification of structures and for chronology.

Excavation work began in the 1970s when the Archaeological Survey of India began a "National Project" of research at Vijayanagara (Michell 1985b). The Karnataka State Directorate of Archaeology and Museums also began excavating in the city at about this time. Both groups have concentrated on the elite core of the city, what Fritz, Michell, and Nagaraja Rao (1985) term the Royal Center. This excavation work is ongoing and has cleared very extensive areas of the city center. Reports of this research can be found in the serial publication *Indian Archaeology—A Review* (Tripathi 1987), and in the *Vijayanagara: Progress of Research* publication series (Nagaraja Rao 1983, 1985; Devaraj and Patil 1991a, 1991b, in press).

In 1980, architectural historian George Michell and archaeologist John Fritz began their work at the site. Their research has stressed careful surface documentation, mapping, and architectural plans of the city. Analyses have been directed toward the urban layout and its symbolic dimensions, and the development of architectural styles (Fritz 1986, 1987; Michell 1985a, 1990). Fritz, Michell, and Nagaraja Rao (1985) have divided the city and its surrounding region into named areas or zones; these terms are now the primary ones used by archaeologists and others in discussing the site. Although their major publication is restricted to the Royal Center (1985; and see Fritz and Morrison in press), Michell has also recently published an inventory of standing structures in the Urban Core (1990).

The first analytical studies of Vijayanagara artifacts were carried out by Sinopoli (1983, 1985, 1986, 1989, 1991a) in conjunction with the Directorate of Archaeology and Museums' excavation in the "Noblemen's Quarters." Sinopoli carried out a metric examination of earthenware sherds in order to study production and to develop functional categories. In conjunction with this study, Sinopoli made extensive surface collections of artifacts from two areas outside the Royal Center: the residential/commercial East Valley and the Muslim quarter (1986). In 1987 I carried out a similar surface study of artifacts and debris in the Northeast Valley (Morrison 1990).

Much research has also been carried out in the fields of art history, architectural history, and archaeoastronomy. Some recent publications and unpublished theses include Blurton (1985), Davison-Jenkins (1988), Dallapiccola (1985; Dallapiccola et al. 1992), Pascher (1987), Purandare (1986), Sinopoli and Blurton (1986), Verghese (1989), and Wagoner (1991, 1993).

The Vijayanagara Metropolitan Survey is an outgrowth of the long history of archaeological and other research in and around Vijayanagara. This project constitutes the basis of chapters 4 and 5, and is discussed in more detail there.

4

The Vijayanagara Metropolitan Survey

THIS CHAPTER DESCRIBES the strategies of the Vijayanagara Metropolitan Survey and reports on some of the results of the project to date. The Vijayanagara Metropolitan Survey has focussed specifically upon the hinterland of the city of Vijayanagara in order to address issues of settlement, land use, and production on a regional scale. Although the survey has not been completed, it is possible to describe some overall patterns in the structure of the regional archaeological record; these patterns are discussed in chapter 5.

METHODOLOGICAL ISSUES

Sample Fraction and Intensity: The "100 Percent Survey"

From the onset of sustained archaeological consideration of sampling (Binford 1964), archaeologists have tended to approach problems of sampling in terms of sites, viewed as replicable units of analysis, rather than in terms of archaeological landscapes, areas that are uniquely structured. Regional surveys do not sample sites or site types (cf. Lycett 1991b). Instead, what is sampled in any archaeological study is *area*—we may or may not know what the past uses of that area were prior to initiating the sampling program. In a recent volume on regional survey (Fish and Kowalewski, eds. 1990), several archaeologists reminisce about their full-coverage surveys, holding up a model of "100 percent survey" as an archaeological ideal. This work appears to be part of a backlash against the emphasis on sampling in regional studies and prompts two separate questions. The first question is: do such studies really bypass the problems of sampling? In answering this question, I consider the variables of sample fraction, intensity, and sensitivity. The second question is equally important. Can we treat the archaeological landscape as a collection of replicable entities (sites of various 'types'), or is each region uniquely structured?

In their introduction, Fish and Kowalewski (1990) argue that although sampling may be necessary because of time and/or budget constraints, full-coverage survey is always preferable. I agree that more continuous coverage is preferable to patchy coverage for most of the questions archaeologists ask of their data, but this discussion has introduced a false notion that such a thing as "100 percent" coverage of the archaeological record of a region can indeed exist. In fact, even the "100 percent" surveys are themselves samples in both time and space. They are samples in time as a consequence of the dynamic nature of the surface record. Although structural remains may be considered relatively stable, artifacts may move about in the soil, the consequence of rodent disturbance, frost action, plowing, erosion, and many other factors (Ammerman 1985; Ammerman and Feldman 1978; Lewarch and O'Brien 1981; O'Brien and Lewarch 1981; Wandsnider 1989; Wood and Johnson 1978). Thus, the surface artifact assemblage may constitute only a sample of the total possible surface assemblage, and the experience of the archaeologist with that surface at a specific point in time is, to some extent, unique to that time. Certainly the archaeological record is in a constant state of transformation, not only as the result of "N-transforms," natural processes such as decay, erosion, and sedimentation (Schiffer 1972), but also due to the growth of cities, the expansion of agriculture, looting, quarrying, and other human actions. Our samples are dependent on the occupational history of the areas we study.

Sample Fraction

The 100 in "100 percent" survey refers to the sample fraction, the proportion of land surface covered at a given level of intensity. Sample fraction has been shown empirically to be extremely important, particularly if archaeologists are interested in rare or unique occurrences, as we often are. Thus, larger sampling fractions are certainly desirable. The underlying distribution of the archaeological record itself is also important. Where archaeological landscapes consist of multiple, similar occurrences, smaller sampling fractions may provide an accurate view of overall distributions. However, where landscapes are uniquely patterned and archaeological features are internally diverse, low fraction sampling may seriously misrepresent underlying distributions.

Intensity

Intensity in regional survey may be conceived of as the grain of surface observations and is primarily a product of crew spacing. It is in the consideration of intensity that the claim of "100 percent" survey may be challenged. Total coverage survey implies total observation. In fact, many of the "100 percent" surveys accomplished 100 percent sampling fractions at the cost of very low intensity coverage. In the Valley of Mexico (Sanders, Parsons, and Santley 1979), for example, crews were spaced 30 to 100 meters apart. Each crew member's success in encountering and observing archaeological remains present in a sampling unit may be considered a factor of at least two variables: the size of the observational unit assigned to the crew member and the visibility and obtrusiveness of the remains themselves. The latter factor is discussed in the next section, but it seems clear that where crew members are so widely spaced that they may not even be able to maintain eye contact with one another, it is unrealistic to believe that they are comprehensively covering the ground surface. Instead, we might consider each person to be surveying an individual sample transect, with the periodicity of the transects determined by crew spacing and the width of the transect by the visual range of the observer combined with the visibility of the archaeological materials. Thus, smaller sites that did not overlap one of these widely spaced transects (the field of view of an individual observer) would not be found. This technique is thus as much a sampling strategy as are lower sample fraction surveys. The difference lies in the choices made in balancing sample faction and intensity. Decisions about sample fraction and intensity may depend on both the goals of the research and the nature of the archaeological record. Where the distribution of large and highly visible sites across a region is the pattern of interest, high fraction, low intensity surveys may be the best strategy. However, if information on small sites or isolated occurrences is desired, very low intensity sampling will be inadequate. In such situations, sacrifices in sampling fraction may have to be made.

Cowgill has attempted to estimate how close crew spacing must be in order to notice unobtrusive sites such as artifact scatters. He suggests: "In order to detect 95 percent of the occurrences 10 meters in diameter, the intensity of survey would have to be increased so that the spacing between observers is only about 16 meters" (1990:255-56).

Sensitivity

Cowgill defines sensitivity as "the probability of detecting an occurrence of evidence of ancient activity" (1990:253) or, in other words, the likelihood of finding the archaeological sites present in an area. Sensitivity is the most difficult survey parameter to measure or describe in that it is somewhat subjective and is contextually specific. According to Cowgill, five factors are relevant in considerations of sensitivity. These include: the nature of the occurrence; the nature of the terrain; the closest approach of the surveyor to the occurrence; the extent to which the observers are sensitized to a certain type of occurrence; and the extent to which special techniques are used to detect subsurface phenomena (1990:253). The first two factors require little discussion. Where sites are large and obtrusive, they will be easier to detect than smaller, more "camouflaged" sites. Where vegetation is dense or alluviation has occurred, sites will be more difficult to detect. The distance of the surveyor from the site is primarily a function of intensity, as discussed above. Therefore, I would suggest that what Cowgill includes here as a variable of observation that is difficult to control is actually a rather straightforward function of crew spacing.

Cowgill's fourth variable, the extent to which observers are sensitized to certain types of occurrences, is of particular importance in the case of the Vijayanagara survey. Because this was the first survey of its type for precolonial southern India, we had very little idea of what to expect in terms of site morphology and content. In fact, we learned a great deal about the Vijayanagara archaeological record as we proceeded. For this reason, some types of features may not have been consistently recorded, particularly in the first season. Most notable, perhaps, were the chipped stone artifacts found in association with Vijayanagara sites (Lycett 1991a, 1994; Morrison and Lycett 1989). Chipped stone artifacts are not, according to traditional systematics, supposed to persist in time periods past the Iron Age, and thus we did not expect to encounter them in the context of Vijayanagara-period remains. However, stone tools were consistently encountered in Vijayanagara sites, and we eventually became habituated to that association and became more aware of the occurrence of such materials. At that point, we also noticed stone tools among the surface artifact assemblages of the city in areas that had been studied previously (Morrison 1990; Sinopoli 1986). Cowgill's (1990) point that sensitivity, or learning, is an important parameter of recovery is well taken.

THE VIJAYANAGARA METROPOLITAN SURVEY

Beyond the walled city of Vijayanagara lies a fortified area more than 350 km^2 in extent that we have termed the greater metropolitan region of Vijayanagara (figure 4.1. Unless otherwise indicated, north is at the top of all maps). The greater metropolitan region is contained within extensive fortifications and constitutes a significant portion of the agricultural sustaining area of the city. The boundaries of this region are partly arbitrary, and we recognize the economic importance of areas outside the metropolitan region (Morrison and Sinopoli 1992; Sinopoli 1994). A portion of the metropolitan area has been divided by previous researchers into 25 blocks of 2.5 minutes of latitude by 2.5 minutes of longitude (Fritz and Michell 1985). Each of these blocks is approximately 4.5 km on a side and is designated with a letter (A to Z, excluding I). The city is located in block N, near the center of the grid. We have expanded this system to include areas outside the original grid, so that the entire metropolitan region can be discussed in terms of a uniform spatial reference system. In the expanded system, the blocks are nested within a series of larger blocks, so that the original grid is contained within block N of a larger grid. Each block in the larger grid is divided into 25 smaller blocks so that, for example, block N in Fritz and Michell's system is [N] N, and the block to the immediate south of block Z in Fritz and Michell's system is block [S] E.

Because it was not possible to intensively survey the entire study area, the eight blocks surrounding the city were selected for detailed examination. These blocks were chosen for several reasons. First, since we wished to examine the relationship of the city to its immediate agricultural and demographic hinterland, these blocks seemed a logical starting point. In addition, we wanted to survey contiguous blocks so as to be able to trace out distributions of settlements and features that may be uniquely patterned. Thus, the outer edges of the eight blocks in no way constitute a natural boundary but are arbitrary limits of the intensively surveyed area.

Areas outside of the eight blocks but within the study area have been studied less intensively. Previous researchers have described structures from some of these areas (Filliozat and Filliozat 1988; Fritz, Michell, and Nagaraja Rao 1985; Michell 1990). This information, together with the results of a study of the Daroji Valley (partly contained within Blocks [N]W through [N]Z) and of the Vijayanagara canal network, will be discussed in more detail in chapter 5. In this chapter, material from outside of the intensively surveyed blocks is not described in detail.

Sampling Strategies

Within the eight blocks intensively surveyed, an explicit sampling program was followed. Each block is approximately 4.5 km on a side or 20.25 km^2. The total survey area is therefore 162.0 km^2.

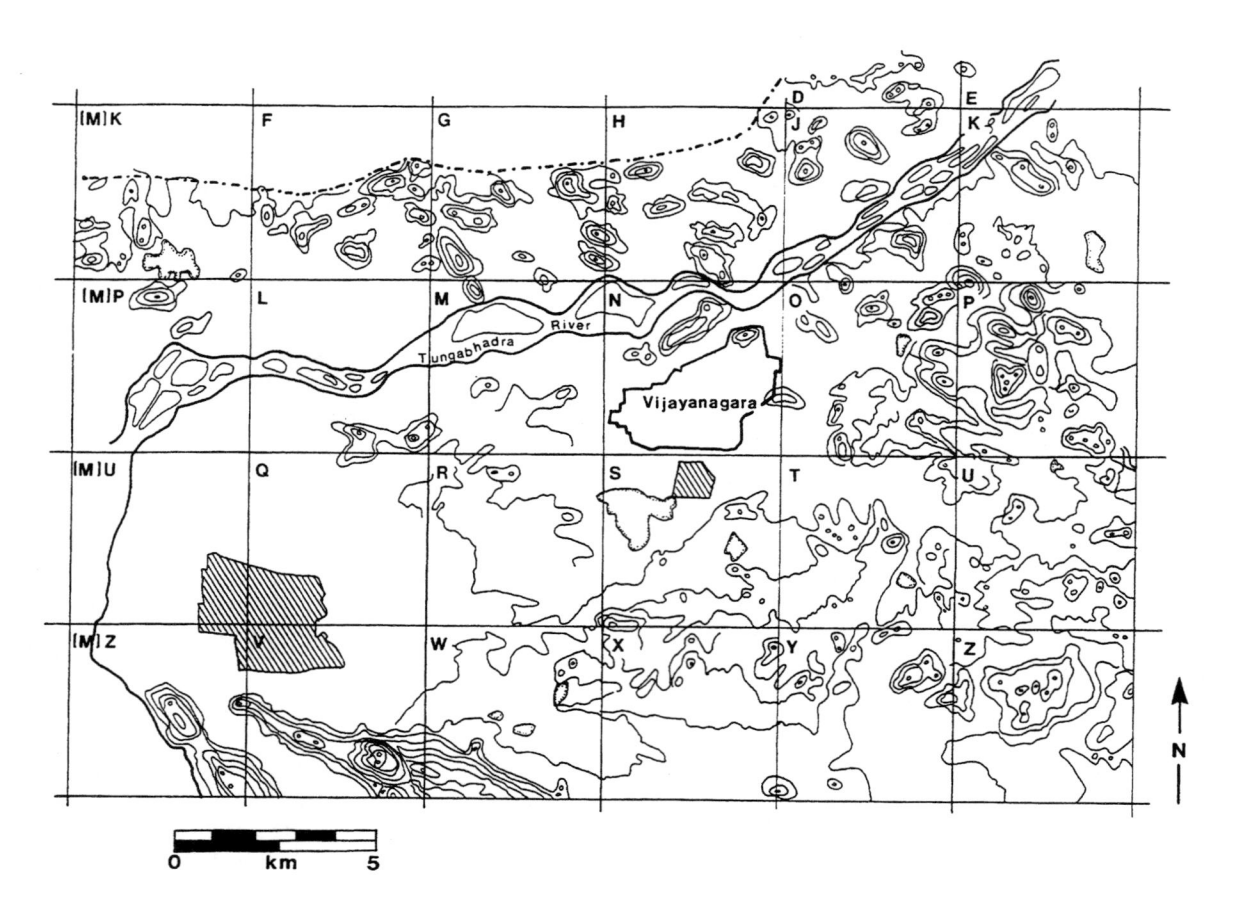

FIGURE 4.1 The Vijayanagara Metropolitan region, showing block boundaries.

We expect the archaeological record of this landscape to be uniquely structured. That is, the settlement pattern is dominated by a single large city, and is constrained by the Tungabhadra River and surrounding rocky uplands. In order to capture spatial patterning in the archaeological distributions of this area, we adopted the largest feasible sampling fraction, 50 percent. Each block within the metropolitan region was treated as an individual sampling stratum, sampled at a fraction of 50 percent. In consideration of experimental studies of sampling unit size and shape (Judge, Ebert, and Hitchcock 1979; Plog 1976; and see Cowgill 1975b), we selected 250-meter-wide transects as the sample unit. Such units are relatively easy to locate in the field and to survey. Each block was divided into 18 north-south transects. In order to avoid potential problems associated with regularly spaced, or periodic site locations, transects were selected using a table of random numbers. Half of the transects within each block were randomly chosen for study.

Because we are interested in the location and distribution of small and unobtrusive as well as large, highly visible sites, a relatively high observation intensity was chosen. Crews were spaced 20 meters apart at all times, so that each observer was responsible for monitoring an area 10 meters on either side of his or her survey path. In practice, survey intensity was slightly higher than 20 meters, as crews had to crisscross and backtrack in order to find ways through or over the many obstacles in the study area. These obstacles included: canals, thorny field boundaries, outcrops, modern structures, and fields planted in wet rice or mature sugarcane.

The high granitic outcrops in the survey area presented a special problem. These hills are composed of piles of huge rounded boulders and are often extremely steep and difficult to climb. Often there are a limited number of routes over an outcrop. In order to cover a 250-meter-wide transect at a 20-meter crew spacing, it is necessary for a crew of three to make four passes (plus an extra 10-meter-wide sweep) up and down a transect. Where outcrops block the transect, crews often had to travel repeatedly over the same limited route. For this reason, the sample fraction on high outcrops was reduced to approximately 25 percent, or to one 60-meter-wide pass. It is generally possible to visually survey an outcrop for larger sites from its peak. While some smaller sites may have been missed, this strategy was adopted in the interests of safety and time. Notes were kept on the locations of reduced sample-fraction areas.

A few additional comments on sampling are in order. Whenever a site overlapped a transect boundary, even slightly, it was fully documented. Thus, many sites are situated largely within unsurveyed transects. Further, many sites could be observed from the vantage of a neighboring transect or were found when crews crossed over areas outside the sample in order to reach sample transects. The presence and locations of these sites were noted, and when possible, the sites were documented. Thus, a portion of the recorded sites are located outside the sampled area. However, I do not assume that such sites constitute a total or representative sample of sites in unsurveyed transects.

Site Definition and the Continuous Record

In the last fifteen years the site concept has been subject to a spirited critique (Dunnell and Dancey 1983; Ebert 1992; Foley 1981; Lewarch and O'Brien 1981; Thomas 1975). Critics of the site concept point out that human use of landscapes is continuous, and that past human activities may not always produce patterns of material remains that conform to archaeological systematics. In response to this problem, various alternative survey strategies have been suggested and tried out, strategies that have been termed "non-site," "siteless," or "off-site" surveys.

Most of these studies have been concerned with relatively low-density archaeological landscapes. The Vijayanagara archaeological landscape presents many of the same problems as continuous, low-density landscapes in that it represents a continuously transformed and reworked environment and cannot be easily separated into discrete "packages" of archaeological material. The Vijayanagara situation differs from those discussed by critics of the site concept in its scale and complexity. Surface artifacts, especially ceramics, occur throughout the survey area, albeit in variable densities. It is not obvious how such a continuous and yet variable scatter should be treated. Breaking it up into individual "sites" would have been arbitrary at best, and further, would have produced many hundreds (or perhaps thousands) of additional "sites." It was not feasible, as has been done elsewhere (e.g. Lycett 1991b), to record the location of each artifact. As discussed in the following section, a compromise strategy was followed, combining traditional site systematics with more continuous observation.

Artifact distributions constitute only one aspect of the archaeological record, however. The Vijayanagara region also contains other consequences of past human activity, from formal structures to minor modifications of rock surfaces to large-scale modifications of soils and slopes. It is fairly easy to break up some archaeological features into sites, for example, a walled temple complex. Other cases are less straightforward. It is necessary, however, to divide the record in order to record its attributes, and we felt that changing the name of each division from "site" to "feature" or some other ostensibly neutral term (such as "occurrence," cf. Cowgill 1990) would not actually address the fundamental difficulty. For this reason, we have employed site terminology, but we recognize that this is partly a recording convenience. Moreover, we are aware of the fundamental interrelation of different sites to one another, and of the potential for interpretive manipulation that the strategy allows. As discussed below, field books were intended to minimize some of the problems inherent in the division of a continuous record into separate units.

Field Recording

Once sites are located and defined, they must be described and recorded. In the Vijayanagara survey, we recorded information about archaeological occurrences several different ways. These included: standardized site survey records, feature forms, field notebooks, photographs, base maps, and site plans. The basic document for each site was the site survey record. This form was designed, in part, to guide the recorder through a number of descriptive categories in order to insure that basic information for each site would be recorded consistently. At the same time, the form includes space for description and interpretation. The site survey record includes information about the context of the site, both in terms of natural features of the landscape and of other sites. Short descriptions of contemporary land use and the apparent effects of modern activities (such as erosion, vandalism, etc.) are required. Basic information on each site includes site measurements and orientation, architectural descriptions (where appropriate), and general layout. The site survey record also contains information about associated artifacts and artifact collection strategies. It serves as the central record for each site, and identifying numbers of additional forms, maps, and photographs are recorded on it.

The feature form was occasionally used for large and complex sites. This form provided additional space for descriptions of structures or other portions of a site designated as a feature (a subset of the archaeological material constituting the site). In addition, the feature form contained prompts for description of formal architectural elements such as mouldings and columns (see also Fritz, Michell, and Nagaraja Rao 1985; Fritz and Morrison in press).

Field notebooks were kept by each crew chief. Notebooks were, in part, a daily log of crew size and composition, weather, and other factors deemed relevant by the crew chief. Field notebooks also represent an attempt to get around the difficulty of breaking up a continuous archaeological record into individual sites. In each field notebook are observations about the distribution of artifacts across transects, whether or not the artifacts were considered to be part of a numbered site. In addition, the possible relationships between numbered sites were discussed in field notebooks.

Each site was photographed with both black-and-white and color film, providing a documentary record that cannot be duplicated by any other medium. All photographs were recorded on the site record forms.

The location of each site was recorded on a series of base maps. The Survey of India 1:50,000 topographic maps were enlarged and redrawn in order to create the 1:25,000 base map series. Each block is represented on a separate map for use in the field. Individual block maps with site locations were combined after survey (figure 4.2). Sketch maps of most sites were also prepared. In most cases, plan view maps were prepared using Brunton compasses and measuring tapes or pacing. Larger and more complex sites such as villages and agricultural terraces were mapped using a theodolite. Not all of the site plans could be accommodated in this chapter, and only a small sample is included.

Collection Strategies

Whenever possible, controlled surface collections of artifacts were made from each site. The collection strategies were formalized only after the initial season, so that the size, shape, and number of collection units from sites in Block O are more variable than those from other blocks. In general, collection strategies were based on the size of the site and the density of surface remains. For very small sites, such as an isolated wall, or for very sparse sites (huge terrace systems may contain only a single sherd, for example), all artifacts observed on the surface within 5 meters of the site boundaries were collected and provenienced by site. For larger sites with denser surface scatters, artifacts were collected along transects oriented to the cardinal directions (preferably north-south). Transect spacing could vary, but it was never more than 20 meters. Along each transect, 2-by-2 meter collection units were placed at regular intervals. Again, interval distances could vary, but they were never greater than 20 meters. Additional "judgment" 2-by-2 meter units could be placed on the transects, and off the transects, 2-by-2 meter "diagnostic" units could be collected. The location of all collection units are indicated on the original site plans.

SURVEYED AREAS AND THE LAYOUT OF THE CITY

All of the areas intensively surveyed to date lie south of the river. Only areas to the east and south of the city are reported on here. The inner portions of Blocks O, S, and T (that is, the portion nearest the city) may be considered the outermost portions of the city of Vijayanagara itself. Except for the northwestern quadrant of Block O, all of the surveyed areas described here also lie within generally drier upland areas. Data from the survey may be compared with detailed surface documentation of portions of the city (Fritz, Michell, and Nagaraja Rao 1985; Michell 1990) and scattered documentation elsewhere (Purandare 1986). More detailed discussions of areas surveyed can be found in Lycett (1991a, 1994), Means (1991), Morrison (in press), Morrison and Sinopoli (in press), Sinopoli and Morrison (1991, in press) and Sinopoli (1991b, 1993).

FIGURE 4.2 Blocks N, O, S, and T with locations of recorded sites

Three preliminary transects were surveyed in 1987 in order to gather baseline data and establish appropriate field recording techniques (Morrison 1991a). These transects ran through blocks O, R, and H, locating six sites (VMS-1 to VMS-6). The sites were not recorded using the same set of guidelines that have become standard in subsequent field seasons. Consequently, these sites are being re-recorded during the course of the survey, as they are encountered.

To date, four survey blocks have been completely documented. Block O, located to the east of the city, was surveyed in 1988 (Sinopoli and Morrison 1991), and the majority of Block S, to the south, in 1990 (Morrison and Sinopoli in press). Block S was completed in 1992. Block T was also completed in the 1992 season. In 1994, Block R and portions of Block M were studied (Morrison and Sinopoli in press), but these are not described here.

Surveyed Blocks: Overview

Significant differences exist between the three survey blocks, differences that are reflected in the types and distributions of sites. In all areas, primary factors influencing site location appear to include topography and soil, proximity to the city, and routes of transportation. There are limited expanses of level ground in the study area, consisting of the narrow alluvial strip of the Tungabhadra River and colluviated valleys between granitic outcrops. These granitic outcrops are one of the most striking features of the landscape, and range from fairly low hills with natural terraces of shallow red soil to extremely high and steep edifices that support only a few clinging bushes. Outcrops are defensively important and also constitute barriers to movement, sacred places, and the primary catchment areas for runoff-fed reservoirs, terraces, and check-dams. As figure 4.2 indicates, Block O contains numerous high steep granitic outcrops, while S is relatively open and flat. Block T is more similar to O, in that it contains a single broad valley enclosed by granitic outcrops. Like Block O, the southeastern portion of Block T is bisected by rocky hills.

Topography and soils, together with the route of the Tungabhadra River, partially determine the locations of different types of agricultural land. Land under permanent, wet cultivation tends to be low-lying since it must fall within the reach of the Vijayanagara irrigation channels. Dry farmed areas are more topographically diverse, and make opportunistic use of topographic variation. The form of agricultural regime itself may itself strongly constrain the locations of other sites. Wet fields and reservoir beds, for example, prevent movement of traffic, while the raised embankments of reservoirs may be used as roadways.

The city of Vijayanagara greatly influenced the arrangement of smaller sites and features in the study area. The city's massive enclosing walls (VMS-10, VMS-123) exerted an almost magnetic attraction, so that most of the recorded settlement areas lie within the city walls or huddled up against them. After one passes out of this urban zone, residence appears to have been almost exclusively concentrated in nucleated settlements. The areas of most intensive agriculture recorded in the survey—the Turtha Canal zone of Block O and the land under the Kamalapuram reservoir (VMS-231) in Block S—are also the closest to the city. In part, this is due to the topographic possibilities for such agriculture, though transport costs may also have been a consideration in their planning.

Vijayanagara site distributions also appear to be highly constrained by transport considerations. As a "primate center" (Smith 1976), Vijayanagara dominated the regional settlement hierarchy. The survey area immediately surrounding the city also reflects this dominance, with a radial pattern of roadways leading into and out of the city. As noted, transport routes are influenced by topography and by agricultural regime; settlement distributions mirror those of roads. The Tungabhadra River is not considered navigable (Kelsall 1872), and thus presents more of an obstacle to transportation than a conduit. A massive stone bridge set on stone piers once spanned the Tungabhadra River north of the city, near the Vithala temple complex. Deloche (1984:26) notes, "According to some inscriptions in the XIVth century, the kings provided stepping stones (or was it a causeway) to cross the Tungabhadra River (Mysore Archaeological Survey 1920(35); Annual Report of Indian Epigraphy for 1958-1959, 94)." A second river crossing exists at Talarighat (Tolara), opposite the settlement of Anegundi. This crossing, made by small, round basket coracles is still important today. That this area was a coracle crossing in the Vijayanagara period is evident from a sixteenth century copper plate inscription, detailing a grant of land made to the boatmen enabling them to give free passage to holy people (Filliozat and Filliozat 1988:vii).

Block O: Introduction

Block O lies to the east of the city and is described by Lycett (1991a), Means (1991), Morrison (1991b), Sinopoli and Morrison (1991), and Sinopoli (1991b). It is bisected by a major roadway that runs southwest-northeast. The block contains a moderate density of sites, the majority of which are found near this major roadway.

Approximately half of Block O consists of low-lying colluvial and alluvial soils, with high granitic inselbergs looming above the relatively flat northwestern portion of the block. This portion of the block is watered by the Vijayanagara-period Turtha Canal (Turtha is the contemporary name for this canal, which was known in the Vijayanagara period as the *Hiriya Kaluve*, or "big canal;" see chapter 2). Site densities are very low in this area. In the southeastern portion of Block O, granitic outcrops are connected by high rocky uplands, forming a large zone of rugged topography. The rocky uplands of the southeast contain numerous dryland agricultural features, evidence of lime processing, and a few shrines.

Site densities in Block O are fairly high in its southwest corner, where an incomplete segment of the city's fortification wall (VMS-10) encloses numerous small structures, wells, and shrines. Outside this area, three nucleated settlements were identified (VMS-2, VMS-35 to 37, and VMS-101). Two of these were located on the major roadway that led from the city toward the town of Kampli along a course very close to that of the modern road. One hundred and eleven sites were recorded in Block O.

Block S: Introduction

Block S lies to the south of the city and is described by Lycett (1994), Morrison and Sinopoli (in press), Morrison (in press), and Sinopoli and Morrison (in press). Survey block S is located in an area of fairly low relief. Both red and mixed black-and-red soils occur in this area. The high granitic outcrops of the Hampi-Daroji Hills are virtually absent, with surface elevation rising gradually from north to south. Sites in Block S tend to be larger and more internally complex than those in Block O, with significant differences in the distribution of settlement and agricultural facilities. While Block O site distributions are almost entirely constrained by environmental and agricultural features, site locations in Block S strongly reflect the influence of the city, as a portion of the block is located within the massive city walls. As in Block O, land in Block S is fairly sharply demarcated by irrigation regime. In the former, permanent cultivation was restricted to land under the river-fed Turtha Canal. In Block S, permanent cultivation was carried out under (to the north of) the Kamalapuram reservoir (VMS-231), which is supplied by the river-fed Raya Canal as well as by seasonal runoff. Elsewhere, dry and seasonally dry farming and grazing predominate. The huge Kamalapuram reservoir dominates the western half of the block. Water levels in the reservoir vary throughout the year, so that in some seasons it is surrounded by marshy ground with aquatic and semi-aquatic vegetation. The embankment of the reservoir, besides having an agricultural function (see below), serves as both a fortification wall and a roadway.

Block T: Introduction

Block T lies to the southeast of the city and is described by Brubaker (in press) and Sinopoli and Morrison (1992, in press). Block T, unlike either S or O, lay completely out of reach of Tungabhadra water during the Vijayanagara period. Thus, all of the agricultural facilities in this mixed red and black soil area relate to either dry farming or wet-cum-dry production. A modern canal now cuts through the center of the block, and canal construction has disturbed many sites in this area.

Topographically, Block T represents a transition between the rocky uplands of Block O and the level expanses of Block S. Block T contains extensive level areas, now mostly under dry cultivation, but several high granitic outcrops tower over the level ground. The northern half of the block consists of a broad valley, running east-west, while higher land to the south promotes northward draining runoff. Block T contains numerous reservoirs, including two very large ones in its northern half. Routes of movement are well defined, with a fortification wall and radial roadway as well as agricultural features serving to channel traffic through the area. Two nucleated settlements and numerous smaller structures attest to the intensity of occupation and land use in the area.

FORTIFICATION

The entire Vijayanagara region was, in a real sense, a fortified zone. In the city, the elite zone of monumental architecture termed by Fritz, Michell, and Nagaraja Rao (1985) the Royal Center consists of numerous walled enclosures and is contained within a circuit of high masonry walls. The Urban Core (Fritz, Michell, and Nagaraja Rao 1985) is also contained within strong walls, many of which are built over and integrate granitic ridges. The walls of the Urban Core are broken by numerous monumental gateways (Fritz 1983) and are guarded by projecting square bastions. Many short "label inscriptions" (Patil and Balasubramanya 1991:19) identify strategic locations as guard posts and lookout points. All of the abovementioned fortifications are located in Block N.

The morphology of Vijayanagara fortification walls in and around the city is worth noting, in part because we have assumed that similar walls in the survey area also belong to the Vijayanagara period. Fortification walls consist of two faces of well-fitted square, rectangular, or irregular blocks, often of quite massive dimensions (up to two meters long). The blocks themselves are commonly triangular or pie-shaped in plan, so that the pointed ends of the blocks of each face meet in the center of the wall. The intervening space is then filled in with earth, rubble, or other fill material. Occasionally rectangular "ties" join the two faces of the wall. Walls may be plastered, but it is rare that mortar is used. Sometimes walls are surmounted by a cap of brick and plaster. A few heavily built walls in the city do not use pie-shaped blocks, but these are less common.

Outside of Block N, an outer ring of massive fortification walls with numerous square bastions follows the Urban Core circuit rather closely, lying up to one kilometer to the south of the Urban Core circuit in Block S. This outer wall (VMS-123) is well preserved in Block S, where it encloses a densely settled area. In the western portion of Block S, the wall joins with the embankment of the Kamalapuram reservoir (VMS-231). The latter clearly functioned as a fortification, as is evident from the two bastions built into it. West and north of Block S, the fortification wall curves up through the northeast corner of Block R and into Block M. To the north and east of Block S, the fortification wall intersects the junction of Blocks S and O (where the wall is renumbered VMS-10). The wall ends abruptly in Block O (figure 4.2), less than 500 meters from a high, northwest-southeast trending ridge.

Features related to fortification and defense are also found outside of the walled area of the city. There are numerous other types of features designed to control movement across the region and to restrict access to specific locations. These include smaller walled settlements, isolated bastions or towers, isolated walls, and "horse stones" and are discussed individually by block.

Block O

VMS-10, a fairly short (90 meters) but well-built segment of fortification wall located in the southwest corner of Block O, was mentioned above. This wall is constructed of two faces of pie-shaped blocks with an earthen core and contains several square bastions. The present northern end of VMS-10 lies in an area of intensively farmed irrigated land (a consequence of the twentieth century dam project). The northern end of the wall may have been destroyed by farmers clearing their fields. If the wall had continued along its present course, it would have run up to the edge of a granitic outcrop. To the north of the outcrop is VMS-25, a wall segment composed of large, pie-shaped blocks, which runs for 178 meters in an east-west direction before turning south to meet the outcrop. This wall segment may have met VMS-10, forming a continuous arc of fortification around the outcrop. The wall would have then left Block O, possibly joining the Urban Core wall on the west. A short wall segment, VMS-20, is located atop the outcrop.

Block O contains the remains of three settlements (see below). Of these, two (VMS-35 to 37 and VMS-101) contain fairly clear evidence of having been fortified. VMS-2 is heavily disturbed. If it had been enclosed or otherwise fortified, no traces of walls, towers, or bastions are preserved. The evidence of fortification at settlements in Block O is discussed below.

Several isolated walls (VMS-19, VMS-27, VMS-32) may have served defensive functions. The complex of sites and features (VMS-42, VMS-43, VMS-44, VMS-45, VMS-46, VMS-47, and VMS-50) associated with the temple VMS-42 and a pathway over a high outcrop (Sinopoli 1991b) include a long, well-built wall (VMS-45) that served to restrict and channel the movement of traffic over the outcrop. This important pass near the city linked the valleys of Blocks O and T and was carefully protected.

VMS-62 is a 130-meter-long feature that may have been a fortification wall-cum-embankment spanning a low-lying area between outcrops (figure 4.2). It is badly disturbed, however, and is more likely to have been a reservoir. VMS-85 is located approximately 60 meters west of the settlement VMS-101 and an associated temple complex, VMS-83. VMS-85 appears to be an isolated square bastion and is 18.4 by 13.6 meters. This structure was built of quarried rectangular blocks and may have been associated with an outer wall of the settlement. A small segment of cobble wall, double faced and with an earthen core, is located immediately south of VMS-85. It prevents easy access to the outcrop containing the temple, VMS-83. Thus, if the access route to the outcrop and its temples were guarded or watched, VMS-85 may have served as a watchtower or lookout post for the area. VMS-85 would have been located either on or near the major roadway running through Block O.

Block S

Block S also contains walled settlements. These include Kamalapuram (VMS-259) and the entire northeastern corner of the block enclosed by VMS-123. These sites are discussed below.

One isolated bastion, VMS-247, is located amid the irrigated fields south of the Kamalapuram reservoir (VMS-231). This round bastion is 10 meters in diameter and does not appear to be associated with Vijayanagara-period walls, roads, or other features. However, the recent extension of irrigated fields to the area (watered by electric pumps) may have caused the destruction of such features. A modern dirt road runs past the site; perhaps this road follows the course of an older route.

VMS-158 (figure 4.3) is located just outside the circuit of walls (VMS-123, VMS-10) and is adjacent to the Penukonda Road (see below). This site consists of a row of closely spaced upright slabs, set on end and partially buried. Adjacent to the row of upright slabs are hundreds of small and medium boulders set into the ground. These boulders are not organized into well-formed rows but are scattered thickly throughout an area up to 10 meters south of the uprights. The feature ends at the edge of the Penukonda Road. VMS-158 is morphologically similar to features known as "horse stones," barriers described by contemporary visitors to the city, and known from the site of Kummata Durga (Patil 1991c). "Horse stones" are mentioned by Paes (Sewell 1900:253) in about A.D. 1520 and by Abdur-Razzak in about 1443. Abdur-Razzak wrote (Sewell 1900:88) "Around the first citadel are stones the height of a man, one half of which is sunk in the ground while the other half rises above it. These are fixed one beside the other in such a manner that no horse or foot soldier could boldly or with ease approach the citadel."

Other possible fortification-related features in Block S include the long walls VMS-279 and VMS-284.

Block T

Block T contains several very long fortification walls and these, together with such barriers as outcrops and reservoir beds, make this block one of the most carefully protected in the survey area. The northern part of Block T consists of an east-west valley. A major roadway leading into the city runs through this valley. This road runs near the village of Nallapuram and is thus called the Nallapuram Road. Along the roadway are several features related to defense, including a bastion or watch tower, VMS-327. This circular masonry structure sits atop a small outcrop commanding a good view of the road and abuts a wall that runs downslope toward the long roadway, VMS-326. Further west along the course of the road lies VMS-321, a small structure or wall fragment that may have been defensive. The entire course of this roadway is both

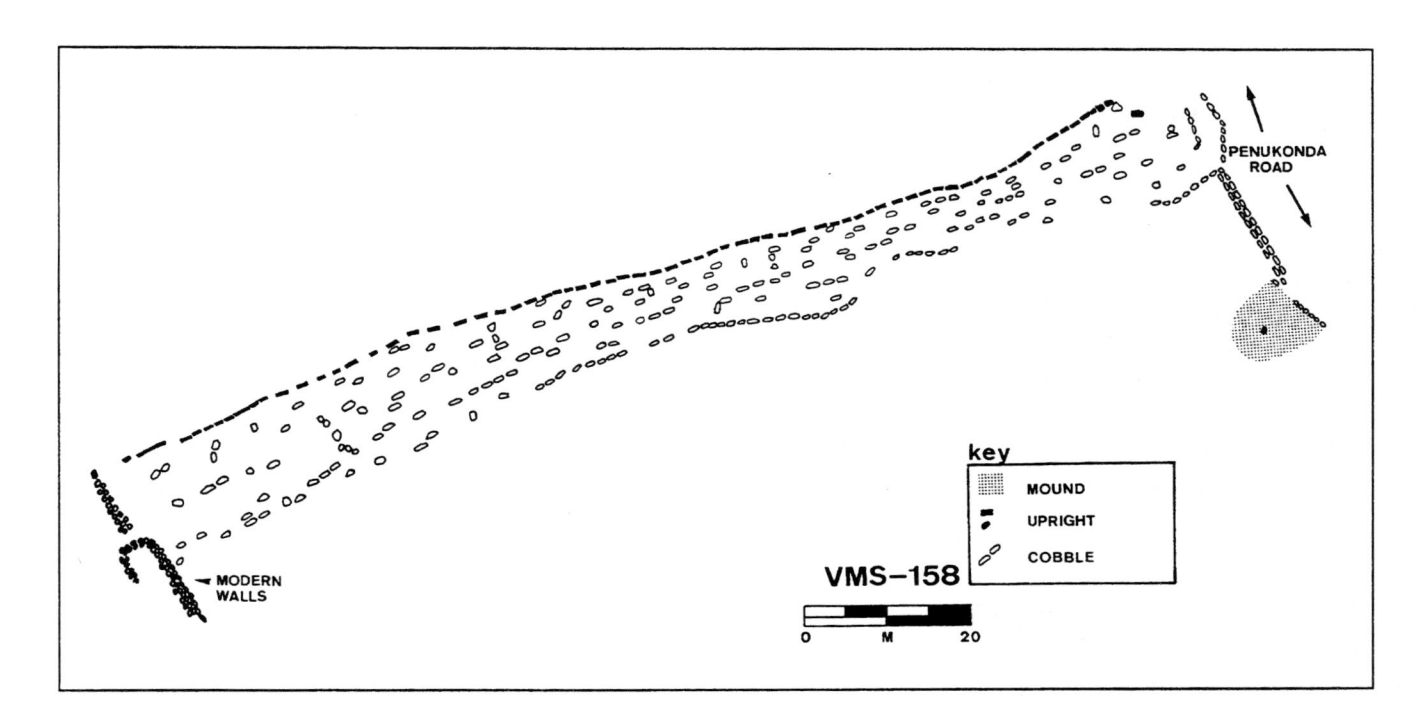

FIGURE 4.3 "Horse Stones," (VMS-158) lying outside city walls, Block S

well defined and well controlled.

VMS-339 is a 2-km-long rubble wall which runs northwest-southeast across the southern half of Block T (figure 4.2). This wall, up to 10 m wide and 3 m high in places, certainly served both for defense and boundary demarcation. The wall extends from a high rock outcrop on the south and spans a level expanse, perhaps compelling traffic to move along the Nallapuram Road. Several other walls (VMS-348, VMS-353, VMS-345) run along the base of the outcrop that defines the southern end of VMS-339 and apparently served to define roadways and paths along the base of the outcrop. At the foot of the outcrop near the present southern end of VMS-339 is VMS-365, a fortified settlement (below). VMS-339 now bisects the course of the road along the outcrop near VMS-365 and thus appears to postdate this route. At the northern end of VMS-336 lies VMS-306, a curved wall segment that runs approximately east-west. This short but substantial wall would have blocked traffic moving north along the base of the long wall VMS-339 on the east side. This feature, VMS-306, may have compelled those taking this route to take an acute turn to the east.

Finally, in between the massive wall and fortified settlement (VMS-339 and VMS-365) on the south and the Nallapuram Valley on the north, the landscape is broken by high outcrops separating moderately hilly zones. In this area are numerous isolated wall fragments, at least one which (VMS-325) seems to have been defensive.

Other Areas

Numerous features related to defense are found throughout the study area. These include walled settlements, forts, and segments of walls and gateways. Walled settlements include: Anegundi (Purandare 1986), Malpannagudi, Hospet (Tirumaladeviyara-Pattana; Filliozat and Filliozat 1988:13), and probably Anantasayanagudi. Major temple complexes themselves resemble walled settlements. Temple complexes were named and conceived of as independent settlements, and often contained large resident populations in and around the temple. Large temples are invariably enclosed within strong and high *prakara* walls (Meister and Dhaky 1986) not dissimilar to fortification walls around cities. Such walls would not only have served to delineate the sacred space of the temple and to prevent unauthorized entrance to the temple but would also have protected the occupants and treasures associated with the temple from attack.

VMS-6 is located in Block W (Morrison 1991a) and consists of a high, isolated granitic outcrop topped by a thick-walled fort. At the base of the hill are a large step well and an extensive complex of masonry rooms. This complex appears to consist of many small square or rectangular rooms arranged around courtyards or open areas. This layout is unlike any other known from the study area. The complex of rooms may be related to the fort on the hill, possibly as an area where soldiers were housed. A second fort is located atop another outcrop near the modern village of Daroji, south and east of the survey area.

Isolated walls are situated throughout the study area and well beyond it. Such walls tend to be heavily constructed, and many contain gateways. Walls are often placed across strategic passes and points of entrance into the region. For example, in order to approach the city through Block O, passing along the Kampli Road, one must enter through a narrow pass in the rocky hills. This pass is blocked by a double line of masonry walls. VMS-370 in Block [O]Q (to the east of Block P) is another such fortification wall, restricting access to the Nallapuram Valley from the west. This 2-km-long wall appears to have been constructed and reconstructed several times and contains two gateways. Similar walls occur well away from the city, guarding the eastern egress into the Daroji Valley.

SETTLEMENT

Although the entire survey area shows evidence of Vijayanagara land use, permanent residences (at least those involving stone construction) seem to have been restricted to nucleated settlements. Such settlements are generally well defined. Unfortunately, many also coincide with locations of modern villages and thus have been heavily damaged.

Block O

Block O contained four major concentrations of settlement. One of these, in the southwest corner of the block, may be considered part of the city itself, being partly enclosed within the fortification wall, VMS-10. This wall is part of an arc that, in Block S, protects Late Vijayanagara settlements and structures. Inasmuch as the wall is continuous, although broken in places and partly dismantled by modern canal construction, it may be the case that the small structures or foundations found in this area also date to the Late Vijayanagara period. Sites in this area include VMS-11, VMS-13, VMS-

14, VMS-15, and VMS-16. VMS-11 is a small rock-cut cistern. VMS-13, VMS-14, and VMS-15 are small, single room structures or foundations. VMS-16 is a pitted area containing a high concentration of ceramics and other refuse.

Several nucleated settlements were also located in Block O. Only one of these, VMS-35-37, is not also the site of a modern village. This settlement is also distinctive in that it is located amid irrigated fields of the Vijayanagara period (watered by the Turtha Canal), and is not situated on an identifiable roadway. The settlement area was separated into several sites partly because each set of habitation structures was spatially segregated and partly for recording convenience. The complex consists of two concentrations of structures, one located on a high and rocky granitic outcrop, and the other, approximately 100 meters to the southeast, on a level area atop a low outcrop. A small temple (VMS-36) lies between the two concentrations (Means 1991; Sinopoli and Morrison 1991).

VMS-35 is a village or hamlet, approximately 200 by 170 meters. It extends from the bottom to the top of a large outcrop, with stairs and paths connecting different levels. Numerous small structures, indicated by cobble wall fall, are opportunistically placed on the available level surfaces, some built up against boulders. Much of the underlying outcrop consists of flat sheetrock, into which stone "horse ties" have been excavated. These ties are common features at Vijayanagara, in which bedrock is pecked away to create a short bar or handle to which things might have been tied. Numerous bedrock and block mortars and small drains are cut into the rock. The site is bounded by walls on all sides (VMS-34 to the southwest, VMS-35 features 25 and 26 to the north, VMS-35 feature 33 on the east, and VMS-35 feature 31 on the south). These walls are solidly, if roughly, built. VMS-34, one of the boundary walls, consists of two faces of quarried rectangular blocks and unmodified boulders separated by an earthen core, 1.45 meters wide. Feature 2, a wall on the highest tier of the settlement is the only formally constructed wall, consisting of well-fitted square and rectangular quarried blocks.

VMS-35 contains abundant evidence of stone working, with large boulders and cobbles of gabbro, which is not naturally occurring at this site, scattered across the settlement. A large quantity of debitage and several finished pegs were recovered in surface collections at the site, perhaps indicating specialized production of gabbro pegs. This raw material is a melanocratic, aphanitic volcanic that occurs as late Tertiary extrusive dykes and sills throughout the Hampi-Daroji Hills (see Lycett 1991a). These black pegs are used throughout the city of Vijayanagara wherever walls are built on sheet rock. Gabbro pegs are inserted into lines of square holes cut all along the base of the wall, anchoring it and preventing it from sliding downhill. Other artifacts recovered in the surface collections included ceramics from a variety of types of vessels, chipped stone debitage, and two schist objects which may be hoe blades (cf. Foote 1914).

VMS-36 is a small, Vijayanagara-period shrine to the god Hanuman. The shrine consists of four dressed columns supporting a simple roof with a carved lotus. To the west of VMS-36 is another concentration of rubble-walled structures, VMS-37. This area is on a fairly level surface atop a low outcrop, and contains at least 18 single or multi-room structures. A "dolerite," or gabbro, dyke runs through this outcrop, which may be the source of the raw material for the pegs. Other evidence of gabbro working is also found at VMS-37. Ceramic densities are lower than at VMS-35. A coin found on the site dates to the reign of Deva Raya II (A.D. 1426-1447; Ramesan 1979) suggesting an Early Vijayanagara attribution for at least part of the occupation.

This entire complex (VMS-35-37) consists of a small, possibly fortified settlement at least partly focussed on gabbro working. It is surrounded by the irrigated fields of the Turtha Canal; it is not clear if the settlement predates the opening of the canal or not (see also Means 1991).

A larger settlement, VMS-2, (figure 4.4) is located midway through the block on the large Kampli Road. Unfortunately, this site now lies between a modern village, Venkatapuram, and the (modern) power canal, both of which have caused considerable destruction of the site. In the small portion of VMS-2 that has survived, there are numerous small informal structures. In addition, scattered architectural elements such as columns and mouldings, as well as quarried blocks, suggest the presence of more substantial elite or public architecture. Several high mounds with fragments of walls are located on the site. One of these, feature 7, is a U-shaped mound, facing east, with two or three stepped levels. This plan corresponds to "palaces" or elite residences found within the city (Blurton 1985). The site also contains a small but well-constructed step well and two shrines or small temples. The Vaisnava shrine has two elephant

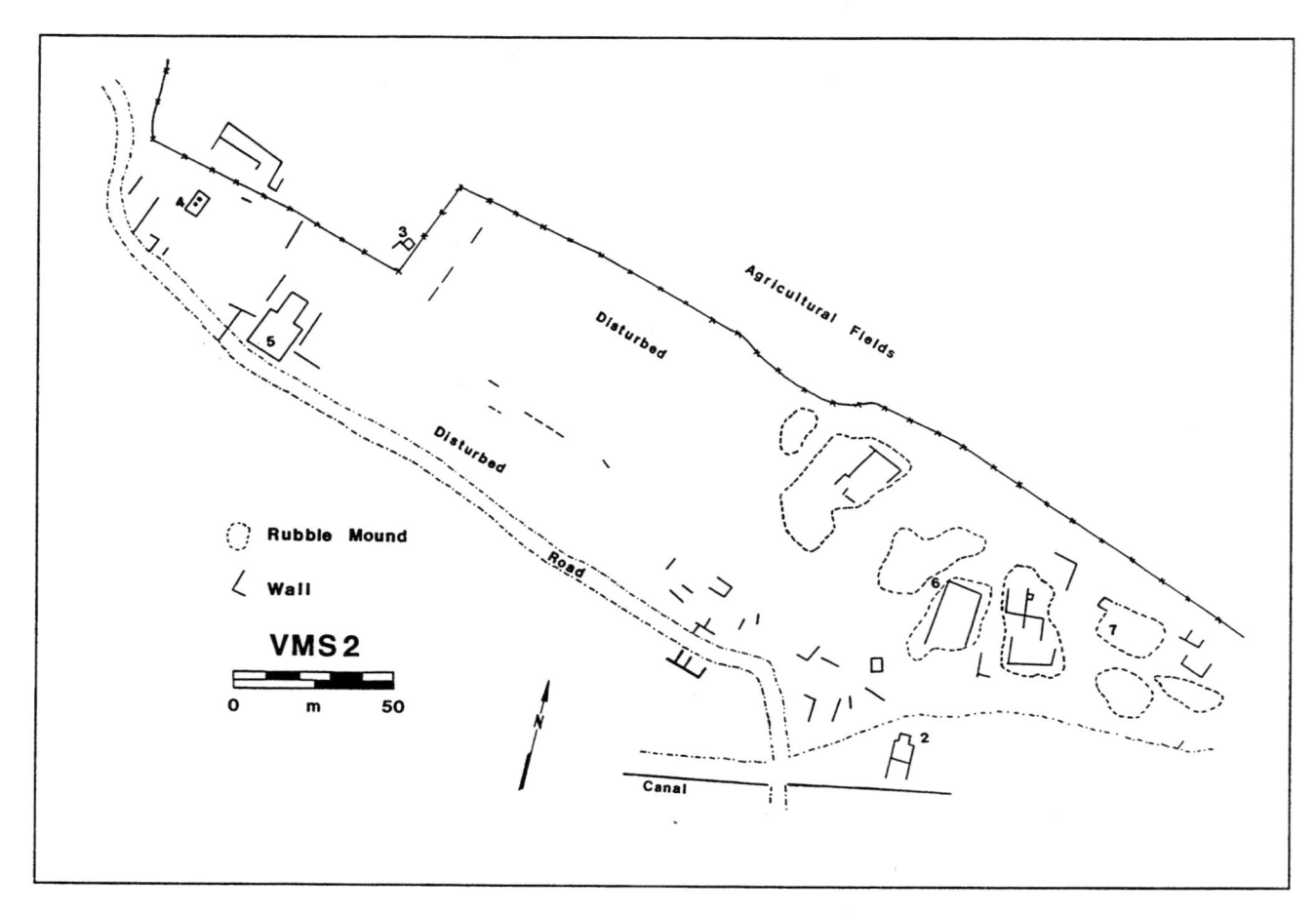

FIGURE 4.4 Heavily disturbed Vijyanagara-period settlement (Venkatapuram), VMS-2, Block O

balustrades in front of it. Similar balustrades in the city are used in the formal architecture of palaces and temples. VMS-2 also contains gabbro-working debris and pegs. There is no sheetrock in the area, so the pegs could not have been for local use. A large number and variety of ceramics were recovered from the site, including one sherd of blue and white porcelain (from China or Southeast Asia, fifteenth to sixteenth century A.D.). Other artifacts included worked glass and iron slag.

Two small boundary markers (Kotraiah 1979) stand in the middle of the visible remnant of the village. One of these contains an inscription referring to a donation made by a resident of the village. The inscription is in a form of Kannada script that was introduced approximately one hundred years ago (Directorate of Archaeology and Museums personnel, personal communication 1988). Thus, it seems likely that this settlement has had a long occupational history in which a fairly substantial Vijayanagara-period village or town was succeeded by a nineteenth to twentieth century settlement. Whether there was continuous settlement from the sixteenth to the nineteenth century is unclear. The contemporary village of Venkatapuram lies adjacent to VMS-2 on the main road from Kamalapuram to Kampli. Because the modern roadway closely parallels a major Vijayanagara-period road, it is likely that VMS-2 lay along this roadway and that Venkatapuram overlies part of the Vijayanagara-period settlement.

VMS-101 is situated on the same roadway, in the northeast corner of the block. It is even more badly disturbed than VMS-2. Like that settlement, it has been bisected by the power canal, and huge piles of fill from canal construction obscure much of the site area. VMS-101 hugs the base of a high outcrop on which a Vijayanagara-period temple complex (VMS-83) is located. At the base of this outcrop is a large masonry-lined spring (VMS-84). This settlement contains traces of several spatially segregated structures. These structures were built of carefully laid unmodified cobbles. Only a few consist of more than one room, but a larger building of four to five rooms with plastered walls can be traced.

Two very long walls may have bounded the settlement. One wall now runs parallel to the modern canal, and it cannot be determined if there were more structures on its northern side. The other wall lies at the eastern end of the settlement, at the mouth of a narrow valley. There are traces of more substantial fortifications nearby. VMS-85, a large stone bastion, lies 60 meters to the west of the spring at the base of the high outcrop. The modern village of Bukkasagara lies just north of the canal. North of Bukkasagara, and north of the Vijayanagara-period roadway, bastions and fortification walls can be seen atop a high outcrop.

The settlement history of VMS-101 may have been similar to that of VMS-2, with continuous or sporadic occupation of the same location from the Vijayanagara period to the present. If VMS-101 had extended as far north as the bastions, much of it would be now underneath the village of Bukkasagara. In fact, several Vijayanagara-period shrines are found within the modern town (VMS-116, VMS-118, VMS-119). The name *Bukkasagara* itself is Sanskrit for "ocean of Bukka," perhaps referring to one of the Vijayanagara kings of that name (Sangama Dynasty; see table 3.1).

Block S

The northern portion of Block S lies just south of the well-built walls surrounding the city's Urban Core (Fritz, Michell, and Nagaraja Rao 1985). This area is itself enclosed within massive fortification walls (VMS-123) that incorporate twenty-nine bastions, and numerous gateways and openings. The only evidence for settlement in Block S is within these walls. Some temporal distinction can be made among settlement areas in Block S. The fort of Kamalapuram (VMS-257, 258, and 259) as well as the large Kamalapuram reservoir (VMS-231) are known to date to the early Vijayanagara period (e.g. Saletore 1982:187; Panchamukhi 1953:*ix*). The Kamalapuram fort (figure 4.5) was later enclosed by and incorporated into the city wall (VMS-123). The embankment of VMS-231 is also integrated into the later city wall, even displaying several large bastions. Within the walls, a late suburb of the city was constructed, and this expanding settlement, probably together with a growing Kamalapuram, eventually coalesced into a continuous distribution of structures and features.

The location of permanent Vijayanagara-period residences and commercial establishments appears to have been confined to rather clearly demarcated areas or zones, very often set off by walls or confined to roadsides. This should not, however, obscure the abundant evidence for the repeated use of the entire surveyed landscape, use that may involve mobility in residence, albeit for limited periods of time (harvesting, for example). The overall pattern of settlement in block S accords well with that from block O, where nucleated settlement distribution predominated. In Block S, areas thought to relate to permanent and fairly dense settlement all lie within the city walls. Numerous structures were found in this area, including *mandapas*, temples and temple complexes, as well as rooms, platforms, walls, and terraces.

Traces of several road segments are evident inside the walls, some lined by raised platforms and small shrines (e.g. VMS-201) similar to bazaar streets in the city associated with the large Vijayanagara temple complexes. Within the walls are many isolated sculptures and architectural elements as well as ten wells or cisterns and over forty bedrock and block mortars, all within a huge and very dense artifact scatter. Only a very limited number of these artifacts could be collected and studied. Although earthenware ceramics dominate the assemblage as elsewhere in the study area, there appears to be a greater concentration of polished wares, both black and red, among the ceramics of this walled zone.

Inscriptions indicate that there were at least two named settlements in Block S during the two hundred years of Vijayanagara occupation. The Early Vijayanagara Kamalapuram fort (VMS-257 to 259) has retained its identity as a settlement, even though it became almost completely enclosed by other settlement areas during the Late Vijayanagara period. Kamalapuram has been continuously occupied since the Vijayanagara period. Thus, it is not possible to trace the layout of the settlement in any detail. Kamalapuram was contained within the high walls of a square fort, approximately 250 by 250 meters. Segments of these walls still exist, and the overall plan can be clearly seen in aerial photos (displayed in the Kamalapuram museum). The north gateway complex (VMS-256, VMS-257) is in good condition. The pillars of the gateway are Late Vijayanagara in style, indicating that the gateway was either constructed or remodelled in that period.

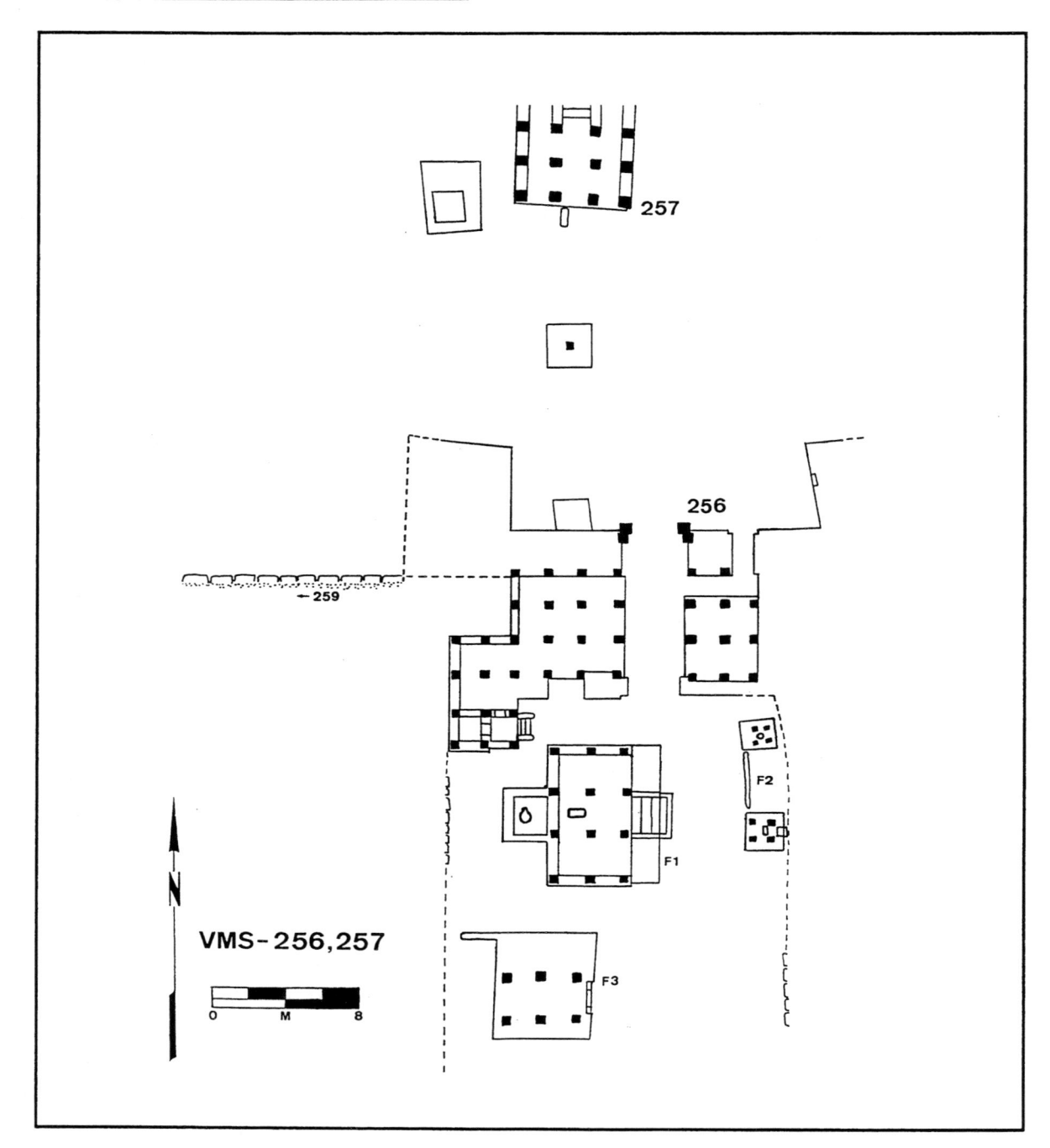

FIGURE 4.5 Northern gateway complex of the Kamalapuram fort (VMS-256) and associated temple (VMS-257)

In the center of the fort is a high, round tower (VMS-258). The tower is solid, except for a stairway leading to its summit.

Filliozat and Filliozat (1988:13) note the occurrence of a second named settlement southeast of the city, Varadadevi-Ammana-Pattana, named after a queen of the emperor Achyuta Raya (ruled A.D. 1529-1542). They describe two inscriptions relating to this town, one dated A.D. 1534 and the other 1539; both were associated with the large Pattabhirama temple complex (VMS-237; see also Pascher 1987). Thus, as noted above, this settlement dates to the latter period of the city's occupation. Archaeologically, settlement appears to have been nearly continuous between Kamalapuram and Varadadevi-Ammana-Pattana, assuming that the latter is located south and east of the Pattabhirama temple.

A long wall, VMS-223, bisects the settled area inside the city, abutting the city wall (VMS-123) on the south and extending to the north for 364 meters, to within 200 meters of the Pattabhirama temple. At this point, the wall makes a ninety degree turn to the west, continuing another 160 meters. East of this turn in VMS-223 is the settlement area VMS-222. This concentration of small structures and artifacts contains a *Saivite* boundary marker (Kotraiah 1979), indicating some formal demarcation of space. Unfortunately, the marker carries no inscription and can be dated only to the Vijayanagara period. Settlement growth in this area appears to have been accretional. Although named settlement areas were established and spatial divisions maintained, the archaeological materials indicate a dense and continuous distribution of settlement across the area.

Block T

The northwestern corner of Block T abuts the outer circuit of the city walls. However, areas of settlement within Block T are confined to well-defined nucleated settlements. VMS-365 is a walled village ca. 600 by 300 m (area inside the walls 140 by 90 m). This Vijayanagara-period settlement contains a small temple with a Hanuman sculpture, a well, and several clusters of multi-roomed rubble-walled structures (rooms and platforms). Two separate concentrations of structures are found. The larger lies inside the circular bounding wall and appears to contain between two and five houses. Some fragments of plaster flooring are visible. Large open areas, what may be courtyards or gardens, also lie within the exterior walls. One lithic artifact was located on the site. The other group of structures is smaller (perhaps one or two houses?) and lies to the northwest of the walled village, separated by about 40 m of open space. VMS-365 is one of the few Vijayanagara-period villages in the study area that has been completely abandoned, and like VMS-35-37, it is well fortified. The reservoir VMS-349 lies adjacent to the village and was undoubtedly an important source of water for domestic and agricultural purposes.

Other structures in Block T may have supported temporary or small-scale residence. One such structure is VMS-343, a single-room rubble-walled structure with no associated artifacts. Other small structures, such as VMS-340, a cluster of platforms, are of uncertain function.

The second nucleated village in Block T is VMS-361. This settlement is situated at a strategic point along the Nallapuram Road. It is adjacent to the bastion, VMS-327, and lies just south of the embankment of the large reservoir VMS-330. As noted, settlements in dry and wet-cum-dry areas are almost always associated with reservoirs. This settlement has been heavily disturbed but is associated with a dense ceramic scatter. Nearby are a step well (VMS-328) and a highly disturbed area containing artifacts and some sculpted columns (VMS-329) that may have once been part of the settlement.

Other Areas

Figure 4.6 shows the distribution of named settlements in the study area known from historical sources and from previous archaeological research (see also figure 3.1). References to Vijayanagara-period structures found in these settlements can be found in Devaraj and Patil (1991a, 1991b), Filliozat and Filliozat (1988), Fritz, Michell, and Nagaraja Rao (1985), Michell (1990), Nagaraja Rao, ed. (1983, 1985), and Purandare (1986).

For the sites identified on figure 4.6, both historical and archaeological evidence coincide, and both location and identification of the settlement are fairly straightforward. However, the historical data on settlement names, dates, and locations cannot be uncritically accepted. The "founding" of a settlement, for example, may refer only to an official naming (or renaming) and to the construction of monumental or elite architecture. Settlements may have been "founded" in (unincorporated) areas where people were already living, merely defining, formalizing, and claiming boundaries. The close association of specific kings and their relatives with specific settlements certainly says something about royal patronage and claims of status, but such associations do not necessarily date the settlement in its entirety.

ROADWAYS

The roadways within the city have been described by Fritz (1983) and by Nagaraja Rao (1983). Outside Block N, many other roads and paths can be identified. These provide important information about the nature of transportation across the study area.

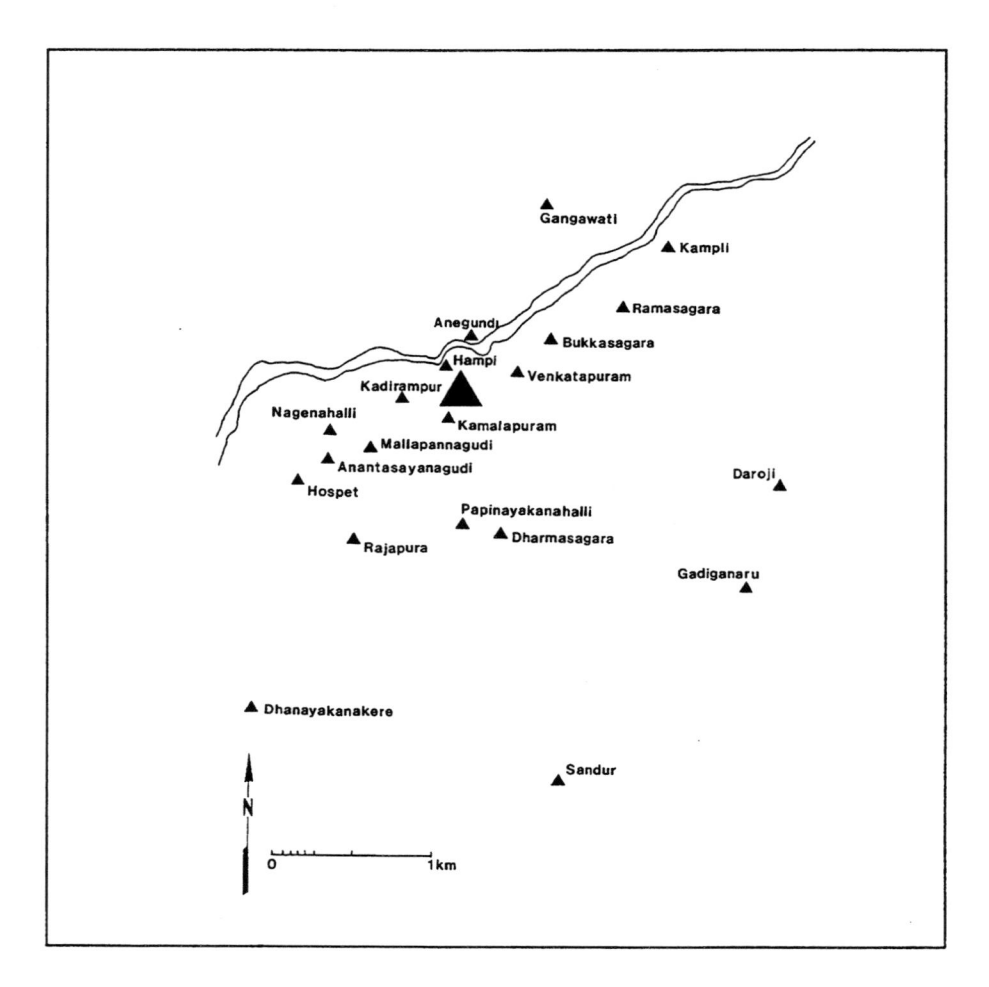

FIGURE 4.6   Distribution of Vijayanagara-period settlements around the city of Vijayanagara

Block O

Block O is dominated by a long roadway which emerges from a gateway in the Urban Core walls and runs southwest-northeast through the block as far as Bukkasagara. Past Bukkasagara, beyond the survey area, transportation was channeled through several narrow passes that are protected by fortifications. The road apparently led through these passes and extended at least as far as the town of Kampli to the east. The route of this roadway is inferred from the distribution of structures that once lined the road. Proscriptions regarding temple placement require an eastern orientation (Dagens 1985), but in practice temples often faced onto roads. Among the structures lining the road are VMS-111, VMS-112, VMS-114, VMS-115, and possibly VMS-64. VMS-93 is a gateway located along the route of the Kampli Road, midway through the block. A wall may once have been associated with this gateway, spanning the flat area between two outcrops here. However, this area has been heavily disturbed by modern canal and road construction and by agricultural clearing.

A second road along the banks of the Turtha Canal now winds its way through the northeastern portion of the block and into the city. This pathway has undoubtedly existed as long as the canal, since it is necessary to have access to the canal for operating sluices, opening and closing feeder canals, and for routine maintenance. Several sites are located near the canal, including VMS-79, a columned structure (figure 4.7) that was only partially finished. This building appears to have been planned as a temple or shrine. It is interesting that the carving of columns for the structure took place on the construction site itself, rather than at a workshop or spatially specialized location (cf. Muller 1984).

Specific reference to the canal road is made in the *Pampamahatmya* (Krishna Das and Dallapiccola, personal communication 1992), a sixteenth and seventeenth century religious text. In this text, a *Saivite* temple known as the Nageswara temple (VMS-80) for the hundreds of *naga* stones (cobra images) it contains, is noted to occur along this road. The Nageswara temple itself is associated with a short road segment (VMS-81; figure 4.8). This road has been heavily disturbed by modern quarrying, but if it had continued at its present orientation, it would have intersected the entrance to VMS-80 on the northwest. VMS-181 runs over a section of relatively flat sheetrock. The roadway here is worn smooth. Where the sheetrock ends on the northwest, a cobbled ramp has been constructed to meet the slope of the rock. Unfortunately, both ends of the road have been destroyed by recent quarrying.

A path or roadway may also have run through a small valley in the northeast corner of Block O. This route would have linked VMS-106 (either a road wall or an erosion control wall), VMS-105 (a step well), and VMS-104 (a shrine).

All of the roads in Block O discussed thus far run approximately east-west, paralleling the general orientation of the Hampi-Daroji Hills. North-south movement through the block would have been, and still is, difficult, as one must cross over successive outcropping ridges of the grey granitic hills. There is evidence of a path over one of these ridges, in the southwest corner of the block (Sinopoli 1991b). This road would have connected the densely settled southwest portion of Block O with the valley to the south in Block T. The road runs over a high outcrop on which a temple (VMS-42) and a temple tank (VMS-43) are placed. Traffic was channeled

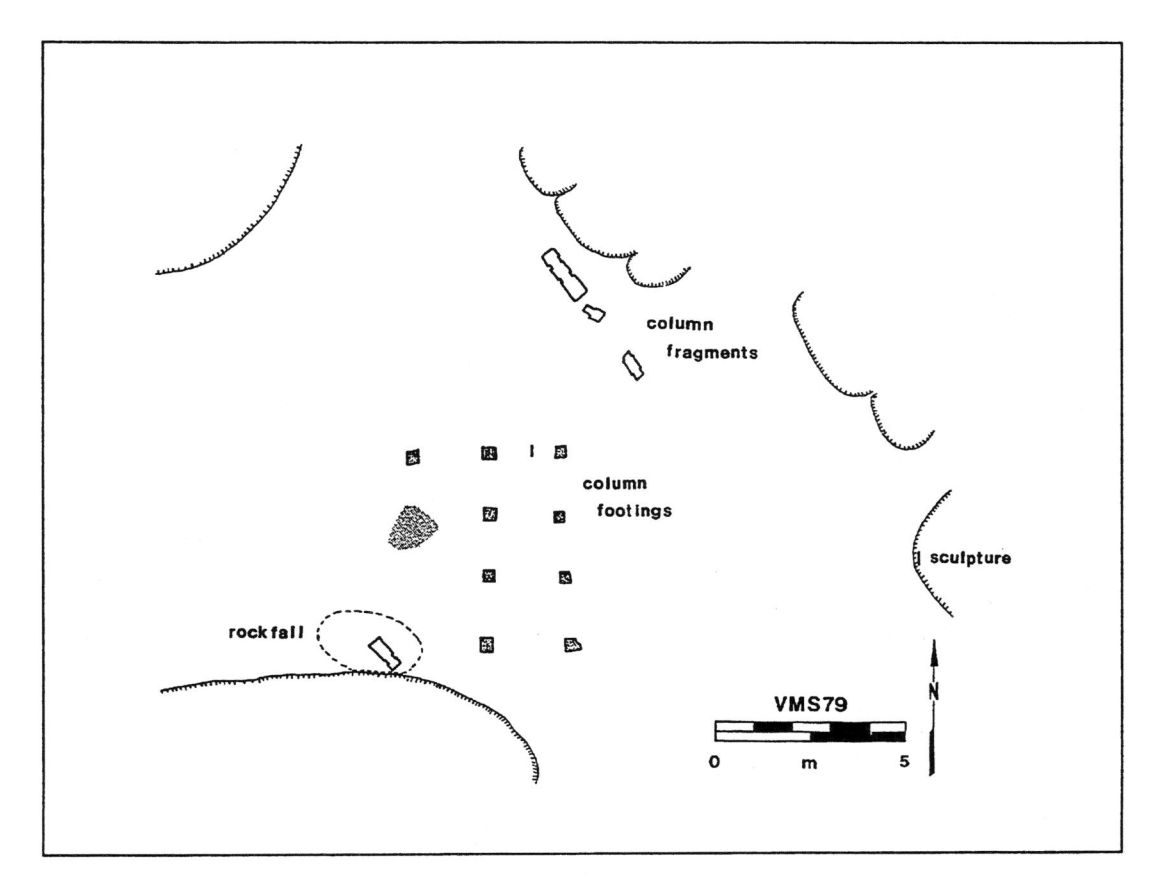

FIGURE 4.7   Columned structure under construction located along canal roadway (VMS-256)

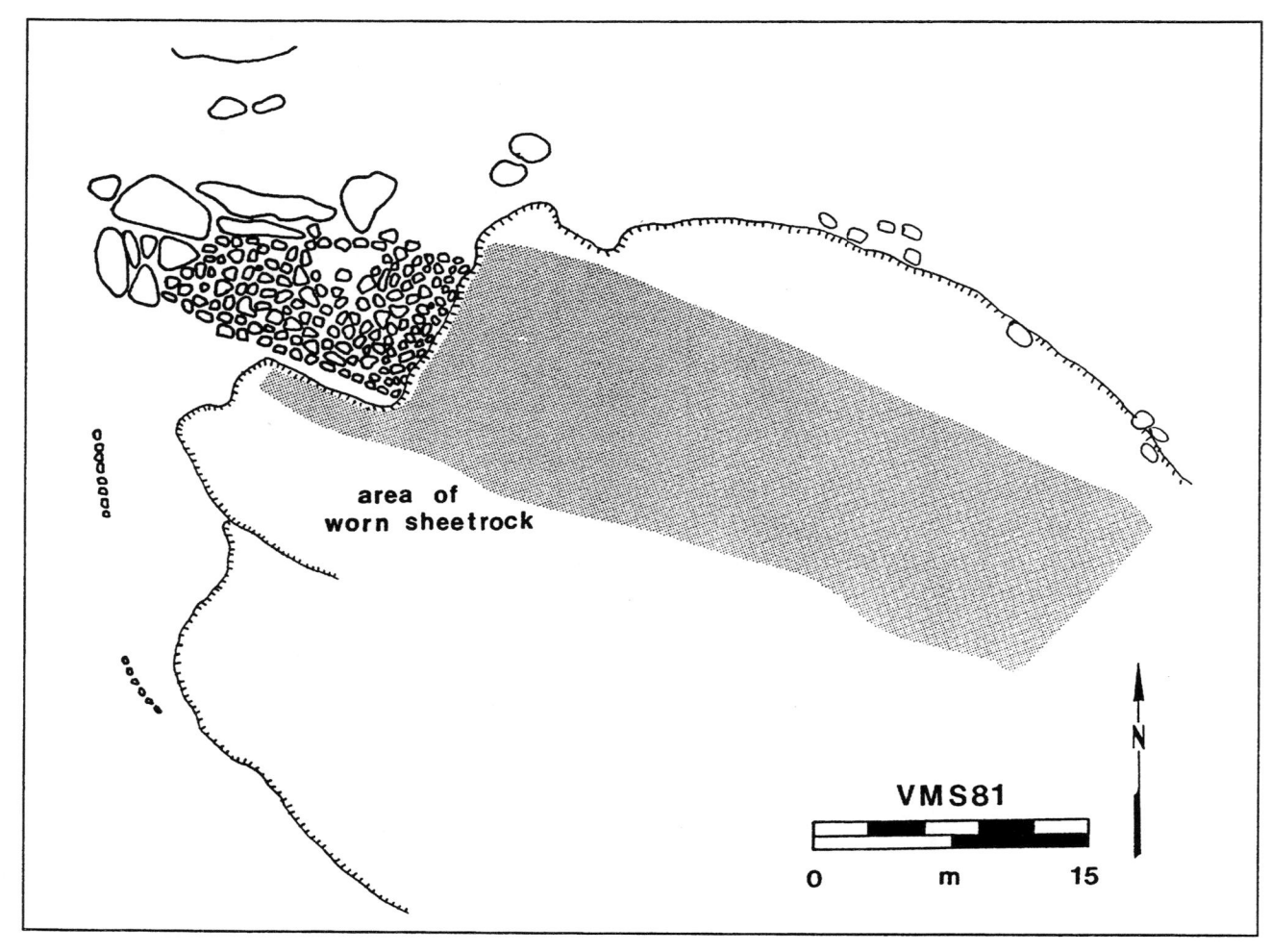

FIGURE 4.8 Road segment leading to Nageshwara temple, VMS-82 (VMS-81), Block O

along a specific and clearly defined route delineated by steps (VMS-44, VMS-46, VMS-47, VMS-50) and walls (VMS-42, VMS-45, VMS-47). A 184-meter-long wall runs along the top of the ridge. This wall is 2.4 meters wide and consists of two faces of boulders and shaped blocks separated by an earthen core. The road evidently passed through a gap in the center of this wall. The formal layout of this route and the heavily built wall at the top of the ridge suggest that this route was well controlled (Sinopoli 1991b).

The outcrop containing the temple complex VMS-83 also has several formal pathways. One of these is described as part of VMS-83 and provides access to the temple from the north via defined pathways. The other, VMS-87, consists of a paved pathway, a carved step, and a terraced walkway leading up the outcrop from the southeast.

Block S

Twelve roadways or road segments were identified in Block S, and several others can be traced using the alignment of structures such as wells, temples, and shrines. Some of these roads differ from those in Block O in that they have a "local" character. That is, they are internal routes within the city walls, or run for only short distances. In contrast, the major roadway identified in Block O connected Vijayanagara with the nearby town of Kampli, 25 kilometers away. As noted, a second long roadway is inferred to have traversed Block O, along the raised north bank of the Turtha Canal. Several of the road segments identified in Block S are described below.

VMS-137 is a raised causeway with masonry sides between 8 and 16 meters apart. It extends for more than 450 meters. Where the road runs over sheetrock, fragments of cobble paving are preserved. A small walled reservoir, VMS-136, is built into the edge of this road (see figure 4.20). VMS-137 winds its way northward from the southeastern corner of Block S. The northern end of the road is cut by a modern canal; it may have been connected to either VMS-214 or VMS-160 on the north. A parallel road segment, VMS-152, runs approximately 700 meters east of VMS-137. This road is not constructed, as is VMS-137, but consists of a long path 10 to 15 meters wide cleared through the surrounding scatter of small granite boulders. Rubble walls have been constructed along the sides of the roadway where gaps in the natural boulder scatter occur.

The east-central portion of Block S is dominated by three large reservoirs (VMS-190, 165, and 132), all of which capture seasonal runoff from the higher ground to the south. The locations of these reservoirs constrained the movement of traffic in this area, at least during the rainy season. North-south passage would have to have been between the beds of the reservoirs, and east-west passage across the raised earthen embankments. Unfortunately, it is not yet possible to precisely date all the reservoirs and all the road segments, so a possible temporal gap between their periods of operation must be considered.

VMS-160, a north-south road segment, is located between reservoirs VMS-132 and VMS-165. This roadway is similar in layout to the formal bazaar streets found within the city. It is defined by two long platforms on either side of an approximately 30-meter-wide road surface. The platforms are constructed of masonry, with earth and rubble fill, and contain visible internal features including stone rings and a shrine with a sculpted female figure. In addition to Vijayanagara earthenware, the ceramic inventory from VMS-160 included a piece of blue-and-white Chinese porcelain.

Another north-south road segment, VMS-214, runs approximately parallel and about 500 meters to the west of VMS-160. This road also passes between two reservoirs (VMS-190 and VMS-165), running north-northwest. This nine-meter-wide road, defined by walls of up to five courses of black gabbro boulders, leads directly to the east gateway of the temple complex VMS-164. South of the temple, the road incorporates a large step well. Although modern cultivation makes it difficult to trace VMS-214 to the south, it may have joined the roadway VMS-152. To the north, the course of VMS-214 can be extended for a short distance to the mandapa VMS-215, and possibly as far as VMS-163, a carved panel and rockshelter. While it is not possible to trace the road past this point, the road segment VMS-183 that passes through the city walls lies only a short distance to the north.

VMS-183 (figure 4.9) is a well-constructed roadway leading into a small passage through the city wall. Associated with it are a step well (VMS-187), small temple, platform (VMS-186; figure 4.10), isolated room (VMS-185), and a cluster of shrines and sculptures (VMS-182; figure 4.11). The structure of this road is complex, and it may have diverged into two or three separate segments as it approached the city wall. The southern portion is defined by raised platforms on either side of the road surface. The road surface, which ranges from 12.5 to 27 meters wide, still contains a few worn cobbles. Further north, the road appears to narrow, though modern fields have encroached on the site and one side of the roadway has apparently been dismantled. The city wall runs along the top of a high outcropping ridge, and two large square bastions loom over the narrow passage of VMS-183 through the wall. There is no evidence of a gateway, but the opening was built into the city wall and not cut through it. The passage constricts to 2.5 meters wide, certainly too narrow for most wheeled traffic. As one emerges into the fortified area on the north, the path narrows further to an approximately one-meter-wide sloping cobbled path lined with small boulders (VMS-182).

VMS-209 is another pedestrian passage into the walled city, but this site is considerably less elaborate and appears to have provided a route over the city wall from a densely settled area to two large step wells (VMS-290/1, VMS-210) just outside the wall. The city wall is constructed atop a high, east-west granitic ridge. The path of VMS-209 is well marked by a paved surface of flat, rounded gabbro boulders. The path ranges from 1 to 2 meters wide, and is about 75 meters long. It incorporates several staircases on its steeper northern end inside the wall. Similar paved walkways run along the top of the granitic ridge just inside the fortification wall.

One roadway that may represent a more regional transport route is the Penukonda Road, so named because it passes through the monumental Penukonda gate complex (VMS-217). Penukonda was a Vijayanagara-period settlement and fortification, located 192 kilometers southeast of the city (an eight-day journey according to Stein 1990:19).

76   *Fields of Victory*

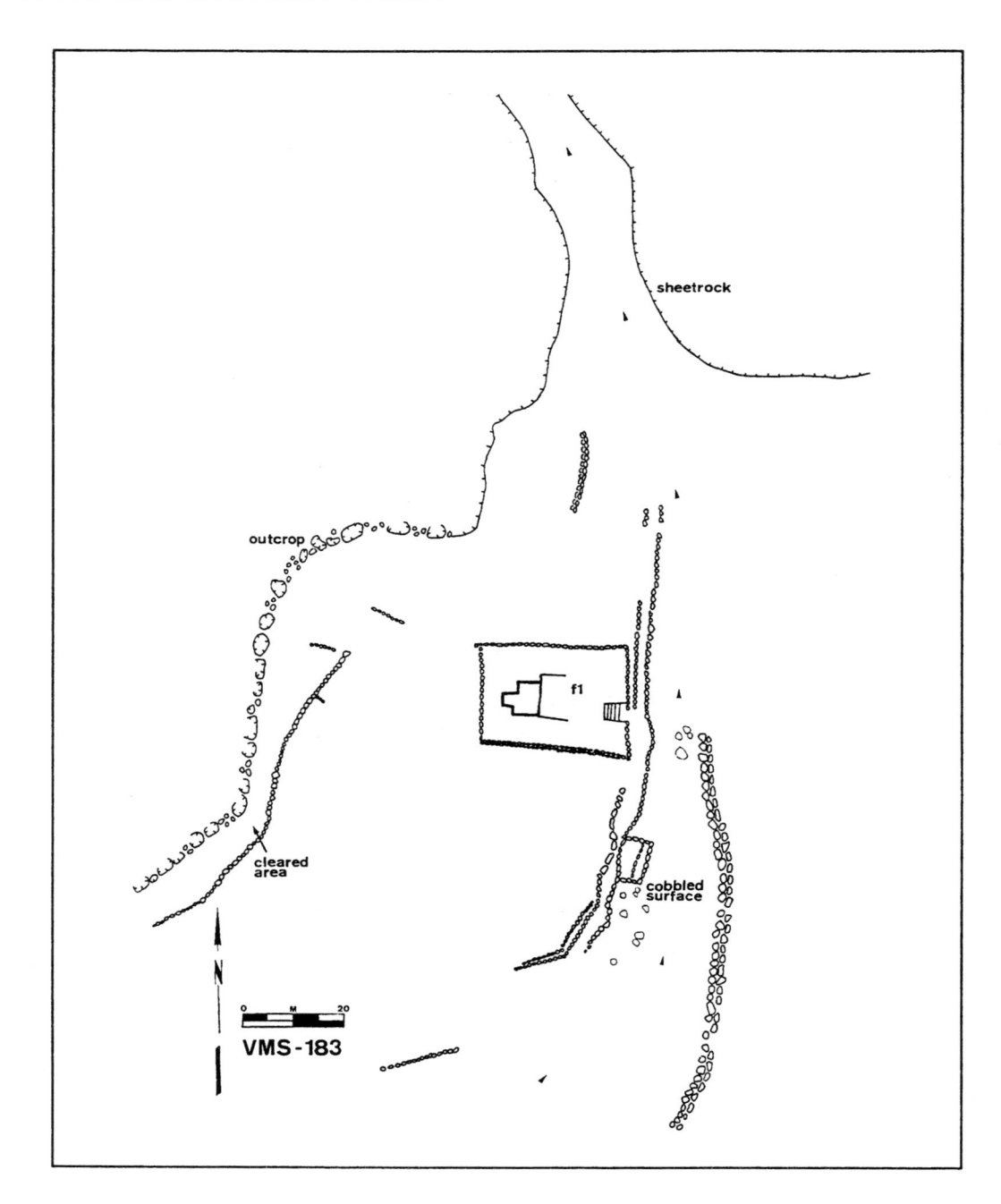

FIGURE 4.9   Roadway complex with cobbled surface flanked by walls and platforms and a small temple (VMS-183), Block S

Following the sack of the city in A.D. 1565, the Vijayanagara court fled to Penukonda. Inscriptions on temples in the gateway complex date it to the late Vijayanagara period, roughly contemporaneous with the naming of Varadadevi-Ammana-Pattana. The Penukonda Road can be traced both inside and outside the city wall. Outside the wall, several temples (VMS-129, VMS-173 [fig. 4.15], VMS-128), a cluster of small platforms (VMS-172), and a step well (VMS-189) define the route of this road.

Further east, a constructed road segment is visible. This short segment, approximately 30 meters wide, is bounded by masonry walls on the north (VMS-130) and south (VMS-158).

Inside the city wall, the Penukonda Road becomes a bazaar street, defined by elevated platforms on both sides (VMS-201). A small *Vaisnavite* temple was built into the platform on the north side of the street. At the present western end of the north platform is a larger temple of the

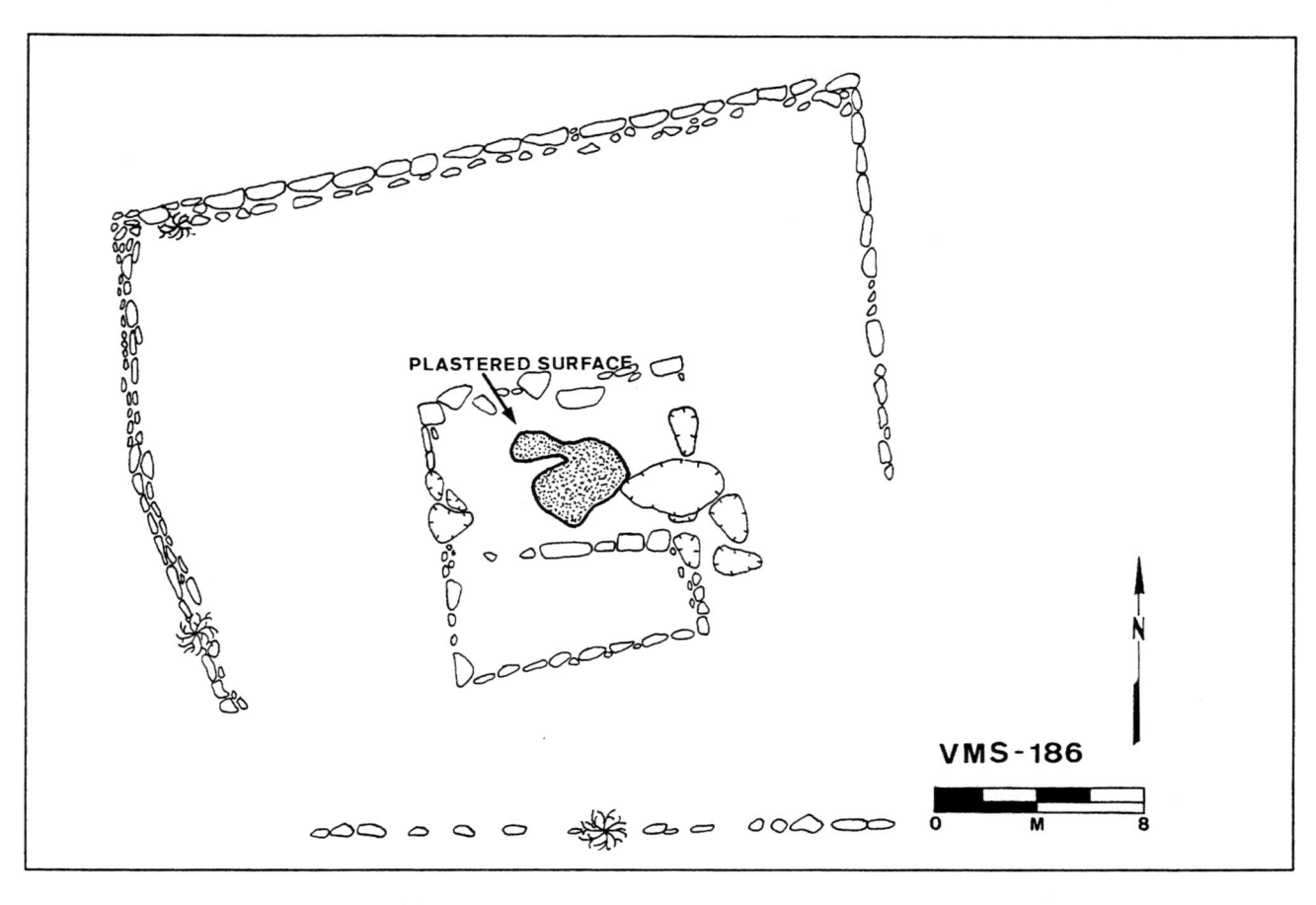

FIGURE 4.10 Two-level platform associated with roadway VMS-183 (VMS-186), Block S

Vijayanagara period. Not far north of this temple the Penukonda Road would have intersected with the road leading from the monumental gateway (VMS-123/1) in the city wall to the north of the Penukonda gateway. Two small *mandapas* (VMS-184) line the roadway between VMS-201 and the Penukonda gate. A shrine (VMS-177) to the god Hanuman, commonly associated with gateways, is situated in the road just inside the gate.

Other road segments from Block S serve to further inform on the circumscription of space within the area of dense settlement inside the city wall. One of these, VMS-224, runs approximately east-west along the base of the high ridge that carries the city wall. VMS-224 is defined by walls on both sides and incorporates a deep rock-cut well. Both the east and west ends of the road are closed off by cross walls; the west end stops just short of the long north-south boundary or fortification wall (VMS-223), which bisects this zone of habitation. The east end of the road does not extend as far as Kamalapuram fort (VMS-257 to 259). Thus, VMS-224 appears to have served a very limited purpose, in an area set apart from surrounding areas.

VMS-225 is a very short, walled road segment with traces of cobbled paving. Had this road continued at its present orientation, it would have led directly to the south door of the Pattabhirama temple.

Another roadway within the city wall can be traced by an east-west alignment of temples (VMS-239, 260, 262, 265-270, 272). This road runs north of the Kamalapuram fort (VMS-257 to 259) and appears to have had a long use-history, as it is edged by both early and late temples. The embankment of the Kamalapuram reservoir (VMS-231) carried a roadway during the Vijayanagara period, as it does now. This is evident from the remains of a gateway at the western end of the embankment. As noted above, the Kamalapuram embankment also doubled as a segment of the outer fortification wall in this area. The road segment along the Kamalapuram embankment is part of the Hospet-Vijayanagara Road (see below).

A north-south road branches off from the Kamalapuram embankment road, heading toward a

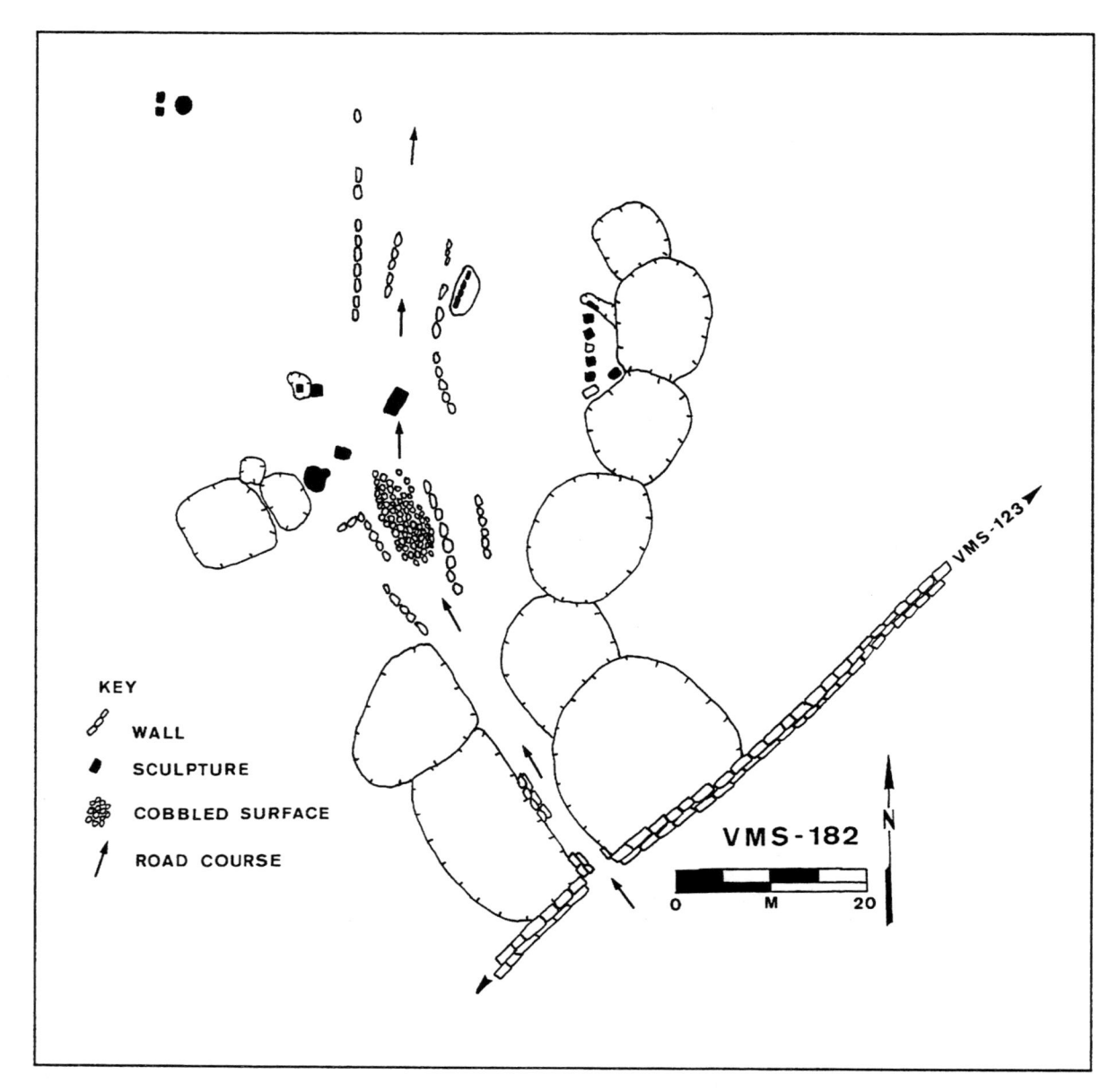

FIGURE 4.11   Opening in the city wall north of VMS-183. The cobbled pathway is lined with boulders, walls, and sculptures (VMS-182), Block S

gate in the Urban Core wall. The route of this road is indicated by a platform (VMS-255), several temples (VMS-238, VMS-239), and a well (VMS-240).

Block T

Block T contains several well-defined routes of movement, not including interior pathways in the settlements VMS-361 and VMS-365. The first of these is a long roadway running approximately east-west through the valley that covers the northern part of the block. This broad valley is partly bounded by high rocky outcrops, but large reservoirs also served to restrict movement. On the east, VMS-360 is a road segment defined by two parallel courses of walls about 20 m apart. The road walls on each side consist of rubble-constructed, double-faced walls. At the eastern end of this 800-meter-long road segment is a masonry-lined spring. The Nallapuram Road continues to the west through the settlement VMS-361 and past the bastion VMS-327. A long section of the road west of the settlement is well preserved. This section, VMS-326, is approximately 1200 meters long and is defined by parallel courses of double-faced rubble walls. The space between the walls is packed with earth and stone. Although the roadway has been disturbed by modern activities, the course is quite clear. Incorporated into the north road wall is VMS-326/F1, a boulder containing several inscribed games and shallow depressions. The northern end of the road has been disturbed, but the structure (bastion?) VMS-321 was almost certainly located right on the roadway, as was the temple complex, VMS-317. Further west, the location of several reservoirs (VMS-319 and VMS-125) served to define movement; the road may have been carried on the embankment of VMS-319 and certainly was carried on the 728-meter-long embankment of VMS-125. If so, this road would have joined to the road in Block S leading from the Penukonda gate. It is also likely that this road split somewhere in the northwestern corner of Block T, with one branch headed to the northwest and into the gateway in the outer city wall, VMS-17.

The second route of movement may be defined by a barrier, the long fortification wall, VMS-339 (and associated walls VMS-306 and VMS-325). Because traffic could not have moved east-west across the broad level fields in this area, it may have been funneled north-northwest by the course of the wall. In any event, people and carts probably moved between the settlement VMS-365 and the city. Thus, there was almost certainly some sort of road or path running north-northwest through the block. This supposition is supported by the evidence of VMS-354 and VMS-356. These are both short fragments of well-built walls incorporating low platforms. If these were indeed parts of a now-destroyed road wall parallel to VMS-339, as their location suggests, then these parallel walls may have defined movement in a northwest-southeast direction across the block.

Finally, several wall segments (VMS-345, VMS-348, and VMS-353) in the southern part of the block define a roadway that runs along the base of a rock outcrop toward the settlement VMS-365. The longest of these, VMS-345, is 750 m long and appears to be an embankment wall that carried an elevated roadway along the edge of the outcrop and above the low-lying fields to the north. The alignment of this substantial wall (up to five courses of boulders and cobbles) is continued on the east by VMS-348 and VMS-353. As noted, the southern end of VMS-339 cuts right through this alignment, and no gateways or openings are apparent. Thus, VMS-339 may postdate this roadway.

Other Areas

Several other major roadways can be identified in the study area. The largest of these is the road leading from Hospet (Tirumaladeviyara-Pattana) to the city of Vijayanagara, via Kamalapuram. This road runs through the villages of Anantasayanagudi and Malapannagudi and is closely paralleled by the modern road. Another modern road branches off from the Hospet-Vijayanagara Road, going through Kadirampuram toward Hampi. The routes of Vijayanagara roads in this area have not yet been investigated.

RELIGIOUS ARCHITECTURE

Block O

Block O contains sixteen temples and shrines of the Vijayanagara period. Two of these (VMS-2/2 and VMS-2/3) are located in the settlement VMS-2, one is found in the small settlement VMS-35, and four (VMS-83, VMS-116, VMS-118, and VMS-119) in or near the settlement VMS-101. In all, seven of the sixteen are associated with settlements, and eight of the sixteen outside of settlements are on identifiable roads.

Both temples in VMS-2 are small structures. Feature 2 is a south-facing *Vaisnava* temple, simply constructed of the type of stone column apparently produced in great quantity (and of low quality) in or near the city. These columns are found by the hundreds—perhaps thousands—in the city. Feature 3 appears to have been a *Saivite* temple. This single chambered shrine now houses an image of Hanuman, but a *nandi* (bull) and an image base with *lingam* (phallus) lie nearby; both of these are *Saivite* symbols.

VMS-42 is a walled temple compound with several associated structures, located on a granitic outcrop in the southwestern portion of the block (Sinopoli 1991b). A pathway leads over this outcrop (see above), connecting the valley of Block O with that of Block T. This two-chambered *Vaisnavite* temple abuts an outcropping boulder and is actually built into the rocky hillside.

VMS-80 is known locally as the Nageswara temple, no doubt because of the hundreds of *naga* stones (cobra images) that lie stacked against the walls of the temple. VMS-80 is one of the larger temples in Block O but is still much smaller than many located in Block S. This east-facing temple is 20 by 8 meters and consists of a covered columned porch, an inner courtyard, and a three by two columned sanctuary.

Another temple located atop a granitic outcrop is VMS-83 (figure 4.12). Like VMS-42, it is built into the rocks of the outcrop. It lies just east of VMS-101 and immediately above VMS-84, a masonry-lined spring. Access to this temple was fairly well controlled (see above) by pathways, steps, and a gateway. Like other temples in Block O, it is difficult to date VMS-83 more precisely than the Vijayanagara period. Defining architectural characteristics include columns, mouldings, brackets, and other elements found only on fairly ornate and elaborate structures. The simple temples of this block contain neither inscriptions nor clear architectural indications of sub-period.

Several other religious/ritual sites are found in Block O. These include VMS-18, a small rockshelter containing religious carvings, and VMS-94, an image of the god Ganesh carved on a boulder. VMS-111 is a small hilltop temple located near the major roadway. The simple shrine is surrounded by rubble-walled rooms, and contains an undated inscription (Morrison and Sinopoli 1992).

Block S

Block S contains a wide range of sculptures, shrines, temples, and temple complexes. Of the twenty-nine temples and shrines in the block, more than half are enclosed within *prakara* walls. In general, temples in Block S are larger and more complex than those located in Blocks O and T. The largest temple complex in the block is the Pattabhirama temple, VMS-237, constructed in the sixteenth century, during the Tuluva dynasty. Two inscriptions from this temple date to the reign of Achyuta Raya (Filliozat and Filliozat 1988:13). Associated with the Pattabhirama temple is an elaborate temple tank, VMS-236. This very large and ornate temple has received proportionately less attention than others in the Vijayanagara region, and is unique in its location. All of the other major temple complexes of the Vijayanagara period are located either in the city or to the north of the city, near the Tungabhadra River. Only the Pattabhirama temple is located south of the city. The architecture and iconography of this temple have been described by Pascher (1987).

Among the very large temples in the block, the VMS-142 complex (figure 4.13) occurs within the city walls, along a roadway leading to the monumental gateway VMS-123/1. This walled *Vaisnavite* complex contains a central and a subsidiary shrine, as well as several smaller structures and numerous rubble-walled rooms. Various grinding implements probably derive from the temple kitchens. West of VMS-142 lies a small *mandapa*; it may be possible to trace a roadway in this area leading to the eastern gateway of the Pattabhirama temple. An inscription on the north gateway of VMS-142 refers to a donation of the emperor Achyuta Raya (Archaeological Survey of India 1904:17), which accords well with the Late Vijayanagara architectural style of the temple, placing it chronologically in the period of the Penukonda gate and the settlement Varadadevi-Ammana-Pattana. The east gate of the complex is aligned exactly with the monumental gateway, VMS-123/1, suggesting that it, too, belongs to the late Vijayanagara period. Thus, almost all of the large-scale construction in this portion of the study area appears to be contemporaneous.

VMS-144 is a smaller *Vaisnavite* temple complex located immediately west and north of VMS-142. This site contains a three-chambered, south-facing shrine and several associated structures, but no enclosing wall. All of the ornate elements appear on the south facade; this side may have faced a roadway. Architecturally, VMS-144 belongs to the Late Vijayanagara period and is similar to (although it is smaller and simpler) VMS-142. However, despite their proximity, the two sites are not in alignment.

VMS-164 (figure 4.14) is a temple complex located along the road segment VMS-214 discussed above. This temple occurs over 750 meters from the walled city. Though much less formally constructed than the VMS-142 complex, VMS-164 is also contained within enclosure walls. The complex has a central *Vaisnavite* shrine, a small *mandapa*, and numerous rubble-walled rooms. Incorporated into the enclosure wall is a simple gate consisting of two platforms on the north, and a more elaborate columned and roofed gateway on the east. Architectural indications suggest that this temple was constructed early in the Vijayanagara period, and the superpositioning of the rubble-walled rooms indicates that they postdate the period of initial construction and use of the temple.

In all, twenty-nine temples and shrines were

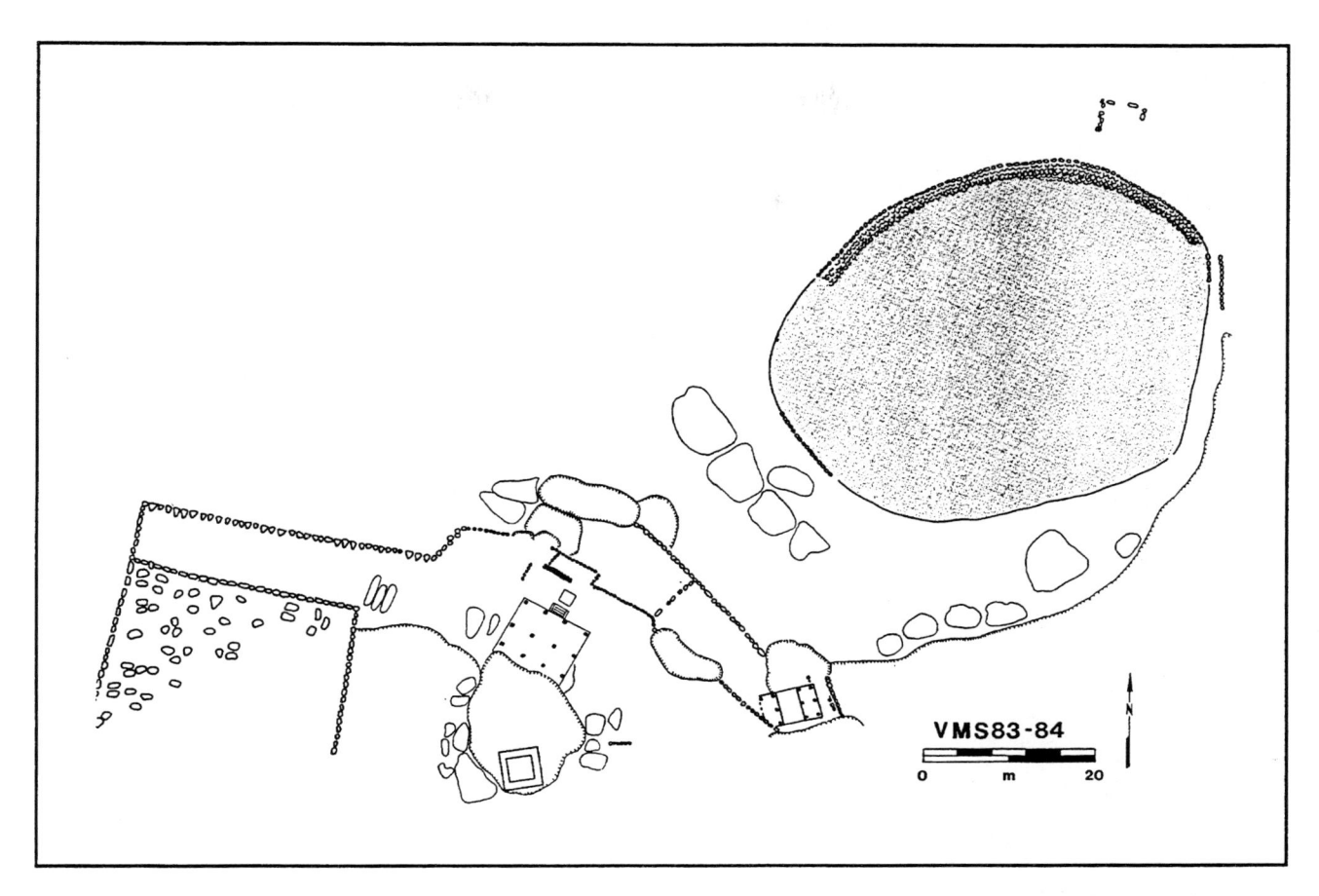

FIGURE 4.12 Hill complex containing terraces, temple, and gateway (VMS-83) above large walled spring (VMS-84), Block O

recorded in Block S, many more than can be described here. Most of these are not large, formal structures. In addition to structures inferred to have a religious function, hundreds of isolated sculptures were located and recorded. The portability of these sculptures, however, makes any attempt to analyze their provenience problematic. Many of the religious structures in the block were located along roads, and the majority were found inside the city wall.

Block T

Block T contains thirteen temples and shrines and an Islamic tomb (VMS-297). As in other parts of the survey area, these features range from small carvings to large complexes. VMS-317 is a temple complex located along the Nallapuram Road. It is centered around an early Vijayanagara *Saivite* temple and contains five associated mandapas (these may have been constructed later). Other associated features include a well and furnace (possibly for iron working). VMS-304 is also a *Saivite* shrine and is perched high atop a rock outcrop in the northern part of the block overlooking the Nallapuram Road. Another elevated shrine, VMS-338, is still in worship but does contain fragmentary images that appear to date to the Vijayanagara period. VMS-293 is a small temple that appears to be an early Vijayanagara *Saivite* shrine. In front of (north) this simple structure is a carved stone basin on a low platform. On the basin is a scene containing *nandi*, *lingam*, and devotees. A lamp column is found further north. Other religious features are smaller, consisting of isolated images or small shrines. With the exceptions of VMS-338, located on a high outcrop, and VMS-316, associated with a reservoir (VMS-315), all of the religious architecture outside of settlements is associated either with the Nallapuram Road or with protected areas contained within (west of) the long wall VMS-339.

VMS-297 (figure 4.16) is a domed Islamic-

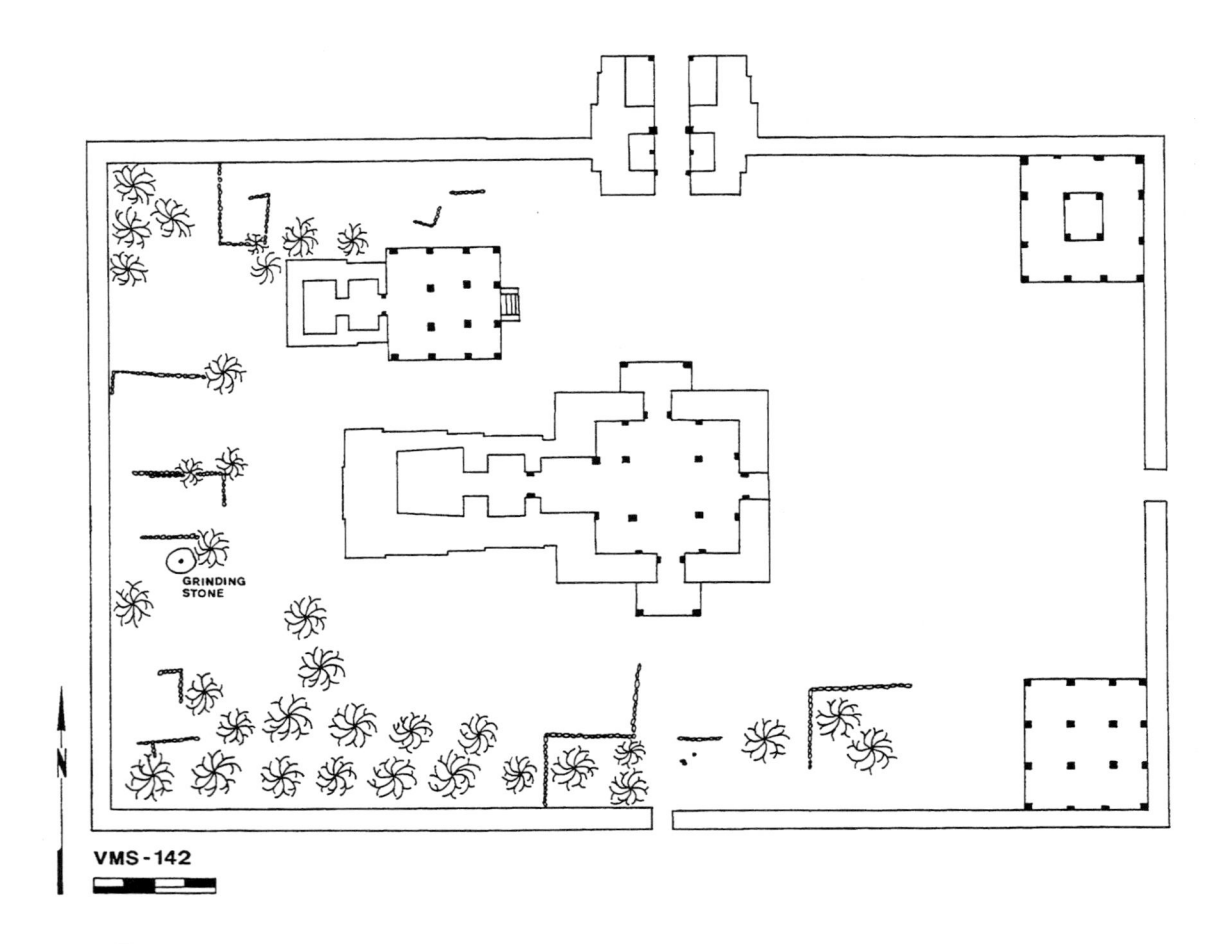

FIGURE 4.13   Late Vijayanagara *Vaisnavite* temple complex (VMS-142), Block S

style tomb located near the edge of the reservoir VMS-319. A pile of rubble is all that is left of what may be a second tomb. No other tombs are located in the immediate area although there are several concentrations of Islamic-style architecture in the Northeast Valley of the Urban Core (Fritz, Michell, and Nagaraja Rao 1985; Michell 1985a, 1990; Sinopoli 1986) and in the village of Kadirampuram (Michell 1985a) to the west of the city.

Other Areas

Hundreds, and perhaps thousands, of temples and shrines are scattered throughout the study area. Virtually every city, town, and village contains at least one temple. Major temple complexes found in and around the city of Vijayanagara include the Ramachandra temple, the Krishna temple, the Virupaksha temple, the Tiruvengalanatha temple, the Vithala temple, and the Pattabhirama temple. These and many others are described in various publications including: Dallapiccola (1985);

Dallapiccola et al. (1992); Devaraj and Patil, eds. (1991a, 1991b); Filliozat and Filliozat (1988); Fritz, Michell, and Nagaraja Rao (1985); Michell (1990); Nagaraja Rao, ed. (1983, 1985); Pascher (1987); and Purandare (1986).

WELLS AND CISTERNS

Water storage was of great importance in the Vijayanagara region. Because the distribution of rainfall is highly seasonal, and overall precipitation is low, about 51 centimeters annually (Singh et al. 1971, and see chapter 2), there exists a limited supply of water, which decreases throughout the winter and spring. Water storage technology was diverse, including such facilities as wells and step wells, cisterns, and reservoirs. Stored water was important for domestic consumption, watering livestock, and for agriculture.

Wells tap the water table, while cisterns merely collect and store water. A wide variety of forms and degrees of elaboration of wells and

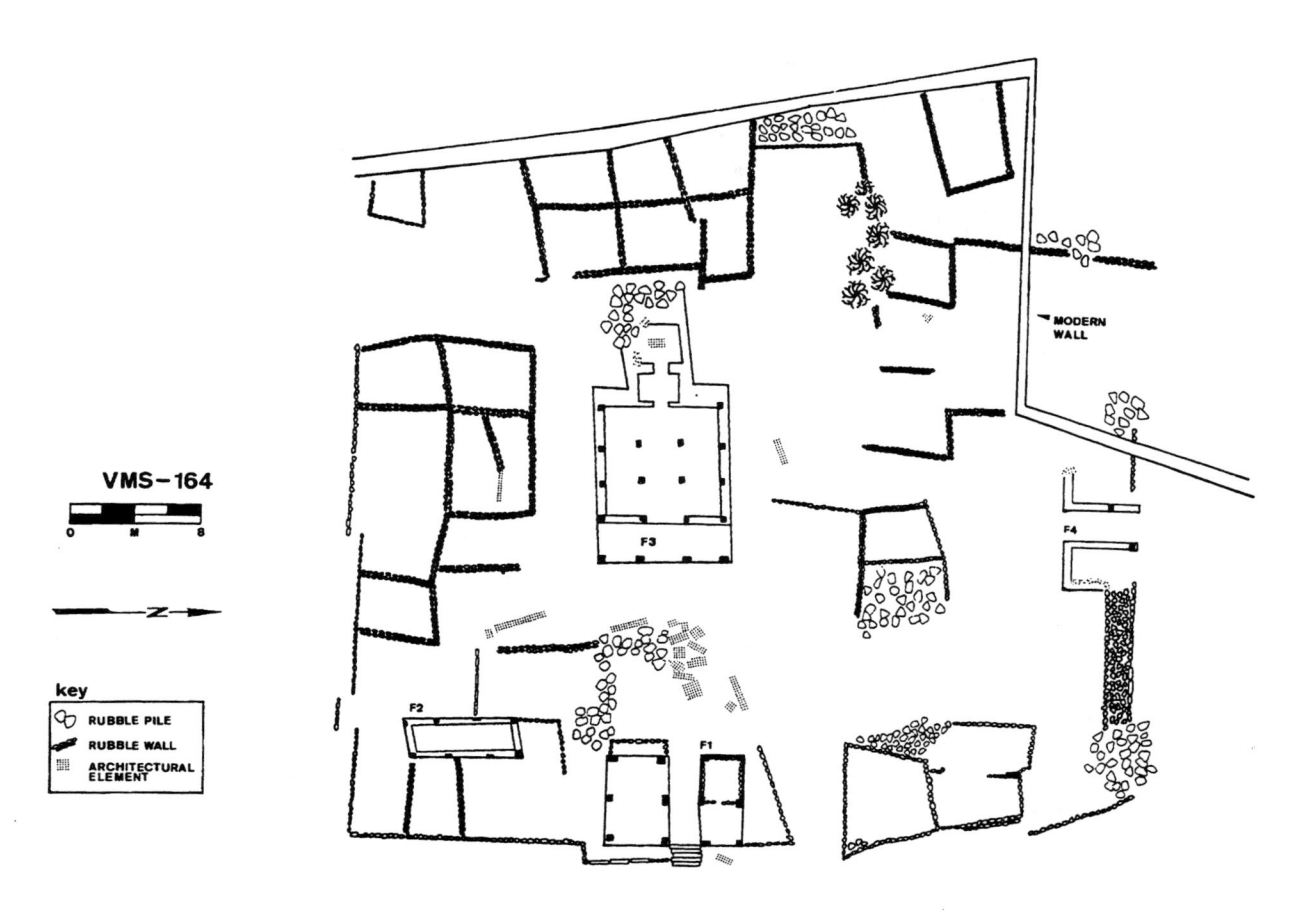

FIGURE 4.14   Temple complex with formal shrine, gate platforms, and *mandapa* surrounded by informal structures (VMS-164), Block S

cisterns are present in the region in and around the city. Wells and cisterns tend to occur in consistently patterned situations. These situations include roadsides, areas near temples, residential and commercial areas, and locations immediately below reservoirs. These are by no means mutually exclusive categories, and many wells served multiple purposes.

Block O

Block O contains ten wells, cisterns, and masonry-lined springs. Five of the ten water storage features are located in areas of settlement, six along roads, and two appear to have been primarily agricultural.

VMS-40 is a large Islamic-style spring and well (and see chapter 2). A spring-fed pool of water is contained within a stone enclosure. Channels lead off to the east directly from the pool. On the west is a large and ornate tower which rises 13 meters above the level of the water. Atop the tower is a platform. Water was raised from the pool by bullocks, who backed up an earthen ramp abutting the tower on the east, and then walked back down the ramp to pull water up out of the pool. The tower, fitted with a superstructure containing pointed arches, contained an elaborate system of pipes and channels for the distribution of water. A chute on the platform funneled water into ceramic pipes, which led down the sides of the platform and into the fields below. In this way, both the fields to the east of the well, which lay at a lower level, and fields to the west of the well, which were higher, could be watered. VMS-40 lies approximately 600 meters from the outer city wall (VMS-10), in an area of dry farming.

Other water storage features in Block O include simple masonry-lined wells and rock-cut storage cisterns, but also elaborate step wells such as VMS-112 (figure 4.17). This well, located along the Kampli Road, included an ornate gateway with two carved *nandis* perched on top.

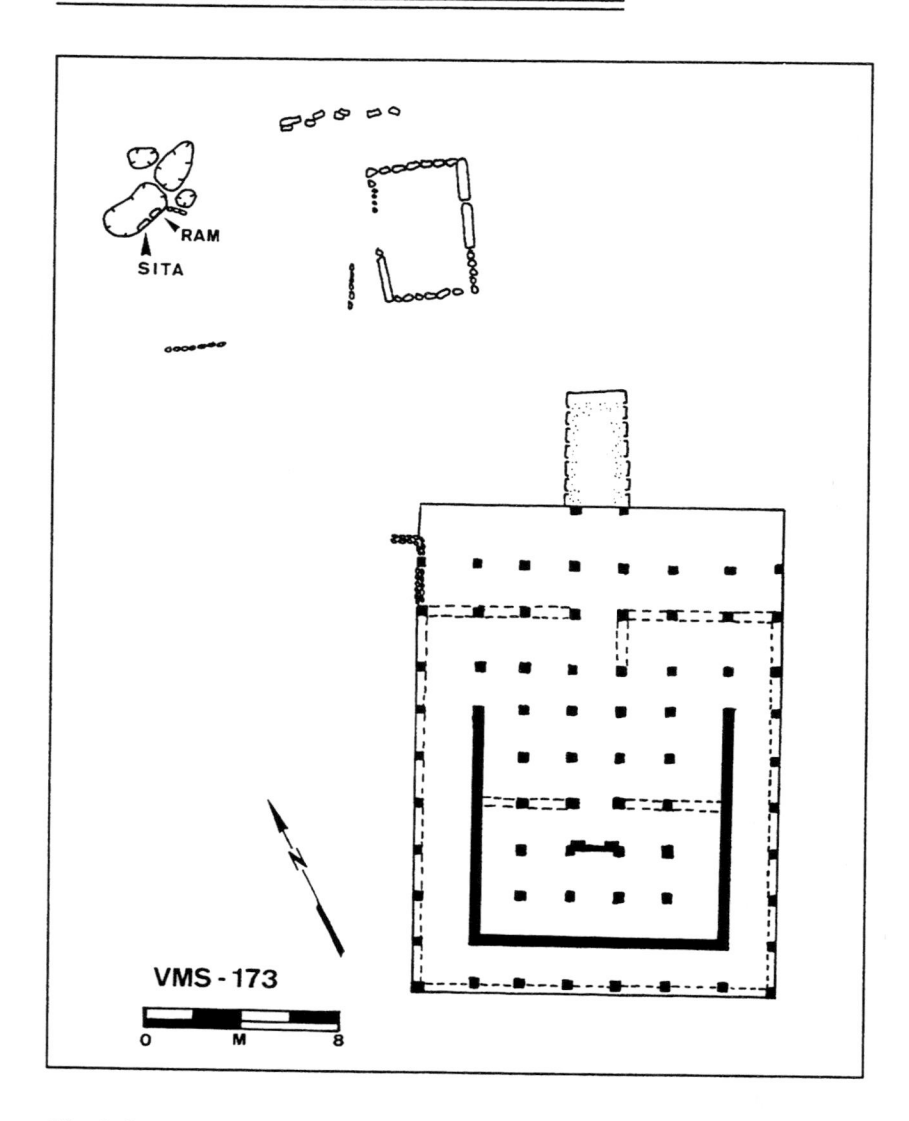

FIGURE 4.15
Temple located along roadway. The location of two rock-cut sculptures is indicated (VMS-173), Block S.

Block S

Of the 26 wells and cisterns recorded in Block S, 10 lie inside the city wall and 16 outside. Considering that a single well may be situated near several different features, 12 of the 23 are located along roads, 8 near temples, 10 in habitation areas, and 2 below reservoirs. This latter figure is very low compared to the number of irrigation-related wells to the east and south of the city in the Daroji Valley. Block S wells and cisterns exhibit a variety of forms, including fairly simple lined wells such as VMS-175 (figure 4.18), more elaborate stepwells such as VMS-210 (figure 4.19), and large walled enclosures such as VMS-136 (figure 4.20).

Block T

Both temple complexes and settlements in Block T were associated with wells. Apart from these, there are four step wells in the block. Of these, three are located on or near the Nallapuram road. VMS-360 is also associated with a masonry-lined spring. One well, VMS-328, lies adjacent to the settlement VMS-361 but was given its own site designation. VMS-294 and VMS-298 are found in the northwest corner of the block. VMS-298 lies right on the postulated course of the Nallapuram road, while VMS-294 is several hundred meters north of the road near the temple VMS-293. The road may have split in this area, with a branch leading up to the gateway VMS-17. VMS-312 is a small keyhole-shaped step well located in the middle of a dry farmed area shielded by the wall VMS-339. This well may have been used for watering livestock and for agriculture as there is no evidence of nearby settlement.

Other Areas

Numerous wells and cisterns are scattered throughout the study area (see, for example Michell

1990). In general, wells and cisterns are found in settlements and along roadways. Wells are also commonly associated with reservoirs, as discussed in chapter 2, and nearly all of the reservoirs in the Daroji Valley are associated with wells. Even when the reservoir does not hold water, the local effect of a raised water table caused by the reservoir ensures that water will be available in the well. Many of the Daroji wells still contain water even though the associated reservoir has been breached and is no longer working. In recent years, wells have become a major form of primary irrigation in the region, thanks to the introduction of electric pumps (cf. Mencher 1978).

NON-AGRICULTURAL PRODUCTION

Block O

Sites related to non-agricultural production in Block O include VMS-1 and VMS-54, which are associated with lime processing. VMS-1 (Morrison 1991a) contains two large mounds of calcium carbonate (*kankar*), which was burned to produce lime. Lime was used in mortar, plaster, iron production, and for many other purposes. Limestone deposits do not occur within the study area. Two circular, clay-lined stone features appear to have been kilns in which the calcium carbonate was fired. The morphology of these features is similar to that of modern lime kilns, which are common throughout the area. These are simple conical structures of brick or stone, open on top, with dual air vents near the ground. The kilns and one of the mounds of *kankar* are set on a platform of rough quartz-pebble concrete, similar to that used in structures throughout the city. VMS-54 is an 8.5 meter diameter pit with calcium carbonate accretions that may have been used for soaking lime. This pit is not located near any known lime kilns, lying 275 meters east of an agricultural embankment, VMS-21. As noted, contemporary lime processing of *kankar* is carried out throughout the study area, and calcium carbonate nodules are widespread in study area soils. Thus, it is difficult to date the lime processing sites with any degree of certainty, particularly VMS-54, which contains no structural remains.

The settlement VMS-35 has evidence of stone working, possibly for peg production, as does VMS-2 (see above). The coarse-grained gabbro of the study area occurs as surface veins in the granitic outcrops, and it does not fracture conchoidally, making it difficult to work out production sequences for pegs and other gabbro objects.

VMS-92 is a rather enigmatic feature. It consists of two large boulders containing hundreds of round shallow pecked impressions, each about four cm in diameter and one cm deep. Some are joined by shallow furrows. The surfaces of the boulders slope down slightly on one side. A small reservoir, VMS-91, is located about 70 meters to the west. Similar features have been observed by Hegde in the context of metal working in western India (Sinopoli, personal communication 1990). Molten metals were poured over the roughened surface and lighter impurities sloughed off.

Block S

VMS-140 is an area of settlement contained within the city wall (VMS-123). Abundant remains of gabbro, both moderately sized chunks and small flakes and debitage, are scattered rather thinly throughout this area. The area around VMS-140 has been heavily disturbed, but it must be consid-

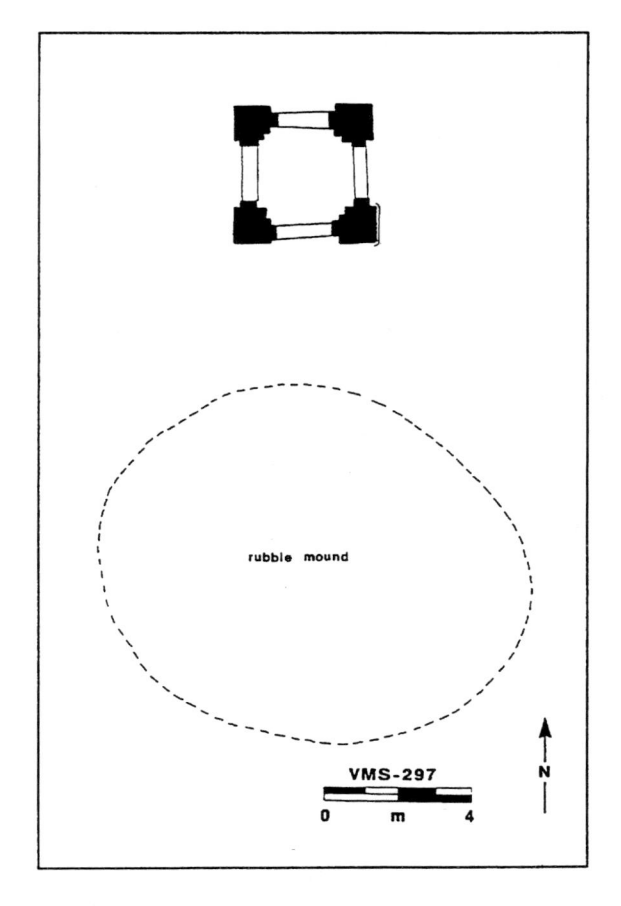

FIGURE 4.16   Islamic-style tomb, Block T

ered a possible production locale for pegs and other stone objects.

Although many types of craft production activities were carried out in the survey area, perhaps the most visible and durable archaeological record was left by iron working. Two iron production sites were identified in Block S. One of these, VMS-121, (figure 4.21) is situated in the middle of the block. The furnace area contains what appear to be vitrified crucible fragments on a low rectangular platform. This feature has been partly broken up and now contains a small shrine. Portions of the furnace, chunks of iron, and slag are incorporated into the fill of the platform of a large, elevated Vijayanagara temple, VMS-7. Thus, the initial construction of VMS-121 predates the construction of the temple. VMS-121 is situated near VMS-122, the very badly disturbed remnant of a small reservoir. This reservoir was superseded by a large step well, VMS-8, apparently associated with the temple. Thus, it is possible that the iron-working site and the reservoir are contemporaneous, and certain that they predate the construction of the temple and step well.

A second iron-working locale, VMS-179 (figure 4.22) is located south of the large temple complex VMS-142. VMS-179 consists of a scatter of artifacts relating to iron working. The scatter contains innumerable small chunks of iron, slag, and overfired red brick. Here, however, there are no *in situ* traces of a furnace. VMS-179 is situated along the route of a road running east-west past VMS-142, and, unusually, is not near any obvious source of water. This site cannot be clearly dated.

Block T

There is very limited evidence for nonagricultural production in Block T, although future study of the settlement areas may alter this view. VMS-317/F7 is a low platform, circa six by three meters, built over outcropping rocks. The platform is constructed of brick and fired earth, and although there are not high slag densities associated with this feature, slag is found elsewhere in the temple complex. It seems that at least some of the temple complex postdates this fragmentary (iron?) production locale, since slag is incorporated into the fill of VMS-317/F6, a *mandapa*.

Other Areas

Evidence of production outside of the intensively surveyed blocks is extremely limited, as such material has generally not been the focus of ar-

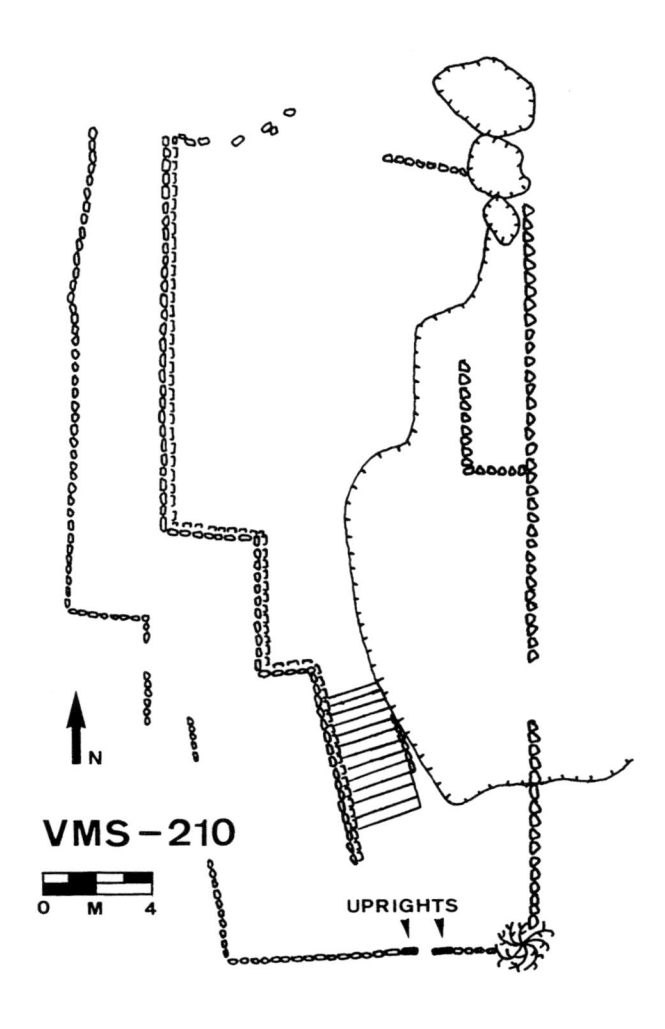

FIGURE 4.19   Step well built into natural rock outcrop (VMS-210), Block S

chaeological investigation. VMS-5 is located in Block R (Morrison 1991a). This site consists of a large scatter of iron slag, vitrified brick, and iron ore. VMS-5 was situated on or near the edge of the reservoir VMS-4 (the Malpannagudi reservoir; Morrison 1991a).

AGRICULTURAL FEATURES

A complete list of agricultural features from Blocks N, O, S, and T is given in chapter 5 (table 5.1).

Block O

The most striking agricultural feature in Block O, and one of the primary determinants of vegetation in the block is the Hiriya or Turtha Canal

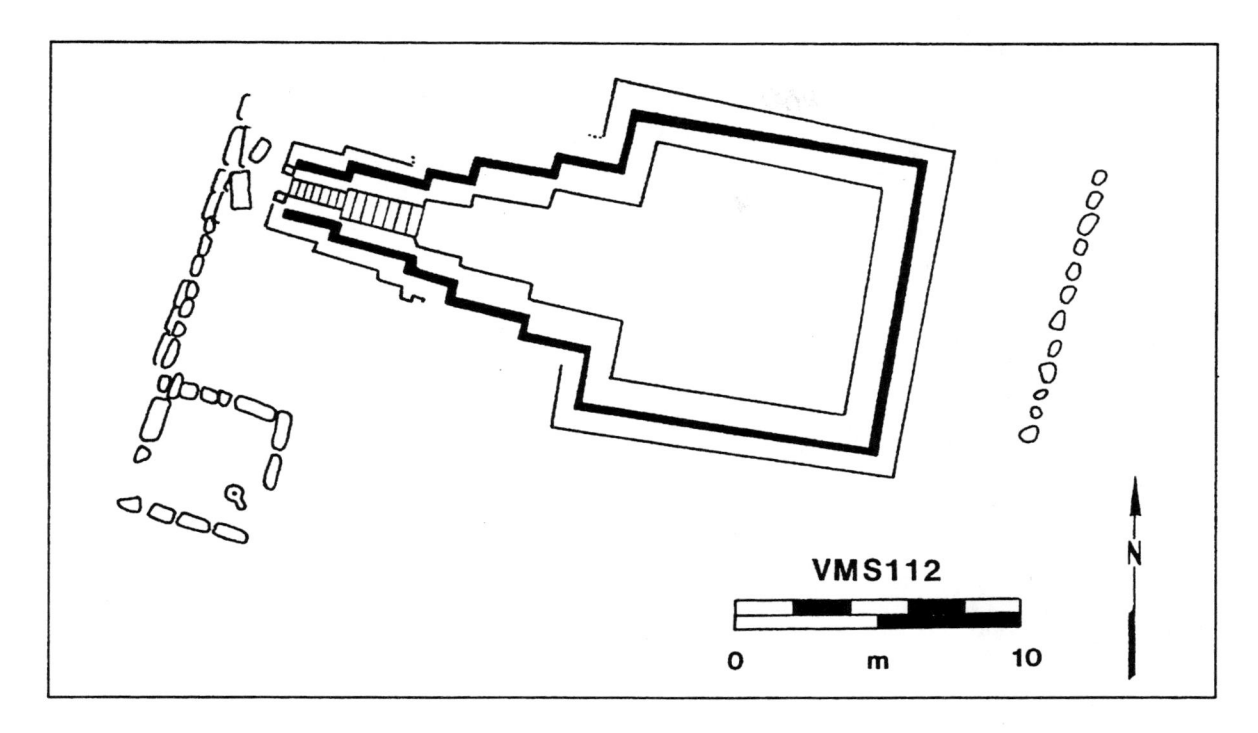

FIGURE 4.17 Elaborate step well with carved *nandi* figures located along roadway (VMS-112), Block O

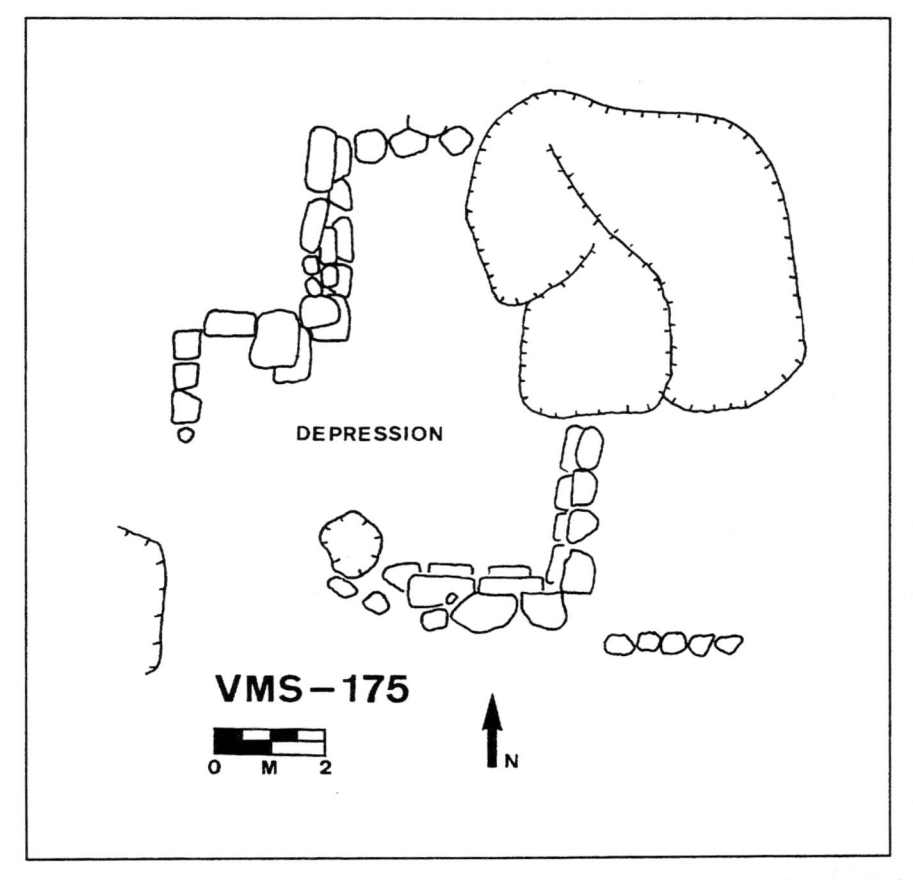

FIGURE 4.18 Small well with stepped masonry sides (VMS-175), Block S

FIGURE 4.20
Masonry-lined spring (VMS-136), Block S

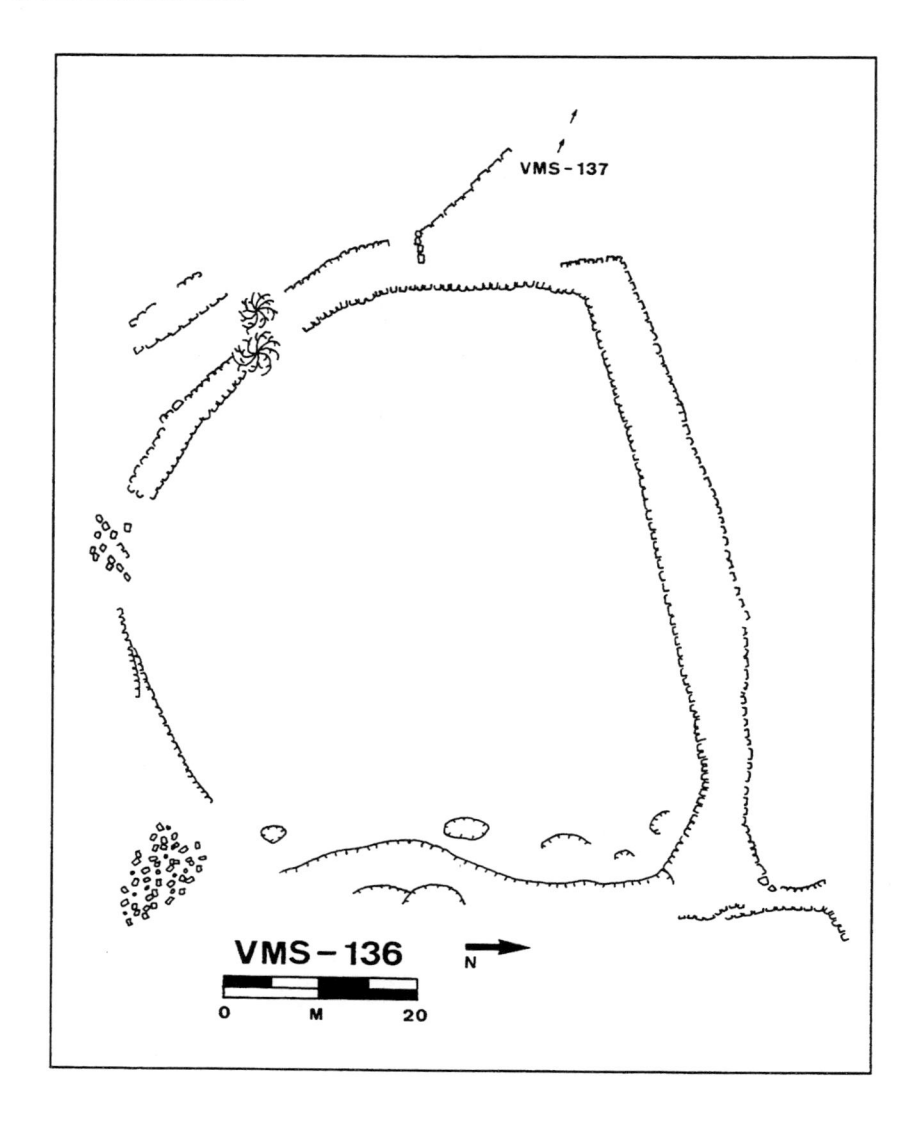

(VMS-120). Hiriya appears to have been the Vijayanagara-period name for the canal, but the name Turtha Canal is in widespread use and has been established in the literature of the site, so I will use it here. The canal begins at a point approximately 2.5 kilometers west of the village of Hampi, where the Turtha *anicut*, a series of low stone walls positioned between the boulders in the river, diverts the flow of the Tungabhadra into the canal. The canal flows back into the river just east of Block O, past Bukkasagara. Fairly detailed description of the Turtha *anicut* can be found in Davison-Jenkins (1988:105).

An inscription of Krishnadeva Raya in A.D. 1524 refers to the donation of produce and of wet lands to a temple located on the canal (Nagaraja Rao and Patil 1985:31). A Portuguese visitor to the city, Nuniz, describes the construction of a canal that seems to match the description of the Turtha Canal. However, although Nuniz visited Vijayanagara between A.D. 1535 and 1537, his account of the canal construction is found within his chronicle of Vijayanagara history. He places the construction during the reign of a nonexistent king, "Ajarao," supposedly the successor to Harihara I (this would be Bukka II, 1399-1406; Sewell 1900: 301, 404). This account cannot be considered reliable. Thus, the canal can only be dated to pre-1524. The Turtha Canal was extremely important to the area near the city. It watered the narrow "irrigated valley" (Fritz, Michell, and Nagaraja Rao 1985) north of the city and ran through the eastern end of the Urban Core itself.

Within Block O, the Turtha Canal has been continuously maintained and repaired, so that not much beyond the route of the Vijayanagara-period canal can be discerned. In general, artifact densities and site densities in the canal zone are very low,

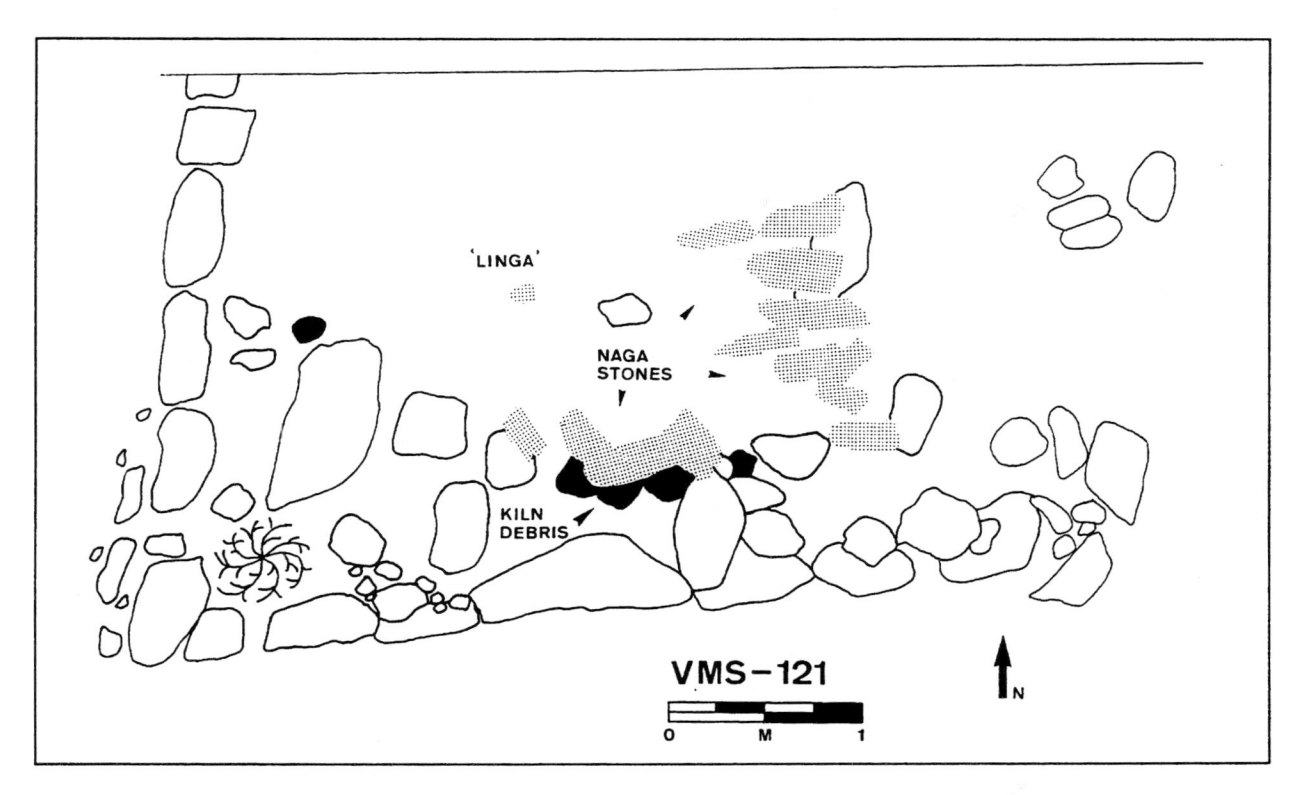

FIGURE 4.21 Furnace/working platform with kiln debris and superimposed shrine (VMS-121), Block S

suggesting that there was minimal nonagricultural use of this area. Important exceptions include the small settlement, VMS-35 to VMS-37, and the pre-Vijayanagara site VMS-26 (and possibly also VMS-28).

Block O contains eleven runoff-fed reservoirs (VMS-21, VMS-48, VMS-59, VMS-62, VMS-72, VMS-91, VMS-97, VMS-108, VMS-113, VMS-117, and VMS-229). These tend to occur near the bases of outcrops and in the narrow valleys around the edge of the southeast corner of the block, which consists of high, dissected rocky hills. VMS-2 is surrounded by a cluster of reservoirs (VMS-72, VMS-117, VMS-229). VMS-59 was a very large reservoir that has now mostly been broken down by construction of the modern canals. This reservoir may have blocked nearly the entire valley through which the modern canals now run. If so, it would have created a significant barrier to the movement of traffic in this area, making the route over the outcrop associated with VMS-42 even more important.

The Block O reservoirs, with the exception of VMS-59 and VMS-117, are relatively small (e.g., VMS-72, figure 4.23). Many of them do not have formal sluice gates but only overflow sluices, and VMS-48 is not faced with masonry. Several of these features were apparently designed for small-scale cultivation within the area of impoundment rather than for downstream distribution of water (Morrison 1991b). One of these embankments is VMS-108. Although solidly constructed, it contains no outlets (aside from a recent breach, figure 4.24).

Informal erosion control walls are often found in association with reservoirs. These generally consist of one or two courses of unmodified boulders or cobbles built at right angles to the direction of runoff. All of the eleven erosion control walls recorded were located either on the edge of granitic outcrops (VMS-82, VMS-98, and VMS-106) or at the base of an outcrop (VMS-52, VMS-53, VMS-55, VMS-58, VMS-60, VMS-61, VMS-63, and VMS-90).

Two sets of check dams (VMS-95 and VMS-100; figure 4.25) were recorded in Block O. Both are located in remote areas, away from roads or settlements. VMS-95 is located in the runoff catchment of the reservoir VMS-117.

The "Islamic style" well, VMS-40, has been

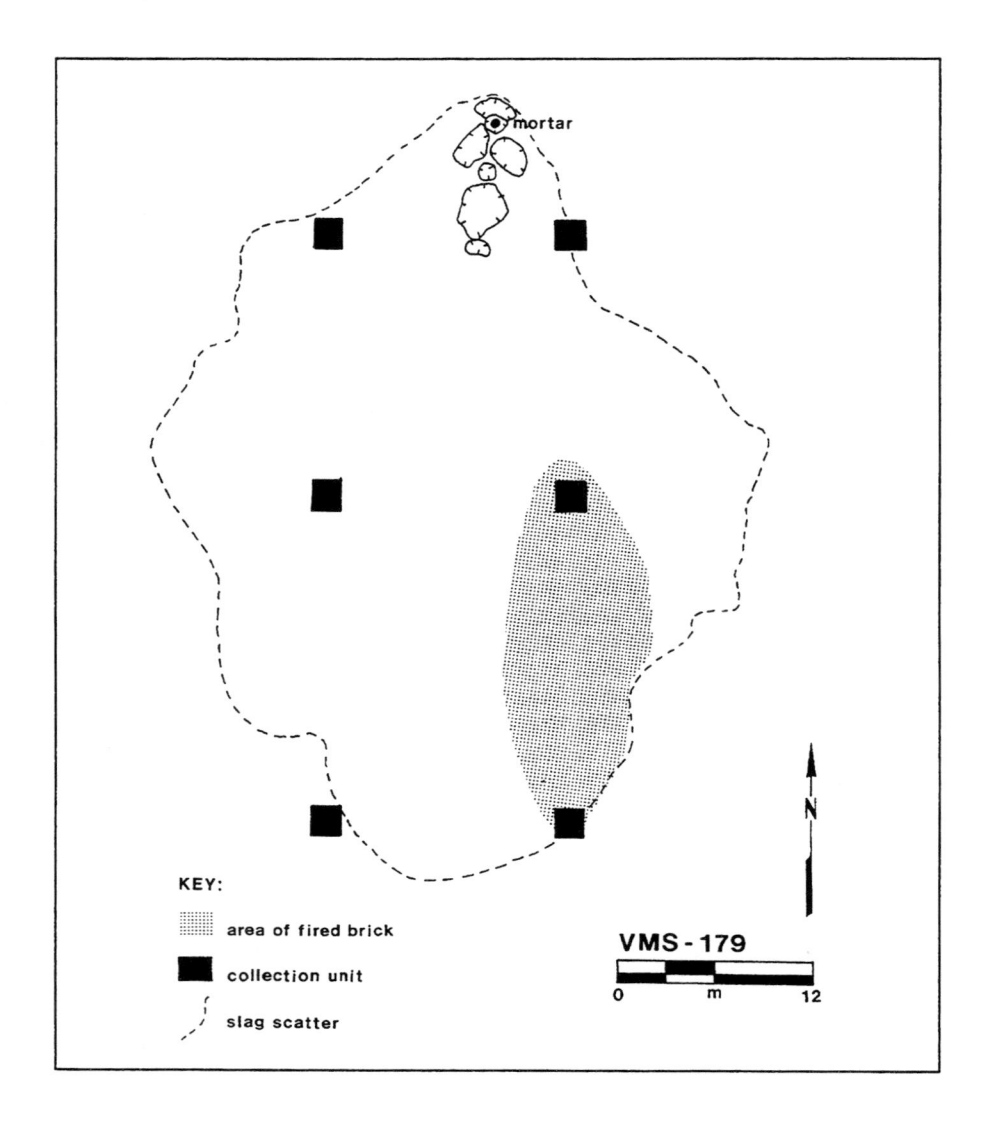

FIGURE 4.22

Scatter of iron slag, iron, and overfired brick (VMS-179), Block S

described above. This feature was associated with agricultural production in a dry zone. The proximity of the site to the city and the labor requirements of such a form of watering may indicate that "garden" crops such as vegetables or orchard crops were grown here. A masonry-lined spring, VMS-99, may also have been used for agriculture (figure 4.26).

Block S

The Vijayanagara agricultural use of Block S was both intensive and diverse. Agricultural facilities identified in the block include a canal-fed reservoir, runoff-fed reservoirs and embankments, terraces, check-dams, gravel-mulched fields, and wells.

The northwestern portion of the block is dominated by the Kamalapuram reservoir (VMS-231, see figure 7.1). Supplied by the river-fed Raya Canal, it provided a year-round source of water for irrigation. Although the land under VMS-231 is enclosed within the city walls, it contains very few artifacts. The primary route that linked the city of Vijayanagara with settlement to the west ran over the raised embankment of the reservoir, passing through a gateway (now mostly dismantled) on the western end of the embankment. A smaller road branched off from this route, extending north to the city. Except for this route, the area north of the reservoir appears to have been used solely for crop production from a very early period. The area watered by VMS-231 was estimated at 182 hectares in 1904 (Francis 1904:282).

The embankment of the Kamalapuram reservoir is nearly two kilometers long, but the easternmost 300 meters or so appear to be a recent addition. The masonry on the south side of the embankment is much-repaired, consisting of

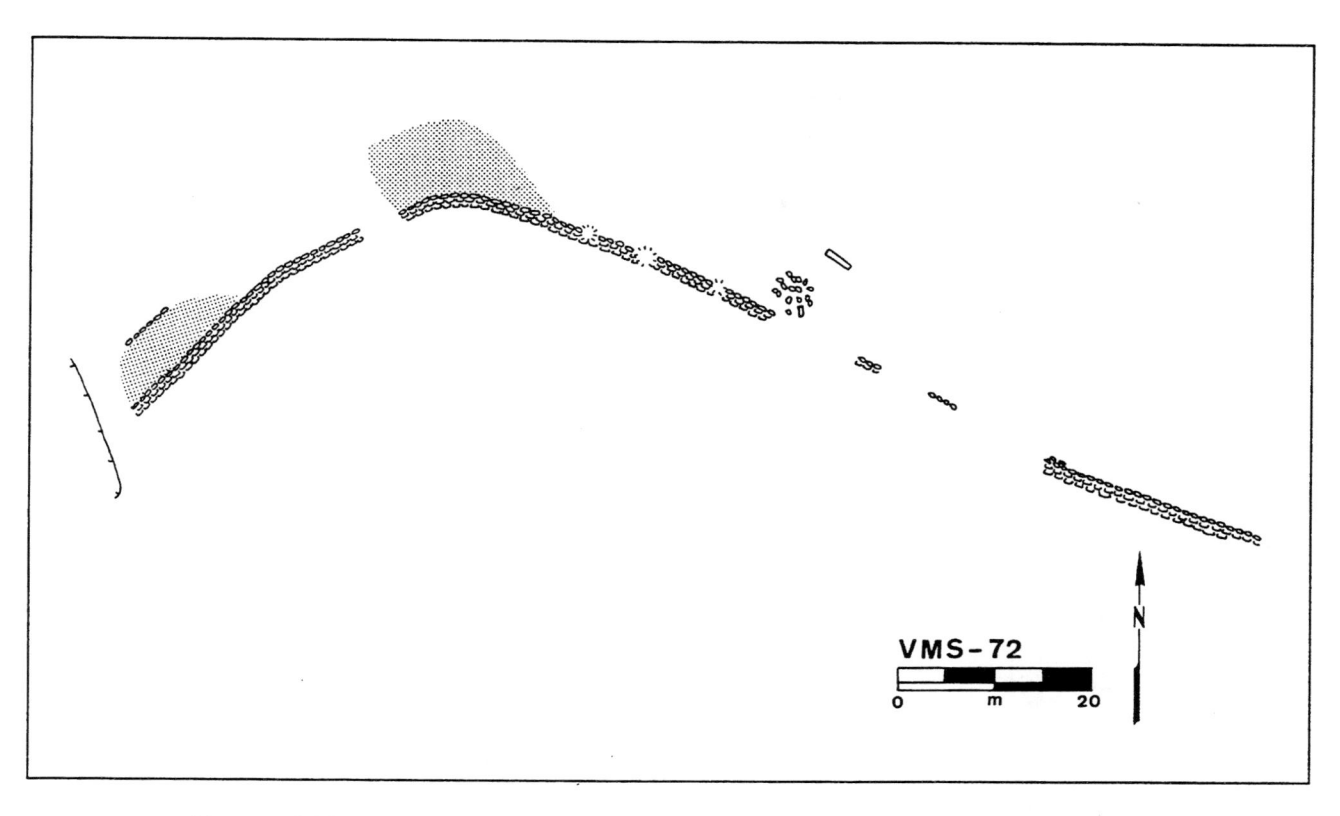

FIGURE 4.23   Heavily disturbed reservoir embankment (VMS-72), Block O

quarried and shaped blocks in the upper courses and unmodified boulders in the lowest courses. There are at present four sluice gates, of which two are from the Vijayanagara period. It is not clear if the westernmost sluice has replaced an original sluice or not; the eastern sluice is part of the post-Vijayanagara modifications to the reservoir. The original sluices are fairly simple, containing two-stepped with angled bevel mouldings with half medallions. This moulding type is extremely common in city architecture. Both of the Vijayanagara-period sluices are associated with stone settling basins below the embankment (see chapter 2).

No inscriptions are located on or near the Kamalapuram reservoir. However, an unpublished inscription of Bukka I, A.D. 1366, is reported to contain a reference to the grant of lands below the reservoir (Manjunathaiah, personal communication 1988). Gopal (1985a:180) reports an inscription of A.D. 1518 located on a boulder northwest of the village of Kamalapuram which records a grant of land to a god (temple) located beside the reservoir of Chikkaraya. Thus, this large and important reservoir appears to have been constructed quite early in the Vijayanagara occupation of the area.

The Kamalapuram reservoir obtains water not only from runoff but also from the Raya Canal, which feeds into the reservoir on the northwest just inside of Block R. The *anicuts* of the Raya Canal (and the Basavanna, which was extended into Block S during the 1940s and 1950s; Davison-Jenkins 1988) have been submerged by the Tungabhadra dam (Kotraiah 1959), and the irrigation department now supplements the holdings of the Kamalapuram reservoir both with the Raya Canal and with a modern canal.

In the eastern portion of the block, wet-cum-dry and dry runoff-dependent agricultural strategies prevailed. Fourteen runoff-fed irrigation reservoirs were recorded (VMS-122, VMS-125, VMS-132, VMS-138, VMS-150, VMS-159, VMS-165, VMS-190, VMS-194, VMS-206, VMS-226, VMS-230, VMS-241, and VMS-242). These reservoirs vary greatly in size, from VMS-230 with a 36-meter-long embankment to VMS-125 with a length of about 728 meters. Block S reservoirs are significantly larger, on average, than those of Block O. Of interest is the relative lack of very small agricultural features common in Block O (Morrison 1991b). Instead, larger and more formal types of agricultural

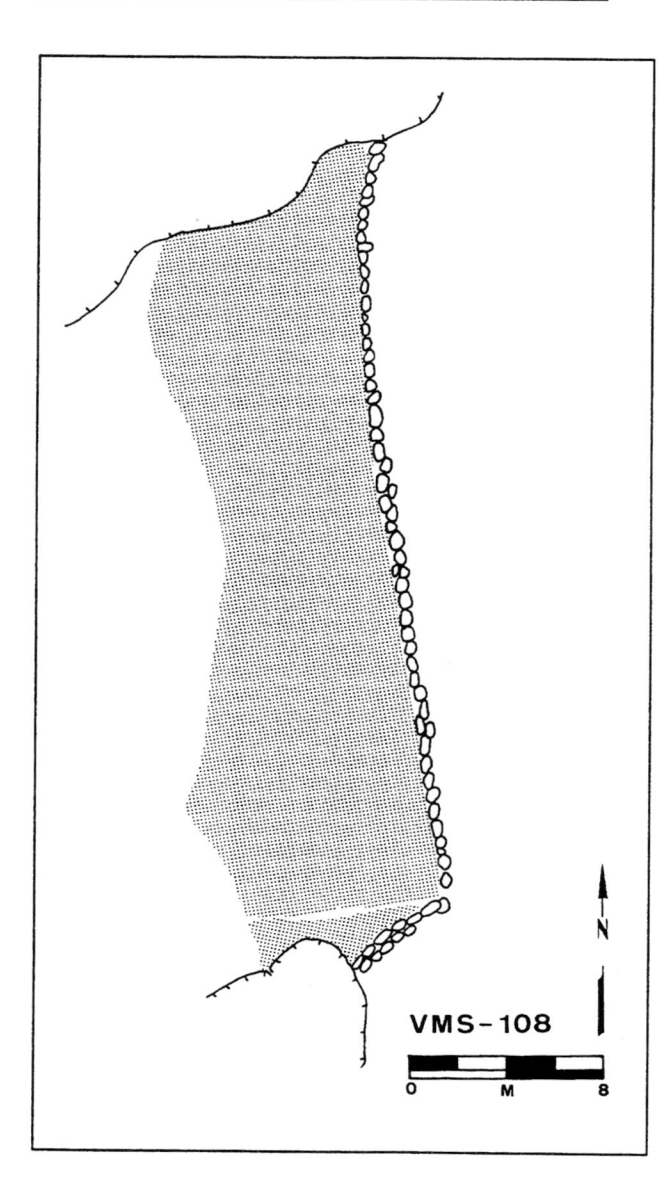

FIGURE 4.24
Masonry-edged earthen embankment (VMS-108), Block O. The only opening is an unlined gap in the embankment.

facilities predominate, and even the dryland features tend to be larger than their counterparts in Block O. However, some very small features do exist, such as VMS-138, a simple embankment with no outlets (figure 4.27).

VMS-190, Halla Kere, is another very large Vijayanagara-period reservoir in Block S. VMS-190 received the overflow from several reservoirs upstream, including VMS-194 and VMS-206. VMS-242 is a large reservoir in the south-central portion of the block. This reservoir has been cut by the modern high level canal and is in poor condition. However, when this reservoir was in operation, the nature of the vegetation and the appearance of the landscape would have been quite different from the scrubby landscape now used only for grazing and collecting, indicating the extent of land use changes in Block S caused by changes in the hydrological regime.

Block S is notable for its extensive terrace systems (figure 4.28). These terraces tend to be shallow and simply constructed, often covering large areas. Most are located in areas that now are used almost exclusively for grazing; some are in areas where dry farming of millets, sunflowers, or cotton are carried out every few years. In a real sense, the categories of check dams and terraces are actually continuous categories. For this discussion, terraces are defined as covering more than one drainage, and check dams only a single drainage. Either may contain walls both parallel and perpendicular to the direction of slope. Terraces and check dams in Block S include: VMS-133, VMS-134, VMS-139, VMS-181, VMS-191, VMS-193, VMS-198, VMS-199, VMS-205, VMS-207, VMS-208, VMS-211, VMS-263, VMS-264, VMS-276, VMS-280, VMS-283, and VMS-287.

As noted in chapter 2, terraces protect areas downstream from excess runoff and the potentially devastating effects of erosion and slope wash. This function may have been as important as the benefits for localized agricultural production. The somewhat unstable nature of the soil cover in the survey area (a consequence both of the topography and rainfall regime as well as of human and animal impact) ensured that agricultural features and practices had consequences well beyond the area actually farmed. The landscape was linked through large-scale movements of soil and water as well as through the social ties of its inhabitants.

Vijayanagara agricultural facilities were often linked to create areally extensive systems of soil and water control. A very striking pattern of association between agricultural facilities can be seen in Block S, where large terraces (VMS-133, VMS-134, VMS-191, VMS-205, VMS-207) cover many of the rocky hillsides forming the runoff catchment for reservoirs below. These terraces are rarely more than two masonry courses high, but they form quite complex systems over large areas.

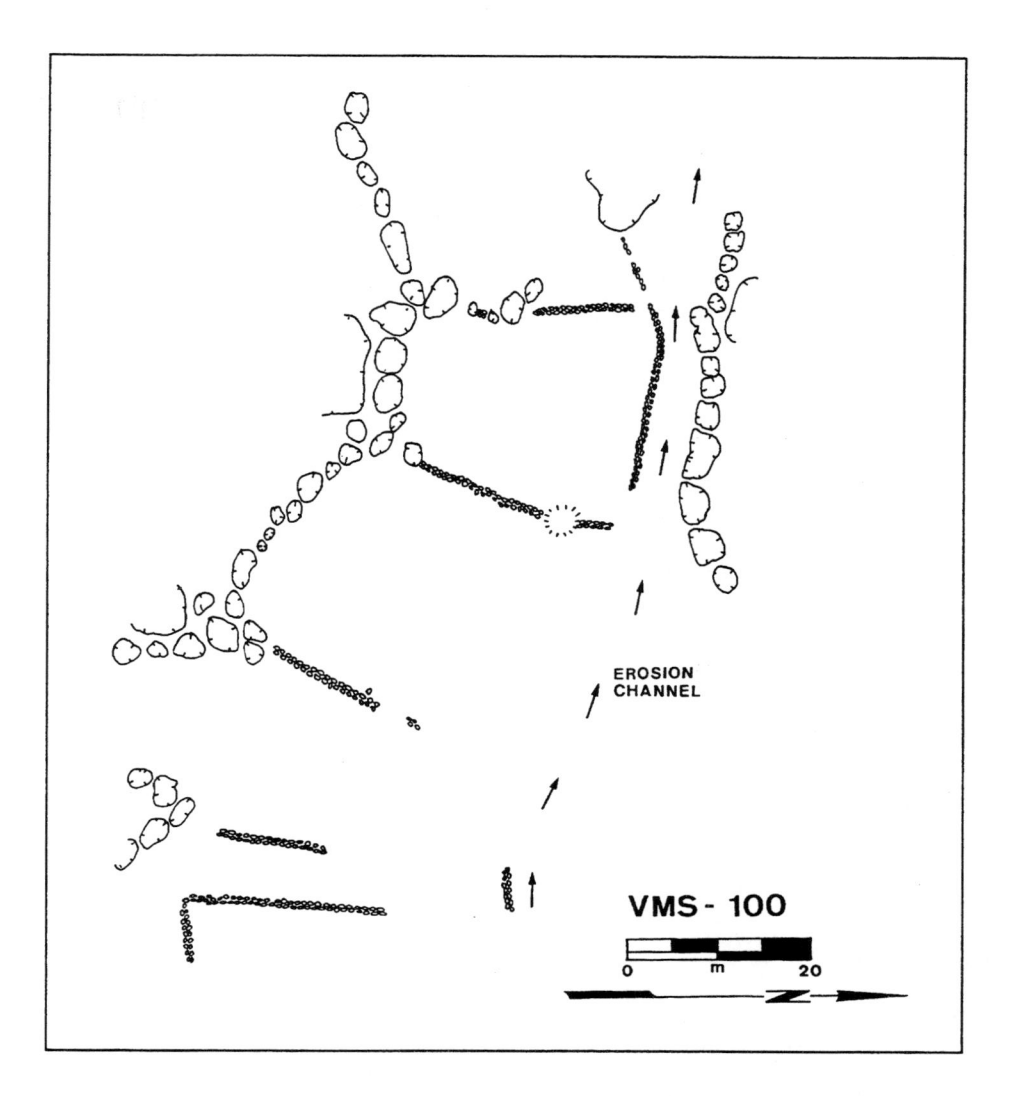

FIGURE 4.25
Check-dams and channel (VMS-100), Block O

Reservoirs are not all located in the flat areas below terraced outcrops, however. Several of the reservoirs recorded in the eastern portion of the block are situated within terrace systems and are an integral part of them. These include: VMS-206 amid the terraces of VMS-205, VMS-226 in the terraces of VMS-133, and VMS-230 in the terraces of VMS-207. Other features such as rooms (VMS-139) and wells (VMS-207) were also built into soil and water control systems.

A number of small erosion control walls, which were often associated with reservoirs, were also found in Block S. A complete list of these is given in table 5.1.

VMS-276 consists of an area of low terraces and gravel-mulched fields. This complex is still in use and may be modern, as it is quite close to Kamalapuram village. However, there is no reason to believe that the gravel-mulched fields contained within the terraces of VMS-263 are modern.

Extensive areas of gravel-mulched fields are also found in the Daroji Valley to the south of the survey area.

In general, the picture of agricultural exploitation of Block S that emerges is one of intensive and opportunistic use of the semi-arid landscape. Although Block O contains a larger area of permanently irrigated land than does Block S, Block S exhibits a greater diversity and density of large, integrated dryland agricultural facilities.

Block T

Although Block T contains large areas that were devoted to dry and wet-cum-dry cultivation in the Vijayanagara period, it is unlike Block S in some respects. The very large terrace systems that are common in Block S are more rare in Block T, although reservoirs are common. No facilities related to wet irrigation are located in the block, as it is out of reach of the Vijayanagara canals. VMS-

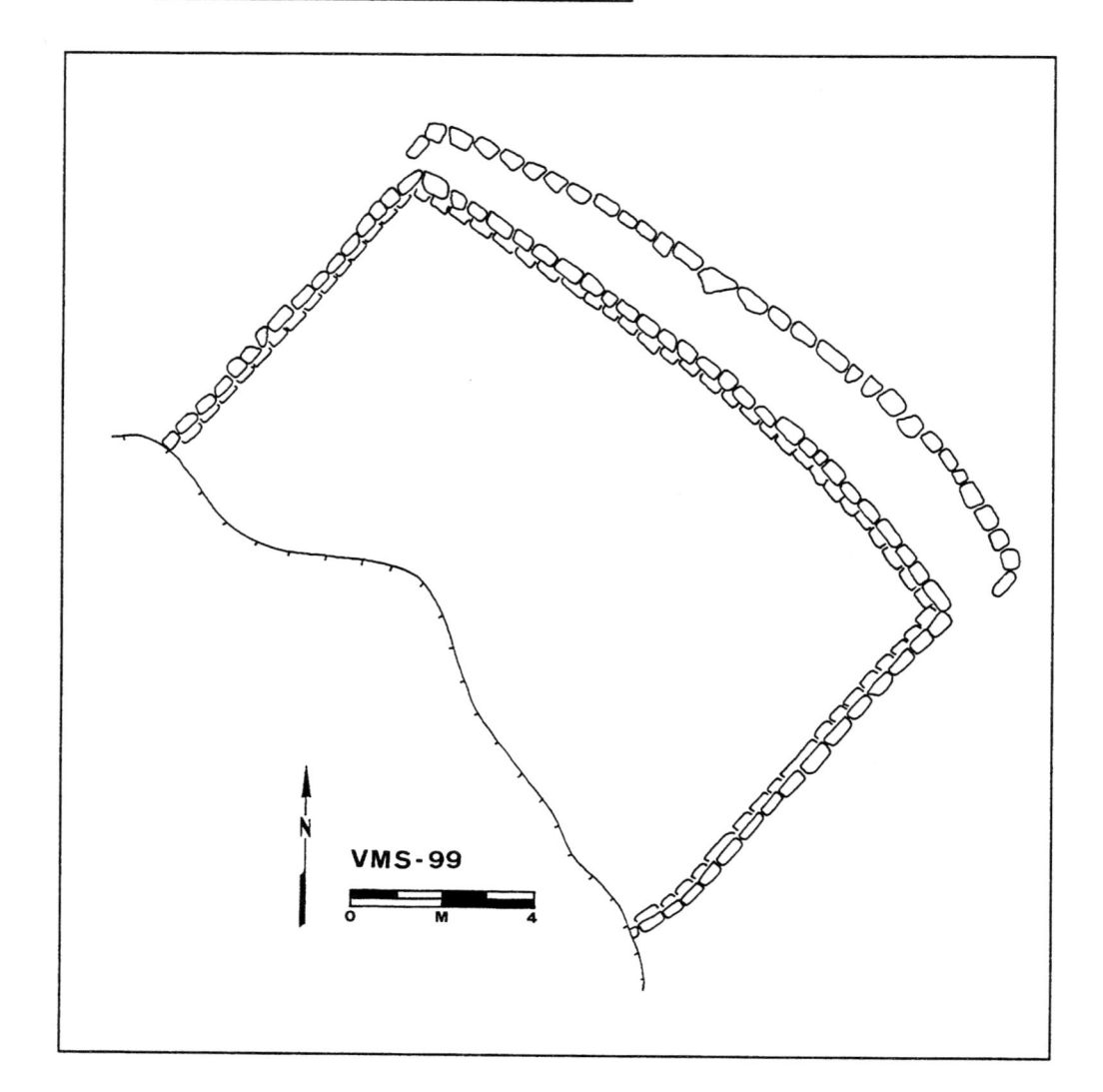

FIGURE 4.26
Spring with stepped masonry edges (VMS-99), Block O

344 is the largest dry facility in the block. This terrace system covers *ca.* 320 by 280 m of an area in the northwest watershed of the reservoir VMS-315. The system consists of five to six long north-south walls spaced 30-50 m apart. The one to two course high terrace walls run perpendicular to the gentle slope and are remarkably straight and long. Silt has built up behind the low walls, and this area was probably used both for immediate cultivation and as a check to erosion into the reservoir below. Abutting the northern end of one terrace wall are two east-west rubble walls parallel to the slope. Adjacent to these is VMS-343, a single room structure. On the southern edge of the terraced area are three other small one-room structures and one inside the terraced area. Artifact concentrations in the area were low.

VMS-299 is a small complex consisting of three square bordered fields (each *ca.* 25 by 25 m) or gardens and five other wall segments. The borders and walls are constructed of piled cobbles. Among the terraced fields are small boulders with petroglyphs—snakes, circles, v-shapes, and letters. There are no artifacts. VMS-299 is located in a dry area of moderate slope inside the long wall VMS-339. Very close to VMS-299 is VMS-300, a series of check dams placed perpendicular to the slope of a narrow area between two outcrops. A second set of check dams, VMS-310, is also found in this dry farmed zone west of VMS-339. This small system (120 by 35 m) consists of five walls perpendicular to a gentle slope and one flanking wall running parallel to the slope, a pattern found in many other similar features in the study area.

Dry farming was also carried out in the level east-central portion of Block T, as attested to by the two terrace walls of VMS-362. The walls of this feature are substantial, with up to four preserved courses of large cobbles holding back soil on a moderate slope. This site may be part of a much

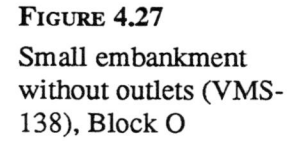

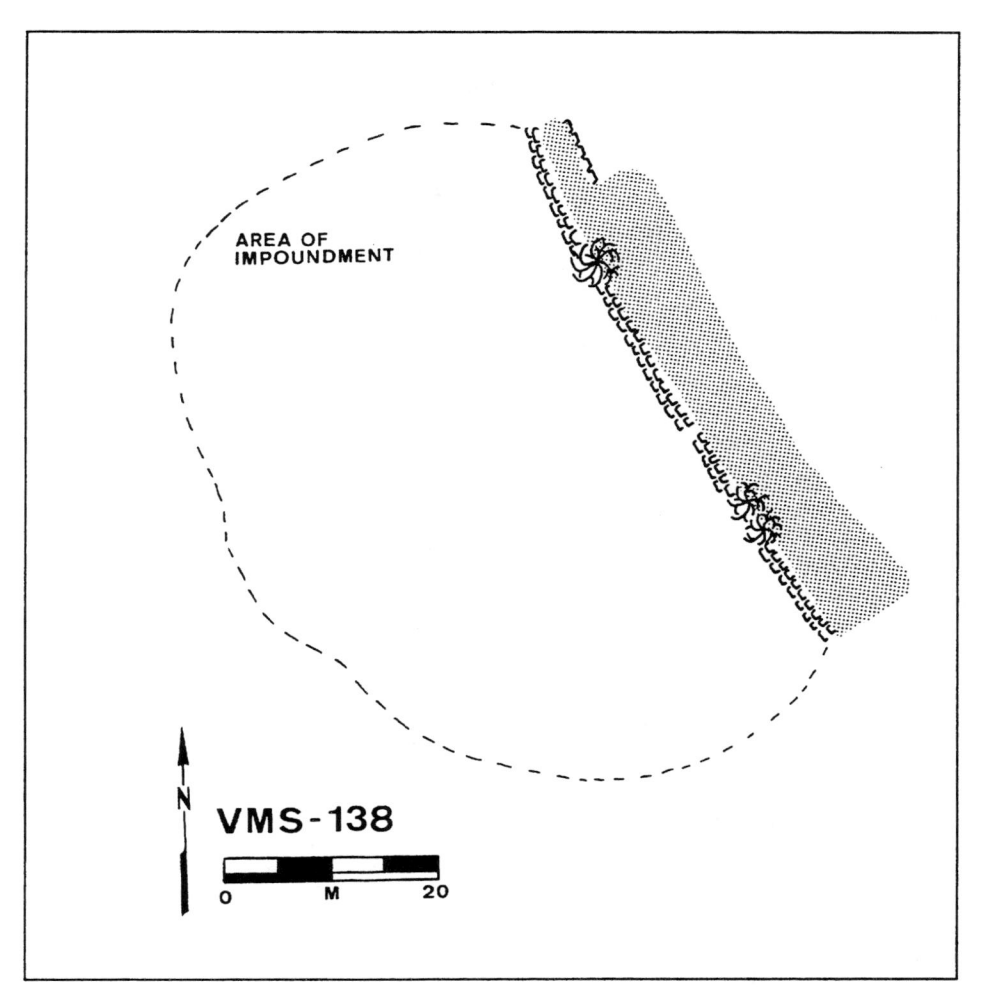

FIGURE 4.27
Small embankment without outlets (VMS-138), Block O

more extensive terraced area containing a well and a one-room structure. VMS-347 is a check dam located on a slope just east of the wall VMS-339.

Block T contains fifteen reservoirs as well as VMS-125 and VMS-132, which span blocks S and T. Thus, Block T contains the highest density of runoff-fed reservoirs in the intensively surveyed area. As noted, features related to dry farming are somewhat smaller (or perhaps only more disturbed and thus not recorded) than in Block S. VMS-125 and VMS-330 are the largest reservoirs in the block. VMS-125 extends into Block S on the west, and its embankment may have carried the Nallapur Road. This reservoir is quite close to the outer circuit of the city walls, and it may predate the expansion of urban settlement into this area. VMS-330 is 650 m long, spanning the northern valley of Block T. Although it has been heavily disturbed, two sluice gates and a brick-and-plaster-lined sluice tunnel still remain. VMS-330 blocks most of the Nallapur Valley and would have watered fields in an area north and west of the village VMS-361. Eight small reservoirs are scattered throughout the area between VMS-125 and VMS-330. Several of these are part of interconnected systems (e.g., VMS-369, VMS-132, VMS-125). The southwestern quadrant of Block T also contains several reservoirs. VMS-349 is associated with the village VMS-365. VMS-315 is a large reservoir, with an embankment 500 m long. The terrace VMS-344 is part of the watershed of this reservoir, and VMS-316, a shrine, is situated next to the reservoir embankment. Most of these southwestern reservoirs are isolated, but VMS-357 and VMS-355 form a small system.

As in other surveyed blocks, a number of sites consist solely of isolated walls and wall fragments. Of these, perhaps seven relate to soil and water control. Many are clearly associated with reservoirs (VMS-332 and VMS-331 with VMS-330; VMS-320 with VMS-297; VMS-350 with VMS-315), although they probably also served more local

96 *Fields of Victory*

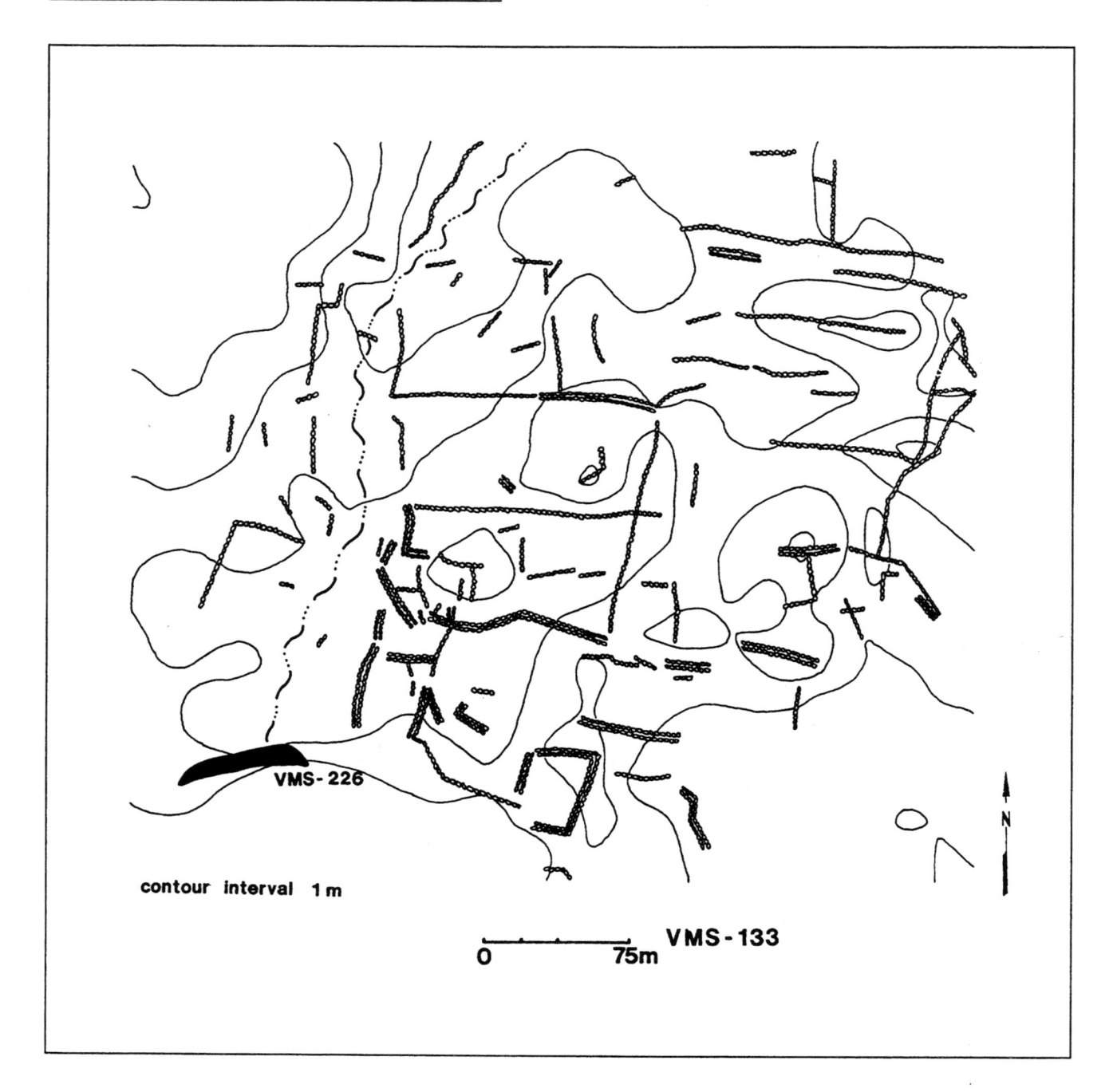

FIGURE 4.28   Integrated system containing terraces (VMS-133) and a small reservoir (VMS-226), Block S

small-scale agricultural purposes. Such walls tend to be quite simply constructed of one or more courses of unmodified cobbles and boulders. A few are more substantial, however. VMS-350 is a 94-m-long wall formed by two parallel alignments of cobbles 1.2 to 1.4 m apart filled with earth and rubble. This wall runs along the top of a low ridge adjacent to an ephemeral drainage leading into the reservoir VMS-315. As the wall turns and extends down the ridge it becomes higher, up to five courses. VMS-363 is 85 m long and may actually be a heavily disturbed reservoir embankment.

The most unusual agricultural feature in Block T is VMS-351, just south of the wall VMS-350 just described. VMS-351, like VMS-350, lies on the edge of a drainage channel leading into VMS-315.

This complex feature consists of a series of walls and platforms and may have been employed as part of a water lift for bringing water up out of the entrenched drainage. The soil and water control features VMS-347 (check dams) and VMS-352 (walls) lie upstream, as does the small reservoir VMS-346. This drainage has been cut by the construction of VMS-339, which may postdate the construction of some of the agricultural facilities.

Other Areas

A diversity of agricultural features are found throughout the study area. Intensively farmed zones of wet agriculture include the areas watered by the Vijayanagara canals and by both the Turtha Canal and by wells within the Urban Core walls. The canal zone stretches approximately from Hospet on the west to Kampli on the east and includes the narrow valley north of the Urban Core. A reservoir was constructed in this valley (Bhupati Kere; Rajasekhara 1985a:112) probably sometime after the Turtha Canal was built. Thus, there were at least three canal-fed reservoirs in the region. Other facilities associated with the canal system include the massive aqueduct, probably dating to the sixteenth century, that carries water from the Anegundi Channel across a branch of the Tungabhadra to a large island, Virupuragadda. A few breached reservoirs in the canal zone attest to the expansion of canal irrigation at the expense of reservoirs during the Vijayanagara period. In most cases, however, different types of facilities did not compete directly since each was suited to a particular environment.

In the larger area around the city, runoff-fed reservoirs were among the most common form of agricultural facility. Hundreds of reservoirs are found throughout the study area (see chapter 5). Of particular interest are the large integrated systems of reservoirs, such as that found in the Daroji Valley, leading into the large Daroji reservoir, and the Dhanayakanakere system, to the south and west of Hospet (figure 4.6). Rare double sluices are found on reservoirs from both systems.

It has not been possible to discuss all of the sites located in the Vijayanagara Metropolitan Survey; instead I have provided an overview of the types of sites and features found and of the diversity of the material remains in the survey area. More detailed discussion is limited to only three survey blocks, a total area of about 75 square kilometers. Clearly, these three blocks represent only a fraction of the productive landscape used by the inhabitants of Vijayanagara and outlying settlements. Even so, it is possible to discern some overall patterns of land use around the city. These patterns are discussed in the following chapter.

5

Archaeological Patterns of Land Use

THE MATERIAL REMAINS of the complex patterns of agricultural land use and settlement around the city of Vijayanagara constitute one of the primary sources of information about the scale and diversity of productive strategies in the region. Although the intensive phase of the survey has covered only a small area to date, the distributions from this area coupled with the less detailed information known about other areas can provide material for some preliminary observations about the nature of agricultural production in the study area and its change through time.

Settlement

In order to understand the distribution of nucleated settlements in the study area, it is necessary first to consider some of the primary locational constraints and opportunities of the region. The course of the Tungabhadra River was clearly very important in structuring settlement. The river was not only a source of water for irrigation and for domestic and ritual use, it was also a significant barrier to north-south traffic and a limited transport route for the west-to-east movement of goods such as logs, which could be floated down the river.

Other topographic features also prevented easy north-south movement; these include the Sandur Hills on the south and the high, rocky granitic hills north of the river. Smaller, parallel ridges of east-west trending granitic hills cross the landscape, making the major direction of roadways east-west, with only short north-south segments connecting adjacent valleys. Temporal trends in agricultural land use in the study area are associated with changes in settlement location. An early settlement concentration near the Tungabhadra River and in zones of wet agriculture reflected the spatial structure of agricultural production in the Early Vijayanagara period, while a later settlement expansion into the dry zones away from the river seems to have been matched by a concomitant expansion in runoff-fed reservoirs. The relationship between settlement location and agricultural strategy is neither simple nor straightforward, however, since both reflect an entire range of locational and organizational constraints. These constraints include, for example, the position of existing settlements, markets, and roadways, as well as the amount and timing of labor demands of different agricultural strategies.

The city of Vijayanagara dominated the settlement distribution of the region, containing high-density residential and residential/commercial neighborhoods. Unfortunately, it is not possible to trace the pattern of population growth (and decline) within the city over its two hundred year occupation, except as it might be reflected in the pattern of construction of monumental structures (see Rajasekhara 1985a). However, it seems unlikely that the tempo of construction of elite architecture unfailingly matched that of the population of the city or of the region. The Urban Core walls were built early in the occupational history of the city (Michell, personal communication 1988); it may be that this walled area was rather sparsely settled at first and filled in only later. The Urban Core did, however, support some agricultural production in the form of economically useful trees and garden plots (Morrison 1989), and one reservoir was actually located within the Urban Core walls (Michell 1990:240, 245). Some of the garden plots in the city were probably watered by the Turtha Canal as it passed through the Urban Core near the "Muslim Quarter" (Michell 1985a).

In the study area as a whole, a clear bimodal pattern of settlement growth exists, with the first mode falling in the fourteenth century coincident with the establishment of the city and of the empire and the second peak occurring in approximately the mid-sixteenth century. The settlements in Block O are not well dated, but VMS-35-37 dates to the early Vijayanagara period and is one of the few settlements in the study area that was not occupied in the Colonial or recent periods. Dates for the establishment of VMS-2 and VMS-101 cannot be determined on the basis of the archaeological evidence. However, both were occupied during the sixteenth century and either have been continuously occupied since or were reoccupied in the eighteenth or early nineteenth century. In Block S, the entire northeastern corner was densely settled. All evidence for the establishment of this settlement points to the mid-sixteenth century, with the founding of Varadadevi-Ammana-Pattana (Filliozat and Filliozat 1988:13) and the construction of the Penukonda gate. The outer city wall (VMS-10, VMS-123) may also have been built coincident with the sixteenth-century expansion in this area. Only Kamalapuram (and the Kamalapuram reservoir, VMS-231) predate the sixteenth-century expansion, but even there, the structure of the gateways of the fort was greatly modified in that time period, as evidenced by the Late Vijayanagara style of columns in the north gateway (VMS-257).

The two nucleated settlements in Block T are not securely dated. Neither contains elaborate architecture nor are any inscriptional records correlated with these settlements. VMS-317 is an early Vijayanagara temple located on the Nallapur Road that runs east-west through this block. Thus, the roadway may have been in use by the fourteenth century, and the small settlement, VMS-361, may even date to this early period. The walled village, VMS-365, is spatially associated with a road system and a system of interconnected dry-land agricultural facilities, both of which are cut by the long wall, VMS-339. Thus, the village probably predates the wall, but it cannot be placed securely within the Vijayanagara period.

Elsewhere in the study area, most settlements have been dated either to the early or the late portions of the Vijayanagara period, but few to the middle of the period (fifteenth century). Locations near the Tungabhadra River seem to have been favored in the earlier periods—Anegundi, Kampli, Hampi, VMS-35-37, the Chalukyan village of Huligi (near modern Muniribad)—all are located on or near the riverbanks. Only Kamalapuram, on the edge of the Kamalapuram reservoir, has a fairly secure temporal assignment to the Early Vijayanagara period and is not on the riverbank. With the possible exceptions of VMS-35-37 and the Chalukyan village of Huligi (the location of the Chalukyan temples), all of these settlements seem to have continued to be occupied into the later Vijayanagara periods or even to the present.

A number of settlements cannot be dated to specific portions of the Vijayanagara period. Examples include VMS-2 and VMS-101 in Block O, VMS-361 and VMS-365 in Block T, and Kadirampuram and Mallapannagudi in Blocks M and R, respectively. The latter two settlements are, however, spatially associated with dated structures. In Kadirampuram, Muslim tombs have been provisionally assigned by Michell to the fifteenth century (1985a:109). Mallapannagudi perches on the edge of a reservoir (VMS-4; Morrison 1991c) dating to A.D. 1412, which, if it also dates the town, would make it one of the very few settlements in the survey area getting its start in the fifteenth century.

The thrust of the sixteenth-century expansion of settlement in the study area was to the west of the city, although the southeastern edge of the city (in Block S) also experienced significant growth (see above). This area to the southeast of the Urban

Core walls was the only area adjacent to the city in which the expansion of urban settlement was possible without significantly encroaching on irrigated land.

Many of the "suburban" (Fritz, Michell, and Nagaraja Rao 1985) settlements in the metropolitan region were founded in the sixteenth century, as indicated both by inscriptions and by architectural style (Filliozat and Filliozat 1988; Rajasekhara 1985a), and the majority of these named and dated settlements are sprinkled along a southwest-northeast axis flanking the zone of canal irrigation. These settlements include Tirumaladeviraya-Pattana (modern Hospet) and Sale-Tirumalemaharaya-Pura (modern Anantasayanagudi [Filliozat and Filliozat 1988:13-14]).

Other portions of the study area may also have experienced settlement expansion in the sixteenth century. The Daroji Valley contains several small villages that date to the Vijayanagara period. Agriculture in this valley was supported entirely by reservoirs, wells, and dry-land features such as gravel-mulched fields and minor terraces. Agricultural facilities in the Daroji Valley were remarkably well integrated, with the excess water from one reservoir channeled into the next reservoir downstream. The largest reservoir in the system (z/1), just above (to the west of) the village of Dharmasagara is dated by an unpublished inscription to A.D. 1509. Thus, the Daroji Valley system, or at least a good part of it, appears to be a manifestation of the larger pattern of settlement expansion in the sixteenth century, and part of the move outward from the Tungabhadra River and from the locus of permanent wet cultivation. A major part of the Dhanayakanakere reservoir system also appears to date to the sixteenth century. Although this area has not yet been systematically studied, all known dated reservoirs are late, and one, at Potalakatte, has large double sluices that are believed to be late Vijayanagara in date.

It is not known whether or not the occupational histories of some or all of these sixteenth-century expansion settlements actually predate the formal founding and naming of settlements and the construction of monumental architecture, but major settlement expansion clearly took place in the mid-sixteenth century. An important future step will be to determine the relationship of local Vijayanagara area population changes to larger scale patterns from southern India. If the volume of inscriptional activity relating to agriculture is any indication of population levels (see chapter 6), then it seems that the study area (Bellary and Raichur districts) experienced a much more marked sixteenth-century expansion than did other areas of what is now Karnataka state.

AGRICULTURAL LAND USE

Zones of Land Use

It is possible to differentiate general zones of land use around the city with a fair degree of certainty. Figure 5.1 indicates the maximal distribution of areas watered by canals and reservoirs in the Vijayanagara period. This map does not show every known reservoir, as many are so small that they would appear only as a speck at this scale. Many others undoubtedly remain to be located and recorded. Further, figure 5.1 represents the combined distributions from the entire two-hundred-year occupation of the area. This temporal dimension will be addressed in more detail below and in chapter 8. A complete list of recorded facilities from the surveyed areas is given in table 5.1.

In general, wet agriculture was limited to a long and narrow strip along the banks of the Tungabhadra, as indicated by the distribution of canal irrigation. Other wet facilities included the canal-fed Kamalapuram Kere, the Bhupati Kere in the "irrigated valley" (Fritz, Michell, and Nagaraja Rao 1985) and another small canal-fed reservoir located to the north of the river, as well as the Setu aqueduct. The areas served by these wet facilities fall within the discrete zone of wet agriculture hugging the riverbanks. Although the zone of wet agriculture had localized areas that were too high or rocky to irrigate or that had dense settlements, in general areas under permanent irrigation had a continuous rather than a patchy distribution.

Wet-cum-dry agriculture, as indicated by the distribution of reservoirs (and wells, most of which are spatially associated with reservoirs), covered a much more extensive area than did wet agriculture. Unlike wet agriculture, however, wet-cum-dry production took place on isolated and discrete units of land; even the interconnected reservoirs of the Daroji Valley were separated by interstitial zones devoted to dry agriculture, grazing, and collecting.

Zones of dry agriculture are not indicated on figure 5.1. These tend to be small and scattered, and the observed distribution of dry fields and facilities probably represents just a fraction of the original dry farmed area since dry farming did not

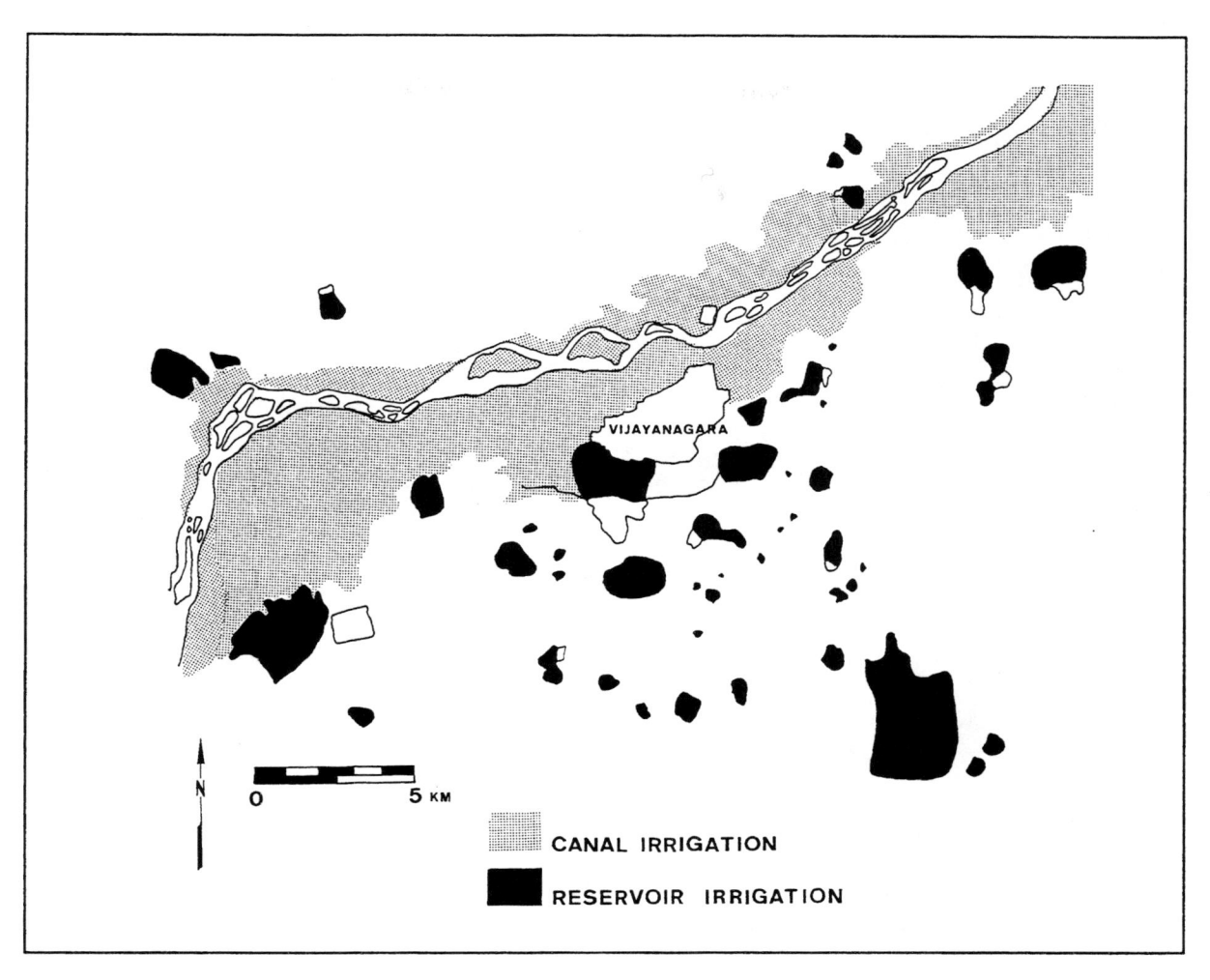

FIGURE 5.1   The Vijayanagara metropolitan area: zones of land use

necessarily result in archaeologically visible landscape modification. Several terraces covering extensive areas were located, however (see chapter 4). These dryland features were often situated near reservoirs and are interspersed between areas watered by reservoirs. Other important forms of land use included grazing of cattle, sheep, and goats; collecting of plants and firewood; and hunting. The forested Sandur Hills, immediately south of the area depicted in figure 5.1, were undoubtedly of great importance for collecting and hunting.

Relation of Settlement to Agriculture

Settlement locations are closely related to the structure of land use. The labor demands of agricultural production are a major consideration in settlement pattern, but these demands constitute only one of the many factors conditioning settlement location. The amount and timing of agricultural and other labor demands might be expected to influence the ways in which farmers situate themselves in space. In the study area, both permanent and temporary habitation sites are indicated, suggesting that although the focus of settlement was in stable, nucleated villages and towns, shorter term camps were also made by agriculturalists and others. Agriculturalists could, and almost certainly did, travel between scattered fields in several different areas and perhaps also in several different production zones. Isolated structures in agricultural areas are often referred to as "field houses." Although this term is problematic, there were certainly a range of features associated with short-term use by agriculturalists, herders, hunters, travellers, and others: shelters, sunshades, caches, caves, and

TABLE 5.1

Agricultural features from surveyed Blocks O, S, and T, and from Block N, by type.

WET FACILITIES (c = canal, a = aqueduct, r = canal-fed reservoir)

BLOCK N	BLOCK O	BLOCK S	BLOCK T
Turtha c	Turtha c	VMS-231 r	—
Bhupati r	—	—	—
Setu a	—	—	—

WET-CUM-DRY FACILITIES (r = reservoir, w = well)

BLOCK N	BLOCK O	BLOCK S	BLOCK T
NYm/14	VMS-21 r	VMS-122 r	VMS-301 r
—	VMS-40 w	VMS-125 r	VMS-302 r
—	VMS-48 r	VMS-132 r	VMS-315 r
—	VMS-59 r	VMS-136 r	VMS-319 r
—	VMS-62 r	VMS-138 r	VMS-322 r
—	VMS-72 r	VMS-150 rw	VMS-324 r
—	VMS-91 r	VMS-159 r	VMS-330 r
—	VMS-97 r	VMS-165 r	VMS-335 r
—	VMS-108 r	VMS-190 r	VMS-342 r
—	VMS-113 r	VMS-194 r	VMS-346 r
—	VMS-117 r	VMS-206 r	VMS-349 r
—	VMS-229 r	VMS-226 r	VMS-355 r
—	—	VMS-230 r	VMS-357 r
—	—	VMS-242 r	VMS-364 r
—	—	—	VMS-369 r

DRY FACILITIES (t = terraces, c = check dams, w = wall, g = gravel-mulched fields)

BLOCK N	BLOCK O	BLOCK S	BLOCK T
—	VMS-52 w	VMS-133 t	VMS-299 c
—	VMS-53 w	VMS-134 t	VMS-300 c
—	VMS-55 w	VMS-139 c	VMS-307 w
—	VMS-58 w	VMS-181 w	VMS-308 w
—	VMS-60 w	VMS-185 w	VMS-310 c
—	VMS-61 w	VMS-191 t	VMS-314 w
—	VMS-63 w	VMS-193 tc	VMS-320 w
—	VMS-82 w	VMS-198 c	VMS-323 w
—	VMS-90 w	VMS-199 tc	VMS-331 w
—	VMS-95 c	VMS-205 t	VMS-332 w
—	VMS-98 w	VMS-207 t/well	VMS-344 t
—	VMS-100 c	VMS-208 cw	VMS-347 c
—	VMS-106 w	VMS-211 t	VMS-350 w
—	—	VMS-263 tg	VMS-351 other
—	—	VMS-264 t	VMS-362 t
—	—	VMS-276 tg	VMS-363 w
—	—	VMS-280 c	—
—	—	VMS-283 c	—
—	—	VMS-287 c	—
—	—	VMS-288 w	—

rockshelters.

Archaeologically, there are consistent patterns of association between settlements and agricultural features. As noted above, much of the settlement in the area, and all of the securely dated early settlement, was situated in or near zones of wet agriculture. Villages recorded in the survey that were not adjacent to the wet agriculture zone were all associated with reservoirs. Reservoirs were important sources of domestic water supply, and the association of villages with reservoirs in South Asia has often been noted (e.g. Leach 1971). Wells also provided domestic water, however, and some densely settled portions of the city appear to have been primarily supplied by wells. Thus, the village-reservoir association may have been related to agricultural practice as well as to domestic water needs. No villages located in zones of exclusively dry agriculture have been located. The explanation for these patterns of association probably relates to the nature of labor demands in the three different forms of production (cf. Stone, Netting, and Stone 1990). Wet agriculture required not only a higher labor input overall than did dry agriculture, but the timing of labor input was also more consistent. Wet rice requires constant monitoring of water levels, as well as a high degree of investment in plowing and weeding. Sugarcane and tree crops have a longer maturation period than do the millets that made up the bulk of the dry farmed crops. Field preparation and facility maintenance may also have been more demanding in wet and wet-cum-dry production than in dry production. Thus, wet and wet-cum-dry agriculture were situated closer to settlements than were concurrently dry farmed or grazed areas used less often or less continuously.

Diversity: Forms of Production

I have discussed Vijayanagara agriculture in terms of a three-part categorization of wet, dry, and wet-cum-dry production and facilities. Notwithstanding the difficulties with this classification, such as the occurrence of forms of production that do not fit easily into a single category, the need for multiple categories highlights the diversity of Vijayanagara productive strategies. Wet, dry, and wet-cum-dry forms of production do not represent points along an evolutionary development of agricultural forms but rather different strategies of production that coexisted within a single point in time and within a single land use system. The key to understanding Vijayanagara intensification lies in understanding this mix of strategies, the organization of this mix, and its change through time.

Even within each category of production a great deal of diversity is evident, moreover. Archaeologically, this diversity is manifest in the forms and distribution of facilities. Information about less visible, but no less important, forms of diversity such as the types of cultigens grown and genetic variation in cultigens, cropping practices (field preparation, weeding, etc.), fallowing, and intercropping either must be inferred from both the archaeological distributions and from ecological knowledge about plant physiology or must be derived from some other source.

Diversity: Agricultural Facilities

As noted in the previous chapter, a great deal of diversity is apparent in agricultural facilities, diversity expressed in the form, size, degree of elaboration, placement, and mode of operation of facilities.

Canals

Formal variability in canals is evident primarily in details of construction rather than in scale. The eleventh century Chalukyan Premogal Canal takes off directly from the river without the assistance of an *anicut* or any headworks (Davison-Jenkins 1988:135). It is only about 8 kilometers long and has not been joined to any other canals. Most of the Vijayanagara canals are somewhat longer, but they do not exhibit the variability in scale that features such as reservoirs do. In part, this scalar consistency may be due to the fact that all of the Vijayanagara canals are still in use and have been subject to some modification (see Davison-Jenkins 1988; Sivamohan 1991), including the extension of some canals and the amputation of others. More important, however, in structuring this similarity were design constraints of *anicuts* and of canals and, possibly, the modes of investment and labor organization in construction.

Anicuts, or small diversion weirs, typically consisted of low masonry walls that filled in gaps between granitic boulders in the watercourse. Boulders were sometimes clamped to each other or to the wall with iron clamps (see chapter 2), and *anicuts* could also support temporary superstructures held in place with stone or iron needles (cf. Sharma and Sharma 1990). This design was well adapted to the braided and rocky course of the Tungabhadra River. Often, one or two channels of the river were blocked to support a canal, leaving other channels unmodified. Dangerous rainy-season floods could then flow down the river relatively unimpeded, causing minimal damage to canal headworks. The force of these summer floods is well illustrated by the massive bulk of the piers of the Setu aqueduct. These piers span the river near Hampi (Block N) and, in spite of their bulk, have been badly damaged by the flowing water. Thus, the rather limited extent of scalar variation in *anicuts* seems to be related primarily to the sizes and orientations of the river channels near the canal headworks. Another physical constraint on canal design is slope. Canals must flow neither too quickly nor too slowly (Sharma and Sharma 1990), and excess water must be drained off into another canal, a reservoir, or back into the river. Vijayanagara canals followed topographic contours rather closely, and where the landscape did not allow the excavation of an earthen canal at an appropriate slope, canals were either rock-cut or were artificially raised, carried by elevated earthen embankments, some faced with masonry. This hierarchy of physical constraints may have ensured that the degree of scalar variation in river-fed canals (as opposed to small inundation canals from seasonal drainage) was relatively limited.

Social and organizational issues were at least as important as construction challenges, however. Canals in the study area were often constructed under royal patronage (Stein 1980 and see chapter 6), using large groups of laborers. Because canals often crossed the boundaries of several villages and the jurisdiction of many local leaders, they required some supraordinate coordination in planning, whether that was facilitated by government bodies, temples, groups of cultivators, or some other corporate group. The organization of construction and of operation were not necessarily congruent, however, and there is little indication of any centralized control over the day-to-day operation of the canal network (Stein 1980, 1982; and see Sivamohan 1991).

Reservoirs

The diversity of form, scale, and elaboration in Vijayanagara reservoirs has been noted in the previous chapter (and see Morrison 1993). Reservoirs range widely in size, from a few meters to a few kilometers long and may also vary greatly in width and height (figure 5.2). Equally striking is the variation in degree of elaboration. Masonry facing on a reservoir may consist of unmodified boulders or of cut and even dressed stone blocks. On VMS-190, Halla Kere, stones of different colors were used in alternating rows of masonry to create a striped effect. Some embankments boast elaborate staircases or protruding slabs that serve as steps down to the water, and even support small temples or other structures. Sluices also exhibit a great deal of variability in ornamentation. The simplest form of upright sluice consists of two roughly shaped uprights with a plain lintel and lower cross-bar. The stone elements vary a great deal in the fineness of shape and in the extent of dressing. The lintel (upper cross-bar) may also consist of two parts (made of two slabs) bearing elaborate mouldings of the type found on temples, gateways, and other forms of elite architecture. Several sluices also contain carvings of gods and goddesses, particularly those associated with doorways. Sculpted figures from the survey area include Sita and Hanuman, Ganesha, and Lakshmi.

The two largest reservoirs in Daroji Valley have double sluices, with four upright posts and, instead of simply being capped by a lintel, they also sport peaked roofs. Several other sluices bear carved finials. As noted, the moderately sized Potalakatte Kere near Hospet also boasts elaborate double sluices. Some, but not all, of the decorative variation in reservoirs can be temporally ordered. For example, many of the dated, highly ornate reservoirs were constructed in the sixteenth century, but other dated late reservoirs are quite plain. The degree of reservoir elaboration is also correlated with size to a certain extent, and possibly thus with sponsorship or with mode of investment.

Reservoirs also vary in operation. Although all worked to collect and store water from seasonal runoff, some reservoirs were not designed to then distribute that water to fields below the embankment but rather to contain soil and water for cultivation in the bed (Morrison 1991b). Some contain overflow sluices or waste weirs (spillways) in addition to tunnel sluices; others have only one or the other outlet device.

Dryland Facilities

Dryland facilities vary a great deal in form, size, degree of elaboration, and degree of integration with other facilities. Dry facilities are, in fact, the most variable of the three categories and include such features as isolated erosion-control walls, check dams, terraces, gravel-mulched fields, and

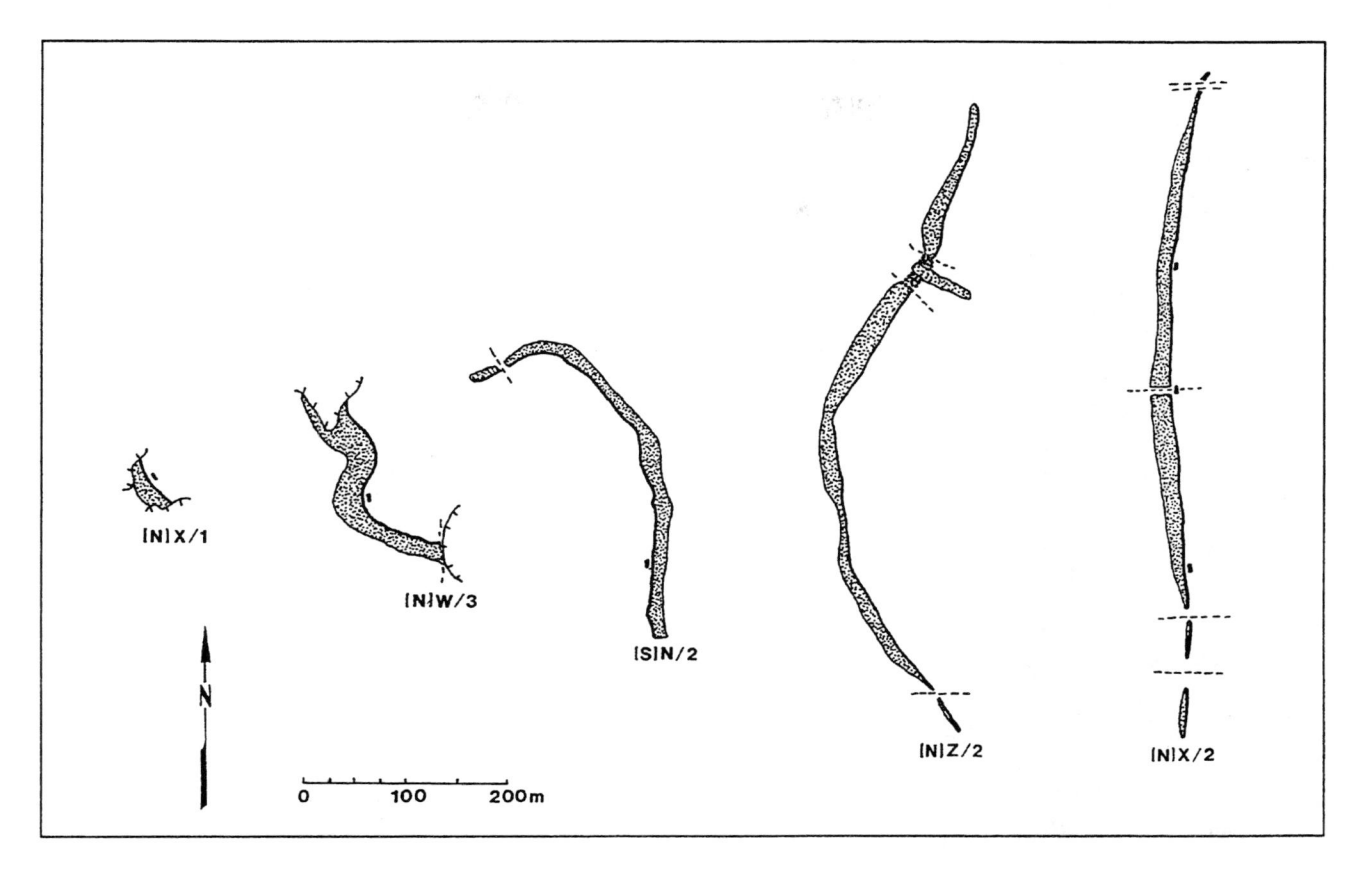

FIGURE 5.2 Selected reservoirs from the Daroji Valley

various combination of these features. Dry facilities do not appear in the inscriptional record (see chapter 6), although dry land as a category was often mentioned. Thus, it seems likely that the modes of investment in the construction and maintenance of dry facilities were quite different, at least in most cases, from those operative for wet and wet-cum-dry facilities. Further, the distribution of dry facilities (and presumably of dry farming) was extremely patchy, and, at least by the end of the period, was restricted to more marginal locales in which neither wet nor wet-cum-dry production could be successfully pursued. Dry facilities must be studied in tandem with the wet-cum-dry facilities they are so often associated with. Because terraces, check dams, and isolated walls often protected reservoirs from slopewash and rapidly moving runoff, the placement, form, and maintenance of these facilities would have been a concern to those using the reservoir even if they were not directly associated with dry-land production.

The Organization of Diversity

The way in which features in the Vijayanagara agricultural landscape actually operated was dependent upon their placement on the landscape—their relation to topography, soils, and to each other.

Topography

The topographic potentials and constraints of canal irrigation were noted above. For these and other features, distributional patterning is largely, although not entirely, explicable in terms of slope and water supply. The Tungabhadra was the only perennial source of water in the region, and thus wet facilities were all ultimately dependent upon the river. All other facilities operated in conjunction with rainfall and runoff. These facilities differed primarily in their success in capturing and storing runoff, and this in turn was dependent upon their placement in relation to potential watersheds. Large reservoirs sometimes tapped nearly the entire surface runoff of a large watershed, while small dry facilities intercepted only a tiny portion of the runoff from any particular watershed. Different watersheds also varied in terms of their reliability, based on their size, relief, and the nature of the substrate and vegetation. The interconnection of facilities was also strongly conditioned by slope. In a reservoir/terrace/well association, for example, the terraces would be placed on the slopes of the hills constituting the watershed of the reservoir, the reservoir at the base of the slope generally blocking a valley, and the well immediately beneath (downstream from) the reservoir embankment.

A striking feature of the study area is its "saturation" of agricultural facilities. It is relatively easy to predict the locations of reservoirs from topographic features. In almost every case that such informal predictions were made, there was in fact a reservoir in that location. Rocks and slope were two major impediments to agriculture outside the alluvial zone. However, a great many very small flat or open patches of soil show evidence of walls or other features associated with agriculture.

Soils

Soils in the study area, with the exception of the narrow band of alluvial soil adjacent to the Tungabhadra River, are shallow and rocky (see chapter 2). The disposition of soils in the area around the city has been greatly modified by human activity during and after the Vijayanagara period. In the city, the granitic ridges have been so heavily eroded and the valleys between them so deeply colluviated that many Vijayanagara-period temples and gateways are now almost completely buried. Further away from the city, soil movement also seems to have been a problem. Erosion control walls and terraces served, in large part, to minimize the movement of sedimentt from the rocky hillsides of watersheds into the beds of reservoirs below, where it clogged up sluices and reduced water-holding capacity. Many reservoirs seem to have been abandoned after they silted in, and nearly all abandoned reservoirs in the study area (unlike the canal system, few Vijayanagara reservoirs are still in use) show some degree of siltation. In extreme cases, sluices (which may be between 2 and 10 m high) were completely buried. Inscriptions describe the removal of silt from reservoirs as a normal maintenance operation, arranging carts for that purpose.

Canals brought, in addition to a consistent water supply, the added benefit of fertile river silt. The open design of Vijayanagara *anicuts* allowed suspended silt to flow through the canal where it could reach the fields, although *anicut* locations ensured that fast-flowing water would be avoided. Like reservoirs, canals required periodic maintenance to remove accumulated sediments and vegetation. The flow of silt-rich water through the Vijayanagara canals was reduced in the mid-twentieth century by the construction of a large dam across the Tungabhadra. Soils in the area tend to have a low overall silt content, but reservoirs created conditions for silt accumulation, and small particle sizes are differentially concentrated in and around reservoirs.

A locally important soil type found near the study area is *regur* (*regada*), or black cotton soil. This fertile soil is well suited for cotton production, as its name implies, and occurs to the east of the survey area where the landscape opens out into a broad plain. This area may have been used for large scale production of cotton, as contemporary visitors to the city observed. Although the black cotton soil tracts have not been intensively surveyed, they do not contain any large scale agricultural facilities. The flat topography severely limits the number of reservoirs that can be constructed, and wells seem to have been the most important agricultural facility in these dry farmed areas. Black cotton soil can also be found north of the study area, in the Raichur doab.

Vegetation

Vegetation cover exerts a significant effect on the hydraulic characteristics of a watershed, affecting both the amount and velocity of runoff as well as of erosion. The natural vegetation of the survey area has been greatly modified by a long history of grazing, collecting, cutting, and clearing. The pollen record (see chapter 7) indicates that deforestation had begun before or coincident with the Vijayanagara period and that the pressures exerted on regional vegetation by the demands of the large and concentrated population of the city for firewood, construction material, and animal fodder were significant. The charcoal record shows that periods of intense burning coincided with periods of open vegetation (Morrison 1994b), suggesting vegetation clearance for agriculture and grazing. This coincidence of grassy, herbaceous vegetation with increased burning no doubt led to increased problems of erosion. Without the stabilizing influence of vegetation, erosion control and siltation would have been increasingly problematic. The denudation of vegetation would also have adversely affected soil fertility on the slopes, although the fertility of colluviated valleys may actually have been enhanced.

Reduced vegetation cover also has microclimatic effects, and the loss of forest and scrub cover may have enhanced the already warm temperatures of the region. In contrast, water and dense vegetation in irrigated zones promoted cooler conditions, humidity, and created environments suitable for breeding mosquitoes. British accounts of the nineteenth century note that cultivators in the Vijayanagara canal zone did not usually live there, due to the prevalence of malaria (Kelsall 1872).

Interconnection of Facilities

I have noted in several places that the archaeological record of the Vijayanagara agricultural landscape must be considered as a whole because of the interconnection and interrelation of agricultural facilities. The material record of agricultural facilities is historically configured, so that the decisions made about agricultural production at one point in time have important consequences for those who come later. Constructed features themselves become part of the productive landscape, modifying and indeed recreating soil, slope, runoff, and vegetation conditions. The diversity of Vijayanagara agricultural strategies, involving different crops, different scales of production, and differential investment in facilities, is partly mitigated by the high degree of integration of forms of production.

The implications of this degree of interconnection are profound. Canal networks are perhaps the most common example of facility interconnection and interrelation, and discussion about the organizational problems of canals is well developed (see discussion in Hunt 1988). Hunt (1988:341) lists six "universally found work tasks" and two "commonly found" ones that are associated with canal irrigation systems, although these could apply equally well to other systems of interconnected facilities:

> construction of the physical system, capture of water from the environment, allocation of water once captured, maintenance of the physical system, conflict resolution and accounting. (Hunt 1988:341)

The "commonly found" tasks include drainage and ritual activities (Hunt 1988:341). Pest control may also be a particular concern in systems of interconnected facilities and interdependent fields. Lansing (1991) describes how large sections of wet rice land in Bali are drained at the same time in order to combat pests that posed a potential threat to the crops of all farmers. Wet rice requires special coordination, since the flow of water through the paddy must be consistently maintained. Thus, both inflow and drainage are ongoing concerns of rice farmers throughout the growing season.

It would be well to consider that interconnected facilities other than canals pose similar organizational problems. Water allocation is a concern in even isolated reservoirs. Those with rights in land underneath a particular reservoir have cause for concern when a new reservoir is constructed upstream, or when facilities upstream are not adequately maintained. It is difficult to isolate this organizational dimension from the archaeological record, and arguments about the organization of past irrigation systems generally rely on ethnographic or historic analogies. Such reliance is problematic, given the apparent absence of any universal "rule" relating system size and complexity to the nature of control over construction and allocation (Hunt 1988; Kelly 1983).

Change through Time

The archaeological record of Vijayanagara agriculture reveals a great and unexpected diversity in form and in scale not evident from the historical record. However, it is difficult to trace temporal patterns in agricultural features based solely on surface remains. Future research must be directed toward excavation and subsurface analysis of a range of agricultural features in order to provide a secure basis for chronological ordering of facilities, including small-scale and dry features that cannot otherwise be securely dated.

At present, we are reliant on the occurrence of inscriptions that date specific agricultural features or, less satisfactory, nearby settlements. As noted above, variation in the degree of ornamentation in reservoir sluices appears to be at least partly temporally ordered. "Simple" sluices, those without mouldings or with mouldings of the type termed two-stepped with angled bevel (without medallions or with medallions or half-medallions; Fritz and Morrison n.d.), occur throughout the period, but thus far all of the dated "ornate" sluices (those with more elaborate moulding styles, finials, capitals, and double sluices) can be assigned to the sixteenth century or the Late Vijayanagara period. These ornate sluices are, unfortunately, rare, and simple sluices cannot be dated on a stylistic basis. However, it is possible to date several of the major agricultural features in the survey area based on both associated inscriptions and on sluice styles.

In defining the patterns of agricultural growth

in the survey area, it has proven difficult to differentiate between fourteenth- and fifteenth-century construction within the canal zone. This confusion arises from disagreement about the association between particular historical references to canal construction (e.g. Sewell 1900:301-302, and see chapter 6) and specific canals. The Kamalapuram reservoir (VMS-231) is known to have been constructed in the fourteenth century and the Malapannagudi reservoir (VMS-4) in the fifteenth century. The pattern that emerges in the chronological ordering of agricultural facilities is strikingly similar to the pattern of settlement expansion in the region. Early facilities were differentially focused near the river, although it will be important to learn more about the specific patterns of change within this riverine area in the early time period. The sixteenth-century expansion appears to have adopted two forms. In one, facilities were built adjacent to the already existing zone of intensive, wet agriculture (and near dense settlements). The major locus of canal expansion (at least, that for which we have dates) took place on the southwestern edge of the irrigated zone, with the construction of the Basavanna Channel and the Korragal and Valabapur *anicuts* in A.D. 1521 (Kelsall 1872:231). Also in this area and near the newly founded town of Tirumaladeviraya-Pattana (Hospet), the Raya Kere was constructed in the early sixteenth century during the reign of Krishnadeva Raya. Further east, a reservoir near the modern village of Nagenahalli was constructed in A.D. 1516 (Gopal 1985a:188). This reservoir watered a small area on the edge of the canal-irrigated zone, drawing runoff from a few rocky hills that prevented the extension of canal irrigation into a small pocket of land.

Just north of the village of Hampi, the sixteenth-century Setu aqueduct carried water from the Anegundi Channel, the major channel north of the river, to a large island. No doubt this island had been cultivated before the construction of the aqueduct, but the provision of a secure supply of water to this high land in the river channel would have dramatically changed the agricultural potential of the island. The monumentality of the aqueduct in relation to the small size of the island is quite striking. Like the pocket of land served by the Nagenahalli reservoir, agricultural land in the vicinity of the city appears to have been highly valued in terms of the effort invested in its cultivation. Unfortunately, the date of the Anegundi Channel itself is not known.

The second form of sixteenth-century expansion involves a movement away from the riverine zone of wet agriculture, as indicated by the chain of reservoirs in the Daroji Valley. The wet-cum-dry agricultural production (and perhaps the associated dry fields as well) in this broad valley appears to have been an outcome of the sixteenth-century intensification process. Many other outlying reservoirs date to the sixteenth century (see chapter 6). Important among these are some or all of the reservoirs of the Dhanayakanakere system. It is not yet known if a major settlement expansion into these areas occurred at the same time, although it seems likely on present evidence.

Clearly, the most problematic temporal pattern is that of the dry facilities. Dry facilities do not appear in Vijayanagara inscriptions, although dry land does but not in sufficient quantity to analyze its temporal distribution. It is likely that dry agriculture was always important in the semi-arid Vijayanagara region, but equally likely that its importance changed through time. It may be that the spatial association of certain dryland features such as terraces with other, dated or dateable, features indicates contemporaneity. If this is the case, then the temporal pattern of dry facilities in the study area followed the same general course as that of wet-cum-dry facilities. However, it is not clear that this assumption can be supported. Additional, subsurface archaeological research is needed to clear up this issue.

Even with the relatively crude chronological control now possible, the Vijayanagara agricultural landscape shows a great deal of spatial diversity in both production strategy and production scale, and through time, both an areal expansion and an intensification of existing lands and strategies. The overall result of this pattern of change is an agricultural landscape that was at once both more intensive and more diverse. The patterns of change are complex; one type of facility was not found in the early period and another in the later period, nor was there a simple locational shift. Rather, diversity was a constant theme throughout, but the organization of that diversity was changeable. The land near the river was utilized from the start, and wet agricultural facilities such as the Kamalapuram reservoir existed from the very beginning of the period. This pattern of land use had consequences for the later inhabitants of Vijayanagara, and the decisions adopted in the fifteenth century built upon those made in the fourteenth century. By the sixteenth century, the large-scale growth in settlement and construction of monumental architecture were reflected by a dual process of agricultural growth. Land use in the wet agricultural zone near the river was intensified; small dry pockets such as that served by the Nagenahalli reservoir were brought under cultivation. The canal zone itself was extended on the southwest, and a more secure water supply was brought to the land on the island north of Hampi. Changes in practice within the wet zone cannot be discerned archaeologically (see chapter 7). Coincident with the continued focus on production in the irrigated zone was an outward expansion of wet-cum-dry production (and dry production?) as indicated by the construction of reservoirs.

Discussion

Archaeological survey in the Vijayanagara metropolitan region has revealed a degree of variation in agricultural practice in type and scale that is not indicated in any other body of information. Dry farming was carried out both on a small and a large scale, and minor wet-cum-dry facilities were extensively employed. Further, in terms of area, the extent of dry and wet-cum-dry production was much greater than that of wet production. The archaeological record of the Vijayanagara area indicates an early concentration of settlement and agriculture near the Tungabhadra River and a later expansion outward from this zone of permanent irrigation. Concurrent with this outward expansion was an intensification of land use around the edges of—and possibly within—the irrigated zone. The archaeological record provides one line of evidence into the nature of Vijayanagara land use. Additional forms of information from the historical and botanical records are considered in the next two chapters.

6

The Historical Record

THE HISTORICAL RECORD of the Vijayanagara period is both rich and diverse, but using inscriptions and documents to understand productive organization is not without difficulties. In this chapter, I discuss three classes of historical documents that relate to the written history of the Vijayanagara region: literary sources, foreign accounts, and inscriptions. For each class of document—here I use the term document to refer to any form of object bearing writing—the nature of the source and the potential information it can provide on the nature of agricultural production in the study area are considered.

Although the use of historic and ethnohistoric materials in archaeology is commonplace, it is well to consider that documents do not represent pure glimpses of historical "fact." They are consciously produced to further the goals or views of elites and are subject to considerable ideological manipulation in presentation (cf. Morrison and Lycett 1994). Anthropologists have been greatly concerned with the analysis of the production of "texts," both historical and anthropological, and the point that foreign accounts of Vijayanagara may be fraught with misunderstandings and were constructed as statements anchored in their own time and culture probably need not be made here. However, indigenous texts such as the stone and copper inscriptions of the Vijayanagara period are equally ideological statements, made by and for a specific stratum of society. Inscriptions reflect the interests and transactions of a portion of South Indian society, and as such provide only a partial view of agricultural and other activities, a view that reflected, and possibly transformed, the attitudes of the literate elite.

LITERARY SOURCES

This rather general category includes all of the non-inscriptional indigenous sources from the fourteenth through sixteenth centuries. This great corpus of material includes poems, songs, religious discourses, and accounts of the activities of great figures, both religious and political (cf. Nilakanta Sastri 1966:340-421). Many of these works were collected by British colonial administrators, such as Colonel Colin Mackenzie (Mahalingam 1940, 1951), in the later eighteenth and early nineteenth centuries. In 1919, Krishnaswami Ayyangar published a selection of this material relating to Vijayanagara history, primarily in Telugu and Sanskrit (with English summaries) in his *Sources of*

Vijayanagara History. In 1946, *Further Sources of Vijayanagara History* was published (Nilakanta Sastri and Venkataramanayya 1946), containing additional extracts (see Stein 1989:8-9 for further discussion).

Literary sources have been preserved on a variety of media, all of which are subject to decay. Thus the preservation of a palm-leaf manuscript, cloth manuscript, or other form of recording is, in part, a matter of chance. More than that, however, important texts are often transcribed over and over (or have been passed on through oral tradition), so that the extant version of a text may actually have been written hundreds of years after its putative date of origin (cf. Leach 1990). Thus, such works must be treated cautiously.

Literary Sources and Agriculture

The literary source material is of great importance for Vijayanagara history as a whole but provides little information about production, focussing instead on genealogies, military sagas, and accounts of the great deeds of patrons of the arts. When these deeds include the construction of agricultural facilities, such documents provide critical information regarding the perception of such activity as meritorious (numerous aphorisms comment on the value placed on the repair and construction of irrigation facilities). Noninscriptional accounts of agricultural patronage might also provide important cross-references to inscriptional notices of the same events. Unfortunately, it was not possible to attempt this sort of cross-reference in this study. Krishnaswami Ayyangar's English summary from the *Annals of Hande Anantapuram* illustrates an account of reservoir construction:

> While Bukka was ruling from Vidynagar [Vijayanagara], his *pradhani* or minister Chikkappa Odeyar constructed an embankment across the river [drainage?] Pandu which rises in the Kambugirisvami hills and formed a big tank [reservoir] filled with its waters in the year Krodhi corresponding to Saka 1286 [A.D. 1364/65]. This was near Devarakonda in the province of Nandela (Nandyal) south of Vidynagar. On each side of the embankment he constructed a village. (Krishnswami Ayyangar 1919:45)

This sort of account varies little from that presented in inscriptions. However, the general corpus of literary works rarely contains this kind of information (but see also Krishnaswami Ayyangar 1919:143, 339), and no attempt has been made to systematically compile such information.

FOREIGN ACCOUNTS

Southern India was a focal point in an extensive network of trade stretching from China on the east to the Mediterranean on the west, and South Indian polities, merchants, and producers were active participants in local and long distance trade. An extensive literature describes this trade and the political and social interaction it engendered (Das Gupta and Pearson 1987; Digby 1982; Mathew 1983; Pearson 1981; Subrahmanyam 1984, 1990). The accounts of foreign visitors to the city of Vijayanagara must be considered within the context of the economic, political, and social relations between Vijayanagara and observers and their countries. Visitors came as ambassadors, traders, or simply adventurers; the concerns and experiences of an ambassador may have differed from those of a horse trader, and these differences must be kept in mind.

Travellers' accounts, not just of Vijayanagara but throughout the region, are also marked by a high degree of conventionality (Pratt 1986:33-35). Certain topics are described again and again, often using the same descriptive devices. For example, the number seven, a culturally significant number for many of the visitors to the city, crops up in virtually every account of the great strength of the walled city of Vijayanagara. It has seven circuits of walls, it is seven miles in circumference, and so on. In part, this conventionality stems from the borrowing of one account from another. Thus, the traveler Nicolo di Conti described diamond mining in South India with a story familiar from another traveller's tale, that of "Sinbad the Sailor" (Sewell 1900:86). The conventionality of description extends beyond overt borrowing, however. Certain themes are repeated: the great wealth of the "Oriental" cities and potentates, the great poverty of the countryside or of the commoners, and the strangeness of indigenous customs. Travellers were generally educated and literate men. As such, they also employed the literary conventions of their day, conventions that become evident when accounts from different traditions, such as those from Europe and those from western Asia, are compared.

Many travellers' stories were written down long after the events in question and were often translated many times. In some cases the extant version is based on a retelling of the saga. Travellers also may also have lacked facility with local languages, making their observations idiosyncratic and depriving them, in many cases, of the ability to cross-check information given to them. Finally, the obvious cultural differences between the observer and the observed may have resulted in many fundamental misunderstandings. This issue lies behind all of the efforts to discern Vijayanagara political economy based on such accounts (cf. Inden 1990; Stein 1989), and is of great importance in interpreting travellers' tales as culturally constructed texts. On a more basic level, this difference in cultural knowledge also resulted in some misidentifications. For example, both Portuguese visitors to Vijayanagara mention the presence of Indian-corn growing in fields around the city, presumably *Zea mays*. It is possible that corn was growing in the area in the early sixteenth century but much more likely that the Portuguese observed *Sorghum* (*Jowar* or *Cholum*), an important dryland grain. Sorghum plants look remarkably like corn plants, even from a relatively short distance away.

In the following sections, I mention a few of the visitors to the city of Vijayanagara and relate some of what they said about agricultural production. Like the literary evidence, the nonindigenous historical sources are extremely important to understanding Vijayanagara history. However, like the literary sources, this corpus of data is primarily anecdotal. It provides interesting and important glimpses into the Vijayanagara period but is difficult to analyze systematically. For this reason and because the existing historical literature contains extensive discussions of this material (Mahalingam 1940, 1951; Sewell 1900; Stein 1980, 1989), I do not cover it in great detail. Every foreign account of Vijayanagara cannot be covered here. For example, the accounts of Ibn Battuta in the fifteenth century (Major 1857) and of Fray Luis (Loschorn 1985) in the sixteenth century are not included.

Nicolo di Conti

Nicolo di Conti was an Italian traveller who visited the city of Vijayanagara during the reign of Devaraya II, in about A.D. 1420 or 1421. His narrative was recorded in Latin by a secretary of the pope (Sewell 1900:81) and was published only in 1723. Thus, Conti's account was actually written by someone else and was recorded some time after he returned home to Europe. Conti provided some description of the city and of its people, describing the city as large and well fortified, containing "ninety thousand men fit to bear arms" (Sewell 1900:82). After discussing the activities that took place at various festivals, he moved on to such diverse topics as diamond mining and the zodiac.

Although Conti's account is interesting in that it portrays the Vijayanagara region as densely populated, it contains little information about agriculture or land use.

Abdur-Razzaq

Kamaluddin Abdur-Razzak Samarqandi (Thackston 1989), an ambassador from Persia to Calicut, was summoned to the court of Devaraya II at Vijayanagara. Abdur-Razzak visited India between A.D. 1442 and 1445. He described the city of Vijayanagara as being of "enormous magnitude and population with a king of perfect rule and hegemony" (Thackston 1989:307) and mentioned the existence of seven concentric rings of fortification. The only overt mention of fields is found in Abdur-Razzak's comment on the structure of the fortified zones:

> Between the first, second, and third walls are orchards, gardens, and buildings. From the third through the seventh is very crowded, with shops and bazaars. (Thackston 1989:308)

Ludovico di Varthema

An Italian traveler, Ludovico di Varthema, left a lengthy account of people and places in South Asia in the beginning of the sixteenth century. Neither Varthema's profession nor his purpose for travelling are known, and doubts have been cast on the verity of his account—in particular on his descriptions of the east coast of India and beyond into Southeast Asia (Temple 1928:xxi). There appears to be no doubt, however, that Varthema spent some time in Calicut and made shorter trips to other cities in western and interior South Asia. Between 1502 and 1508, Varthema visited Vijayanagara, about which he had relatively little to say. He was particularly impressed by the use of elephants in warfare (Temple 1928:51) and was interested in military matters in general. Of the city and surrounding countryside, Varthema said only:

> The said city of Bisnegar belongs to the king of Narsingha [Vijayanagara, after the name of the king, Narasimha], and is very large and strongly walled. It is situated on the side of a mountain, and is seven miles in circumference. It has a triple circuit of walls. It is a place of great merchandise, is extremely fertile, and is endowed with all possible kinds of delicacies. (Temple 1928:51)

Duarte Barbosa

In 1524, a Portuguese manuscript describing the coasts of East Africa and western India was translated into Spanish by Martin Centurion and Diego Ribero (Stanley 1867:*i*). This Spanish edition was then translated into Italian and published in 1554 by Ramusio (Stanley 1867:*iv*), who was the first to attribute authorship of the piece to Duarte Barbosa, a cousin of Magellan and employee of the Portuguese government in India who was known to have lived for several years on the Malabar coast and to have spoken the local language. Whether or not the author of this account actually was Barbosa or not, it does provide some interesting descriptions of India and of Vijayanagara in the period between approximately A.D. 1510 and 1514.

Like many other visitors to the city, Barbosa began his trip on the west coast and journeyed inland, crossing the Western Ghats, noting:

> After passing this mountain range, the country is almost entirely plain, very fertile and abundantly supplied in the inland districts, which belong to the kingdom of Narsinga, in which there are many cities and villages and forts, and many large rivers run through it. There is in the country much cultivation of rice and other vegetables, with which they maintain themselves, and many cows, buffaloes, pigs, sheep, asses, and diminutive ponies . . . (Stanley 1867:85)

Barbosa's description of the city of Vijayanagara is extensive and eclectic, containing a great deal of detail on the appearance and dress of the inhabitants of the city. He had little to say about agriculture or vegetation, though he did note the presence of gardens inside the city:

> Forty-five leagues from these mountains [the Western Ghats] inland, there is a very large city which is called Bijanaguer, very populous and surrounded on one side by a very good wall and on another by a river, and on the other by a mountain . . . [The king] has in this place very large and handsome palaces, with numerous courts in which there are many mounds, pools of water with plenty of fish, gardens of shrubs, flowers, and sweet-smelling herbs. There are also in the city many other palaces of great lords who live there. And all the other houses of the place are covered with thatch. (Stanley 1867:85)

Domingo Paes

Domingo Paes was a Portuguese horse trader who visited Vijayanagara, probably several times, between the period 1520 to 1522. The reigning king was Krishnadeva Raya. Paes's account of the city and of the area around it is one of the longest and most detailed that remains and was written in India. Paes had a great deal to say about the city, but I will focus here on the descriptions of agriculture and of agricultural facilities.

Forests and Fields

On his way to Vijayanagara from the west coast Paes noticed many cities and walled villages (Sewell 1900:237, 242). Of the kingdom as a whole he noted:

> These dominions are very well-cultivated and very fertile, and are provided with quantities of cattle, such as cows, buffaloes, and sheep . . . The land has plenty of rice and Indian-corn, grains, beans and other kind of crops which are not sown in our parts; also an infinity of cotton. Of the grains there is a great quantity, because besides being used as food for men, it is also used for horses, since there is no other kind of barley; and this country has much wheat, and that good. (Sewell 1900:237)

Paes began his description of the city with an account of the fortifications that block strategic passes along the road to the city, describing several zones of encircling hills and fortifications:

> Between all these enclosures are plains and valleys where rice is grown, and there are gardens with many orange trees, limes, citrons, and radishes (rabaos), and other kinds of garden produce as in Portugal, only not lettuces or cabbages. Between these hill ranges are many lakes by which they irrigate the crops mentioned and amongst all these ranges there are no forests or patches of brushwood, except very small ones, nor anything that is green. (Sewell 1900:243)

Several interesting points are raised by this description. First of all, it indicates that fortified areas did contain agricultural fields as well as settlement, a pattern also indicated by the survey results. The association of reservoirs with garden crops such as vegetables that are water and labor intensive is also notable. As Paes travelled through the Vijayanagara region from the west, he would have passed through or near areas watered by canals, although he does not mention these. Several large reservoirs were located between Hospet and Vijayanagara, on or near the main road. These include VMS-4, the Malapannagudi reservoir, and VMS-231, the Kamalapuram reservoir (canal-fed), among others. These "inner" reservoirs (located close to the wet agriculture zone) would also have been important as domestic water sources, and their proximity to densely settled areas and urban markets may have made them attractive for production of garden crops (perhaps with supplemental well irrigation for the runoff-fed reservoirs).

Finally, the sparse natural vegetation noticed by Paes contrasts sharply with his characterization of agricultural fields. Fields are seen as rich and green; other vegetation as brown and bare. This view is borne out by the pollen evidence from the Kamalapuram reservoir (see chapter 7), in which trees and shrubs comprise a very small portion of the pollen record.

Reservoirs

Paes was struck by the relative dryness of the interior plateau compared to Portuguese Goa (on the west coast). Within the first few pages of his narrative, Paes has mentioned both the importance of reservoirs and their insecurity of supply:

> This country wants water because it is very great and has few streams; they make lakes in which water collects when it rains and thereby maintain themselves. They maintain themselves by means of some in which there are springs better than by others that have only the water from rain; for we find many quite dry, so that people go about walking in their beds, and dig holes to try and find enough water, even a little, for their maintenance. The failure of the water is because they have no winter, as in our parts and in India [Portuguese Goa], but only thunderstorms that are greater in one part of the year than in another. The water in these lakes is for the most part muddy . . . (Sewell 1900:238)

That runoff-fed reservoirs were observed by Paes to be ubiquitous, and yet very uncertain sources of water, confirms contemporary and archaeological observations of reservoirs.

Perhaps the most widely quoted sections of Paes's narrative that relate to agriculture are those relating to the large reservoir known as Rayakere located near Hospet (for a brief description of this reservoir see Davison-Jenkins 1988). Nuniz also discussed this reservoir, and the two accounts may profitably be compared (see below). According to Paes:

> Besides this the king made a tank [reservoir] there, which, as it seems to me, has the width of a falcon-shot [a type of artillery, according to Sewell 1900:244] and it is at the mouth of two hills, so that all the water which comes from either one side or the other collects there and, besides this, water comes to it from more than three leagues by pipes which run along the lower parts of the range outside. This water is brought from a lake which itself overflows into a little river. This tank has three large pillars handsomely carved with figures; these connect above with certain pipes by which they get water when they have to irrigate their gardens and rice-fields. In order to make this tank the said king [Krishnadeva Raya] broke down a hill which enclosed the ground occupied by the said tank. In the tank I saw so many people at work that there must have been fifteen or twenty thousand men, looking like ants, so that you could not see the ground on which they walked so many there were; this tank the king portioned out amongst his captains, each of whom had the duty of seeing that the people placed under him did their work, and that the tank was finished and brought to completion. (Sewell 1900:244-45)

Paes went on to describe how the reservoir "burst two or three times" (Sewell 1900:245), and how the king was advised by Brahmans to make a sacrifice. This sacrifice is said to have consisted of the heads of sixty men as well as an unspecified number of horses and buffaloes (Sewell 1900:245).

Paes's description of what is probably Rayakere raises several issues. This reservoir, while not the longest in the study area, is certainly the tallest (about 22 meters high). However, even though it has not been breached, it holds no more than a meter of water in the rainy season, nor did it operate effectively in the Colonial period (Kelsall 1872:16-17). Water apparently percolates quickly through the soft soil beneath the embankment, so that no water is available to be distributed to fields below. Paes notes the "bursting" of the reservoir; this generally is a problem related to water flowing into the facility at too great a velocity or in too great a quantity for the strength of the embankment. Paes apparently did not remain in the area long enough to observe the operation of the reservoir, but this apparent anomaly must be noted.

The placement of the reservoir to capture runoff from the two hills was aptly described, but Paes's comments on a supplemental source of water are interesting and, as far as I can tell, have never been taken seriously as a factual account. Upstream from the Rayakere, near Rajapura, is another smaller reservoir, now breached. To the west of the narrow valley dammed by the Rayakere embankment is a complex system of interconnected reservoirs, what I have called the Dhanayakanakere system after the largest reservoir in the group. The pipes Paes described as bringing supplemental water into the Rayakere may have allowed the reservoir to fill sufficiently for distribution to fields below. These pipes are noted to come from more than three leagues away, "along the lower part of the range outside." This phrase could mean many things. The pipes could have run along the base of the hills "outside" the reservoir, but inside the valley (perhaps from the Rajapura reservoir), or along the base of the hills "outside" the valley (perhaps from the Dhanayakanakere system). No traces of pipes are visible today. Clay pipes were used extensively in Vijayanagara structures, as were copper pipes, but the latter have all been removed for scrap. In general, it is difficult to try and interpret travellers accounts such as Paes's as literal, accounts of historical "fact," but in this situation it is tempting to suggest that the high degree of investment in the reservoir and its proximity and importance to the growing city of Hospet (Nagalapura, according to Sewell 1900:162 or Tirumaladeviyara-Pattana, according to Filliozat and Filliozat 1988:13) made it necessary to ensure its supply at whatever cost.

Fernao Nuniz

Fernao Nuniz was another Portuguese horsetrader who spent several years in the city of Vijayanagara. Nuniz visited the city between about A.D. 1535 and 1537, only fifteen years or so after Paes. Nuniz's account contains a long history of Vijayanagara and its kings; this secondary material appears to be mixed in with observations Nuniz made himself.

Both Paes and Nuniz commented on the types of crops grown in the region and on the number and variety of items they saw for sale in the market. These observations are compiled in table 6.1. Of the area outside (between?) Hospet and Vijayanagara, Nuniz wrote: "Outside these two cities are fields and places richly cultivated with wheat and gram and rice and millet, for this last is the grain most consumed in the land." (Sewell 1900:366)

Reservoirs

Nuniz wrote an account of the construction of a reservoir that most analysts have assumed is Rayakere, the same reservoir described by Paes:

> This King [Krishnadeva Raya] also made in his time a lake for water, which lies between two very lofty *serras*. But since he had no means in the country for making it, nor any one who could do it he sent to Goa to ask the governor to send some Portuguese masons . . . (Sewell 1900:364-65)

This account may be fanciful, since reservoir-building was clearly not unknown to Vijayanagara engineers. Nuniz describes (Sewell 1900:364) how the Portuguese engineer asked for lime but was told that lime was not known about or used. In fact, lime was used extensively in plaster and for other purposes, though generally not in reservoirs. Nuniz went on to describe the construction problems of the reservoir, problems that now have taken on an almost mythic quality:

> The King commanded to throw down quantities of stone and cast down many great rocks into the valley but everything fell to pieces, so that all the work done in the day was destroyed each night. (Sewell 1900:365)

The requisite sacrifices were made, and "with this, the work advanced" (Sewell 1900:365).
The reservoir itself seems to have operated well enough to produce revenue:

> He [the king] made a bank across the middle of the valley so lofty and wide that it was a crossbow-shot in breadth and length, and had large openings [*espacos*, perhaps sluices]; and below it he put pipes by which the water escaped, and when they wish to do so they close these. By means of this water they made many improvements in the city, and many channels by which they irrigated rice-fields and gardens, and in order that they might improve their lands he gave the people the lands which are irrigated by this water free for nine years until they had made their improvements, so that the revenue already amounts to 20,000 *pardaos* [a type of gold coin]. (Sewell 1900:365)

Nuniz's account shifts to the present tense at this point, describing the fortifications around the reservoir, perhaps indicating that he had seen the reservoir itself. Although the story of construction problems and subsequent sacrifices was included by Nuniz, he never suggested that the reservoir did not function.

The similarities between Paes's and Nuniz's stories are worth noting. Both describe the length of the reservoir in terms of the range of a projectile. Whether this indicates borrowing or simply shared descriptive devices is not clear.

Caesaro Federici

Caesaro Federici, an Italian merchant dealing in horses, visited the city of Vijayanagara in A.D. 1567, shortly after the disastrous battle of Talikota in 1565. Federici stayed in the city for seven months, attempting to collect payment for some horses that the retreating court "purchased" but never paid for (Wheeler 1974:136-37). Thus, although the city had been sacked and looted, it must not have been completely depopulated.

TABLE 6.1 Plants identified by Paes and Nuniz in the vicinity of Vijayanagara (data from Sewell 1900)

DOMINGO PAES (1520-1522)		
rice	cotton	oranges
"grains"	betel	limes
Indian-corn	cloves	grapes
horse-gram	mangos	pomegranates
mung	jackfruit	roses
wheat	lemons	grass and straw

FERNAO NUNIZ (1535-1537)		
rice	"oil seeds"	mangos
"grains"	gingelly	jackfruit
millet	cotton	citrons
Indian-corn	betel	oranges
gram	areca	limes
mung	herbs	tamarind
pulses	beans	pomegranate
wheat	brinjals	grapes
barley	radishes	roses

Federici must have had some reason for staying; presumably he believed it would still be possible to obtain payment. Indeed, there were several (unsuccessful) attempts by Arividu kings to resettle the city. He described the state of the city:

> The city of Bezeneger is not altogether destroyed, yet the houses stand still, but emptie, and there is dwelling in them nothing, as is reported, but Tygres and other wild beasts. (cited in Loschhorn 1985:349)

INSCRIPTIONS

The most extensive source of historical information on the Vijayanagara period is the inscriptional record. Contemporary inscriptions were generally made either in stone or on copper plates and refer primarily to what may be called ritual/economic transactions. The most abundant category of inscription is that recording grants to temples, as discussed in chapter 2. However, it would be misleading to characterize all inscriptions as records of temple donations or of other donations. Inscriptions can be thought of as public or private announcements of agreements and transactions (and, rarely, of events). Such agreements included gifts or donations, sales, tax remissions, and exchanges of goods and services. Stone inscriptions are often found in association with temples or on boulders, reservoir sluices, or other public places. In contrast, copper plate inscriptions were portable and probably represented more private records.

QUANTITATIVE ANALYSIS

The Inscriptional Data Base

In the following sections I present an analysis of Vijayanagara-period inscriptions based on a data base of 1538 inscriptions from eleven districts in Karnataka in order to isolate trends in agricultural land use and investment. The complete data base is contained in Morrison (1992).

The inscriptional data base constitutes only a sample of the known inscriptions from the Vijayanagara period. Because inscriptions are published in many different serial and occasional publications, Vijayanagara inscriptions may be found scattered throughout a large body of published work. Unpublished inscriptions are also numerous. Thus, it should be emphasized that the inscriptional data base does not constitute a complete set of inscriptions, or even of published inscriptions from each district in the data base. The principal sources used in the compilation of the data base were Gopal (1985a, 1985b, 1990), Nagaraja Rao, ed. (1983, 1985), Patil (1991a), Patil and Balasubramanya (1991), and an unpublished compilation of inscriptions generously provided by Dr. C. S. Patil of the Directorate of Archaeology and Museums, Karnataka.

Coding

In order to facilitate comparison of a large number of inscriptions, it was necessary to reduce each inscription to a series of coded categories in the data base. Naturally, a great deal of information contained in each inscription is lost in the process. However, the large-scale comparisons made possible by quantitative analysis do provide important adjuncts to the study of individual inscriptions, revealing the timing and tempo of change as well as its form.

The full text of the data base codes is given in table 6.2. Most inscriptions were carved either in stone or copper; a few were found on wooden doors or in other unusual proveniences. Both the language and script of each inscription was coded.

The calendric system used in southern India in the Vijayanagara period differs from the European system in that the cycle of Saka years does not correspond exactly with years A.D. In most cases, sufficient detailed astronomic information is given to allow epigraphers to convert the date precisely into day, month, and year A.D. In a few cases where these astronomical data were not present, or where the inscription was damaged, the *Saka* year could only be converted to a range of years A.D. (eg. 1546-1547). In these situations, the year A.D. was recorded as the first year in the series. The month was recorded whenever possible in order to determine if there were seasonal patterns in inscriptions. No such seasonal pattern could be discerned, either for all inscriptions or for agricultural inscriptions.

TABLE 6.2 Inscriptional Data Base Reference Codes

1. Published Reference.
   KN = B. R. Gopal
   ARE = Annual Report of Epigraphy, ASI
   ARIE = Annual Report of Indian Epigraphy
   ARSIE = Annual Report of South Indian Epigraphy

2. Form of Inscription.
   1 = Stone
   2 = Copper
   3 = Wooden door/other

3. Language of Inscription.
   1 = Sanskrit
   2 = Kannada
   3 = Telugu
   4 = Tamil
   5 = Marathi
   6 = Kannada and Sanskrit
   7 = Kannada and Telugu
   8 = Sanskrit and Telugu
   9 = Persian

4. Script of Inscription.
   1 = Nagari
   2 = Kannada
   3 = Telugu
   4 = Tamil
   5 = Tamil and Grantha
   6 = Grantha
   7 = Grantha, Tamil, and Kannada/Nagari & Telugu
   8 = Kannada and Nagari

5. Date of Inscription: Year (years A.D.).

6. Date of Inscription: Month.
   0 = unknown
   1 = January
   2 = February
   3 = March
   4 = April
   5 = May
   6 = June
   7 = July

con't.

table 6.2 con't.

8 = August
9 = September
10 = October
11 = November
12 = December

7. Location of Inscription: District.
    1 = Bellary
    2 = Raichur
    3 = Kolar
    4 = Chitradurga
    5 = Hassan
    6 = Chikmagalur
    7 = Mandya
    8 = Dharwad
    9 = Tumkur
    10 = Bangalore
    11 = Shimoga

8. Location of Inscription: Taluk.
    1 = Bellary
    2 = Harapanahalli
    3 = Hospet
    4 = Kudligi
    5 = Sandur
    6 = Siruguppa
    7 = Hadagalli
    8 = HGB
    9 = Shrihatti
    11 = Gangawati
    12 = Koppal
    13 = Lingasur
    14 = Raichur
    15 = Yalibargi
    16 = Kushtagi
    17 = Manvi
    20 = Bagepalli
    21 = Bangarapete
    22 = Chikballapur
    23 = Chintamani
    24 = Gauribanda
    25 = Gudibande
    26 = Kolar
    27 = Malur
    28 = Mulbagal
    29 = Sidlaghatta
    30 = Srinivasapura
    40 = Challakere
    41 = Chitradurga
    42 = Davanagere
    43 = Harihara
    44 = Hiriyur
    45 = Holakere
    46 = Hosadurga
    47 = Jagalur

    48 = Molakalmuru
    50 = Alluru
    51 = Arakalagud
    52 = Arasikere
    53 = Beluru
    54 = Channagigapattana
    55 = Hotenarasipura
    56 = Manjarabab
    60 = Chikkamagalur
    61 = Koppa
    62 = Mudagere
    63 = Narasimharajapura
    64 = Srinigeri
    65 = Tarikere
    66 = Krishnarajapete
    67 = Maddur
    68 = Magavalli
    69 = Mandya
    70 = Nagamangara
    71 = Pandavapura
    72 = Srirangapattana
    73 = Bankapura
    74 = Byadagi
    75 = Dharwar
    76 = Gadag
    77 = Hangal
    78 = Haveri
    79 = Hirekerur
    80 = Hubli
    81 = Kundgol
    82 = Naragund
    83 = Navalgund
    84 = Ranibennur
    85 = Ron
    86 = Chikkanayakanahalli
    87 = Gubbi
    88 = Kunigal
    89 = Madugiri
    90 = Ravugaga
    91 = Sika
    92 = Tipatur
    93 = Tumakuru
    94 = Anekal
    95 = Bangalore
    96 = Channapattana
    97 = Devanahalli
    98 = Doddaballapura
    99 = Hosakote
    100 = Kanakapura
    101 = Magadi
    102 = Nelamangala

9. Location of Inscription: Village.

table 6.2 con't.

10. Dynasty.
- 1 = Sangam
- 2 = Saluva
- 3 = Tuluva
- 4 = Arividu

11. King.
- 1 = Harihara I
- 2 = Bukka I
- 3 = Bukka II
- 4 = Harihara II
- 5 = Devaraya I
- 6 = Bukka III/Vijayaraya I
- 7 = Harihara III
- 8 = Devaraya II
- 9 = Devaraya III
- 10 = Virupaksha
- 11 = Narasimha I
- 12 = Narasimha II (Immadi)
- 13 = Vira Narasimha (III)
- 14 = Krishnadeva Raya
- 15 = Achyuta Raya
- 16 = Sadasivaraya
- 17 = Ramaraya/Aliya Ramaraya
- 18 = Venkata(pati) II
- 19 = Venkatadeva I
- 20 = Kampana (Sangama)
- 21 = Praudhadeva Raya (Sangam)
- 22 = Narasa Nayaka (Tuluva)
- 23 = Ramadevaraja (Arividu)
- 24 = Venkatapatiraya I
- 25 = Sriranga I
- 26 = Mallikarjuna (Sangam)
- 27 = Venkatapatiraya IV
- 28 = Timmarakayya (Tuluva)
- 29 = Tirumaladeva (Tuluva)
- 30 = Savamanna Vodeya (Sangam)
- 31 = Ramachandra Raya
- 32 = Venkatesha
- 33 = Jommana Udaiyar, son of Kampana
- 34 = Vira Bukka Bhupati and Devaraya (Sangam)
- 35 = Sriranga III (& 39)
- 36 = sons of Bukka I
- 37 = Tirumala (brother of Ramaraja)
- 38 = sons of Vira Harihara
- 40 = Sriranga IV
- 50 = Ibrahim Adil Shahi II
- 96 = unspecified Devaraya
- 97 = a *Mahamandaleshwara*
- 98 = unspecified Bukka
- 99 = unspecified Harihara

12. Donor.
- 1 = king
- 2 = member of royal family
- 3 = temple/god
- 4 = nayaka/local elite/chief
- 5 = merchant/commercial group
- 6 = villager/nattar/nattavar
- 7 = officer
- 8 = brahmin(s)/agrahara/matha
- 9 = individual
- 0 = unknown

13. Donee. Same codes as donor.

14. First gift/grant mentioned in inscription.
- 1 = gift of village
- 2 = gift of land
- 3 = gift of wet land
- 4 = construction of reservoir (or gift of)
- 5 = maintenance of reservoir
- 6 = construction of canal
- 7 = maintenance of canal
- 8 = tax remission
- 9 = nonagricultural
- 10 = commercial agreement
- 11 = meligolaga rights
- 12 = cash gift for agriculture
- 13 = land transfer
- 14 = land reclamation
- 15 = land below a reservoir
- 16 = gift of office
- 17 = gift of money income
- 18 = gift of dry land
- 19 = founding of village
- 20 = land below a canal
- 00 = unknown

15. Second gift/grant mentioned in inscription. Same as first gift.

16. Condition of Inscription.
- 1 = good
- 2 = damaged/incomplete
- 3 = heavily damaged

15. Association. Where the inscription is located.
- 1 = on or near temple
- 2 = on other structure
- 3 = sculpture or architectural element
- 4 = on or near tank
- 5 = on or near canal
- 6 = in field/outside of village
- 7 = on portable medium
- 8 = within village
- 9 = on or near well

All inscriptions in the data base are located in Karnataka state (see figure 6.1). Within the state, data from eleven different districts were coded. Locational information recorded includes the district, taluk (a subdivision of district), village (name of the nearest settlement), and the subject location, or the smallest named unit of space (village or territorial unit) referred to in the inscription. In many cases, the modern settlements have retained the names of the Vijayanagara-period settlements.

The dynasty and name of the king mentioned in the inscription were also recorded. For the purposes of this analysis, kings were used as supplemental indicators of temporal affiliation. Inscriptions in which no year was given and no king indicated were deleted from the data base. Inscriptions without years but with the name of a king and dynasty were assigned a year on the basis of the mean regnal date for that king, using dynastic data from Nilakanta Sastri (1966; see table 3.1). In all, eighty-seven inscriptions were dated in this way. Only inscriptions dating to between A.D. 1300 and A.D. 1700 were coded. No inscriptions listing Vijayanagara kings (or future kings) occur before A.D. 1300, and although a few post-1700 inscriptions claiming Vijayanagara affiliation do occur, the political situation in Karnataka had become quite complex by this time making the year 1700 a convenient termination point.

The same codes were used for both donor and donee. Donors and donees are usually mentioned by name, and the names of parents and grandparents (usually father and grandfather) are also often noted, as well as any title held by the donor. In many cases, it was not possible to assign the donor or donee to one of the functional classes in the data base. In these cases he or she was simply described as an "individual." This uncertainty has certainly resulted in an undernumeration of certain types of donors, but there is no reason to believe that this undernumeration is differentially concentrated in any single category. Some inscriptions also refer to multiple donors. Unfortunately, multiple donor inscriptions first appeared only after the structure of the analysis had been set, and multiple donors were coded according to the first donor mentioned. The practical result of this decision is that villagers and village assemblies are slightly under-represented, since they sometimes were involved in transactions with local elites, whose names were invariably mentioned first.

The category of gift or grant also includes what may be better termed transactions. Although the majority of the coded inscriptions do refer to gifts or grants, some also relate to transfers of land or other property, or to commercial or other agreements. Many inscriptions referred to multiple grants, and two variables, "gift 1" and "gift 2", were coded. In a few cases, more than two grants were made. In these instances only the first two were coded.

The final category coded is association, which refers to the context of the inscription. Because many of the inscriptions were published without adequate contextual information, the value of this variable could not always be determined.

ANALYSIS

All Inscriptions: Subject

Figure 6.2 shows the distribution of grants (category "grant 1") across the entire data base. The most common grant mentioned in the inscriptional data base is the grant of a village, labelled in figure 6.2 as "income." Villages appear to have had specifically demarcated territories and to have been associated with specific hamlets or subsidiary settlements. In the Vijayanagara period, villages rather than the larger territorial unit, the *nadu*, appear most often as the objects of transactions. Grants of villages refer not to the actual physical territory of the village, but to rights in income or income shares, from various taxes on the village, of which the most important were agricultural levies (cf. Neale 1979). Stein notes:

> Vijayanagara inscriptions are concerned with new and public claims upon shares of village income. To be stressed here is that the 'rights in land' always refer to shares in income, not 'dominion in land,' and that in many cases such shares have always existed but were not before given the public and formal status achieved in the fifteenth and sixteenth centuries. (1980:421)

The second most common category of grant, labelled as "other," is nonagricultural. These grants refer to a variety of activities such as the construction of temples, maths, rest-houses, or other structures; gifts of lamps, money, and other things to temples; or to the bestowing of titles, rights, or tax remissions not related to agricultural production.

Grants of land are the third most common topic of the coded inscriptions, followed by the construction of agricultural facilities, and the expansion or establishment of new settlements. The

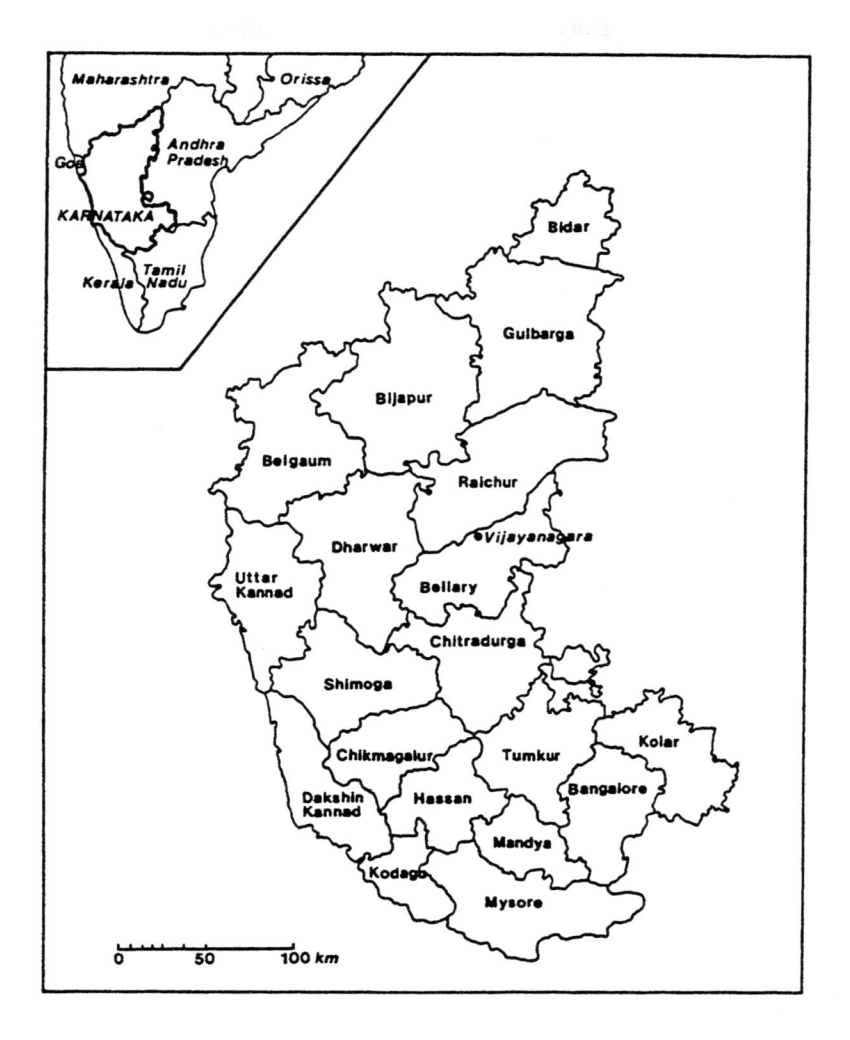

FIGURE 6.1   Districts of the state of Karnataka

subject of some damaged inscriptions could not be discerned; these were coded as unknown. Land grants may be divided by types of cultivation; in figure 6.2 they are taken as a whole. Several inscriptions refer to the construction of agricultural facilities or to arrangements made for their maintenance. In figure 6.2, the category labelled "settlement" includes the clearing of new agricultural land and the establishment of new settlements as well as the resettlement of deserted villages and the reclamation of land for agriculture.

Most inscriptions recorded only one gift, as indicated in figure 6.3. In general, however, the distribution of second gifts follows that of first gifts, at least in overall frequencies. Thus, it is clear that the subject matter of inscriptions relates overwhelmingly to transactions involving agriculture—land, income from land, the construction and maintenance of agricultural facilities, and the clearing of new agricultural land. In the following sections I will disaggregate this distribution by time, district, and topic.

All Inscriptions: Temporal Distribution

Figure 6.4 shows the overall temporal distribution of inscriptions in the data base. The distribution is bimodal, with a lower and more temporally diffuse peak centered around the beginning of the fifteenth century and a higher, more focussed peak in the early to middle sixteenth century. The overall distribution of inscriptions by time, or the rate of inscriptional activity, can stand as a proxy

122   *Fields of Victory*

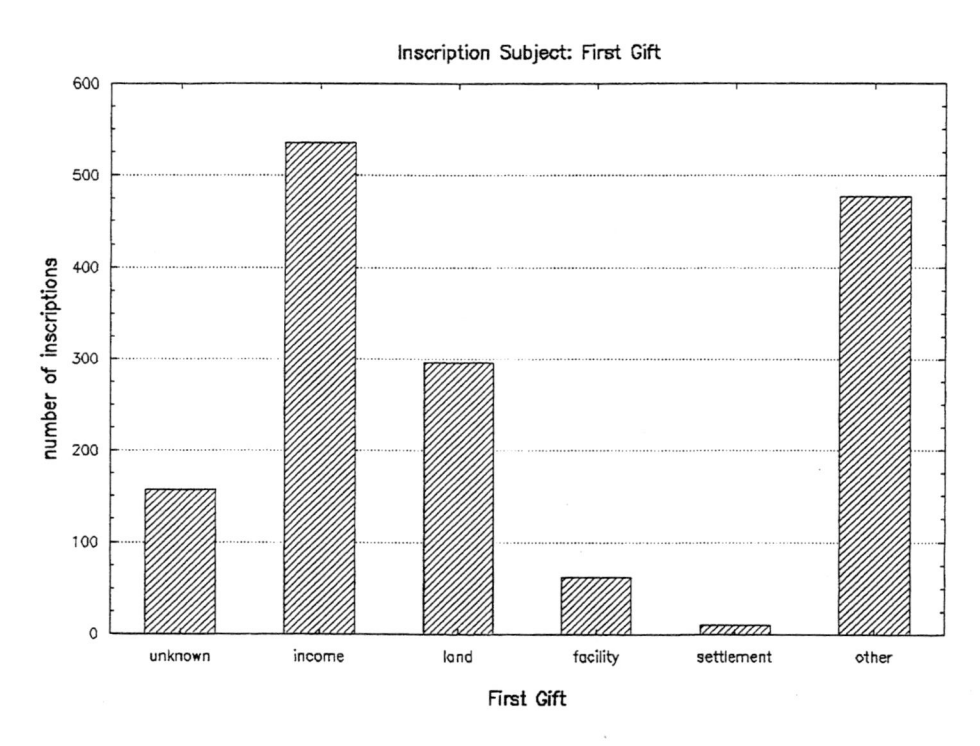

FIGURE 6.2   Major categories of first gift noted in inscriptions, all districts

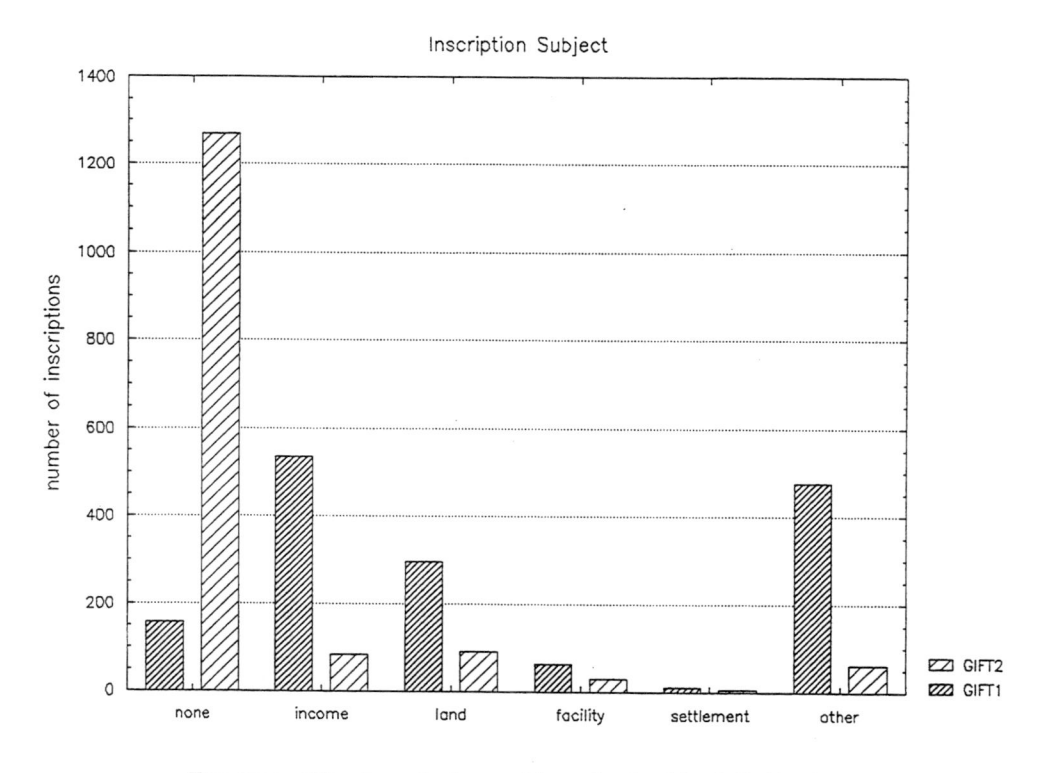

FIGURE 6.3   Inscription subject, both gifts (all districts)

Temporal Distribution of Inscriptions

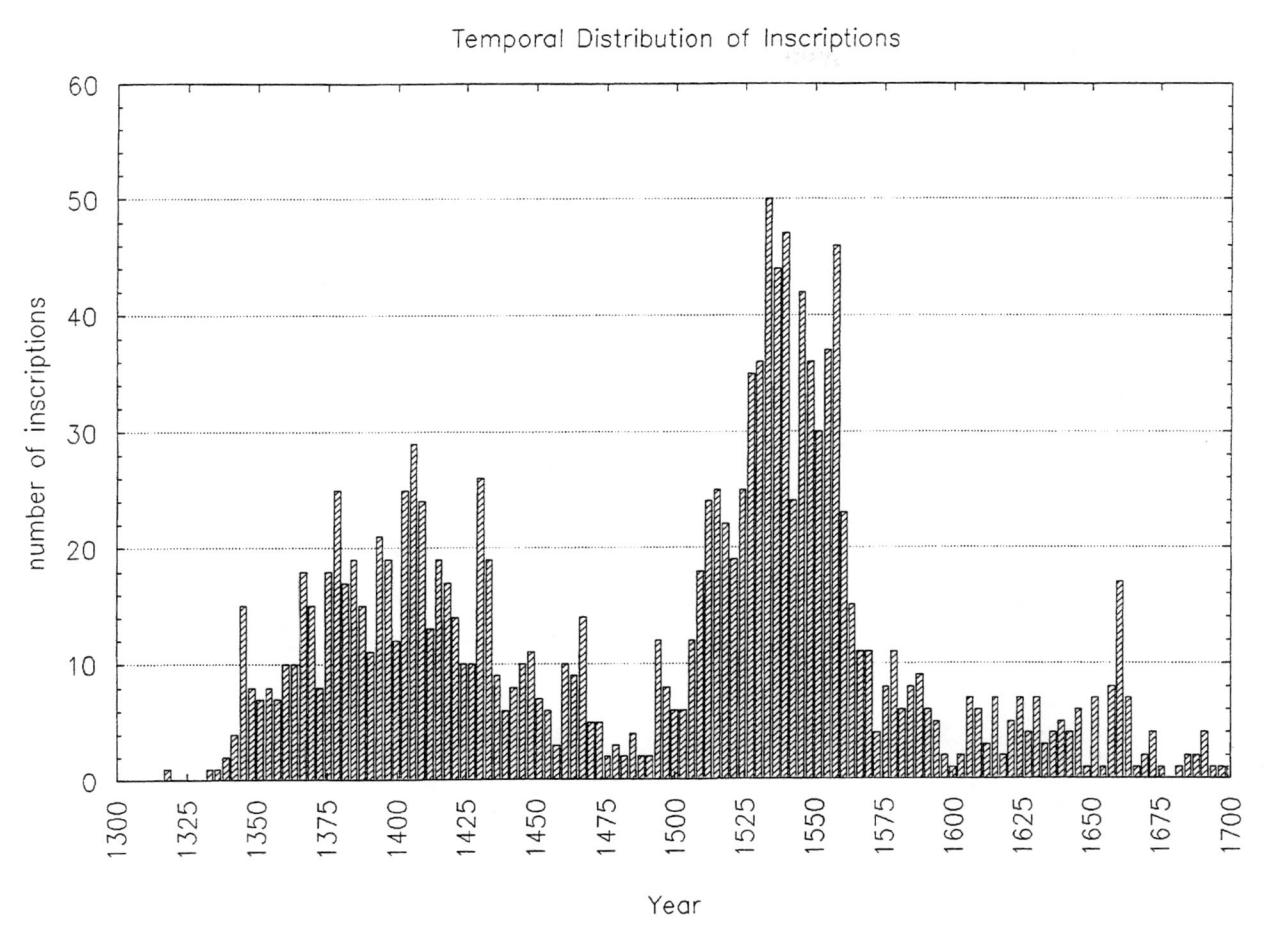

FIGURE 6.4 Number of inscriptions by year, all districts

measure of the tempo of economic/ritual transactions in the region as a whole. The founding of the empire and the establishment of political control over areas both around the city and further south prompted a flurry of inscriptional activity in the late fourteenth and early fifteenth century. In the late fifteenth and very early sixteenth century there appears to have been a lull in inscription-writing, reflecting a slowdown both in gifting and in publicized commercial transactions. In the early to middle sixteenth century, a boom in inscription-writing appears to reflect the dynamic state of politics and the economy. In large part, this sixteenth-century peak in the overall distribution of inscriptions is fuelled by Bellary District, as discussed below. After the battle of Talikota (A.D. 1565), the record is characterized by a slow decline in the number of records. Both the shape and the magnitude of inscriptional peaks are of interest, reflecting both the tempo and the magnitude of gifting through time.

Significant differences between districts exist in the temporal distribution of inscriptions. Figure 6.5 shows the distribution of inscriptions by year by district (see figure 6.1). Bellary District inscriptions are bimodally distributed, but the sixteenth-century peak in this district, which contains the city of Vijayanagara, is particularly marked. Raichur, just north of the Tungabhadra, shows a similar pattern, although the number of inscriptions is much greater in Bellary District. Dharwar and Chitradurga are the two districts closest to the "core area" of Bellary/Raichur. Inscriptions from these two districts are bimodally distributed, as are most of the others. Shimoga is notable for the number of early inscriptions it contains; many of these are "hero stones," which commemorate deaths in battle or skirmishes. Thus, although the overall temporal

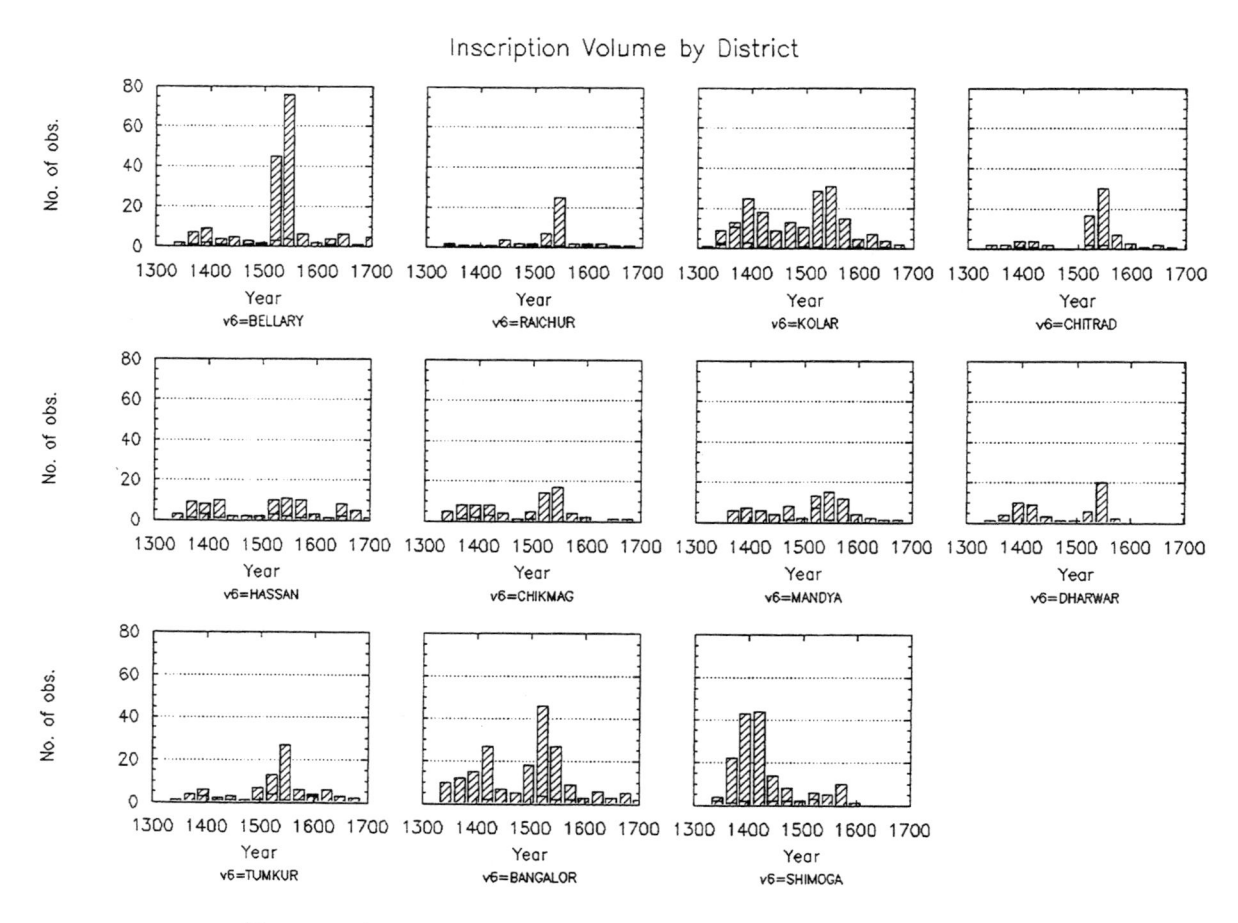

FIGURE 6.5 Number of inscriptions by year for each district

pattern of all districts is bimodal, the areas nearest to the city show a particularly strong sixteenth-century peak in the occurrence of records.

Donors and Donees

Who were the people involved in the transactions reflected in inscriptions? Donor classifications were simplified (see table 6.2) into six categories: royalty, which refers to either the king or his family; religious groups, including temples and Brahmins; local elites, including *nayakas* and "chiefs;" others, such as merchant groups, groups of villagers, and groups of craftspeople; unknown, which includes the categories of unknown and "individual;" and officers, restricted to royal officers. Figure 6.6 shows the distributions of inscriptions by donor category through time. Local elites are the most common donors, followed closely by unknown donors. Many of these individuals known only by name and not by status may,

in fact, qualify as local elites. The pattern of royal gifting is striking, particularly if both royalty and royal officers are considered. Inscriptions involving royal officers as donors peak sharply in the middle to late sixteenth century, as do all inscriptions, but in the former case the strength of this late peak contrasts sharply with the relative unimportance of officers as donors in the early period. An early peak in donations by "others" contrasts with the increased importance of both local elites, kings, and royal officers in the later Vijayanagara period (see Morrison 1994a for a more detailed analysis).

The patterns of donees are almost mirror images of the donor curves (figure 6.7). Kings never appear as donees, and local elites and royal officers are similarly unimportant. Not surprisingly, religious institutions—and temples constitute the majority of this category—appear as the major recipients of gifts. Many donees cannot be as-

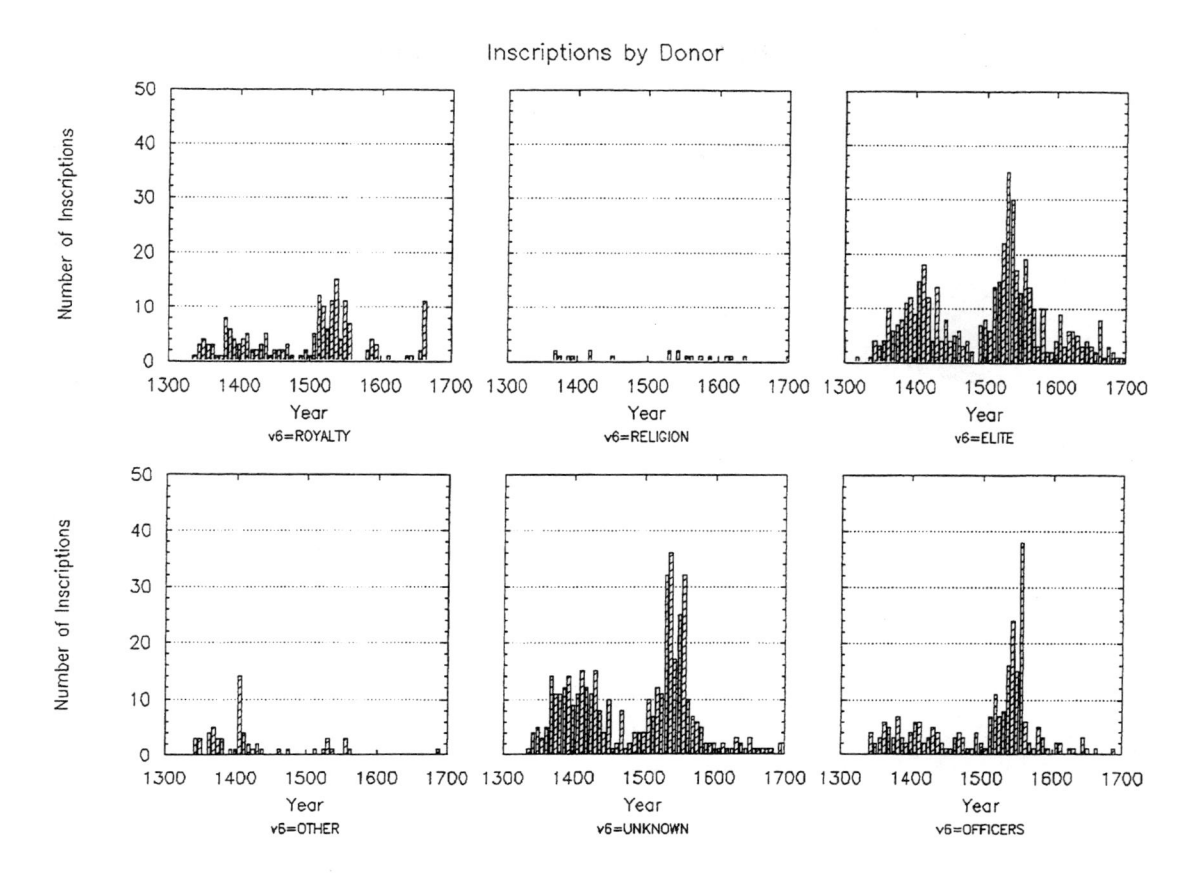

FIGURE 6.6 Number of inscriptions by donor category, all districts

signed to functional categories, but the shape of the "unknown" curve closely follows that of the religious institutions. In a few types of transactions, such as the construction of agricultural facilities, donees are not routinely listed, presumably because the facility benefits many different people and is in a category of action different from that of a simple land grant. "Others" appear more often as donees in the sixteenth century and as donors in the late fourteenth and early fifteenth. The low number of inscriptions with "others" as donors or donees makes it difficult to dissect this pattern, but several of the early inscriptions with others (in this case villagers) as donors refer to communal construction of agricultural facilities, while many of the later inscriptions with "others" as donees (mostly nonagricultural specialists, primarily barbers) relate to tax exemptions.

The distribution of donors is not uniform across districts. A crosstabulation of donor types and districts reveals significant differences (chi-square equals 256.9, with 50 degrees of freedom, significant at the p<.0001 level). When only royal donors, their officers, and local elite donors are considered, significant district-wise differences still exist (chi-square equals 94.89, with 20 degrees of freedom, significant at the p<.0001 level). Royal donations are more important in the Bellary District than elsewhere, though donation by royal officers are important in a number of districts.

Gifts and Grants

Figures 6.2 and 6.3 indicated the distribution of gift categories in the data base as a whole. Significant differences also exist in the overall pattern of gifting through time (chi-square equals 118, with 35 degrees of freedom, significant at the p< .0001 level). Figure 6.8 shows the temporal distribution of the first gift by year. Most gifts conform to the now-familiar bimodal temporal pattern, except for gifts of land which, although they increase in the sixteenth century, do not

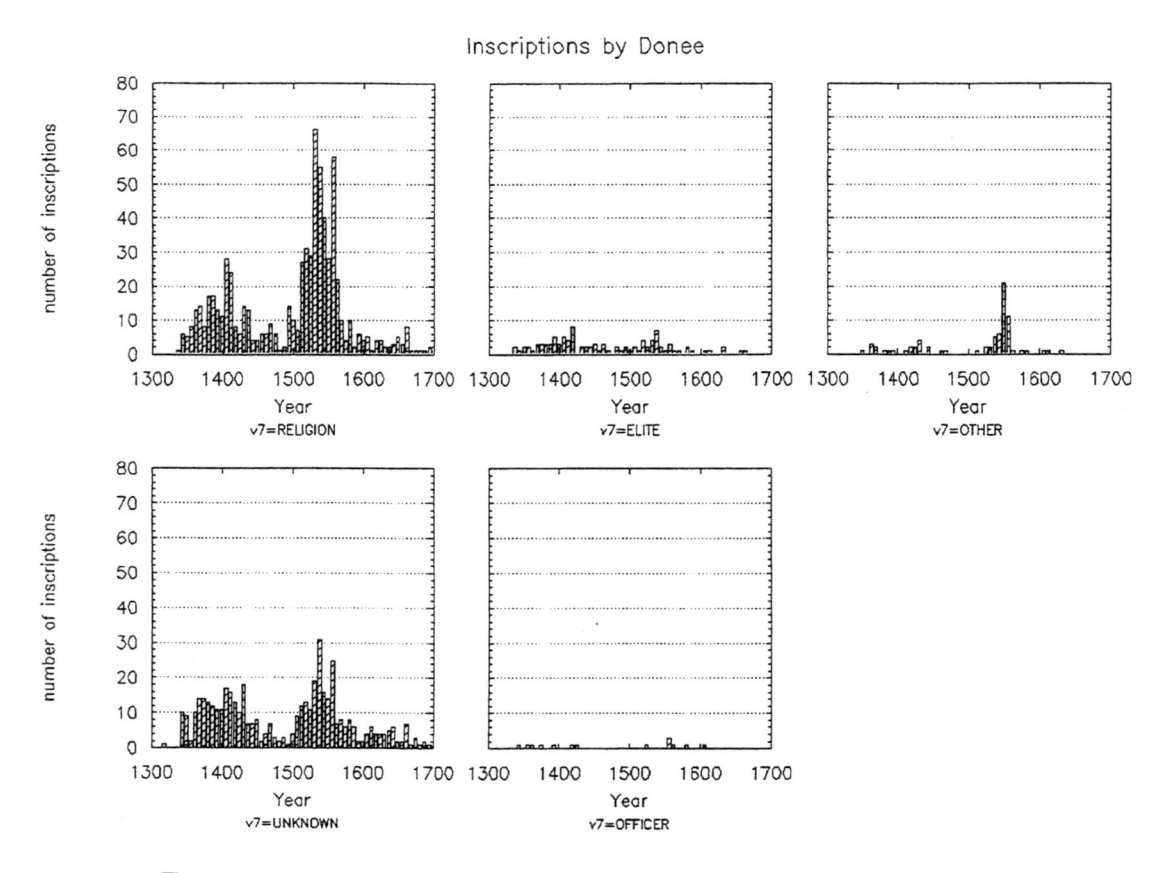

FIGURE 6.7 Number of inscriptions by donee category, all districts

exhibit the strong peaks that gifts of villages and nonagricultural gifts do.

Agricultural Inscriptions: Land

Land grants in the inscriptional record are sometimes differentiated as either wet land, dry land, land below a reservoir, or land below a canal. Unfortunately, many inscriptions do not distinguish between different types of land (or else the translators do not). Figure 6.9 shows the temporal distribution of land grants by district, where the general category of "land" incorporates all types of land. More than any other district, land grants in Bellary District are temporally clustered, concentrated in the period between 1515 and 1570. The pattern for Raichur District is weaker, but similar, as indeed are those for all three of the districts adjacent to Bellary. The variation between districts in land grants is quite striking, however. In both Kolar and Shimoga districts, early land grants are more common than late grants, even though Kolar, at least, contains more inscriptions overall from the later period.

Irrigated land includes all land described as being wet, below a reservoir, or below a canal. If the temporal distribution of irrigated land grants by district (figure 6.10) is compared with that of land in general (figure 6.9), several interesting patterns emerge. In Bellary District the sample size is fairly low, but a strong sixteenth century peak is evident, with only one mention of irrigated land before the beginning of the sixteenth century. Inscriptional references dating from before the sixteenth century and referring to wet land in the district do occur, but these are all unpublished. In no other district, however, is there a late peak in donations of irrigated land of the magnitude and suddenness of that in the Bellary District. The atypical pattern of Kolar District in overall land grants is clarified by the distribution of irrigated land. In Kolar, a small sixteenth century increase in irrigated land donations contrasts sharply with an overall decline in

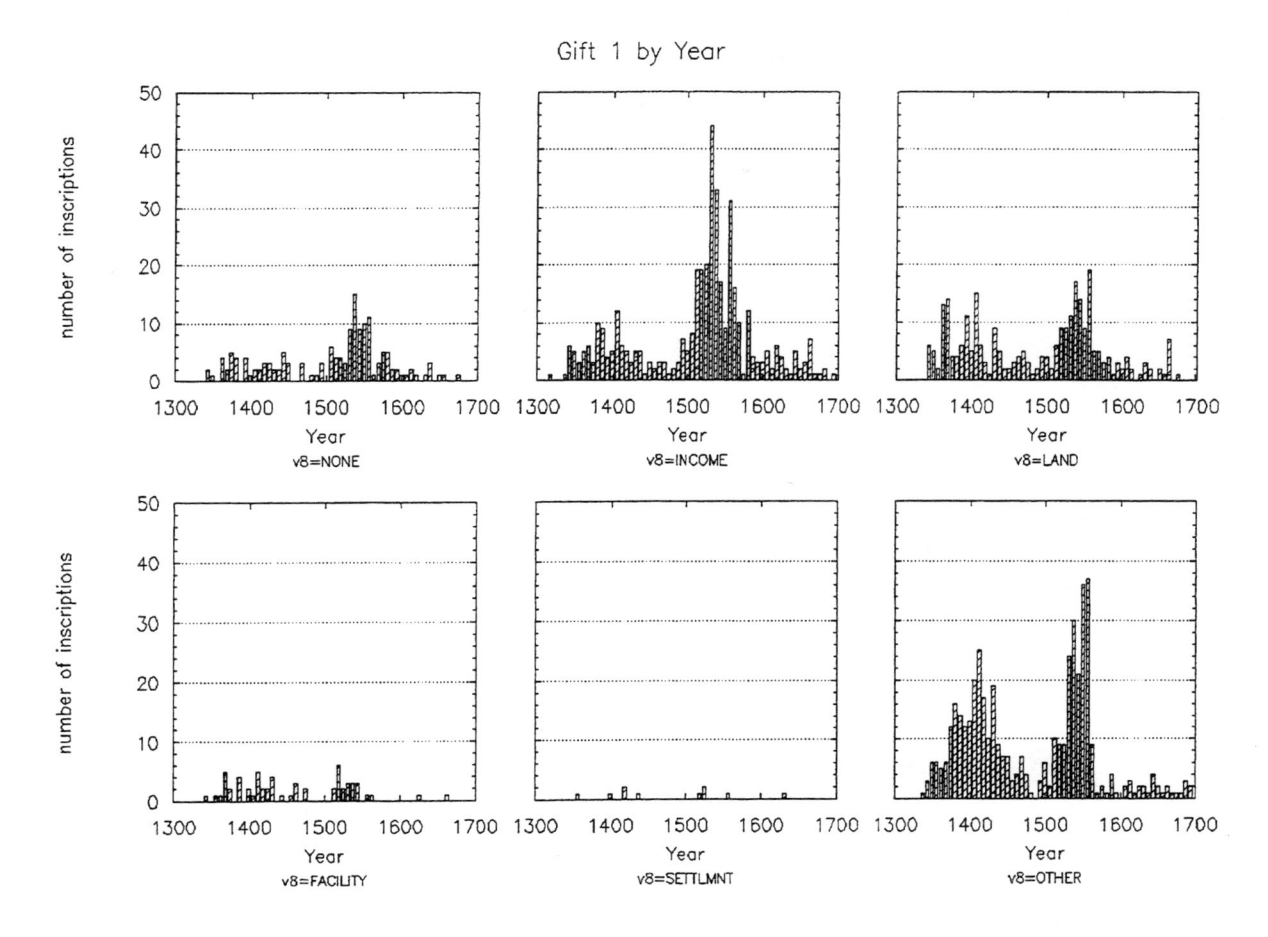

FIGURE 6.8 Temporal distribution of gift one, divided by gift category

gifts of land.

Agricultural Inscriptions: Facilities

Ninety-one inscriptions referred to the construction of canals, reservoirs, and wells, the only types of agricultural facilities represented in the inscriptional record. In other cases, inscriptions were built into agricultural facilities, or lay near them, but did not refer directly to the construction of the facility. Figure 6.11 indicates the proveniences of coded inscriptions. Temples are the most common location for inscriptions, followed by fields and villages. Inscriptions placed on rocks in fields may be underrepresented in the data base, since these are the hardest to locate. "Copper" refers to portable copper plate inscriptions, "architec" to inscriptions on isolated architectural elements such as columns, and "agricult" to inscriptions on or near agricultural facilities. Unfortunately, the number of inscriptions associated with agricultural facilities was insufficient for more detailed analysis. In Bellary District, however, four of the five inscriptions located on reservoirs or other facilities fell between the years 1536 and 1556; the fifth dated to A.D. 1661. Thus, the distribution of these inscriptions supports and supplements that of other inscriptions directly recording facility construction.

The temporal distribution of inscriptions recording canal construction for all districts is shown in figure 6.12. Of importance is the early cluster of five dates between A.D. 1375 and 1415. Five more inscriptions are found in the period between A.D. 1475 and 1560, while several additional unpublished inscriptions also fall within this latter range. It was not possible to disaggregate the data on canal construction given the very small sample size.

References to reservoir construction were more numerous. The combined distribution from

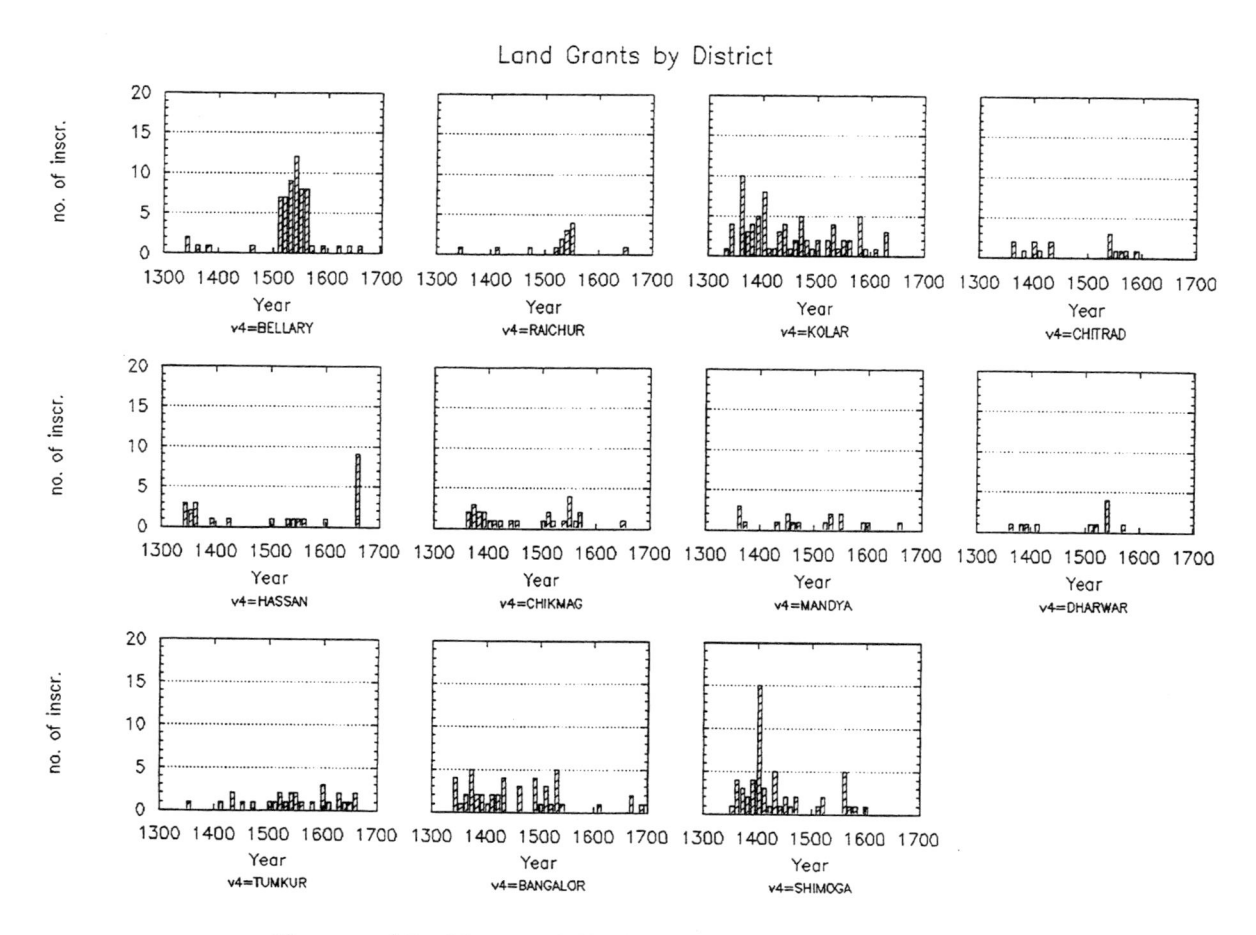

FIGURE 6.9 Temporal distribution of land grants by district

all districts is bimodal, with the larger peak falling in the early period. Thus, reservoir construction in central Karnataka as a whole (figure 6.13) seems to have been an important Early Vijayanagara activity that came back into importance in the middle sixteenth century. The late fourteenth- to early-fifteenth-century boom in reservoir construction actually achieved a magnitude greater than that of the sixteenth century. When reservoir data are categorized by district, however, a different picture emerges (figure 6.14). The distribution of inscriptions referring to reservoir construction in Bellary District is idiosyncratic compared to other districts. In Bellary District, construction references bunch tightly together in the middle sixteenth century, a pattern seen in no other district containing more than two inscriptions. In every other district for which a pattern can be discerned—and sample sizes are quite small for all districts—reservoir construction appears primarily as an early strategy.

QUALITATIVE ANALYSIS

A great deal of information on Vijayanagara agriculture and land use contained in inscriptions was, of necessity, collapsed into fairly general categories in the process of coding inscriptions for the data base. While it is not possible to discuss all of this information in detail, I will comment on several inscriptions relevant to understanding agricultural intensification. Because the inscriptional record is largely focused on the disposition of land and of its products, volumes could be (and have been) written regarding the structure of Vijayanagara agriculture based on inscriptions (Breckenridge 1985; Mahalingam 1951; Randhawa 1980; Saraswati 1984; Stein 1980; Viswanath 1985).

Land Classification

The tripartite classification of agricultural production into wet, dry, and wet-cum-dry was discussed in chapter 2. As noted in that chapter, an

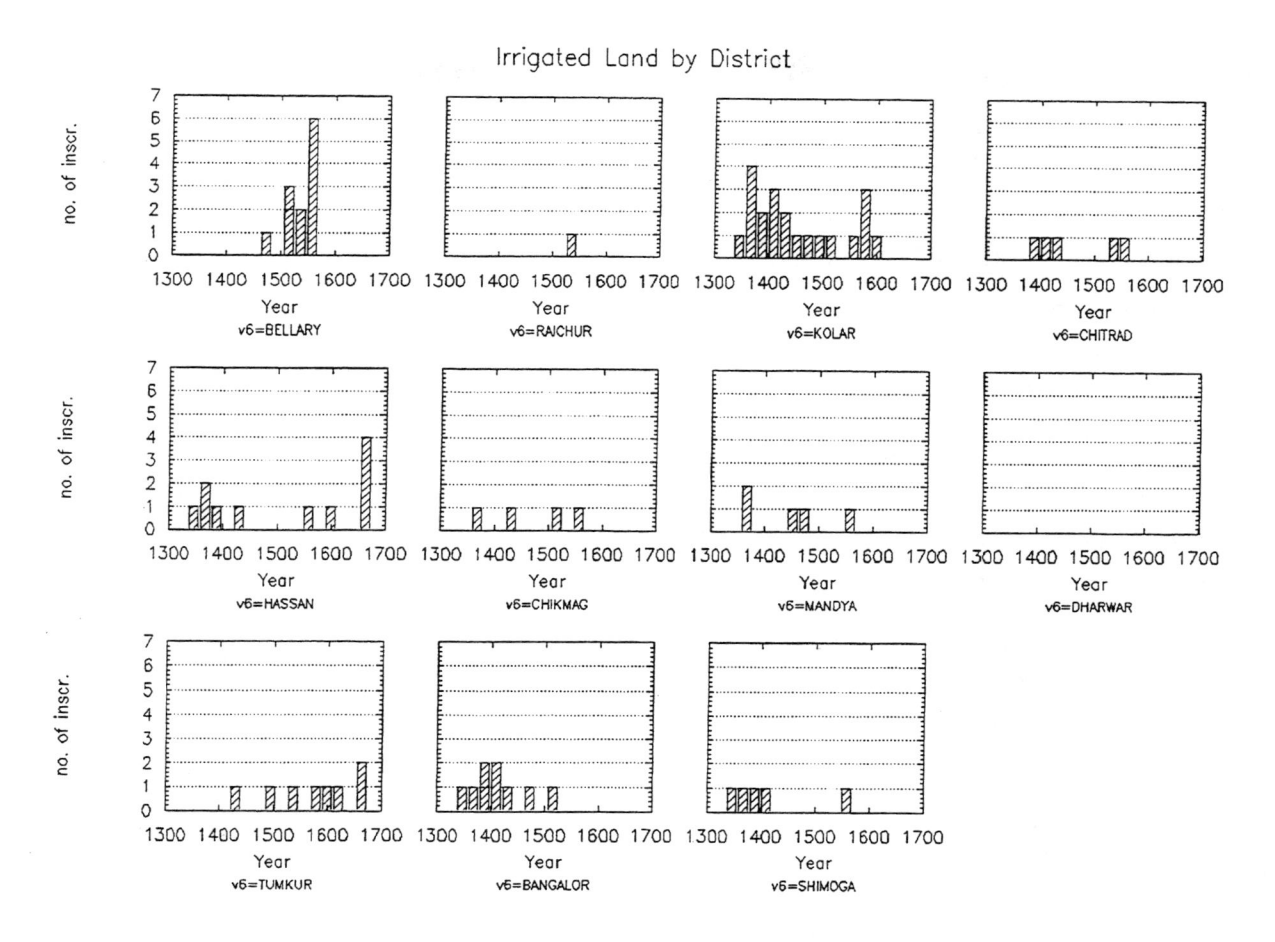

FIGURE 6.10 Temporal distribution of irrigated land grants by district

additional category, garden land, has been employed in revenue classification schemes since the Colonial period, while wet-cum-dry production has not been consistently employed as a revenue category. This variable categorization of agricultural production raises several issues. First of all, what were the categories of land classification in the Vijayanagara period? Were forms of production associated with specific plots of land? That is, is it legitimate to speak of dry lands as well as of dry agriculture? Finally, can such categorization be useful for understanding Vijayanagara intensification; and how can these forms of land use be detected archaeologically?

Indigenous land and land use classification during the Vijayanagara period may have been somewhat regionally and temporally variable. Thus, analyses that treat the entire period and all of southern India as a single field of information must be approached with caution. Where land types were differentiated in the inscriptions included in the data base, the three most common categories were wet land, dry land, and land beneath a reservoir. Land beneath runoff-fed reservoirs is wet-cum-dry land *par excellence*, suggesting that this three-part classification may have some utility. However, it is clear that much more precise divisions also existed. Based on his reading of inscriptions from the entire empire, Mahalingam (1940:41-42) has classified categories of land taxes into those on wet crops and those on dry crops. For revenue purposes, the form of tenure was considered, as well as the success of the crop and its stage in the fallow cycle:

> In the taxable land a distinction was made between paddy fields, uncultivated waste (newly brought under cultivation), forests reclaimed, and *kadaippu* lands (land on which only the last crop is raised) and lands irrigated by lifting water. The government also considered if they were wet lands on which were grown plantain and sugarcane, or were *padugaitakku* (banks of rivers)

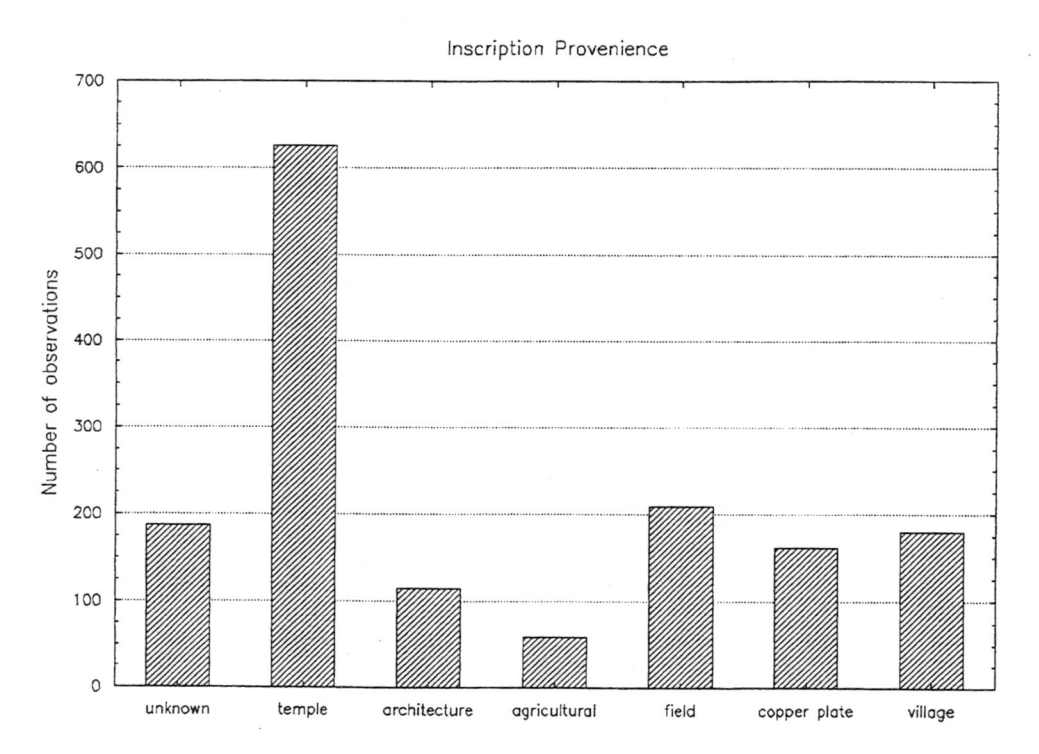

FIGURE 6.11 Provenience of coded inscriptions

where these were grown or marshes in which red lotuses were grown or lands producing... a large number of other crops. There was also some differentiation made between wet crops being raised on wet lands and wet crops being raised on dry lands. (Mahalingam 1940:42)

Several inscriptions from the data base inform on land classification. In an inscription from Hassan District (A.D. 1360; Gopal 1985b:136-37), two villages were granted to a temple in order to support the activities of various ritual specialists. The villages were described as yielding a certain amount of revenue. In addition to the villages, garden lands below a reservoir (or reservoirs?) were included in the gift. What appears to have been given in this case was, in fact, not the land itself but the income from certain specified taxes on that land. The word garden may have been added by the translator, since it appears in parentheses. An inscription of A.D. 1417 from Shimoga District indicates the importance of perennial crops in determining land value as well as the situation of a plot of land vis-à-vis agricultural facilities:

> Naganna-haggade, his brothers, ... and all the members of the family of Megaravalli...together agreed and sold the land and arecanut trees below the tank at Mumbale and at Lokavalli for 42 *hons* and five *hanas*.... (Gopal 1990:393)

In an inscription located near a reservoir in Kolar District (A.D. 1371; Gopal 1990:20), a grant of rice land was received as *kattu-godagi* (or *kattu-kodaga*, see chapter 3) by a *nayaka* for having constructed a reservoir in the name of his mother. The specific designation of rice land may indicate something about the security and abundance of supply of that particular reservoir. Specific plots of land were viewed as "belonging to" or being associated with agricultural facilities. It is particularly interesting in the light of the interconnection of features in the study area that reservoirs and canals were said to be associated with both wet and dry land. Another inscription associated with a reservoir embankment in Kolar District (A.D. 1428; Gopal 1990:48) "registers the gift of the tank excavated by Danakanidevi... with all the wet land below irrigated by it, and the dry fields attached thereto" (Gopal 1990:48). Even canals were associated with some dry lands (A.D. 1660, Hassan District; Gopal 1985b:157).

Maintenance of Facilities

The burden of maintenance of canals and reservoirs seems to have most often fallen on the villagers whose lands were watered by them (Gopal 1985b:*lvii*). However, others were sometimes

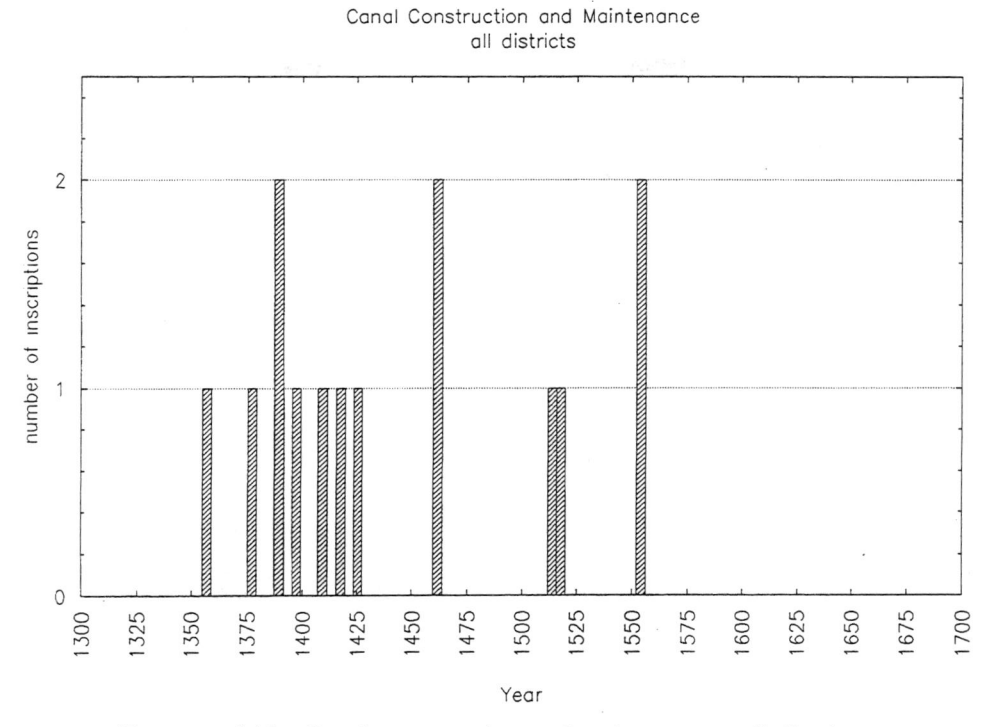

FIGURE 6.12 Canal construction and maintenance, all districts

involved. Several inscriptions refer to grants of land or land tax for maintaining carts for reservoir repair and maintenance. Such carts were used for hauling away silt from the bed and for bringing earth and stones for strengthening and repair of the embankment (Gopal 1985b:147). These maintenance gifts were made by *nayakas* (Gopal 1985a:13-14), members of the royal house (Gopal 1985b:147), or villagers themselves (Gopal 1985b:139-40, 146). In the two cases in which villagers arranged for the maintenance of carts (Gopal 1985b:139-40, 146), income from specified taxes (and exemption from others) was provided to several individuals responsible for the work. In a Hassan District inscription of A.D. 1371 (Gopal 1985b:139-40), "it was stipulated that the beneficiaries themselves were to meet the expenses of the buffalo (*kona*), wooden implements (*kirumuttu*), iron (*kabbuna*), and oil for the carts (probably castor oil; see Gopal 1985b:146). The tax demands imposed on cultivators to cover the cost of repairing breached reservoirs could be heavy, and an inscription of A.D. 1527 from Chitradurga District describes how farmers migrated away from their village as a result of the heavy tax burden for facility repairs (Gopal 1985b:74). Specialists may have been called in for repairs to sluices. In an inscription of A.D. 1400 in Bangalore District, a stone mason was rewarded with wet land, dry land, and a house for his work in repairing a reservoir sluice (apparently during construction; Gopal 1985:86).

Two records from Chitradurga District dated to A.D. 1410 and 1424 (Gopal 1985b:61-62) describe the complex transactions and obligations involved in the construction and repair of a canal and anicut. These two inscriptions are worth quoting in detail, but several terms must first be defined. *Mahajanas* have been variously defined as the "Brahmana residents of the entire village; all the members of the village assembly . . . [or] members of a village council" (Sircar 1966a:177). *Vrittis* are units of land measurement, as are *kolagas*:

> This record is described as a . . . (deed of transactions). The *mahajanas* of Harihara-kshetra, having at their own expense built a dam to the river Haridra within the boundaries of ([the land of?] the temple of) god Harihara and dug a canal through the god's land to Harihara [village], the king granted two parts of all the land irrigated by the said canal for god Harihara and the third part was gifted to those *mahajanas* who got built the canal. The land for the *mahajanas* was divided into 111 *vrittis* and distributed among several Brahmanas...The canal passed through the villages of Bannikodu, Beluvadi,

Reservoir Construction and Maintenance
all districts

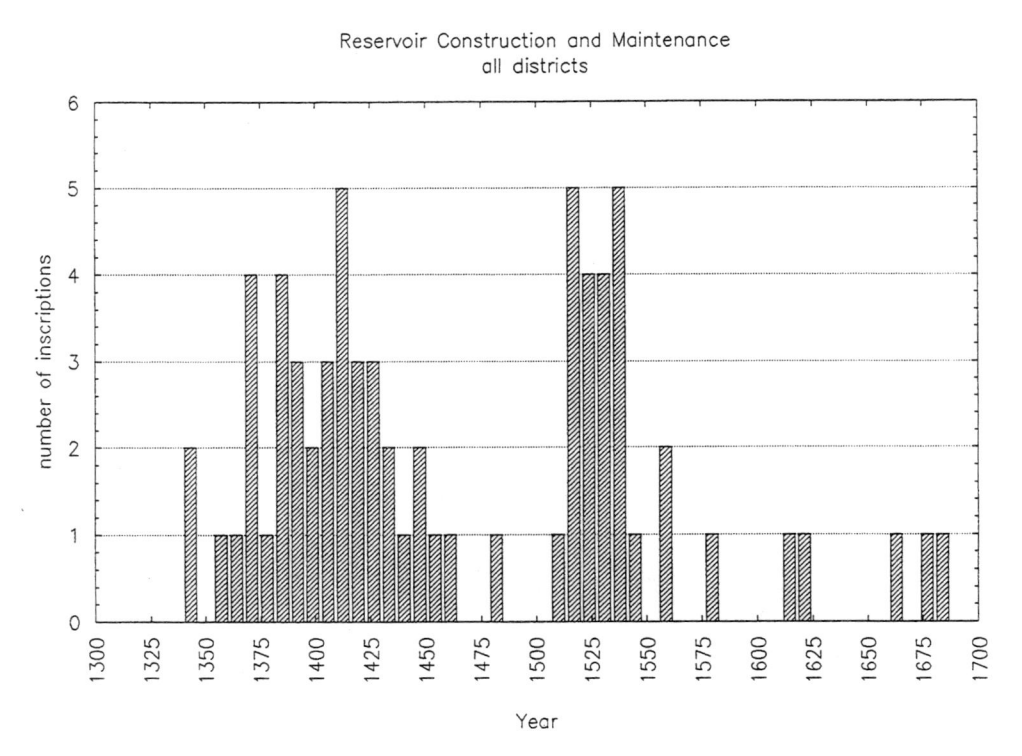

FIGURE 6.13 Reservoir construction, all districts

Hanagavadi, Harihara, Gutturu, and Gamganarasiyakere the lands in which were distributed as shown above. It is stipulated that the donees and the temple were to bear the expenses for the maintenance of the canal and its repair in case of break down etc. in the same proportion.

The later portion . . . records that Jagannatha, the minister (*mantri*) . . . with the permission of the king . . . entrusted the work of construction of the dam on the Haridra to his son Bullapa who carried it out to the satisfaction of the *mahajanas*. (Gopal 1985b:61)

The work of the contractor Bullapa turned out not to be so satisfactory, since the anicut breached just fourteen years later. The *mahajanas* and the temple did not, however, finance the repair:

The strong dam on the river Haridra earlier built by Bullaraja [Bullapa], at the instance of the king and *mahapradhana* Nagana-dannayaka having breached, this Bullarasa met Chamanripala, the army commander . . . and persuaded him to get it repaired. He having agreed to bear the cost of repair, the dam was reconstructed by Bullarasa. Chamaraja is eulogized. (Gopal 1985b:62)

Although the king figures prominently in both inscriptions, his role was not as donor or investor. Although the king is said to have distributed the newly irrigated land, the *mahajanas* financed the initial construction of the canal on their own initiative, and the the army commander financed the repairs. The contracting out of the construction to the son of the king's minister is interesting, suggesting that the initiative of the *mahajanas* was at least controlled by political leaders. Two inscriptions from Bellary District (A.D. 1465-1466; Annual Report on South Indian Epigraphy 1923-24, No. 434 of 1923; Annual Report on Indian Epigraphy 1977-78, No. B 105) record the repair of an anicut by *nayakas*.

Finally, inscriptions about agricultural facilities may indicate construction dates and sequences. Several canals and reservoirs in the study area were dated by associated inscriptions (chapter 5). In Kolar District, an inscription from A.D. 1389 records the construction of a canal to an apparently pre-existing reservoir in order to provide a secure supply of water to the city of Penukonda (Gopal 1990:42).

Settlements, Expansion, and Agriculture

The construction or renovation of a reservoir seems to have been a fundamental aspect of resettling or founding a village. Nearly every village was associated with a reservoir, as reflected in the number of place names ending with kere, samudra, sandra (apparently a corruption of samudra), or

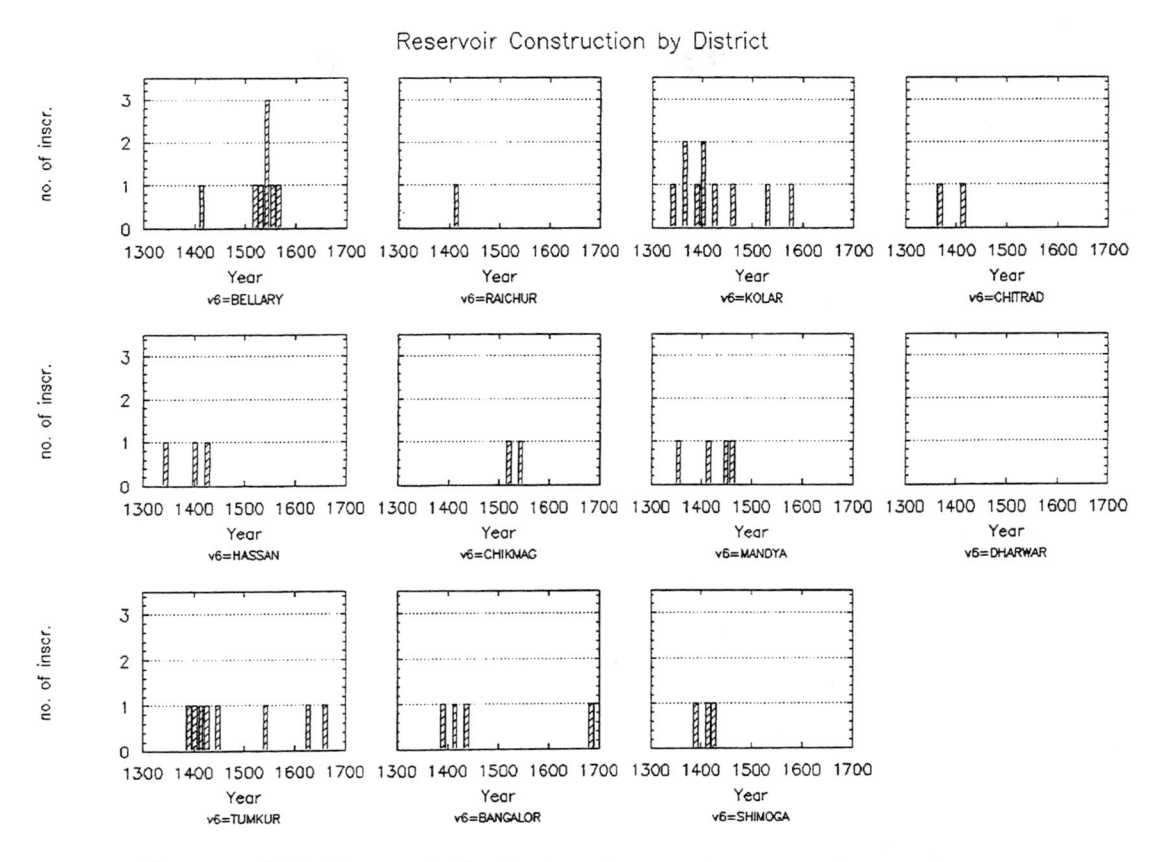

FIGURE 6.14 Temporal distribution of reservoir construction by district

sagara. The establishment of the village of Mallasamudra (now Mallsandra; Gopal 1990:94-95) in Kolar District in A.D. 1399 involved the excavation of a reservoir, the raising of a garden, and the planting of trees in the village, which was established by an officer (of the king?). Two inscriptions (A.D. 1438 and 1416) from Bangalore District (Gopal 1985a:44,45) mention the excavation of new reservoirs in conjunction with the resettlement of abandoned villages. The exemption of land below a new reservoir from various taxes indicates some of the crops that could be grown, as in this inscription from Bellary District (Harapanahalli Taluk, A.D. 1419):

> On the occasion of a solar eclipse, this Hariyanna [a local leader or administrator] gave to several *mahajanas* like Bachappa, son of Bommarasa of Rik-sakha, Singanna, son of Vithappa of Vasistha-gotra and the like, forest land near Arasiyakere which they converted into a *pura* named Hariyasamudra, a *srotrya-agrahara* [a rent-free Brahman village]. Thereupon they founded it by reclaiming the forest and excavating a tank, at the cost of 1000 *hons*. The land under the tank was made free from taxes on wet land, dry land, arecanut, jack fruit, mango trees, sugarcane, plantain trees, betel creepers, saltpan (*uppinamole*), harvest grain, ploughs of bullocks...and other imposts. (Gopal 1985a:148-49)

In all cases in which the official establishment or re-establishment of villages is commemorated, some reference was made to a reservoir. Settlements without associated reservoirs do certainly exist; it may be that these settlements were never formally founded or never received donations or investments.

DISCUSSION

The historical record of Vijayanagara constitutes an important body of information relating to agricultural production and reveals a great deal about public (or publicized) investment in agriculture and about the collection and disposition of various rights, taxes, and obligations. Inscriptions may be considered as descriptive of some agricultural and economic practice but not as normative, since they refer disproportionately to the activities and concerns of elites, even within the general classification of agriculturalist. Brahmans, in particular, were often the recipients of gifts, and are thus prominent in the record even though they almost certainly did not constitute the majority of the population. Historical sources contain little information on the actual practice of agriculture other than that plows and bullock traction were used, as were carts, iron tools, and so on. The classification of land into wet and dry categories is evident, and the specification of land below reservoirs as a category supports the three-fold classification into wet, dry, and wet-cum-dry production. The category of garden land is not as clearly indicated in the inscriptional record.

Historical accounts of the construction and maintenance of agricultural facilities are limited to the larger-scale features of canals and reservoirs. Occasional references to wells occur, but these more often than not refer to wells located in villages or along roads and thus perhaps primarily for domestic consumption. Analysis of the inscriptional data base has revealed clear temporal patterns in the construction of agricultural facilities, with the first peak period of construction occurring in the late fourteenth and early fifteenth century, and the second in the middle to late sixteenth century. In Bellary and Raichur districts, the districts surrounding the city of Vijayanagara, the sixteenth-century peak dominates, in contrast to the pattern from other districts. Thus, reservoir and canal construction attain special importance as agricultural strategies in the study area in the sixteenth century. The temporal distribution of land grants, too, is anomalous in Bellary District, concentrated in and increasing in magnitude in the middle sixteenth century. Clearly, general patterns of agricultural donation and investment in the examined area exist, and just as clearly, the patterns found in Bellary District are unique in several respects.

Travellers' accounts provide a level of detail not present in inscriptions, but they also present many problems of interpretation and comparability. All of the travellers cited drew a picture of extensive and lush fields, which contrasts rather markedly with the scanty natural vegetation. Many described large urban produce markets and the great quantity and variety of goods available there.

Certainly, both foreign and indigenous sources are invaluable for assigning dates to specific structures, sites, and features, but there are also limits to the information provided by written sources about production in the study area. Only large-scale features are routinely discussed in the inscriptional record. Without archaeological knowledge of the range of type and scale of agricultural facilities in the study area, the role of small-scale and dry farming in the agricultural repertoire would be severely underestimated. The numerous and well-dated Vijayanagara inscriptions do, however, provide an almost unparalleled opportunity to examine the tempo of change on both a local and a regional scale.

7

Identifying Land Use: Pollen and Charcoal

THE SEDIMENTARY RECORD of Vijayanagara reservoirs constitutes the third source of information on past agriculture and land use employed in this study. In this chapter, I discuss two techniques that may inform on past land use in the Vijayanagara region: pollen analysis and microscopic charcoal analysis. Information derived from these analyses may provide data on vegetation and vegetation change, fire history, soil erosion, and on the hydrological regime of reservoirs.

Botanically oriented studies of archaeological sites and regions have sometimes maintained an uneasy relationship with human action, either focussing primarily on the human use of plants or, where research has been directed toward investigating regional vegetation and climate, viewing human impact on vegetation as disturbance. In part, this unease is based on the research problem pursued. Ethnobotanists must, however, come to terms with background patterns of vegetation and vegetation change, and palaeobotanists with the significant and long-term impact human beings have had on plant distributions. I seek to avoid this paradox by considering the regional vegetation record as an artifact of both ecological and human forces, as a record of a transformed landscape. Agricultural landscapes are both "natural" and "made" environments, and interpretations linked to environment or vegetation as well as to agricultural practice must integrate this dual identity.

POLLEN ANALYSIS

Pollen analysis, the study of "fossil" (that is, non-contemporary, although the material is not truly fossilized) pollen for the purposes of environmental reconstruction, is one way of detecting and analyzing past agriculture. Environment, in this sense, may include factors such as soil, temperature, and rainfall as well as the activities of human beings. Human impact on vegetation is variable at different scales, and diverse agricultural strategies might be expected to shape local and regional vegetation in fairly complex ways. Thus, it is important to pursue multiple scales of sampling and analysis (cf. Dimbleby 1985).

Pollen grains consist of two layers. The inner layer, or intine, is composed mostly of cellulose (Moore and Webb 1978:31) and is not particularly resistant to decay. The outer layer, or exine, is composed of cellulose, hemicellulose, lignin, pectic substances, and sporopollenin (Bryant and Holloway 1983:194). Sporopollenin is highly resistant to decay (Moore and Webb 1978; Faegri, Kaland, and Krzywinski 1989). Identification of pollen and spores rests on the observation that each family or genus (and sometimes species) produces a morphologically distinctive product, with specifiable size range, number and arrangement of pores and apertures, and exine characteristics.

Production, Dispersal, and Preservation

The methodological bases for interpretation of fossil pollen profiles consist of bodies of information drawn from the operation of contemporary processes in plant biology and ecology, hydrology, and sedimentology. As discussed below, differential pollen production, dispersal, and preservation, as well as specificity of identification, sampling, and even forms of data presentation intervene between the observed patterns and our ability to make statements about past vegetation. Much recent research has been directed toward understanding these processes, and the impact they have on the fossil pollen record (cf. Birks and Gordon 1985; Roberts 1989).

Part of the appeal of pollen analysis is that it represents a quantifiable, albeit indirect, measure of past vegetation. Unlike macrobotanical analysis, where deposition often depends on human intervention (whether intentional or not), and preservation may be quite variable even within a single isolated location, pollen continuously accumulates in soils (Dimbleby 1957, 1985) and, importantly, in lakes, bogs, and other bodies of water, providing a stratigraphic record of vegetation. This record is far from pristine. Beginning with the point of origin—the plant—it is certainly not possible to make the equation of one grain to one individual. Different species vary significantly in the volume of pollen they produce. In part, this disparity is related to the mode of pollen dispersal. Anemophilous, or wind-pollinated, plants must produce large quantities of pollen to reproduce. For this reason, and because of their wide distribution, they tend to dominate the pollen record (Bryant and Holloway 1983:194). Zoophilous pollen grains are coated with a layer of sticky lipids so they can adhere to their animal vectors (Bryant and Holloway 1983:194). Zoophilous species produce far fewer grains, and these grains are less likely to find their way into the fossil record. Some hydrophilous, or water-pollinated taxa, lack resistant exines and thus generally are not preserved (Bryant and Holloway 1983:195; and see Cox 1993). Finally, cleistogamous, or self-pollinated species, also produce few grains, which are not often deposited in fossil contexts.

The historical development of pollen analysis in Europe and North America is not coincidental; species diversity is lower than in Africa (Livingstone 1984:23) or Asia (Chanda 1972:340; Vishnu-Mittre 1985), and many taxa are anemophilous. In Asia some of the major cultigens, such as rice (*Oryza sativa*) and sugarcane (*Sacharrum officinarium*), are cleistogamous (Chanda 1972:338; Vishnu-Mittre 1972:353). Tropical environments, in general, (e.g. Byrne and Horn 1989; Livingstone 1984:23) also contain many more zoophilous species than temperate environments (see also Tilak 1989). Knowledge of dispersal modes provides the analyst with expected frequency trends, so that deviations from these trends can be explained. For example, anomalously high concentrations of zoophilic pollen may occur in human coprolites (Bryant and Williams-Dean 1975), or in archaeological sites.

Morphological differences contribute to the potential for long-distance transport of a pollen grain. Factors such as shape, size, and weight converge in determining the buoyancy of a pollen grain. Some large, heavy pollen grains such as those of *Zea mays* and *Abies* do not travel far from their parent plant (Bryant and Holloway 1983:195). Others, such as *Pinus* (which has two large air sacs or "bladders") are notable for their mobility (Erdtman 1969; Moore and Webb 1978:2-3). Studies of dispersal mechanisms and distance-density patterns for specific species under a variety of atmospheric conditions and topographic settings are necessary to evaluate the representativeness and catchment area of the fossil pollen record (Tauber 1965; Wright 1967; Webb, Laseski, and Bernabo 1978; Birks and Gordon 1985). No such studies have been carried out in South India.

Even anemophilous pollen may not be transported solely by wind. For most sediments, the contribution of water transport is significant (Swain 1973; Cwynar 1978; Patterson, Edwards, and Maguire 1977). For example, in a simulation study of Lowland Maya agricultural practice, Wiseman (1978) generated an expected maize pollen influx value based on the expectation of maize monocropping (and studies of modern maize pollen dispersal). The actual maize pollen concentration from his study of lakes Petenxil and Eckinxil was, however, even higher than the monocrop simulation projection. This becomes less surprising when it is noted that the parameters of the model specified only airborne pollen transport. It seems clear that the role of runoff in pollen transport is a significant factor in dispersing (or focussing) pollen (Dimbleby 1985; Peck 1973). Pollen is also only one component of sediment, whether in a lake, field, or archaeological site. Thus, the more general processes acting on sediment, including erosion (Butzer 1982:127-33), faunal mixing (Dimbleby 1985:101,122), and sediment focussing (Davis and Ford 1982), are relevant to understanding pollen stratigraphy. The resolution of soil pollen stratification (Dimbleby 1957, 1985) is even less than that of lake sediments, as it.is more prone to disturbance.

Preservation issues, while important in pollen analysis, are not as crippling as those of macrobotanical analysis. Pollen of some taxa such as *Populus* are differentially degraded in lakes and bogs (Webb, Laseski, and Bernabo 1978:1157). Mechanical abrasion may affect certain shapes of pollen grains more than others (Bryant and Holloway 1983:193). The poor preservation of pollen under conditions of alternate wetting and drying may be partly accounted for by mechanical weathering, although chemical conditions are also important. In general, pollen survives well under conditions of low pH (Moore and Webb 1978; Faegri, Kaland, and Krzywinski 1989; Dimbleby 1957), but preservation under more basic conditions is not unknown (Bryant and Holloway 1983:193; see also Martin 1963). Tschudy (1969) argues that, in fact, oxidation potential (Eh) is a more important predictor of pollen preservation than is pH, since certain hydrogen-producing bacteria occur in low Eh environments, and this reducing environment is favorable for pollen preservation. Biological agents can also be highly destructive. Certain aquatic and soil phycomycetes degrade pollen, and this degradation is not uniform for all species (Bryant and Holloway 1983:197).

Pollen Analysis: Interpretation

In light of the complex of factors that act on the pollen record, it is not particularly surprising that few pollen analysts attempt to describe past vegetation except in the most general way. However, while Barker and Gamble (1985:10) complain: "We do not yet have a reliable route to follow from counts of pollen grains to statements about plant biomass, primary productivity, or other ecological measures that provide an essential basis for assessing past human adaptations to the environment," several methods for transforming pollen counts into ecological statements about past vegetation are being developed.

Moving from pollen to vegetation requires two steps. The first involves developing an understanding of the ecology of the species involved (Birks and Gordon 1985:41). The second step involves determining the nature of the relationship of modern vegetation to its contemporary pollen spectra (Bryant and Holloway 1983; Birks, Webb, and Berti 1955; Davis and Goodlett 1960; O'Sullivan and Riley 1974; Prentice and Parson 1983; Parson and Prentice 1981; Webb et al. 1981; Webb, Laseski, and Bernabo 1978). Surface pollen sampling of contemporary pollen is thus very important (cf. Davis 1969). Birks and Gordon (1985:141) note that "a quantitative relationship is assumed to exist between the numbers of pollen grains of a taxon deposited in the sediment at a site and the number of individuals of that taxon in the vegetation surrounding the site," but this quantitative relationship is extremely complex. The usual approach to the problem involves skipping over the intermediate effects of differential pollen production, dispersal, and so forth, and directly comparing the modern pollen rain with its vegetational source area to arrive at pollen "signatures" for vegetation (Birks and Gordon 1985:142). This approach sometimes tends to lump vegetation into plant communities (Webb, Laseski, and Bernabo 1978). Birks and Gordon term this the comparative or analogue approach (1985:143; for a fuller discussion see Davis 1969; Birks and Birks 1980).

An alternate procedure, which emphasizes individual plant taxa, involves the derivation of numerical "transfer functions" (Bryant and Holloway 1983:209) for translating pollen counts to plant counts. A basic component of this analysis is the calculation of modern "pollen representation factors" (Davis 1963), which are defined by comparing the proportion of pollen of a specified taxon observed in a surface sample with the proportion of that taxon in the surrounding vegetation. The vegetation proportions must sum to one. That is, pollen representation factors must be derived for all species contributing to the sample (Birks and Gordon 1985:7). More recent work has greatly expanded and improved Davis's initial formulation (Parsons and Prentice 1981; Prentice and Parsons 1983; Webb et al. 1981).

Both the analogue approach and the pollen representation approach require definition of the pollen source area (Birks and Gordon 1985:145) or vegetational catchment. This definition can be problematic since, for example, pollen grains of some species may travel long distances. Modern pollen studies may require definition of a discontinuous catchment, with local individuals contributing strongly to the pattern, intermediate individuals less strongly, and perhaps distant individuals of only certain species playing a part. Thus, experimental studies and studies of contemporary pollen provide means of evaluating the basic assumptions of pollen analytical methods (Birks and Gordon 1985:146). Unfortunately, analyses of contemporary pollen spectra and their relationship to vegetation are absent in South India, except for a few studies from the Ghat forests (Blasco and Thanikaimoni 1974), and it has not proved possible in the present study to use either pollen signatures or pollen transfer functions to specify vegetation patterns more accurately.

POLLEN ANALYSIS AND AGRICULTURE

Archaeological applications of pollen analysis have focussed on one of two scales: the individual site or the region. Unlike macrobotanical analysis, where the cultural association of materials (but see Covich 1978:151) has largely confined research to the intra-site scale, pollen analysts have had a long history of evaluating the impact of human activities on a regional scale. Early identification of prehistoric forest clearance, or *Landnam*, in Europe was made by Iverson (1941) on the basis of pollen evidence (and see Godwin 1944a, 1944b; Simmons 1969a, 1969b). Iverson's inference was based on an initial increase in herbaceous plants and a slight decline in arboreal taxa such as lime, elm, oak, and ash. This was followed by a short-lived maximum of willow and ash, and then birch and hazel (Iverson 1941), the latter two indicating secondary succession. In the final phase, forest trees except elm (*Ulmus*) (Bryant and Holloway 1983:192) regained their former importance (for a review, see Birks 1986). The interpretation of a period of *Brandwirtschaft*, or shifting cultivation (Forni 1984), preceding more intensive forms of agriculture in Europe has been widely accepted. Indeed, shortly after Iverson published his 1941 paper, numerous other similar studies appeared on England (Godwin 1944a, 1944b, 1956), Ireland (Mitchell 1951; M. Morrison 1959), Scotland (Donner 1962), and elsewhere (cf. Birks 1986).

Evaluations of the *Landnam* hypothesis have addressed a number of issues. As Covich (1978:145) discusses for the Maya area, the assumption that swidden agricultural practices can be unambiguously discerned from pollen diagrams is predicated on the assumption that such agricultural regimes require extensive deforestation and that they are the only determinant of such deforestation. Such an assumption clearly requires some grounding in measures of the "base" stability of an ecological system and the alternate causes of, and periodicity in, vegetational shifts (Rowly-Conwy 1984b). The *Landnam* interpretation has also been challenged on archaeological grounds (Rowly-Conwy 1984b), and one pollen analyst has even suggested that subsequent pollen zonations have been unduly influenced by this interpretation (Edwards 1979). It may also be significant that the notion of an earlier phase of swidden agriculture preceding settled agriculture fits easily into a unilinear view of agricultural intensification, in which land extensive strategies necessarily preceded more land intensive strategies. The demise of the swidden hypothesis for early European agriculture has, then, significant implications for studies of agricultural change throughout the world.

Palynological indications of past agriculture do not consist solely of plant successions. Direct pollen records of cultigens are sometimes preserved (Byrne and Horn 1989), but the identification of economic plants is often hampered by problems of specificity of identification. Many of the important domesticated foodstuffs belong to the grass family, Gramineae (Poaceae). Different genera of grass pollen are distinguished chiefly on the basis of size, and considerable overlap exists between sizes of wild and domestic grass pollen in many parts of the world. *Zea* can be readily distinguished from other grasses in the New World (Irwin and Barghoorn 1965). In Europe and Western Asia it has proved possible to distinguish a "Cerealia type" of pollen from that of wild grasses (Dimbleby 1985:149) on the basis of size statistics (Faegri, Kaland, and Krzywinski 1989:235). In Africa (Livingstone 1984:23-24; Bonnefille 1969), wild and domestic grass pollen cannot be statistically separated, although the pollen of several indigenous domesticates (not grasses) can be identified. Guinet (1966) examined pollen from several South Indian grass species and found that it was not possible to distinguish wild from cultivated grasses on the basis of size alone (see also Chanda 1972; Vishnu-Mittre 1972). Caratini and Tissot of the Institut Francais de Pondichery, on the other hand, have found differences in pore size and morphology between modern hybrid rice (*Oryza sativa*) and other grasses (personal communication 1992). It is not known, however, if other cultivated Gramineae can also be distinguished on the basis of pore size and morphology, or if traditional rice varieties are similarly identifiable.

The use of weeds (cf. Harlan and de Wet 1964; Tadulingam and Venkatanarayana 1932) as indirect cropping indicators is an important part of palynological investigation of agriculture (e.g. O'Connell 1986), particularly where direct evidence of cultigens is absent. In the New World, the presence of *Ambrosia* as a field weed appears to provide a marker of intensity of clearing. In North America, indigenous maize agriculture is not characterized by *Ambrosia* pollen (Bryant and Holloway 1983:217; McAndrews 1976), while colonial European agriculture is. In Mesoamerica, where indigenous population densities were much greater and where there is archaeological indication of intensive agriculture, the association is reversed (Byrne and Horn 1989). Even within cultural groups, fields of the same species treated in different ways may create a variable pollen record. For example, the field weeds of dry rice are quite distinct from those of paddy rice (Barrett 1977). In Europe, weed assemblages have been used to distinguish cropland from pasture land, the so-called "arable-pastoral index" (Dimbleby 1985:145). Dimbleby suggests that anomalously high (*vis-à-vis* local vegetation) pollen concentrations of particular species or types of species in archaeological sites may relate to direct consumption or use of that species not only by humans but also by animals. For example, high ivy (*Hedera*) concentrations in some European Mesolithic sites are suggested to be associated with red deer husbandry (1985:142; see also Jarman 1972).

More secure interpretations of agricultural practices on a local scale might include evidence of field manuring. Dimbleby (1985:144) discusses the pollen taxa found in the chalk soils of the south of England, a locus of intensive agriculture. Species included, among others, a high concentration of *Pteridium* (bracken), which does not grow on such soils, and of insect-pollinated Liguliflorae. He suggests that these were introduced as fertilizer from farmyard manure and household refuse, noting the coincident distribution of small sherds and charcoal in the fields (1985:144; and see Wilkinson 1982, 1989). Pollen analysis, combined with distributional archaeological data, may prove to be an effective means of identifying manuring practices. Barker, for example, marshals a combination of ethnographic, documentary, and archaeological arguments to make a case for field manuring near settlements in prehistoric Europe (1985:52). Other crop management practices may also be amenable to pollen analytical investigation, given an understanding of these practices and their effects in the pollen and archaeological records, and an attention to sampling and analysis at the appropriate scale for the research issue.

Although percentage diagrams of pollen assemblages convey important information, absolute counts and influx measures (Davis 1963; Stockmarr 1972) are also important for the investigation of early agriculture, since changes in sedimentation rates may signal geologic processes associated with vegetation clearance (Butzer 1972, 1982). In addition, more minor vegetation changes may be discernible only with absolute diagrams, since the values of a dominant species in a percentage diagram may mask trends in rarer species. For example, Holloway, Bryant, and Valastro (1981) were able to isolate a vegetational shift in their record using absolute values that was not apparent in the percentage calculation. Microstratigraphic studies have also been successful in tracing small-scale patterns of human impact (Sarmaja-Koronen 1992).

Pollen Analysis from the Vijayanagara Region

Pollen analyses were made from a 57-cm-long core extracted from the sediments of the Kamalapuram Kere. The Kamalapuram Kere (VMS-231, see chapter 4) is a large reservoir which contains water year-round. Water is retained by a masonry-faced earthen dam nearly 2 kilometers long (figure 7.1). Approximately 1700 meters of the embankment appear to belong to the Vijayanagara-period reservoir; recent additions in concrete have extended the embankment on either end. Three sluices date to the Vijayanagara period, and two of these are connected to stone basins beneath (to the north of) the embankment (one of these is illustrated in figure 2.7).

The Kamalapuram Kere is one of the few reservoirs in the Vijayanagara metropolitan region that is not solely dependent on runoff from seasonal or semi-permanent water sources. Instead, its holdings are supplemented by the Raya Canal, which

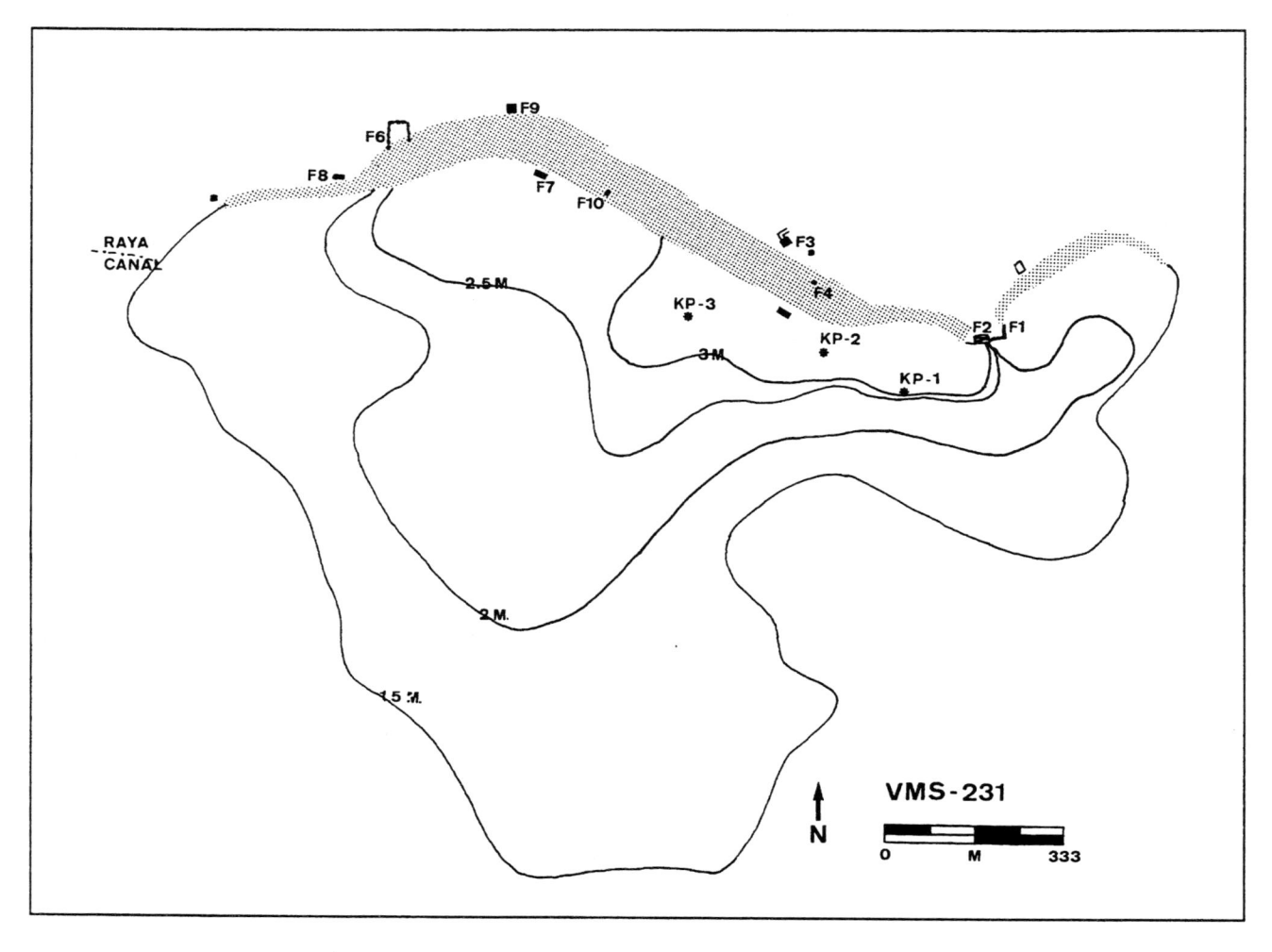

FIGURE 7.1   VMS-231, the Kamalapuram Kere. Map of water depths and core locations.

itself is supplied by an *anicut* from the Tungabhadra River. Thus, the Kamalapuram Kere contains a much more certain water supply than other reservoirs in the region. It has never been completely dry within local memory (about forty years). Only if the canal source were somehow blocked, diverted, or otherwise stopped, might the reservoir dry out. Even so, some water from seasonal runoff still would have flowed into the reservoir along with the overflow from several Vijayanagara-period reservoirs upstream. This constancy of water supply has important implications not only for agricultural production, but also for pollen preservation. Pollen grains are more likely to be preserved where conditions are either uniformly wet or dry; pollen degrades rapidly under conditions of alternate wetting and drying. Samples taken from the fill of several seasonal reservoirs in Block O, for example, did not contain any pollen.

The Kamalapuram reservoir was probably constructed in the early fourteenth century (chapter 5; an inscription of A.D. 1518 also appears to refer to the Kamalapuram Kere; Gopal 1985a:180). This would put its construction in the very beginning of the Vijayanagara period, giving this body of water the potential to provide information on the entire span of Vijayanagara, Colonial, and Post-Independence vegetational history.

The Raya Canal *anicut* was submerged in the Tungabhadra dam project of the 1940s and 1950s (Kotraiah 1959; Davison-Jenkins 1988), and the flow through the canal is now regulated by the irrigation authorities at the Tungabhadra dam. Currently, a moderate but consistent supply of water is released into the reservoir each year from the Raya Canal. Because of the submergence of the Raya *anicut*, it is not possible to detect its elevational position in relation to potential variations in water height—the Tungabhadra River used to rise dangerously high during the monsoon season (Kelsall 1872) and fall quite low in the dry season before the construction of the dam—and thus to assess its reliability. It is assumed that the Raya, like other Vijayanagara canals, provided a fairly secure, year-round flow of water.

The date of the Raya Canal is not entirely clear. Davison-Jenkins (1988:97) argues that the *anicut* and canal mentioned by Nuniz in his recap of Vijayanagara history is the Raya Canal, which thus dates it to the fifteenth century. However, this argument is unconvincing. Even if Nuniz's account is treated as a simple, factual, historical account, he mentions a canal that was "brought inside the city" (Sewell 1900:301), a description that matches the route of the Turtha and not the Raya Canal. It may be that the Raya Canal and the reservoir are contemporaneous, but the occurrence of the inscription from Penukonda (chapter 6) referring to the construction of a canal in order to supplement a reservoir's supply should indicate that this contemporaneity cannot be assumed.

Vegetation

As discussed in chapter 2, the study area is characterized by vegetation of the xeric *Albizia amara-Acacia* series. The slopes of the Sandur Hills support vegetation of the *Hardwickia-Anogeissus* series, while the hilltops contain plants of the *Anogeissus-Terminalia-Tectona* series (Gaussen, et al. 1966). The vegetation in the area has, however, been greatly modified by human activity and cultivated species today constitute a significant proportion of the regional flora (N. P. Singh 1988).

Blasco and Thanikaimoni have argued that the interpretation of South Indian pollen diagrams must be made somewhat differently from temperate zone records:

> In South India, we cannot follow the conventional division of arborescent group and non arborescent group, because surface samples from Nilgiri and Palni have shown that certain forest types may be represented even if pollen grains of herbaceous plants are found in abundance (Guinet 1966). (1974:633)

The reason for this pattern appears to relate both to the relatively low pollen production and the limited dispersal of pollen from many common trees and shrubs. Thus, pollen from the 'characteristic' species of the three vegetation series found in the study area are not necessarily prominent in the pollen record. Many of these genera are insect pollinated, while others such as *Acacia* are also very heavy and are generally not transported for any distance. The most acute problem in interpreting pollen diagrams from the dry interior zones of southern India is, however, the lack of studies relating to pollen production and dispersal and to pollen-vegetation relationships.

The Kamalapuram Kere receives input from a wide catchment area, particularly since the water of the Raya Canal is ultimately derived from the Tungabhadra River. The runoff catchment of the Kamalapuram Kere is also large. Overflow from the smaller reservoirs VMS-241 and VMS-242 upstream was channeled into the Kamalapuram Kere; the watershed of these reservoirs included the Sandur Hills. Thus, the pollen source area for the Kamalapuram reservoir is likely to have been quite large, including all three of the vegetation series found in the region, and the pollen record from this reservoir ought to provide a large-scale, regional record of past vegetation.

Sampling Program

Three sediment cores were extracted from the Kamalapuram Kere; only one of these (1KP) is discussed here. The reservoir was cored in early June 1990, at the height of the dry season. In spite of this, and despite several years of drought in northern Karnataka, the water level was only slightly below the average, perhaps one meter less, judging from water staining on the masonry embankment. The reservoir was not very deep, ranging from less than one meter at its marshy edges, to the deepest area near the sluice, where the water depth was about four meters. Water depths and core locations are indicated in figure 7.1. All cores were taken from a raft, using a modified version of the "UNAM" corer developed by Roger Byrne of the University of California, Berkeley. The corer used on the Kamalapuram sediments was constructed under the direction of Dr. Phadke at the Department of Instrumentation Science, University of Poona, India, and was christened "UNAM Dho" (UNAM two). Because the length of the core's barrel was only 30 cm, it was necessary to obtain several overlapping cores, or "slugs" of sediment. Additional samples currently being studied were obtained using a corer with a longer barrel.

Core Description

The upper 2.5 cm of the core 1KP consists of red silt and clay, followed by 4.5 cm of red silt and clay mixed with black silt. Particles of the two different colors are well mixed, showing no stratigraphic separation such as layering or banding. Silt is the predominant grain size in this stratum. Red silt and clay recur at this point and continue for 22.5 cm. A distinct stratigraphic break is evident in the transition to brown sand and silt at this point in the core. This level is 16.5 cm thick. The basal 11 cm of the core are composed of heavy brown clay. This stratum probably extends to a greater depth than the recovered core; however, it was not possible to push the corer any deeper into this dense sediment.

The cause of the color variation in the upper red and red-black silty levels of the core is not entirely clear. Nevertheless, the overall zonation of the core from clay to sand to silt, a shift from smaller to larger and then to medium particles, is of interest. All strata, of course, actually consist of admixtures of particle sizes, but the general pattern of size sorting is clear. The stratigraphy of a core taken from Halla Kere, a small reservoir to the east of Kamalapuram Kere, exhibits a similar zonation from clay to sand to silt dominated layers. Figure 7.2 shows the stratigraphy of cores 1KP, 2KP, and 3KP in relation to one another and to the depth of the reservoir. Munsell color determinations of the wet sediments are indicated next to each stratum. Where a stratum spanned more than one "slug," Munsell determinations were made on each section. As is clear from the figure, all of the silty layers are very close in color, in part as a consequence of the difficulty of assigning a single color term to a variegated sediment. In fact, the same color category used to describe a red silty level in 3KP (2.5YR 3/6) is used to describe a mixed red-and-black silty level in 2KP. Thus, it is difficult to assign much relevance to Munsell colors, except in very general terms. All of the silty levels were in the 2.5 YR range (red/dark red), and all of the sandy levels and clay levels were in the 5YR range (yellowish red).

Processing

Pollen were extracted from the sediments using 10 percent HCl, 49 percent HF, 70 percent HNO_3, and acetolysis. All samples were processed in the same way; a complete account of processing steps is given in Morrison (1992). Several points are worth noting here, however. First of all, the clay rich sediments presented a minor processing problem requiring several rinses with detergent to deflocculate the clay. More problematic, however, was the presence of resistant organic materials that necessitated the use of concentrated (70 percent) nitric acid. Nitric acid may be harmful to pollen, causing degradation or even destruction of the grain. Because exotic pollen grains (*Lycopodium* tablets; see Benninghof 1962; Stockmarr 1972) were added to the samples during processing, it is possible to assess the potential effects of nitric acid on the fossil pollen by determining if, in fact, the *Lycopodium* grains were damaged. In some cases, *Lycopodium* grains were affected by the processing, with their long spines "burned" off by the acid. Most grains were unaffected, however. Thus only minor degradation of the fossil pollen might be expected.

Concentration

Pollen concentrations in 1KP were quite low, consistent with results obtained from other semi-arid environments (e.g. Clary and Dean 1992). Clary and Dean (1992) have argued that a minimum of 1000 grains per gram of sediment is required in order to make a reliable count. The Kamalapuram pollen concentrations fall well within this range. The generally low pollen concentrations did, however, slow down the counting process considerably, since entire slides or even multiple slides per level had to be counted to locate the minimum number of 200 grains/level used in the analysis.

Core Chronology: Radiocarbon and Introduced Species

Six radiocarbon samples from macroscopic organic material (seeds, leaves, twigs) were submitted for analysis, the results of which are listed in table 7.1. All of the samples were quite small and were analyzed by accelerator mass spectrometry by Geochron Laboratories of Cambridge, Massachusetts. Although small radiocarbon series from rather closely spaced samples are expected to yield a few anomalous dates (Michels 1973:156), the dates reported are difficult to interpret since they exhibit a wide range of variation and their stratigraphic and chronological orders are not coincident. The two uppermost dates were reported to be less than 100 years old, a result that was expected based on their stratigraphic position. At 32 cm, a

TABLE 7.1 Radiocarbon dates from Kamalapuram Core 1. Dates are uncalibrated.

Level	Sample Number	Date (B.P.)	Date (B.C./A.D.)
6.5	GX-17505-AMS	<100 years	recent
22	GX-17506-AMS	<100 years	recent
32	GX-17507-AMS	719 +/- 93	A.D. 1231 +/- 93
36	GX-17508-AMS	1,723 +/- 90	A.D. 218 +/- 90
44	GX-17509-AMS	494 +/- 90	A.D. 1456 +/- 90
46	GX-17510-AMS	1,418 +/- 90	A.D. 532 +/- 90

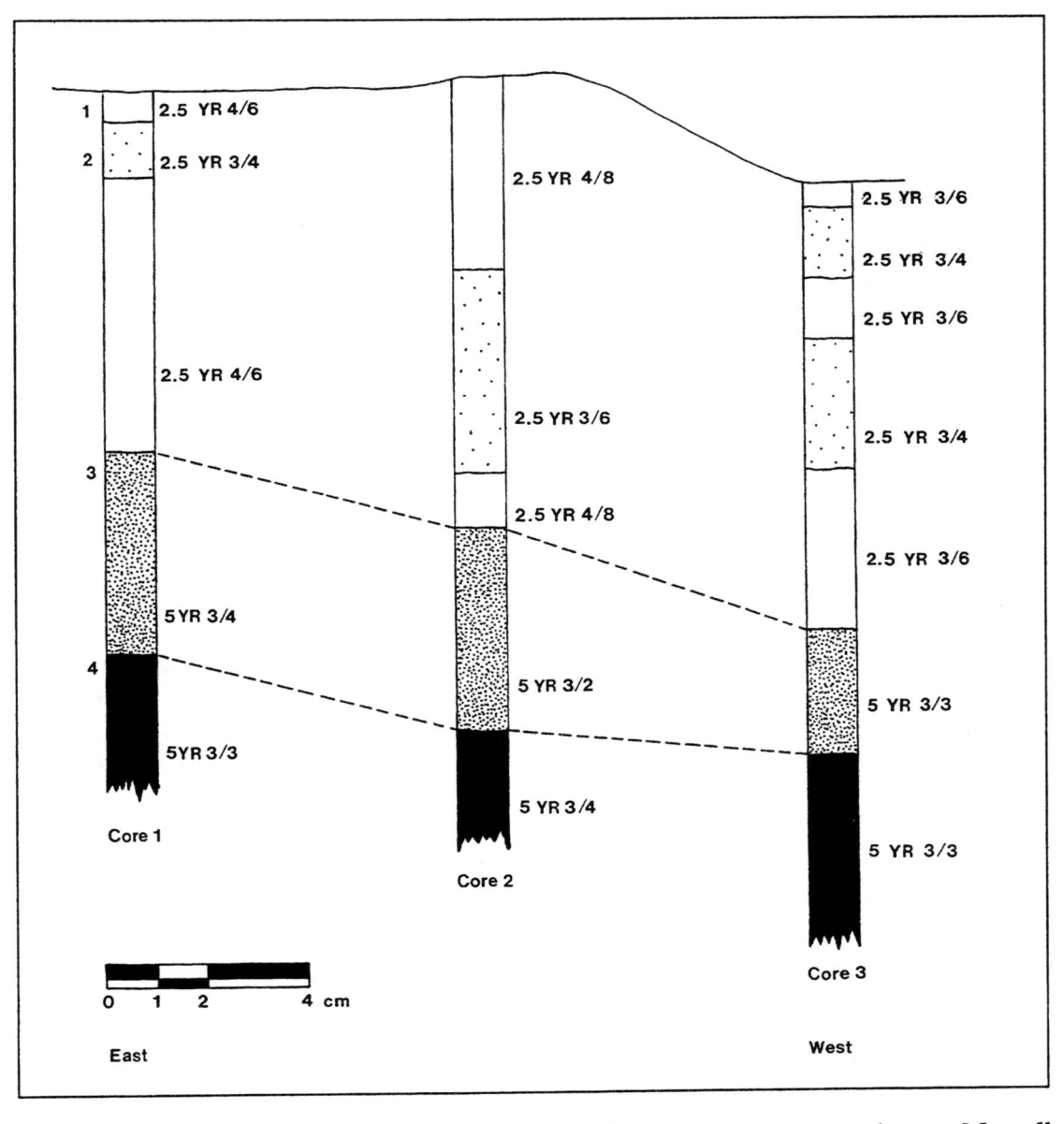

FIGURE 7.2 Kamalapuram Kere, cores 1-3 stratigraphy. Stratum colors are given as Munsell readings. Symbols are discussed in text.

single seed was reported to date to between A.D. 1138 and 1324, somewhat older but within the general range expected. At 36 cm, a date of between A.D. 128 and 308 was reported. These four dates, while surprising, are at least in temporal sequence. At 44 cm, however, material from that level dated to between 1366 and 1546, squarely within the Vijayanagara period. Although this date, along with the two recent dates, constitutes the best "fit" with the other temporal indicators, it is younger than dates from the two higher levels. Finally, the material from the 46 cm level returned a date of A.D. 442 to 622, which, again, is out of sequence since it is older than level 44 but younger than level 36.

Several factors must be considered in assessing the radiocarbon dates. First of all, radiocarbon dating is often problematic within the time range of interest. The real problem, however, probably lies with the context of the macrobotanical material sampled, which has likely undergone humification and thus has been subject to reworking of its carbon compounds (Michels 1973:159).

The stratigraphy of the core provides a broad framework for chronological assessment. The reservoir was probably constructed in the early fourteenth century, and the core almost certainly did not reach the original land surface (or the base surface, since the reservoir was likely to have been excavated into the original soil), so that the base levels are thought to post-date the early fourteenth century, but perhaps not by much. The Kamalapuram reservoir is still in operation, watering a large area under rice and sugarcane. The uppermost levels, then, date to the twentieth century. Thus, if there are no gaps in the core—and none could be discerned stratigraphically through visual inspection or by x-ray of the core—the pollen record should extend from the fourteenth to the twentieth centuries. The lowest portions are suggested to date to the Vijayanagara period, and the higher portions to the Colonial and Post-Independence periods. It cannot be assumed that the length of core represented by each century is of equivalent length, since that would require that the sedimentation rate of the reservoir be constant through time. This assumption cannot be supported, and in fact, the archaeological and historical evidence suggests, quite to the contrary, that erosion was more of a problem at some times than at others, as the differential grain sizes in the sediment also suggest.

In addition to stratigraphy, the presence of plants introduced into India from other parts of the world provides an additional temporal control. *Ricinus*, the castor oil plant, is a native of Africa. Many economically important South Asian plants, including *Sorghum* and many of the millets, are African in origin and were present in India probably by the second millennium B.C. (Possehl 1986). *Ricinus* is present throughout almost the entire core. New World plants provide a more precise marker of time, since they all post-date A.D. 1500. *Alternanthera* appears in the core at 28 cm. Thus, the portion of the core above 28 cm should date to the sixteenth century or later. *Casuarina* was introduced into India in the 1780s (Tissot, personal communication 1992); it appears first at 18 cm and occurs consistently in the upper portions of the core. Thus, if there are no gaps in the sequence, the portion of the core between 18 and 0 cm should represent the eighteenth, nineteenth, and twentieth centuries. As noted, a constant sedimentation rate cannot be assumed, so this sequence cannot be retrodicted.

Vegetation Groups: Identification

The identification of pollen grains and spores from 1KP was facilitated by use of the excellent pollen reference collection of the French Institute, Pondicherry, India. Much of the pollen from the Kamalapuram core could only be identified to family, although some genus and species-level identifications were possible. Families characterized by a single form of vegetation such as herbs, shrubs, or trees were grouped together in figures 7.3 and 7.4. A few families are quite variable in form; these were not included in the overall groupings. The most serious difficulty is presented by the grasses, which dominate the pollen assemblage. The most important agricultural crops of the Vijayanagara period: rice, sorghum, millets, and possibly sugarcane, are all grasses. In Bellary and Raichur districts alone, 97 species in 63 genera of noncultivated Gramineae were reported by N. P. Singh (1988). Most of these occur in disturbed zones such as cleared areas and cultivated fields, and as weeds around habitations and along roads. The great diversity of grasses defies precise ecological categorization, however. General trends can be discerned in both the proportion of grasses to other types of vegetation and in the absolute amount of grass pollen deposited in the reservoir through time (see below).

Appendix 2 lists all of the families identified in the analysis of 1KP, and, where identification was made only to family or genus, all of the poten-

Kamalapuram Kere: Core 1

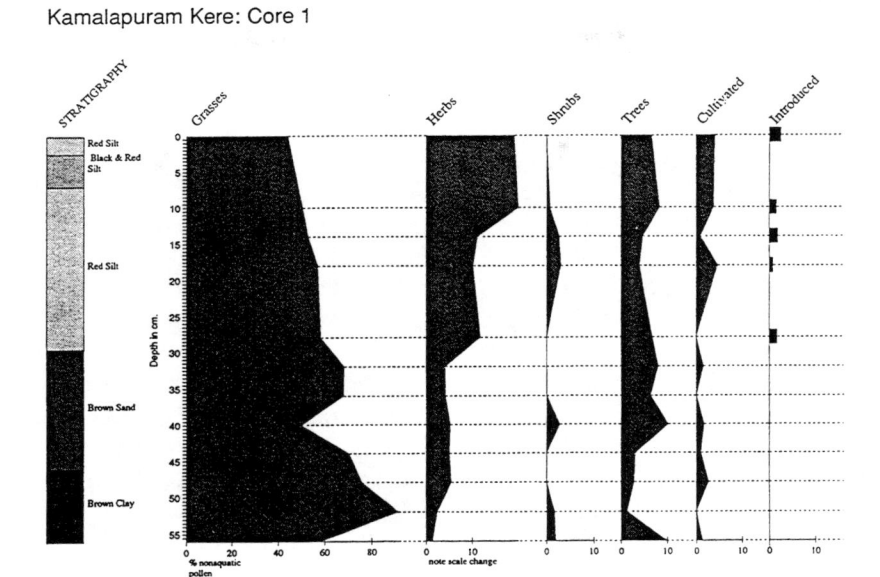

FIGURE 7.3 Vegetation groups: percentage

Kamalapuram Kere: Core 1

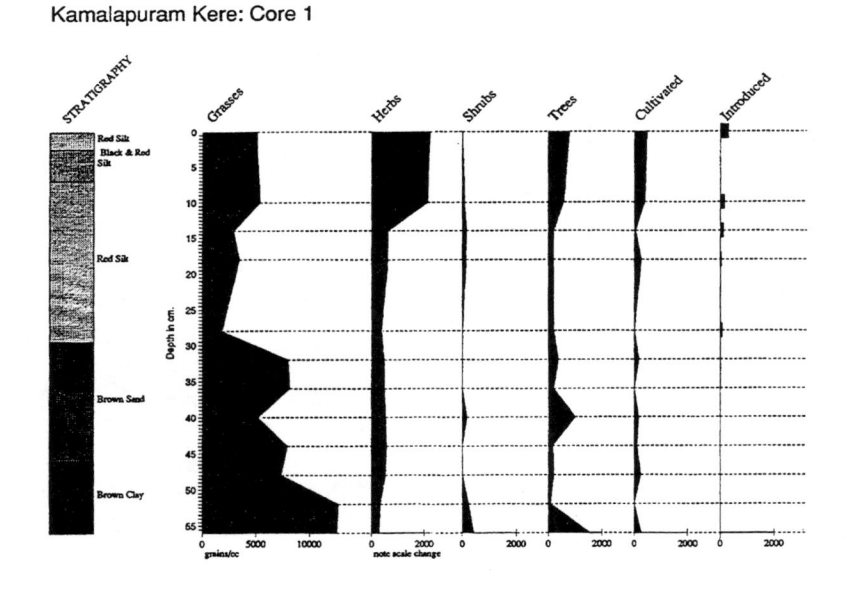

FIGURE 7.4 Vegetation groups: concentration

tial species represented by that identification are listed. The list of potential species is based on the distribution of contemporary vegetation in Bellary and Raichur districts, as reported in N. P. Singh (1988). Although modern vegetation distributions may not reflect past vegetation types exactly, they constitute the best data available for the region.

There is no indication of climate change between the Vijayanagara and modern periods, and changes in species distributions are likely to have been primarily influenced by human activity.

Vegetation Groups: Results

The overall results of the Kamalapuram pollen

core are presented in figure 7.3, which indicates relative abundance of taxa, and figure 7.4 indicating pollen concentrations. It can be seen that grasses dominate the assemblage, followed by herbs and trees. The category of cultivated species refers to non-grass cultigens. On the far right of the diagram are species introduced into India from the New World.

Figure 7.4 shows a decline in overall pollen concentration in the middle portion of the core, between approximately 28 and 14 cm. This decline can be seen quite clearly in the grass curve (Gramineae), the dominant pollen type, but it is a general feature of this portion of the core. The declining concentration of pollen in the core could have been caused by an increased sedimentation rate at this time. At the 24 cm level, the core contains almost no pollen, and counts from this level were not included in the diagram. Except for the extremely low pollen concentration (nine grains counted on one slide, as compared to between 65 and 618 grains per slide for the other levels), there is nothing else of note about the 24 cm level. It contains charcoal (see below), and there is no visually apparent stratigraphic break. There are several possible explanations for this lack of pollen. One may be that the reservoir actually dried out during this period, and the consequent wetting and drying destroyed pollen in sediments near the surface. Alternately, the low pollen concentration could be seen as an extreme example of the low concentrations in nearby levels.

What can be seen in the grass curve is a marked peak near the base of the core that rises to a very high proportion of the total assemblage, approximately 90 percent. This peak undergoes a long and sustained decline, until it reaches a minimum at about 40 cm. Following this low point, grasses rebound somewhat between 40 and 28 cm, after which they again undergo a slow and sustained decline. Because of the composite nature of the grass curve, it is difficult to interpret this pattern. It is tempting to suggest that the dramatic increase in grass pollen between 56 and 52 cm is a consequence of agricultural intensification, caused by the expansion of cultivated fields and the concomitant growth of both weeds and crops, and by the clearing of non-grass vegetation. Figure 7.4 indicates, however, that grass was dominant in the pollen record from the very beginning of the sequence, and in fact, the relative increase of grass at 52 cm is largely a product of a relative decrease in unidentified grains. However, these unknown types are quite unlikely to be grasses, which are easily identified. Thus, the proportional rise in grass pollen actually does relate to a decrease in other taxa. The preponderance of grass at the base of the core is significant. At no other level does the relative or absolute abundance of grass pollen reach the levels it attains near the base. It is not possible to assess the proportion of vegetation types directly from the proportion of pollen types, but it is very striking that the contemporary landscape—deforested, overgrazed, virtually denuded of natural vegetation and covered by agricultural fields—does not create as strong a grass signal.

The basal grass maximum declines between 52 and 40 cm, with only a slight rebound at 42 cm. This decline is evident in both relative and absolute pollen counts, and represents a change in environment conducive to grass growth. The cause of that change is open to interpretation; it may represent a decrease in cultivated grasses, or in open habitats favored by wild grasses, or some combination of factors. Between 14 cm and the top of the core, grass pollen increases in absolute terms but continues to decrease as a percentage, largely due to the increase in Compositae (see below).

Herbaceous plants exhibit a very clear pattern of incidence in the upper portion of the core. Proportionally, they peak at approximately 10 and 28 cm. The initial peak actually seems to reflect the striking decline in numbers of grass pollen grains deposited, however, and the concentration of herbaceous plants in the core is very consistent before the upper 10 cm, with only a slight increase between 48 and 44 cm. The record of herbaceous plants, many of them field weeds, is considered in more detail below.

Shrubs constitute only a very small proportion of the pollen record, and in several levels no shrub pollen at all was counted. For this reason, it is difficult to assign much significance to the distribution of shrub pollen. There are three periods during which shrubs appear in the record. The first two of these correspond with periods of increase in arboreal pollen, and it is probable that both trees and shrubs were responding to similar conditions at these times. Both the tree and shrub curves exhibit a decline between approximately 52 and 44 cm during the period of most significant change in the grass curve. The loss of trees and shrubs is not precisely aligned with a growth in grass pollen, although there is a slight increase in herbaceous plants. At the base of the core, grasses already dominate the record, and tree and shrub pollen is already undergoing a precipitous decline. The proportion of trees and shrubs remains low until about 40 cm, when it begins to increase. This pattern may indicate pressure on the woody vegetation in the study area from the beginning of the record, followed by a period of more open vegetation, with a later (and limited) regeneration of trees and shrubs. Trees are discussed in more detail below.

The curve representing cultivated plants does *not* include any cultigens belonging to the family Gramineae. Only pollen grains which could be securely identified to genus, and which are known to have been cultivated (that is, they do not occur naturally in the area and are cultivated today), are included in this category. The cultivated genera are discussed in more detail below.

Grasses and Aquatic and Herbaceous Plants

Figures 7.5 and 7.6 indicate the percentages and concentrations, respectively, of grasses, aquatic plants, and herbaceous plants in the Kamalapuram core. The grass curve is the same as that represented in figures 7.3 and 7.4. Next to the grass curve is the record of pollen from aquatic plants, which exhibits a very striking pattern. There is a well-defined peak in aquatic vegetation (with a slight decline at 40 cm) between about 44 and 32 cm. The rapid growth in aquatic plants corresponds with a decline in grasses, and begins somewhat before the period in which trees and shrubs begin to reappear in the record. Normal maintenance of reservoirs includes cleaning out aquatic plants, so that the rapid growth in aquatic vegetation almost certainly indicates a period during which the reservoir was not well maintained. By the time trees and shrubs began to regenerate, the reservoir had become choked with aquatic vegetation. The rapid decline in the concentration of pollen of aquatic plants (at about 28 cm) occurs at the same time as the first introduced species appear in the record, and shortly before the possible drying out of the reservoir at the 24 cm level. Thus, the postulated drying out period follows the beginning of renewed maintenance of the reservoir. Because the Kamalapuram Kere is supplied by both seasonal runoff and the river-fed Raya Canal, virtually the only way the reservoir could dry out (seasonally) would be to block, divert, or otherwise stop the flow from the canal. Today, canals are periodically blocked in order to clean out silt and vegetation. Perhaps the potential drying out actually represents maintenance of the reservoir, including the removal of aquatic plants.

Most of the aquatic plants are represented by plants belonging to just three families, Typhaceae, Cyperaceae, and Potomagetonaceae (figure 7.7). *Typha angustata* is an aquatic or marshy-habitat herb which grows in shallow water around the edges of reservoirs and other bodies of water (appendix 2). Similarly, the five genera of Cyperaceae that are found in the study area grow in shallow water. In contrast, *Potomageton nodosus*, although it also grows in shallow water, can grow partially or almost completely submerged (appendix 2), so that it has the potential to invade more of a reservoir than simply its edges. The strong pattern in aquatic plants is created almost entirely by *Potomageton*, with some contribution by Cyperaceae. *Typha* concentrations are remarkably consistent throughout the core, with a slight increase near the top and a decrease in the lowest levels.

The strong pattern exhibited by the aquatic plant concentrations in the core also raises questions about the pattern of the grass curve. Below 48 cm, there appears to be no relationship between the concentration of Gramineae and of aquatic plants in the core. During the period of maximum aquatic plant growth, however, smaller peaks in the grass curve co-occur with those of aquatic taxa. It is possible that some of the grasses making up the overall curve are aquatic species, and in the areas where grass pollen patterns echo those of aquatic plants, the possibility is even stronger. If this were the case, then the pattern of non-aquatic grass decline above 52 cm would be even more marked.

Figures 7.5 and 7.6 detail the pollen record of the more common types of herbaceous vegetation. By far the most ubiquitous of these is Compositae (Asteraceae), of which twenty-seven genera are found in the study area today, eight of them New World introductions (appendix 2). All of these genera are characterized by herbaceous plants favoring open habitats, and a great many of them occur as weeds in cultivated fields, though some favor wetter and other drier environments. The pollen of Compositae can be divided into categories on the basis of several characteristics; one of these is the length of the spines, with grains often sorted into "low spine" and "high spine" categories. As indicated by figures 7.5 and 7.6, the recent increase

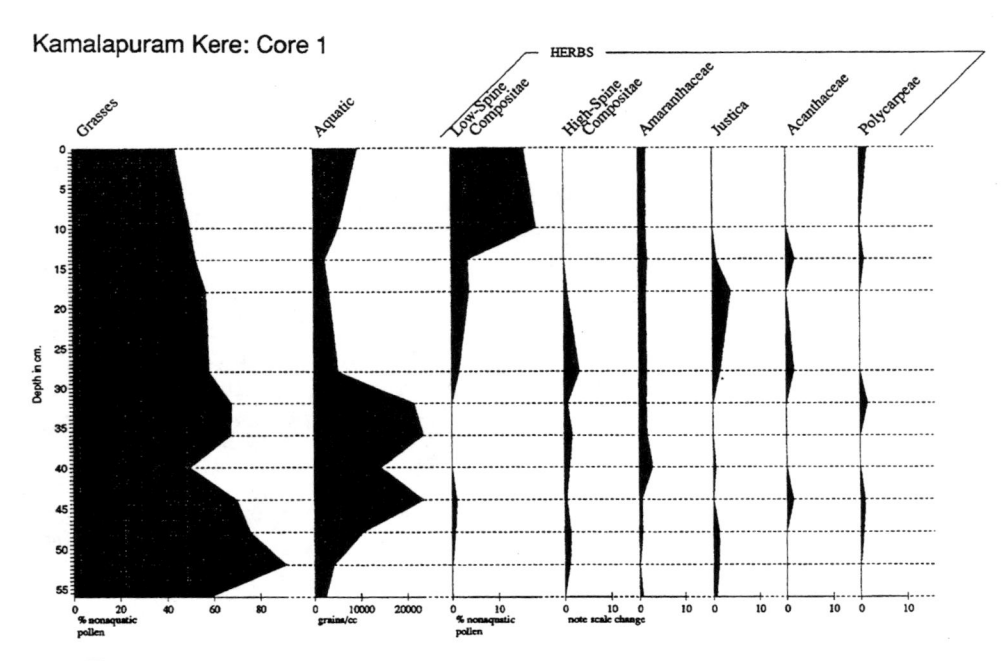

FIGURE 7.5 Grasses, aquatic and herbaceous plants: percentage

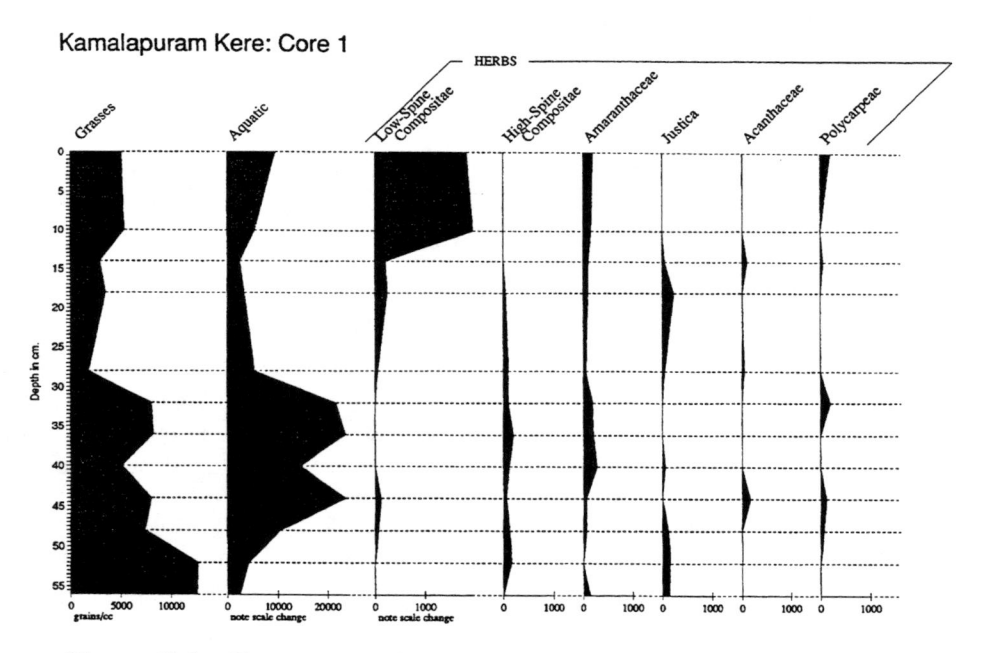

FIGURE 7.6 Grasses, aquatic and herbaceous plants: concentration

in Compositae pollen consists entirely of "low spine" types, and in fact, the distributions of "low spine" and "high spine" pollen are nearly exclusive, with a small "low spine" peak at 44 cm falling in a "high spine" trough. It would be worthwhile knowing what, if anything, these differences relate to. The eclipse of "high spine" by "low spine" types near the top of the core is also interesting in light of the number of introduced genera of Compositae, such as *Xanthium*, which is a low-spine introduced genus (N. P. Singh 1988; Saldanha 1984). Whatever genera of Compositae are represented, however, the marked peak in Compositae pollen near the top of the core is significant and

Kamalapuram Kere: Core 1

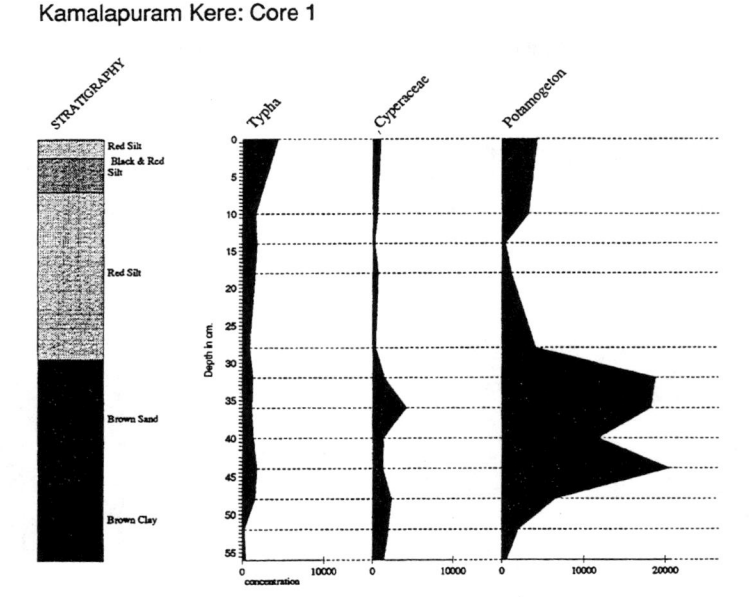

FIGURE 7.7 Aquatic plants: concentration

indicates that late Colonial and/or recent land use is quite different from that of the Vijayanagara period in that it is marked by a somewhat different weedy flora.

The record of Amaranthaceae is quite consistent through time, with only minor changes evident. Most genera of Amaranthaceae present in the study area occur as weeds in cultivated fields. The genus *Justica* belongs to the family Acanthaceae. Both of these occur in figures 7.5 and 7.6, since genus-level identifications were not always possible. In the study area, two species of *Justica* are found (appendix 2). One grows in moist, open areas at low elevations such as open patches in deciduous forests, and the other is found exclusively in the Sandur Hills (N. P. Singh 1988). The exact provenience of the *Justica* in the core cannot, of course, be determined, but its association with open patches is significant since the two periods during which it occurs in the core correspond to what are postulated to be the Vijayanagara period and the Colonial period, respectively. Non-*Justica* Acanthaceae is a minor component of the record. Other Acanthaceae genera tend to prefer moist situations, and one (*Hygrophila*) is often associated with reservoirs. *Polycarpaea* is a member of the family Caryophyllaceae, and is found in sandy soils in cultivated fields and other disturbed areas (appendix 2).

Trees

Trees are not well represented in the Kamalapuram pollen core, but it is difficult to make any assessment of the relative importance of trees in the vegetation of the region given the lack of information about pollen production and dispersal of local plants (and see Blasco and Thanikaimoni 1974). Figures 7.8 and 7.9 give the breakdown of the most common tree types in the sample. *Acacia* and *Phoenix* are numerically predominant, and at least for *Acacia*, that probably also reflects its importance in the vegetation. I have already noted the period of decline in trees and shrubs; this pattern is exhibited by many of the groups in figures 7.8 and 7.9. Pollen labelled as *Acacia* may also belong to the genus *Albizia* (family: Mimosaceae). The ten species of *Acacia* and *Albizia* in the study area all occur in dry situations in thorn scrub forests, with some also found in deciduous forests. *Acacia chundra* constitutes a major component of the vegetation in Bellary and Raichur districts (N. P. Singh 1988). The initial decrease in *Acacia* near the base of the core corresponds with the increase in grasses, and the regeneration of *Acacia* with a decline in grasses. *Phoenix*, or wild date palm, occurs naturally in the area in dry deciduous forests, growing in dense stands in valleys (Saldanha 1984:19). The distribution of *Phoenix* pollen is similar to that of *Acacia*. *Casuarina*, as noted above, was introduced into India and is sometimes grown in large stands for charcoal. Not all pollen from palms (Palmae or Aracaceae) could be identified; these are classified as a single group in figures 7.8 and 7.9. Other families such as Bignonaceae (probably *Dolichandrone*, see appendix 2) and Combretaceae make up minor components of the pollen record. A few grains of *Azadirachta indica* (the *Neem* tree) were also identified.

Non-Gramineae Cultivated Plants

The combined pattern of non-grass cultivated plants shows little significant patterning through time except for a slight increase in the upper levels of the core. However, some interesting patterns do

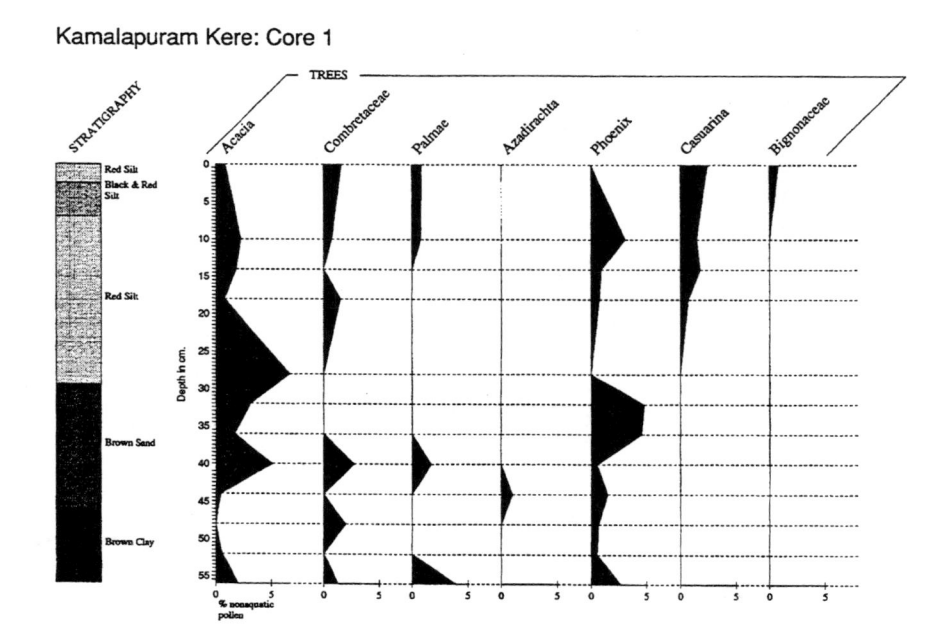

FIGURE 7.8 Trees: percentage

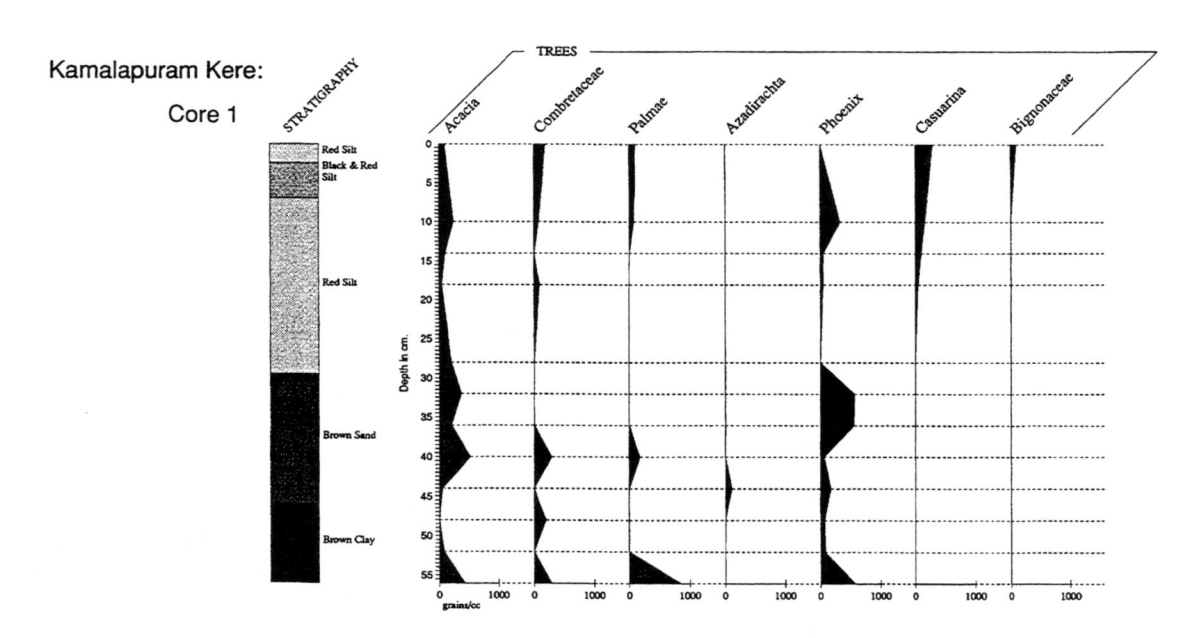

FIGURE 7.9 Trees: concentration

emerge when this composite curve is separated into its component taxa (figures 7.10 and 7.11). These data should be treated with caution because of the small amount of pollen they reflect. *Arenga pinnata* (Gomuti palm; Ambasta 1986:51) and *Jasminum auriculatum* (Jasmine) are very rare in the sample. More common are *Cocos nucifera* (coconut) and *Ricinus communis* (castor oil plant). *Cocos* is an important cash crop in the area today, and this dominance is reflected in the larger amounts of coconut pollen between 10 cm and the top of the core. *Cocos* has its second highest concentration at the base of the core, but it quickly declines in importance before reaching a small peak between 44 and 40 cm. This pattern may simply be a product of the small sample size of coconut pollen at the base of the core, but it is at least qualitatively interesting as it indicates the production of

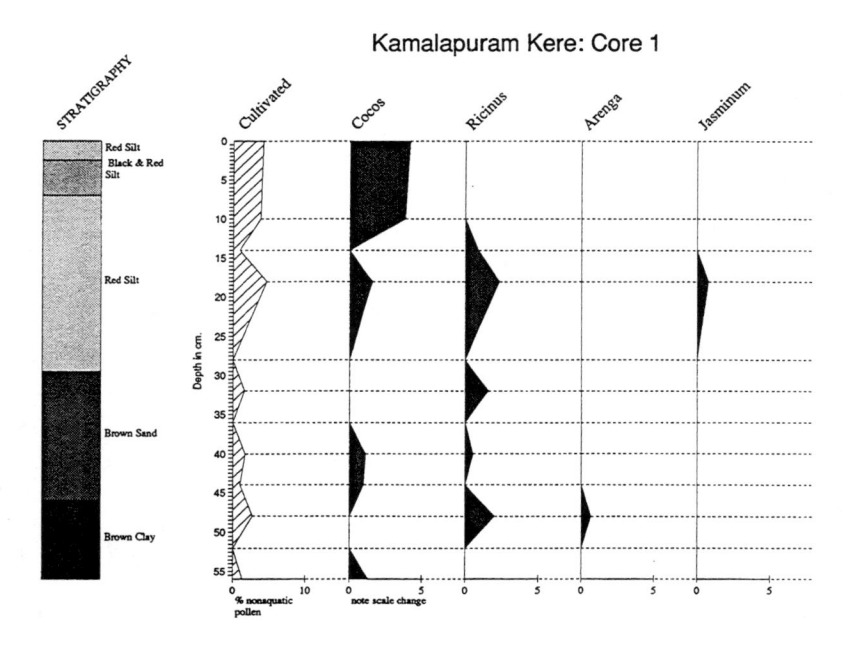

FIGURE 7.10 Non-grass cultivated plants: percentage

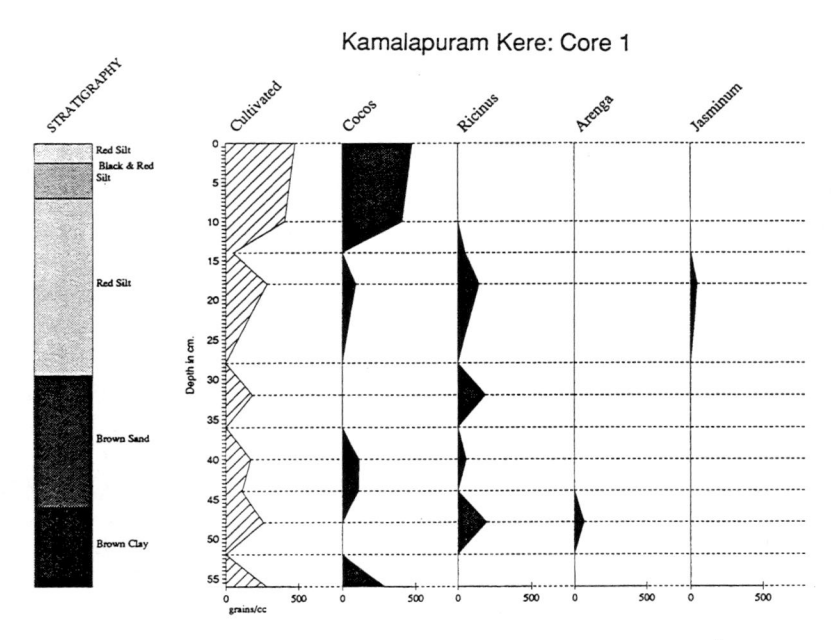

FIGURE 7.11 Non-grass cultivated plants: concentration

coconuts in the Vijayanagara period (also noted in historical sources, see chapter 6). Whether or not the apparent decline in *Cocos* in the lower third of the core is a "real" phenomenon or just a sampling fluctuation, it is apparent that overall the earlier record of coconuts indicates that they were of less importance than in the later record. The more recent focus on *Cocos* production occurs at the time of the first New World species and during the period in which it was suggested that renewed maintenance of the reservoir was taking place. *Ricinus* may originally have been a native of Africa, as are many other Indian cultigens, although some botanists feel that *Ricinus* may be indigenous to India (see discussion in Narain 1974). The distribution of *Ricinus*, which may be grown as either a dry or an irrigated crop, is strikingly different from that of *Cocos*, occurring neither in the earliest nor in the latest portions of the core. The context of *Ricinus* cultivation thus appears to have been quite different from that of coconut cultivation.

Charcoal Analysis

Just as the types and quantity of charcoal from archaeological contexts are used to make inferences about the human use of fire within settlements, regional records of fire history may be preserved in lake or reservoir sediments. Quantitative analysis of charcoal content in sediment cores has the potential to inform on both natural fire history and on the frequency and intensity of fire in the context of agricultural practice and in settlements.

Fire in Context

Fire plays an important role in the contemporary agricultural practices of South India. The stubble remaining in sugar cane fields after harvesting is regularly burned off, and the ashes are either plowed back into the soil or carried off to other areas and distributed on the fields. Because of the long maturation period of sugar cane, eleven months, and its reliance on irrigation water, planting, weeding, harvesting, and burning of cane fields occur more or less simultaneously across large areas in a patchwork fashion. Areas under cane production have a mosaic-like appearance, with multiple crop stages simultaneously represented. Groups of several neighboring fields served by a single water source are often at a similar stage of development. Thus, the need to coordinate water flow to fields requires some coordination of scheduling but not on a supraregional scale. While individual cane fires are usually small, burning less than ten hectares at a time, fires are frequent wherever it is possible to grow sugar cane.

Fire is also employed to control weed and shrub growth along field borders, roadways, and near settlements. Fire may be an important tool for forest clearance, although this is no longer a concern in the Vijayanagara region. At present, no crop grown in the study area other than sugar cane is regularly burned.

Undoubtedly, the most well-known role of fire in agricultural production is in "slash and burn" or swidden agriculture (Iverson 1941; Stewart 1956; Mellars 1976; Jacobi, Tallis, and Mellars 1976; Simmons, Kershaw, and Clark 1981). Swidden agriculture was widely practiced in India and is well documented in the literature of the Colonial period from the seventeenth to early twentieth centuries. Chola inscriptions of the eleventh century from the state of Tamil Nadu refer to swidden plots (*kummari*) of "forest people" (Stein 1980:26). Stein (1980:75-76) discusses the tensions between lowland peasants and the non-peasant inhabitants of the hills and dry forests, a tension well documented into the sixteenth century. In the Vijayanagara region, swidden cultivation could have been supported on the slopes of the Sandur Hills. There is, at present, no evidence of this agricultural regime during the Vijayanagara period.

Finally, the non-agricultural use of fire was also significant. Both wood and dung were probably burned in domestic contexts. Some forms of craft production also employed fire extensively, either in kilns or open burns. Charcoal, which is produced locally, is often used as the fuel for ceramic, lime, and metal kilns. Thus, we must guard against assuming that the fossil record of fire relates solely to agricultural burning (cf. Patterson, Edwards, and Maguire 1987:4). This point is taken up below in the discussion of charcoal transport.

Proxy Measures of Fire

Given that information on fire history may be of interest in reconstructing Vijayanagara land use, the question arises how best to investigate the fossil record of that history. Archaeological investigations in the Royal Center have revealed evidence of fires that destroyed numerous buildings in the "Noblemen's Quarter" area. Investigators have attributed this evidence to the burning and sacking of the city following the battle of Talikota in A.D.1565 (Balasubramanyam personal communication). Other, more localized ash levels are evident in excavated sections, but these do not inform on regional scale fire history. As with pollen, the action of lakes (or reservoirs) as regional or even supraregional sediment traps provides the best possibility for reconstructing Vijayanagara fire history.

The most common measures of fire history from lake sediments include microscopic and macroscopic charcoal; pollen assemblages and accumulation rates, chemical digestion of elemental carbon, geochemistry of lake sediments, and sedimentological measures (J. S. Clark 1988a, 1988b; R. L. Clark 1982; MacDonald et al. 1991; Patterson, Edwards, and Maguire 1987; Swain 1973; Tolonen 1986; Waddington 1969; Winkler 1987). A growing literature, mostly concerned with the reconstruction of boreal forest fire histories, discusses each of these methods in detail. Several recent studies have compared the efficacy of different methods using documentary history and fire scars on trees as controls (e.g. MacDonald et al. 1991; J. S. Clark 1988a). MacDonald and others (1991:65) found little consistency between proxy measures of fire history and documented fires. Pollen records provided some indication of vegetation succession but presented a limited picture of postfire recovery. The results of carbon digestion-combustion techniques were not consistent with microscopic and macroscopic charcoal patterns and may be affected by very small charcoal particles, which are not counted in visual studies, and by changes in sediment types (see Winkler 1985:319). Visual studies of charcoal, both microscopic and macroscopic, provided fairly good indicators of fire history in a region up to 120 kilometers from the sediment source (MacDonald et al. 1991:62, figure 8). The following discussion is limited to visual studies of charcoal from lake sediments.

From Fire to Lake: Production, Dispersal, and Deposition

Fires may vary a great deal in the amount of charcoal they produce and in the extent of dispersal of that charcoal. Relevant variables include the type of fuel, the size of the fire, and weather conditions. It is often assumed that larger fragments of charcoal are found nearer the source of the fire and smaller fragments farther away. Patterson, Edwards, and Maguire (1987:5-7) present a simple zonal model of the effect of distance on the quantity and size of charcoal fragments deposited after a fire. They tentatively suggest that the deposition of a set of concentric rings of charcoal size classes in the absence of wind, with multiple sources causing overlapping patterns.

In practice, however, the dynamics of charcoal transport are much more complex. In an important study of the physics of charcoal transport, J. S. Clark (1988b) has shown that wind has fundamentally different effects on different size classes of charcoal. Clark identifies three major forms of wind transport: (1) suspension; (2) saltation, in which moving particles strike other particles lifting them from the surface and moving them downwind; and (3) traction, or movement along the surface. Smaller particles are more subject to suspension, intermediate size classes are moved by saltation, and larger particles are moved by traction. Clark notes:

> mineral particles approximately 100μm in size are most easily entrained by wind; cohesive forces and aerodynamic properties of smaller particles make them difficult to pick up, and larger particles are too massive. Although difficult to entrain, smaller particles tend to be transported long distances, if they are suspended. Source areas for dust fallout at a given point may be subcontinental or even global, depending on particle size and atmospheric conditions. 'Coarse dust' (5-50μm) transported by dust storms is generally deposited within 100 km of the source. 'Fine dust' (2-10μm) is frequently transported hundreds to thousands of kilometers, remaining in suspension until washed out by precipitation. (1988b:69)

Charcoal particles have a much lower density than mineral particles, so that charcoal fragments in the 130 to 150 μm range are the most readily lifted by the wind (Clark 1988b). Most charcoal fragments examined microscopically fall well below this size category and thus must be considered representative of burning over a large spatial scale. Clark (1988a) describes a method for examining macroscopic charcoal using thin-sections of sediment cores. This method is, however, appropriate only for annually laminated or varved deposits. Such deposits, which do not include the Kamalapuram sample, are rare, especially in the tropics. Macroscopic analysis of charcoal holds great promise for studies of fire history, particularly since larger pieces of charcoal are also the most readily identifiable to genus or type (e.g. Byrne, Michaelson, and Soutar 1977, 1979; Hutchinson and Goulden 1966). Future analyses of the Kamalapuram material will include macroscopic as well as microscopic charcoal studies.

The second major contribution made by J. S. Clark's (1988b) study is the identification of a finite "skip distance" between the point where most particles of a given size leave the ground and where they settle back down. Indrafts and convection in the rising hot air of a fire create turbulence in which particles are suspended, and the specific skip distance depends on the height of the convection column created by a particular fire. In general, the higher the convection column the larger the skip distance and the larger the particle size, the smaller the skip distance. Clark (1988b) fails to stress, however, that this skip is applicable only for airborne particles. Even for easily entrained smaller particles, some proportion is left *in situ* in the burn location. Further, his model is based on wildfires, which may differ significantly from small, controlled burns in several ways including type of fuel and height of the smoke plume (cf. Patterson, Edwards, and Maguire 1977). Most fire history studies attempt to find fossil evidence for individual large forest fires, events of high intensity, short duration, and variable periodicity (see J. S. Clark 1988b for a discussion of fire periodicity and sampling intervals). Many of these analyses have failed to isolate individual fires. However, the overall importance of fire during different periods are just the sort of broad patterns likely to be isolated in charcoal studies.

Charcoal size categories must be carefully considered in light of the recent scholarship on the dynamics of charcoal transport. Different size classes do not always co-vary (MacDonald et al. 1991:61, table 2), and size categories may have to be individually studied and interpreted. A size-based analysis of the Kamalapuram charcoal record can be found in Morrison (1994b).

Clark's (1988a, 1988b) studies focus exclusively on air transport of charcoal, and, in fact, he asserts that air transport is the most important mechanism of charcoal deposition in lakes, at least for areas with uncompacted forest soils. Swain (1973:391) suggests that slope wash of charcoal into lakes may be quite important even in forested areas (see also Cwynar 1978; Patterson, Edwards, and Maguire 1977). Fires themselves may increase surface runoff and erosion (Tsukada and Deevey 1967; Swain 1973; Cwynar 1978). In either case, it is clear that water-assisted movement of soil must be considered in the case of the Kamalapuram Kere, where no forest cover exists, rainfall is highly seasonal, erosion severe, and soils are compacted (cf. Bonny 1976; Peck 1973). Thus, fires in the reservoir catchment to the south of the reservoir are expected to contribute disproportionately to the charcoal record in the reservoir sediment.

Fossil Fuels and Soot Balls

The burning of fossil fuels can produce opaque, black spheres, alternately referred to as "opaque spherules" (J. S. Clark 1988b) or "soot balls" (Winkler 1985:319), which can be confused with charcoal from plant tissues. Morphological studies of opaque spherules have been carried out by Clark and Patterson (1984) and Renberg and Wilk (1985). These spherules, approximately 5 to 35 μm in diameter and composed of iron oxide (Patterson, Edwards, and Maguire 1977), have been recognized in sediments less than 100 years old from eastern North America (Clark and Patterson 1984). If such objects are limited to industrial sources and automobiles, then their occurrence in South Indian reservoir sediments should signal quite recent time periods, perhaps less than fifty years. However, Patterson and others (1987) warn that opaque spherules may be produced by wildfires or domestic burning. If the latter is true, then the distribution of opaque spherules should be variable throughout the Kamalapuram core, and they should occur in the earliest levels.

Pollen Processing and Charcoal

Because of its composition, charcoal is not destroyed in the process of pollen extraction. There is some indication that samples treated with nitric acid, such as the Kamalapuram samples (see below), contain a significantly smaller proportion of charcoal than samples not treated with nitric acid. Nevertheless, the relative proportions of charcoal in each stratum appear to be stable even with nitric treatment (Singh, Kershaw, and Clark 1981; Patterson, Edwards, and Maguire 1987). Nitric acid treatments, necessary for the pollen extraction in the Kamalapuram case, also have the benefit of removing opaque pyrite crystals (Waddington 1969; Patterson, Edwards, and Maguire 1987). Thus, the Kamalapuram samples can only be compared internally or to other samples processed in a similar fashion.

CHARCOAL FROM THE VIJAYANAGARA REGION

Charcoal analysis from the Kamalapuram core was carried out using the same slides employed for pollen analysis (see discussion above). Most previous studies of microscopic charcoal have been made either by counting the number of charcoal particles or the measurement of their areas by point counts (Patterson, Edwards, and Maguire 1987). An eyepiece graticule, which divides the field of view into grid squares of known size, may be used. Charcoal fragments are then counted by grid square class (1 square, 2 squares, etc.) (Waddington 1969). The charcoal counts or area determinations can be calculated as a percentage of the total pollen sum, or as a ratio to the pollen sum (Patterson, Edwards, and Maguire 1987; Swain 1973). Charcoal counts can also be expressed in relation to absolute quantities and influx (Byrne, Michaelsen, and Soutar 1977), just as pollen can (MacDonald et al. 1991:57).

Charcoal counts of the Kamalapuram Kere slides were made using an automated system that analyzed the level and uniformity of darkness of particles on a microscope slide. This automated system is described in detail by Horn, Horn, and Byrne (1992). Five hundred randomly selected fields of view were analyzed for each slide. Views were selected from within a 12 x 12 mm area in the center of the coverslip (22 x 22 mm) in order to avoid problems of slide variation at the edges of the coverslip. Only particles with a minimum linear dimension of 25 µm and a minimum area of 156 µm^2 were counted. Images on the slides were analyzed by the computer as containing grey shade values between 0 and 63, where 0 is black and 63 is white. All pixels in a particle image were analyzed individually and mean grey shade value and standard deviations were calculated. Only objects having a mean grey shade value of 3.5 or less and a standard deviation of 5 or less were considered. Thus, particles had to be quite dark and uniformly dark in order to be counted as charcoal. Periodic visual monitoring of the procedure provided a high level of agreement between the occurrence of charcoal and its fit with these criteria. Magnification was set at 160X. MacDonald and others (1991) also used an automated counting system, but they counted every particle larger than 10 µm long and 10 µm wide. Because of the high frequency of long, thin charcoal particles in the Kamalapuram sample, these parameters would have excluded a great deal of charcoal. As it is, charcoal counts are probably somewhat low due to bleeding of light onto the edges of the particles, which leads to higher mean grey shade values. More problematic, perhaps, is the computer's inability to distinguish between superimposed objects. Where small pieces of charcoal lay atop clumps of cellular material, the resultant form was counted as one object, generally with a high grey value standard deviation. Such charcoal was not counted by the procedure. For this reason, slides were made as thin as possible.

Charcoal Results

Special scans of the charcoal slides were made in order to count *Lycopodium*. These values were then used to calibrate the charcoal counts, which are indicated in figure 7.12. The charcoal record from the Kamalapuram core shows a great deal of variation through time, with several major peaks and many more minor ones. Figure 7.12 gives charcoal data both in terms of the number of charcoal particles (minimum size cutoff 156 µm^2) and the area of charcoal (mm^2). Both methods yield similar results with the exception of two peaks at 16 and 10 cm.

Beginning at the base of the core, a small charcoal peak can be seen in the lowest level, followed by a decline and then a major peak at about 52 cm. At this same level a decline in trees and shrubs and an increase in grasses were also recorded. Thus, although some of this charcoal may be attributable to domestic burning in the Vijayanagara period, it is likely that it also relates, at least in part, to land use practices which led to the creation of a more open, less wooded landscape. The context of Vijayanagara-period burning is less clear than is recent burning. Trees and sometimes shrubs were collected for firewood to be used in domestic contexts, but fuel was also needed for charcoal production for use in such craft activities as metallurgy. Sugarcane or other crops may have been burned off, and burning may also have been employed for the clearance of thorny vegetation and the eradication of weeds, as it is today. Charcoal peaks in this densely settled region undoubtedly relate to periods of intensification of human burning activities, and many of those were probably related to agricultural operations.

Following the marked charcoal peak at 52 cm, the amount of charcoal in the sample drops off, and then rises again into two minor peaks between 46 and 26 cm. Above this point, the difference between the count data and the area data become much more pronounced. Table 7.2 gives descriptive statistics on charcoal area data from each level. At 8 and 10 cm the mean area of charcoal in the sample rises sharply in response to an increase in

TABLE 7.2 Charcoal in 1KP: level, number of charcoal particles, minimum, maximum, mean, and standard deviation of area

Level	N	Minimum area (μm^2)	Maximum area (μm^2)	Mean area (μm^2)	Standard Deviation
0	18	174.4	2361.5	699.4	581.9
8	102	228.1	15372.4	3005.6	2969.5
10	77	163.7	14375.6	2875.1	3226.0
12	69	158.3	6853.7	991.0	1374.1
14	47	158.3	5058.4	880.4	1013.9
16	443	158.3	5952.0	612.2	581.6
18	213	161.0	3574.4	536.9	470.6
20	67	158.3	3767.7	824.9	880.5
22	30	169.1	1132.4	297.9	187.7
24	211	158.3	4613.0	473.8	542.7
26	65	158.3	8114.9	681.4	1160.3
28	43	161.0	5283.8	710.4	889.6
30	43	158.3	1800.6	552.2	427.7
32	144	163.7	5884.9	521.6	704.6
34	49	158.3	2906.2	660.0	596.6
36	38	169.1	1084.1	456.5	263.8
38	164	161.0	9263.5	731.2	1333.4
40	69	158.3	6711.5	638.6	986.3
42	10	169.1	3222.9	682.7	919.2
44	24	166.4	2756.0	446.3	519.0
46	50	158.3	1663.8	466.0	361.9
48	84	163.7	5643.4	652.2	855.2
50	253	161.0	2699.6	454.7	387.9
52	235	158.3	4723.0	592.6	667.7
54	179	158.3	9384.2	645.7	992.3
56	41	166.6	2954.5	690.4	676.1

the size of the largest charcoal particles. It may be that this increase in particle size relates to a change in the distance between some burning activities and the reservoir. Today, the area around the Kamalapuram reservoir is almost all planted in sugarcane, which is burned off after each harvest. If there were a shift in the pattern of agricultural land use around the reservoir from some other crop or crop mix (dominated by rice?) to the commercially important sugarcane, then an increase in both the quantity and size of charcoal in the reservoir sediments might be expected. That this pattern of increased charcoal size does not continue into the uppermost level is troubling in light of the sugarcane hypothesis, but the very small size of the sample (N=18) makes it difficult to evaluate the hypothesis. Future analyses of both macroscopic and microscopic charcoal from other Kamalapuram cores should clarify this issue.

The most pronounced charcoal increase occurs at approximately the 16 cm level, during a period of very low overall pollen concentration but before some of the vegetation changes associated with the uppermost levels of the core. This peak is not characterized by larger particles but by an increase in the number of particles.

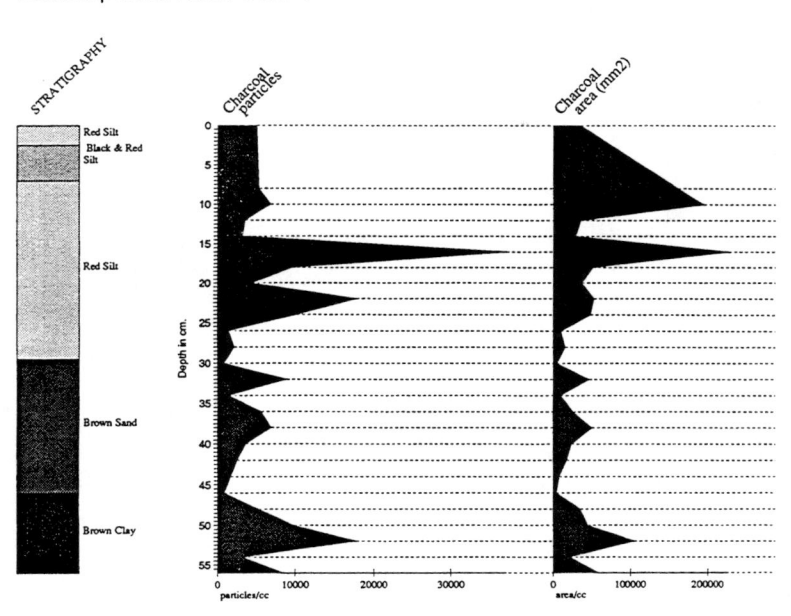

Kamalapuram Kere: Core 1

FIGURE 7.12 Charcoal concentrations by count and by area

In general, the pattern that emerges from the charcoal analysis is similar to that of grasses and herbaceous vegetation, with initially high values in the lower portions of the core followed by generally lower values in the middle part of the core and a resurgence of high values in the upper portion of the core. Thus, charcoal patterns correspond, at least in a general way, with the patterns of open, transformed vegetation. Both burning and open vegetation are indicated in the Vijayanagara period and again in the Colonial to recent periods, when agricultural production was the most intensive. In the period during which the reservoir sediments contained a large amount of aquatic pollen, the charcoal record reaches its minimum, with both measures perhaps indicating a cessation of maintenance activities in and around the facility.

DISCUSSION

Interpretation of the pollen analysis from the Kamalapuram core is hampered by the imprecision of dates from the core and by the lack of detailed studies relating modern vegetation in dry interior South India to the pollen record. Nevertheless, several strong patterns have emerged from the pollen and charcoal analyses. These patterns include very high values for grass pollen at the very beginning of the record and a concurrent sharp decrease in the pollen of trees and shrubs. The quantities of tree and shrub pollen were reduced significantly in what is suggested to be the Middle or Late Vijayanagara period, only to undergo a rebound, probably at the end of the Vijayanagara period. In the post-Vijayanagara period, the reservoir became choked with aquatic vegetation. About the time the reservoir was cleared of swampy vegetation, the first introduced New World species appear in the record, and the concentrations of pollen also decreased, possibly as a result of increased erosion (associated with renewed clearance of vegetation?). At 24 cm, the reservoir may have dried out completely for a time.

Toward the top of the record, probably the later Colonial or the Post-independence periods, agricultural production seems to be of renewed importance, but this agricultural landscape appears different form the Vijayanagara period landscape in several important respects. First of all, the grass-dominated Vijayanagara record is not duplicated in the record of modern commercial agriculture. Instead, herbaceous plants appear much more important, and specifically, Compositae (with "low spine" pollen grains) come to constitute a significant proportion of the pollen flora. Coconut pollen also appears in greater quantities. While coconuts did appear in the Vijayanagara period record, their numerical importance in more recent sediments is striking and is consistent with their current value as a commercial crop. Thus, the impression of Vijayanagara agriculture is one of a pattern of land use that was already intensive from the beginning of the pollen record. Grasses did increase proportionally at the beginning of the record, but the concentration of grass pollen at the base of the core was consistently high.

The record of charcoal is generally consistent with the pollen record, with periods of more intensive burning occurring near the bottom and top of the core. Unfortunately, charcoal peaks cannot be dated precisely, but it is very interesting that, in the lowest levels of the core, two charcoal peaks occur. The first, smaller peak is found in the lowest level (56 cm), followed by a larger peak at 52 cm. The larger peak falls in the period of grass pollen maximum and tree and shrub minima (during the period of sixteenth century intensification?).

Pollen analysis of Vijayanagara area sediments is still at a preliminary stage, and significant problems of chronology and interpretation remain to be addressed. Future research will include analyses of the pollen and charcoal records from additional cores and from additional sampling locations in order to place the record from this single Kamalapuram core in context.

8

Conclusion: Intensification at Vijayanagara

IN THIS ANALYSIS I have approached Vijayanagara land use and intensification from the different perspectives afforded by three different and independent lines of evidence: archaeological surface survey; historical documents; and pollen analysis. Each of these bodies of information informs on the nature of Vijayanagara land use and environment—both natural and constructed—and its change through time, and each offers a different view of the possible dimensions of Vijayanagara intensification.

INTENSITY

Before the process of intensification can be discussed, it is necessary to consider more closely the measurement of intensity. I have asserted that of the three categories of production identified in this study, wet production may be considered the most intensive, followed by wet-cum-dry and dry production. This rather simple progression is based on consideration of both labor and land, and, as noted below, although it obscures a considerable amount of variation, the general relationship between production category and intensity level holds.

Intensity of agricultural production relates both to land and to labor, and as such, can be divided into the forms and frequency of working (land intensity) and the intensity of working (labor intensity). Agricultural intensity is thus multidimensional and may be more profitably conceived in terms of organization rather than simply effort.

Labor and Intensity

I have noted that the facilities associated with both wet and wet-cum-dry agriculture—canals, aqueducts, and reservoirs—all require substantial investments of labor for construction. The Anantarajasagar inscription discussed in chapter 2 provides just one illustration of the enormous scale of effort required in the construction of a large reservoir, and the accounts of travellers such as Paes and Nuniz (Sewell 1900) also evoke the often massive efforts involved in construction. Although it is clear that labor for the construction of these facilities was mobilized in large work groups, it is not known if wage labor was employed or if workers were under some sort of labor obligation to local leaders (cf. Karashima 1992) or perhaps to temples. Certainly construction financing was generally arranged through temples for these large projects.

The initial construction effort for the larger dry facilities must also have been laborious, although there is little information on this point that is specific to the region. Large dry facilities such as terraces may have been constructed all at once by large groups of workers—perhaps through cooperative organizations since the inscriptional record is silent on this point—or may have grown accretionally, the product of more intermittent and long-term efforts of a smaller group. Like dry facilities, historical documents do not describe the organization of labor involved in the construction of smaller wet-cum-dry facilities.

Overall, in terms of the initial effort of construction, both wet and larger wet-cum-dry facilities rate very high in comparison to dry and smaller wet-cum-dry features. However, construction costs, both of labor and capital, are only one aspect of the labor intensity of an agricultural strategy, and even these initial costs must be considered historically contingent. A canal or reservoir is constructed only once, and even though it may require extensive maintenance or repair (see below), the facility, once constructed, becomes part of the landscape. Thus, for a farmer with access to land watered by an extant reservoir, wet-cum-dry agriculture could actually be a less labor intensive activity than dry agriculture.

Facility maintenance creates additional labor demands. All facilities require some sort of periodic or occasional maintenance, and some of the inscriptions described in chapter 6 outlined arrangements for the provision of people and carts for such routine maintenance. Facilities were also subject to the potentially devastating action of surface runoff in a region where rainfall is highly seasonal and vegetation cover sparse. Breached reservoirs, terraces, and other features could and did give way to the force of erosion induced by monsoon runoff. Again, quantitative information on labor requirements for maintenance and repair is sparse, but it seems that wet and wet-cum-dry facilities again demanded the greatest amounts of labor. Further, the demands of facility maintenance would have been strongly conditioned by the individual placement of the facility, not just the size and type of facility. Some small reservoirs, for example, were more subject to breaching by virtue of their topographic, edaphic, and geological context.

Although agricultural facilities are the most archaeologically visible product of past land use, most effort expended in agricultural production was spent on farming activities and not on facilities. Contemporary and historically documented agricultural practices associated with different crops in southern India provide guidelines for assessing the labor requirements of different forms of agricultural production in the Vijayanagara period. Activities such as plowing, levelling, mounding, planting, weeding, watering, manuring, harvesting, and processing were part of all farming, but in terms of total labor required the demands of wet crops were greater than those of dry crops, particularly where more than one crop per year was grown. Some crops, such as wet rice, were particularly demanding. In a sense, there are no wet-cum-dry crops as such, since either irrigated or unirrigated crops could be grown under wet-cum-dry regimes. However, irrigated counterparts of "traditionally" dry crops often produce much more, and perhaps such crops were treated with particular care, as, for example, irrigated cotton is today. Thus, the correlation of labor intensity with cropping regime is only broadly correct.

The timing of labor demands, as well as their magnitude, influence how labor will be mobilized, whether in larger work groups or in small family groups (cf. Stone, Netting, and Stone 1990). Wilk and Netting (1984:7) distinguish between "linear" labor, in which tasks are performed sequentially, and "simultaneous" labor, which is carried out all at once by a large group. In this scheme, labor demand bottlenecks associated with tasks such as cane cutting or rice transplanting would demand simultaneous labor, while more intermittent chores such as repairing terrace walls could be carried out with linear labor.

For both wet-cum-dry and dry production, the timing of agricultural activities is closely tied to the weather, while producers on wet fields have a somewhat greater degree of independence from the timing of the monsoons and thus have the potential, at least, to more closely control the timing of periods of peak labor demands. However, farmers involved in larger scale systems of facilities must also cooperate with other producers in the system, whether that system is a canal network, a system of reservoirs, or simply a string of adjacent dryland features. As noted above, Conelly's (1992:214-15) study of the growth of wet rice agriculture in Napsaan, Philippines showed that this course of intensification did not lead to reduced farm diversity since the temporal labor requirements of wet rice were compatible with other forms of production such as arboriculture and swidden cropping. He notes, "While there is some overlap in the timing of labor requirements in the two systems, the periods of *peak* labor do not coincide" (1992:215 emphasis in original). More work could be done to compare the timing of agricultural operations for traditional rice varieties and those of dry crops in southern India; however, several points might be made here. First of all, the periods of peak labor demand for wet production could rarely have been met by individual households. Thus, some form of labor mobilization was necessary. Such labor demands undoubtedly helped to structure the organization of settlement in the region. Second, the timing of dry operations is often annually very variable, given the uncertainty and variablity of the monsoons in the region.

Labor demands of different forms of production are mirrored in the social composition of South Indian communities. In the wet coastal deltas of the far south, large numbers of low-caste people work as agricultural laborers, since even small rice farms have difficulty managing with only household labor (Mencher 1978). In the drier inland regions, where reservoir irrigation is more important, local social profiles reflect the lower demand for casual labor. The Vijayanagara region, although within the dry zone, is somewhat of an anomaly given its extensive area of canal irrigation, and thus might be expected to have required a somewhat larger than usual labor force for agriculture.

No simple measure of labor intensity for different forms of production can be devised, since so many factors must be taken into account in determining labor requirements, including temporally variable considerations such as the amount and distribution of rainfall in any given year. However, it is possible to roughly order the three forms of production wet, wet-cum-dry, and dry into a relative ranking of labor intensity involved in production, keeping in mind the potential complexity of the issue.

Land and Intensity

Intensity can also be measured from the perspective of land, as is done in the Boserupian measure of fallow period. Here the sequence from wet to dry also holds and is, perhaps, even more clear-cut. Because the primary limiting factor in agricultural production in the Vijayanagara area is water, the potential length of cultivation of a given plot depends entirely on its water supply (see Stone, Netting, and Stone 1990 for a discussion of the temporal extension of agricultural chores into the dry season as a strategy of intensification).

On wet lands, water might be available year-round. Irrigation water from canals carried fertile silt and suspended nutrients to wet fields. Wet rice is particularly interesting in that production can be sustained, apparently indefinitely, without fallowing due to the unique conditions of the paddy field. Two crops per year of rice are possible from canal-irrigated fields. Such well-watered areas can also support crops with longer maturation period such as sugarcane and tree crops. Wet-cum-dry fields probably rarely achieved this level of cropping frequency, except where water supplies were particularly reliable. Dry fields are even less frequently planted. In a dry year, and dry years come quite often, no crop may be possible and some fallowing is necessary to restore soil fertility.

The pattern of change in Vijayanagara land use was not temporally ordered with respect to these three categories. Thus, they can in no way be considered "stages" or steps in a unilineal process of intensification. Instead, multiple strategies and scales of production characterized agriculture in every period. The process of intensification was itself complex, involving changes that can be discussed under the headings of intensification proper, specialization, and diversification.

THE COURSE OF INTENSIFICATION

The Sequence

Although humans have used and occupied the Vijayanagara area for a great deal of time, it was not until the Vijayanagara period that the study area became the focus of a large population concentration and an area of highly intensive agricultural production. With the founding of the city in the early to middle fourteenth century, regional population, as reflected in urban and rural settlement, expanded quickly and dramatically. The large walled area of the Urban Core was constructed at this time, marking the initial shift away from the small, nucleated pre-Vijayanagara settlements near the river. The early Vijayanagara period saw a major expansion in the area covered by archaeological remains. Thus, it seems that land use was at once more extensive as well as intensive. Many of the canals date to the Early Vijayanagara period, as does the Kamalapuram Kere. During the late fourteenth century there was a peak in the number of inscriptions generally, as well as in the number of those relating to the construction of facilities and to land transactions. Figure 8.1 shows the temporal distribution of published inscriptions relating to the construction of agricultural facilities for all districts studied (see chapter 6); figure 8.2 shows references to both construction and maintenance for Bellary District only. Published inscriptions, and inscriptions generally, reflect only a portion of the actual construction and maintenance activity.

The earliest portions of the pollen record may date to the Early Vijayanagara period. This record indicates a landscape already dominated by grasses, but also a time in which the relative proportion of grass pollen rose sharply. Trees and shrubs appear to have been subject to considerable pressure and began a decline which was not checked for some time. A moderate charcoal peak also shows up in the lowest level of the core.

The fifteenth century, or Middle Vijayanagara period, appears to have been a plateau of sorts, with few new monumental structures built and few new settlements established. Of the admittedly few dated settlements, only Malapannagudi may date to this century. The number of inscriptions referring to the construction of agricultural facilities—indeed, of all inscriptions—is lower in the fifteenth century than in any other part of the Vijayanagara period. It is difficult to date the changes in vegetation precisely, but the pollen record immediately above the lowest levels of the core shows a continuation of trends already started. Trees and shrubs continued to decline, and grasses reached a maximum. The quantity of charcoal decreased dramatically, only to rise again to an even larger peak a short distance up the core.

By far the most dramatic changes are those associated with the sixteenth century. By this time, the general layout of the city and of the agricultural landscape around it was already established, but in the early to middle sixteenth century, both settlement and agricultural production underwent a variety of changes. Many new monumental structures were built in and around the city and, importantly, a large number of small settlements were founded. The population of Vijayanagara expanded out beyond the Urban Core walls with the extension of settlement into the area north and west of VMS-123, the outer circuit of the city walls. The new Basavanna Canal was constructed along with several new *anicuts*. The Raya Kere, the massive reservoir near Dharmasagara in the Daroji Valley, and innumerable other reservoirs were constructed. Dryland features near sixteenth-century settlements and reservoirs may also date to the Late Vijayanagara period.

The largest peaks in the inscriptional record of the study area all occur in the sixteenth century, a pattern not mirrored by some areas further away from the powerful effects of the city. The construction of agricultural facilities, the transfer of land, and the overall level of inscriptional activity were at their maximum in the Late Vijayanagara period, dropping off quickly but not dying out altogether after the destruction of the city in A.D. 1565.

By the seventeenth century, there is little that is new in the archaeological record. No new settlements, monumental architecture, or agricultural facilities can be dated to the immediate post-Vijayanagara period. At some point the process of tree and shrub clearing, or the pressure on woody vegetation, was reduced, and trees and shrubs enjoyed a period of regeneration also marked by a decline in grasses and an overall low concentration of charcoal deposited in the sediments of the Kamalapuram reservoir. Maintenance of the reservoir appears to have been neglected, and the reservoir became choked with aquatic vegetation. By the time of the first introduced New World species, the concentration of pollen in the core had also dropped, perhaps indicating an increased sedimentation rate caused by increased erosion of unmaintained terraces or by breached reservoirs upstream. Later, the reservoir was cleaned out, trees and shrubs again cleared, and a new phase of agricultural production begun. In this re-established agricultural landscape, extending probably from the Colonial period to the present, grasses were (and are) no longer as dominant, and a modified weedy flora was established. Coconuts, an important cash crop, gained a new importance.

Many settlements in the survey area were occupied in the Colonial period and continue to be occupied today, sustained both by the Vijayanagara channels and, since about 1950, by lands watered by the Tungabhadra reservoir. The locus of settlement has shifted away from the Vijayanagara area toward the west, and now the city of Hospet, established in the sixteenth century (Tirumaladeviyara-Pattana; Filliozat and Filliozat 1988:13), is the major population center of the region.

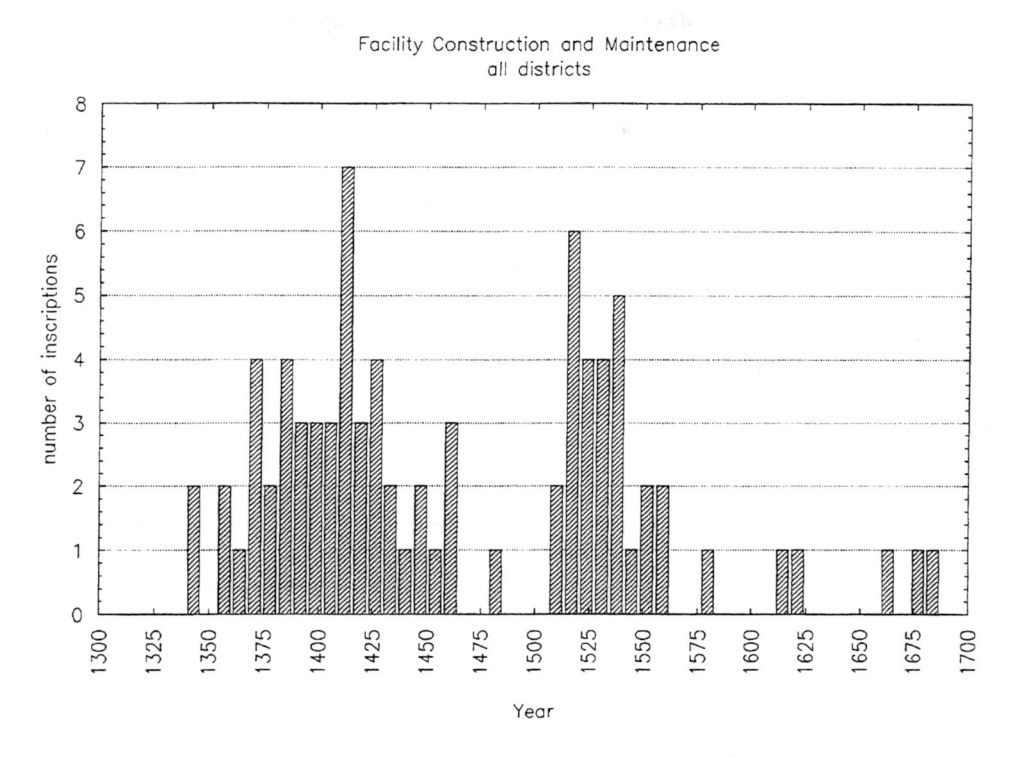

FIGURE 8.1 Temporal distribution of the construction and maintenance of agricultural facilities, all districts

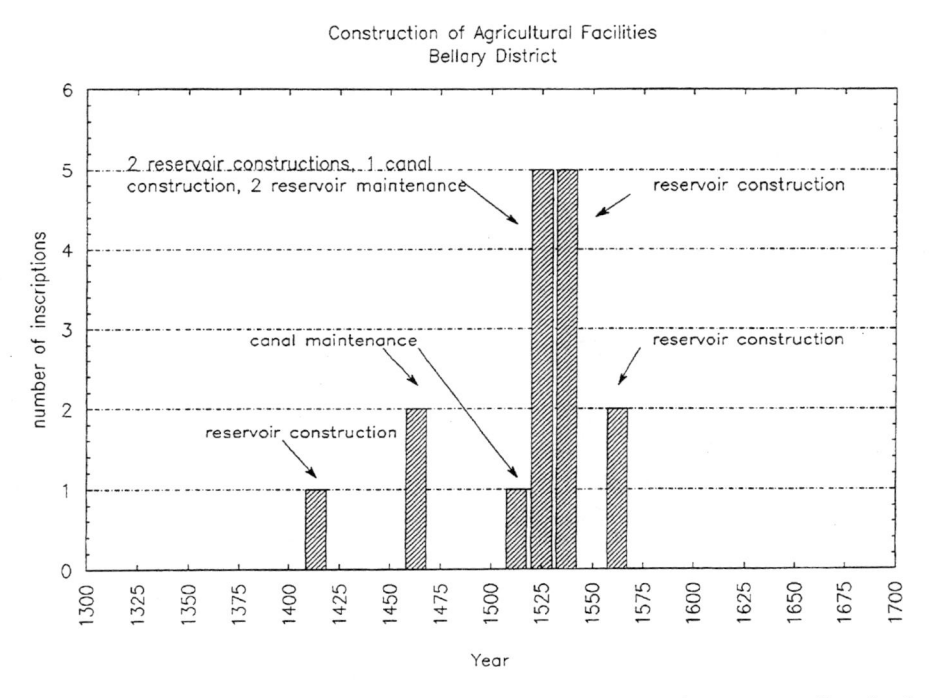

FIGURE 8.2 Temporal distribution of the construction and maintenance of agricultural facilities recorded in published inscriptions, Bellary District

Intensification Proper

The construction of wet agricultural facilities and the extension of wet agriculture clearly constitute strategies of intensification proper. The land that was watered by canals in the Vijayanagara period had certainly been exploited for a long time, as the pre-Vijayanagara (and, in part) early Vijayanagara distribution of settlements near the river attests, but in the Vijayanagara period this same land was used more intensively. Crops could be grown more often, and more labor was invested in the construction, maintenance, and repair of facilities, and almost certainly also in farming practices.

Many of the Vijayanagara canals date to the early part of the city's occupation, but there are also a number of Late Vijayanagara, sixteenth-century constructions in the zone of canal irrigation. The Kamalapuram reservoir dates to the Early Vijayanagara period, but facilitates some of the most intensive agriculture in the region. Dates for the unnamed canal-fed reservoir north of the river and for the Bhupati Kere are not secure, but the massive aqueduct that carried water from the Anegundi Channel probably dates to the sixteenth century. Thus, there seem to be two primary periods of activity in the construction of wet facilities in the region (and see chapter 6), the fourteenth and the sixteenth centuries, and thus two periods also of archaeologically recoverable examples of intensification proper.

A great deal more remains to be learned about the types and proportions of crops grown and about actual cultivation practices. It is tempting to view the overwhelming domination of the pollen record by grasses at the base of the core as indicative of a Vijayanagara-period focus on the production of food grains, and even to see the initial proportional increase in grasses as a consequence of fourteenth-century intensification, with the later grass maximum as reflective of the sixteenth-century peak in intensification. Clearly, the data do not allow such precise assignments. Modern rice and sugarcane varieties are cleistogamous and thus would not be expected to contribute much pollen to the record.

In order to address some of these questions raised by considering intensification proper, several different research avenues could be followed. We must obtain information from domestic contexts of processing and consumption in non-elite contexts and, just as importantly, on the subsurface contexts of agricultural facilities. It is important to continue efforts to identify pollen types more precisely (especially grasses) and to explore other techniques such as macrobotanical and phytolith analysis of sediments from domestic, agricultural, and lacustrine deposits. Did intensification proper involve the use of improved crop varieties or the addition of manuring, transplanting, additional weeding, or other types of agricultural practice? Were fallow periods in dry and wet-cum-dry fields reduced? We are not yet in a position to answer these questions. The course of intensification proper through the Vijayanagara period can, at present, be only roughly sketched out, but it is clear that strategies that can be classified under the rubric of intensification proper occurred throughout the entire period, even the very beginning. A definite bimodal pattern of intensification proper can be outlined, a pattern similar to that evinced by strategies grouped under the heading of diversification (see below).

The category of intensification proper included what, for Boserup, *was* intensification—the reduction of fallow periods. However, as I have argued elsewhere (Morrison 1994a), fallow length is difficult to measure archaeologically and, in any case, constitutes only one single strategy of intensification. Given that wet agriculture is generally associated with shorter fallow periods than dry agriculture in South India, the early significance of wet production would seem to violate Boserup's (1965) postulated sequence of intensification.

Specialization

Of the three strategies of intensification, evidence for specialization in the Vijayanagara period is perhaps the most circumstantial. Because agriculturalists and others had to meet demands for cash revenues increasingly through the period, and because we know of the existence of large urban markets, it seems probable that producers met some or all of these cash demands by production for and participation in these markets. A wide variety of products were offered for sale in the bazaars, indicating the production of a diverse assemblage of crops and probably also indicating the presence of garden land (a form of wet production, see chapter 2) in and around the city. Although there is a minor peak in coconut pollen at the base of the Kamalapuram core, the concentration of coconut pollen never reached anything like that produced by the limited commercial production of coconuts in the area today.

Further out from the city in the broad plains to the east, toward Bellary, are extensive areas of *regur*, or black cotton soil. These level plains are not suitable for reservoir construction and are too far from the river for wet agriculture. Thus, these areas may have been devoted to specialized production of cotton, a dry crop. Cotton was an essential raw material for the weaving industry, which achieved great economic and political importance in the Vijayanagara period (Ramaswamy 1985a, 1985c). Although we know that there must have been production for markets, we do not know to what extent commercial farming affected subsistence production. It may be that the expansion in cultivated area in the sixteenth century, especially of wet-cum-dry and dry lands further away from the city, permitted wet lands nearer the city to be turned over to market production. If there were indeed a rise in specialized production for markets in the Vijayanagara period, and particularly during the period of sixteenth century intensification when cash demands seem to have begun in earnest, then it would also seem that this particular strategy of intensification was driven by nondemographic considerations.

Diversification

Diversification as a strategy of intensification is clearly indicated in the case of Vijayanagara. The expansion of cultivated area in both the Early and the Late Vijayanagara periods increased the spatial diversity of the archaeological landscape around the city. Cultivators outside the zones of wet agriculture and alluvial soils faced different constraints on production and transportation than they did in the perennially irrigated zones. Spatial expansion on a large scale is indicated in the historical record of the sixteenth century, with many inscriptions recording the clearing or reclamation of land and the founding of new settlements.

Expansion of cultivation cannot be contrasted with intensification, however, since it often also incorporated intensification, both of land and labor. Reservoirs were an important component of the agricultural landscape, supporting, along with wells, that variable category of production classified here as wet-cum-dry. The construction and maintenance of reservoirs was a relatively labor-demanding strategy, but reservoirs were able to use the local landscape with its rocky hills and heavy seasonal runoff to maximum advantage. Either wet or dry crops could be grown, depending on the situation of facility and on seasonal precipitation. In a real sense, then, the expansion of reservoir irrigation in the Vijayanagara region can be considered as both an extension of wet and dry cultivation, extending wet agriculture into areas out of the reach of canals, and intensifying dry agriculture, and as the extension of a unique *form* of production in its own right. Reservoirs were not a new "invention" in the Vijayanagara period, and they were present throughout the entire sequence, but the dramatic expansion of reservoir construction in the sixteenth century (and to a lesser extent, in the fourteenth century) represented a diversification and elaboration of production strategies.

Just as important in promoting spatial diversification in agriculture was the mechanism of temple investment. As discussed in previous chapters, temple donors and thus holders of rights in produce were often scattered over large areas, so that investors had rights in produce from a variety of locations in ecologically diverse zones.

Diversity was not simply something that was added to Vijayanagara productive strategies, but instead was present from the beginning, with wet, dry, and wet-cum-dry production occurring in all periods, and only the relative quantities and proportions changing. It would be helpful to know if the overall level of diversity in agriculture actually increased throughout the Vijayanagara period or not. In terms of the number of types of facilities, only the Late Vijayanagara aqueduct was a feature "new" to the area (but then, there was ever only one). Unfortunately, it is not possible to tell whether or not the number of different crops grown or of varieties of a single crop changed through time, or whether households balanced agricultural and non-agricultural activities in different ways.

Producers and Production

The previous sections have highlighted several of the important questions about the organization of agricultural production in the study area that cannot be answered at this point, given our information about the nature of Vijayanagara productive systems. It has been possible to make a number of generalizations about production but very few about producers. It would be possible to say much more about diversification and specialization, for example, if we knew more about the nature of landholding. Did farmers work a number of scattered plots under different types of irrigation regimes, or did they focus on only one type of field? Did farmers construct and maintain the small-scale facilities themselves? Decision making about water distribution even in the canal system was apparently not centralized—to what extent were local corporate bodies such as *urs* and *nadus* involved? How was access to different types of land structured? How was labor for production mobilized? Many important questions about the relationship "on the ground" between producers and production in the metropolitan region persist, largely because we still know very little about the nature of and variability in productive activity in non-elite domestic contexts. Allied to questions about production in such contexts are concerns about distribution and consumption. Clearly, structures of access to land, to resources, and to opportunity were not the same for all members of Vijayanagara society, and the production of food is only one aspect of its eventual disposition and consumption.

Discussion: Independent Lines of Evidence

A key aspect of this analysis has been the use of three different, independent lines of evidence. Inscriptional data were relied upon to date surface archaeological material much more than I would have preferred, but the analysis of inscriptions in chapter 6 extends beyond the few dated features in the survey area. In general, the three lines of evidence proved to be complementary, and notwithstanding the chronological difficulties involved in trying to match evidence from the three data sets to obtain information on the shape of a single pattern of change, the approach has proven a valuable one.

Small-scale and dryland features were completely absent from the historical record, but prominent in the archaeological record. Pollen analysis of the area revealed just how important such extensive activities as grazing and burning were in shaping the regional vegetation, and pointed to the potentially dramatic effects of erosion on the landscape (seen also in the surface record of hundreds of silted up reservoirs). Historical documents, on the other hand, were valuable for developing an understanding of the processes of agricultural investment and of the socio-political context of agricultural production. All three lines of evidence show remarkable agreement in the overall form of Vijayanagara intensification—an initial spurt of growth in the fourteenth century, followed by a relative lull in the fifteenth century and a dramatic period of expansion and intensification in the sixteenth. Then, the intensity of agricultural land use and of settlement appears to have dropped off until some time in the Colonial period, with the twentieth-century dam project finally prompting the present period of maximum population and productive intensity.

Discussion: Boserup and the Course of Vijayanagara Intensification

The primary focus of Boserup's (1965) account of intensification was on causes, rather than courses of intensification, but because of the overwhelming importance of the Boserupian model in shaping anthropological discussions of intensification, her conception of the path of intensification as characterized by a simple, linear progression of decreasing fallow periods and improved technology has also shaped anthropological research to a great extent (and see Morrison 1994 a). In fact, in the Vijayanagara case, a Boserupian sequence of change is not supported. There is no simple progression of form in agricultural production, and no single measure of intensity is sufficient to capture the diversity and flexibility of the system. Contra Boserup, agricultural systems consist of multiple strategies which may be flexibly employed by producers. This is a normal state of affairs in nonindustrial productive systems, and not an anomaly caused by viewing a process of unilineal, evolutionary change at a single point in time. Further, there seems no reason to believe that Vijayanagara agriculturalists followed the Law of Least Effort—clearly a whole suite of constraints and opportunities structured agricultural choices, and in the earlier periods of the city's occupation, agricultural activities seem to have been organized to minimize distance from the settlement rather than to minimize labor investment, with intensive, wet agriculture present from the very beginning. Considerations of risk in this region of low and annually variable precipitation (which was also the location of almost constant warfare) may also have been a consideration in the early focus on wet agriculture. Factors influencing the organization of agricultural production were complex, and the course of change reflected this organizational complexity.

Causes

If the courses of intensification turn out to be more complex than a simple progression of fallow reduction and technology improvement, then what of the causes? It is always difficult to isolate causes with any degree of certainty, but in the case of Vijayanagara, the "cause" for productive intensification was actually a complex and interconnected suite of factors. Demography was certainly very important in shaping agricultural land use, and both periods of intensification were marked by population increases (certainly in the Early period and probably also in the Late period), but demographic forces were mediated by other factors. Indeed, the demographic changes at work in this period followed the exigencies both of resource distributions and political pressures, with migration to the city playing a major role, if not *the* major role, in its population dynamics. These other, nondemographic variables were of great consequence in shaping the course of change and included demands for revenue, monetization, and commercialization. Demands for cash payments of revenue obligations may have forced participation in a market economy (cf. Morrison 1994c). Increasing military spending may have prompted increased revenue demands on producers. The causes of Vijayanagara intensification were complex, related to forces at once commercial, political, and ritual, with demography playing an important if indirect role.

Conclusion: The Study

This analysis of land use and intensification constitutes a beginning inquiry into the topic of productive systems and strategies in the Vijayanagara period. Certain limitations of the study are evident and indicate future research directions. Archaeologically, the study is hampered by a poorly developed chronology and by the limited area surveyed. Both of these problems are being addressed by ongoing research. Surface studies are ongoing, and we have begun a program of excavation to complement the surface studies already carried out.

The analysis of pollen and charcoal provides a very promising, if preliminary, look at past vegetation and burning. Because this study was the first ever analysis of reservoir pollen from pre-Colonial India, and one of the very few studies of pollen from the dry interior of South India, only very general interpretations could be made. Ecological studies of the relationship between modern vegetation and pollen rain are urgently required. Additional cores from the Kamalapuram reservoir and from other sampling locations are being analyzed for comparison with 1KP, and additional radiocarbon determinations will be made. Studies of macrobotanical material from sediment cores have also begun, and extensive macrobotanical and sedimentological studies of excavated contexts are planned.

Quantitative analysis of inscriptions from the study area proved to be useful in defining chronological patterns as well as for the more traditional detailing of qualitative information on political and economic context. The inscriptional data base is currently being expanded to cover newly discovered and translated inscriptions, a larger sample area, and more fine-grained analysis of content. The latter includes, for example, more careful analysis done of donor/donee identities (gender, caste, occupation, etc.). The locations of donated villages and lands could be profitably mapped out along the lines of the study done by Heitzman (1987) in order to detail the spatial patterns of land control through time (see Morrison and Lycett 1994 for a more detailed spatial analysis of inscriptions than given here).

The focus of this study has been on production, but in the end a more balanced view of Vijayanagara land use and economy must also include information about the domestic contexts of production and consumption: the household. Current archaeological research in the city of Vijayanagara on elite contexts would be complemented by studies of the households of agriculturalists and other producers.

In the Vijayanagara region, the course of agricultural change as well as its causes have proved to be complex and diverse. It has not been possible to support a view of a unilinear progression of change nor to devise a single measure of intensity that would adequately capture the variety of productive strategies and scales employed at a single point in time. If the path of intensification at Vijayanagara is not simple, then it is unlikely to be simple in any other case, and the cause or causes of such an internally diverse process are thus bound to be equally complex.

APPENDIX 1

List of Recorded Sites

SITE	BLOCK	DESCRIPTION
1	O	lime kiln
2	O	village
3	N	aqueduct
4	R	reservoir
5	R	slag scatter
6	W	fortified hilltop and step well
7	S	temple
8	S	step well
9	O	single-room structure
10	O	fortification wall
11	O	cistern
12	O	single-room structure
13	O	L-shaped wall
14	O	single-room structure
15	O	single-room structure
16	O	artifact scatter
17	O	gateway
18	O	rockshelter
19	O	fortification wall
20	O	fortification wall
21	O	reservoir
22	O	shrine
23	O	cistern
24	O	wall and mortar
25	O	fortification wall
26	O	Neolithic ash mound
27	O	fortification wall
28	O	lithic scatter
29	O	single-room structure
30	O	single-room structure
31	O	ceramic and lithic scatter
32	O	linear rubble pile
33	O	rockshelter
34	O	fortification wall
35	O	village
36	O	temple
37	O	village
38	O	single-room structure or well
39	O	two-room structure
40	O	well and superstructure
41	O	single-room structure
42	O	temple complex
43	O	step well
44	O	stairway
45	O	isolated wall
46	O	rock-cut stairs
47	O	rock-cut stairs and wall
48	O	reservoir
49	O	isolated walls
50	O	rock-cut stairs
51	O	rock-cut stairs
52	O	erosion control walls
53	O	erosion control walls
54	O	lime processing site
55	O	erosion control walls
56	O	wall segment
57	O	wall segment
58	O	erosion control wall
59	O	reservoir
60	O	erosion control wall
61	O	erosion control wall
62	O	reservoir
63	O	erosion control wall
64	O	structure
65	O	L-shaped wall
66	O	ceramic scatter
67	O	terraces
68	O	long wall
69	O	temple
70	O	rock shelter
71	O	sculptures
72	O	reservoir
73	O	single-room structure and wall
74	O	erosion control wall
75	O	rockshelter
76	O	ceramic and lithic scatter
77	O	isolated wall
78	O	ceramic scatter
79	O	temple
80	O	temple
81	O	road segment
82	O	erosion control wall
83	O	temple complex
84	O	masonry-lined spring
85	O	bastion
86	O	fortification wall
87	O	pathway
88	O	terraced area

SITE	BLOCK	DESCRIPTION	SITE	BLOCK	DESCRIPTION
89	O	isolated wall	146	S	erosion control wall
90	O	erosion control wall	147	S	rock shelter
91	O	reservoir	148	S	structure
92	O	carved boulder	149	S	ceramic scatter
93	O	gateway	150	S	reservoir
94	O	sculpture and inscription	151	S	well
95	O	check dams	152	S	road segment
96	O	isolated wall	153	S	artifact scatter
97	O	reservoir	154	S	sculptures
98	O	erosion control wall	155	S	cistern
99	O	masonry-lined spring	156	S	inscribed slab
100	O	check dams	157	S	inscribed sheetrock
101	O	village	158	S	road segment
102	O	terraces and shrines	159	S	reservoir
103	O	shrine	160	S	road segment
104	O	shrine	161	S	ceramic scatter
105	O	step well	162	S	sculptures
106	O	erosion control wall	163	S	rockshelter
107	O	single-room structure and walls	164	S	temple complex
108	O	reservoir	165	S	reservoir
111	O	temple complex	166	S	isolated wall
112	O	step well	167	S	wall and artifact scatter
113	O	reservoir	168	S	structure and hero stone
114	O	mounded area	169	S	artifact scatter
115	O	mounded single-room structure	170	S	rockshelter
116	O	temple complex	171	S	sculptures
117	O	reservoir	172	S	platforms
118	O	temple	173	S	temple
119	O	temple	174	S	isolated wall
121	S	iron processing site	175	S	structure or well
122	S	reservoir	176	S	residential terraces
123	S	fortification wall and gate	177	S	sculpture
124	S	isolated walls	178	S	habitation area
125	S	reservoir	179	S	iron-processing site
126	S	games and peg holes	180	S	step well
127	S	isolated wall and peg holes	181	S	erosion control wall
128	S	mandapa	182	S	roadway and shrines
129	S	temple complex	183	S	roadway and temple
130	S	isolated wall	184	S	mandapa
131	S	shrine	185	S	isolated wall
132	S	reservoir	186	S	platform
133	S	terraces	187	S	step well
134	S	terraces	188	S	single room
135	S	ceramic scatter	189	S	step well
136	S	reservoir	190	S	reservoir
137	S	road system	191	S	terraces
138	S	reservoir	192	S	wall and rooms
139	S	one-room structure & check dams	193	S	terraces and check dams
140	S	settlement	194	S	reservoir
141	S	sculptures	195	S	lithic scatter
142	S	temple complex	196	S	isolated walls
143	S	step well	197	S	artifact scatter
144	S	temple	198	S	check dams
145	S	rock shelter	199	S	terraces and check dams

SITE	BLOCK	DESCRIPTION	SITE	BLOCK	DESCRIPTION
200	S	step well	254	S	temple complex
201	S	bazaar street	255	S	platform
202	S	residential area	256	S	gateway complex
203	S	room or platform	257	S	temple
204	S	well	258	S	bastion
205	S	terraces	259	S	fortification
206	S	reservoir	260	S	temple
207	S	terraces and well	261	S	shrine
208	S	walls and check dams	262	S	wall footings
209	S	roadway	263	S	gravel-mulched fields & terraces
210	S	step well	264	S	terraces
211	S	terraces	265	S	shrine
212	S	artifact scatter	266	S	temple
213	S	well	267	S	temple
214	S	step well and roadway	268	S	temple
215	S	mandapa	269	S	temple
216	S	well	270	S	temple
217	S	gateway and temple	271	S	temple complex
218	S	temple	272	S	shrine
219	S	terraces	273	S	temple
220	S	mandapa	274	S	isolated wall
221	S	terraces and walls	275	S	shrine
222	S	settlement	276	S	gravel-mulched fields & terraces
223	S	long wall	277	S	cistern
224	S	roadway and well	278	S	ceramic scatter
225	S	roadway	279	S	fortification wall
226	S	reservoir	280	S	check dams
227	S	well	281	S	cistern
228	S	settlement area	282	S	isolated wall
229	O	reservoir	283	S	check dams
230	S	reservoir	284	S	fortification wall
231	S	reservoir	285	S	ceramic scatter
232	S	sculptures	286	S	isolated walls
233	S	wall and sculpture	287	S	check dams
234	S	well	288	S	isolated wall
235	S	platform	289	S	columns
236	S	temple tank	290	S	petroglyph
237	S	temple complex	291	S	step well
238	S	temple	292	T	shrine
239	S	mandapa	293	T	temple
240	S	well	294	T	step well
241	S	reservoir	295	T	inscribed stone
242	S	reservoir	296	T	inscribed sheetrock
243	S	rockshelter	297	T	Islamic-style tomb
244	S	roadway	298	T	step well
245	S	isolated wall	299	T	check dams
246	S	artifact scatter	300	T	check dams
247	S	bastion	301	T	reservoir
248	S	erosion control wall	302	T	reservoir
249	S	lithic scatter	303	T	mandapa
250	S	erosion control wall	304	T	shrine
251	S	artifact scatter	305	T	embankment
252	S	temple	306	T	isolated wall
253	S	shrine	307	T	erosion control wall

SITE	BLOCK	DESCRIPTION	SITE	BLOCK	DESCRIPTION
308	T	erosion control wall	339	T	fortification wall
309	Y	reservoir	340	T	round and rectangular structures
310	T	check dams	341	T	quarrying locale
311	T	rubble mounds	342	T	reservoir
312	T	step well	343	T	rubble wall structure
313	T	erosion control walls	344	T	terraces
314	T	erosion control walls	345	T	road wall
315	T	reservoir	346	T	reservoir
316	T	shrine	347	T	check dams
317	T	temple complex	348	T	road wall
318	T	shrine	349	T	reservoir
319	T	reservoir	350	T	erosion control walls
320	T	erosion control walls	351	T	platform/water control
321	T	defensive wall	352	T	isolated wall
322	T	reservoir	353	T	isolated wall
323	T	erosion control wall	354	T	(road?) wall and platform
324	T	reservoir	355	T	reservoir
325	T	fortification wall	356	T	(road?) wall and platform
326	T	road system	357	T	reservoir
327	T	round structure/watch tower	358	T	road walls
328	T	step well	359	T	single-room structure/lookout
329	T	columned structures	360	T	road
330	T	reservoir	361	T	village
331	T	erosion control walls	362	T	terraces
332	T	erosion control wall	363	T	erosion control wall
333	T	rock cairn	364	T	reservoir
334	T	rock cairn	365	T	village
335	T	reservoir	366	T	shrine and isolated sculptures
336	T	rock shelter	367	T	shrine
337	T	rock cairn	368	T	temple
338	T	shrine	369	T	reservoir

APPENDIX 2
Vegetation

DICOTS

ACANTHACEAE

Andrographis	*echinoides*	herbs among boulders & grasses on slopes, along roads, in open scrub forests to 700 m (482)
A.	*lineata*	herbs among grasses on hilltops and slopes at 800 to 1050 m (483)
A.	*paniculata*	herbs in open patches, sometimes among grasses in deciduous & scrub forests at low elevations (483)
Asystasia	*dalzelliana*	herbs in moist situations (484)
Barleria	*cristata*	herbs, often cultivated and as escape from cultivation, among grasses in deciduous forests to 700 m (486)
B.	*cuspidata*	shrubs along roads in poor soils, and among boulders (487)
B.	*prionitis*	undershrubs or shrubs along forest edges, in rocky open situations, along watercourses or roads, often grown as hedges (487-88)
Blepharis	*maderspatensis*	herbs among rocks and grasses in open tracts of cleared or scrub forests (489)
Dipterocarpus	*patulus*	herbs in moist and irrigated lands (490)
Dyschoriste	*vagans*	herbs in shade of undergrowth of deciduous forests at 900 to 1050 m (490)
Gantelbua	*urens*	herbs along roads & in cultivated fields like cotton and jowar, in plains (491-92)
Haplanthodes	*verticillatus*	herbs found in Sandur Hills (492)
Hemigraphis	*crenata*	herbs endemic to peninsular India (492)
H.	*latebrosa*	herbs along water channels and rocks in scrub forests & cleared deciduous forests to 1000 m (493)
Hygrophilia	*auriculata*	herbs in moist places along nullahs (drainages) and around ponds, to 800 m (493)
Justica	*diffusa*	herbs in deciduous forests and open patches to 750 m (495)
J.	*glabra*	herbs found in Sandur Hills (495)
Lepidagathis	*cristata*	herbs along roads in waste places, often on raised borders (bunds) of nurseries & plantations at low elevations (497-98)
Peristrophe	*bicalyculata*	herbs along roads in waste places, around cultivated fields, and in forest undergrowth in deciduous forests to 800 m (498-99)
Rhinacanthus	*nasuta*	herbs or under shrubs among grasses, on poor soils on hills to 900 m (499)
Rungia	*repens*	herbs among grasses in moist situations, along roads, in waste places, & among rocks on hill slopes & tops in deciduous forests to 600 m (500)

APOCYNACEAE

Carissa	*spinarum*	shrubs in scrub forests on poor soils, sometimes a major component of the vegetation (401-402)

Catharanthus	*pusillus*	herbs along rivers in sandy soils, & as a weed in cultivated fields to 500 m (402)
Holarrhena	*antidysenterica*	small trees or large shrubs on hilltops and slopes among boulders in sandy soils at 800-1000 m (403)
Wrightia	*tinctora*	shrubs or trees in deciduous & scrub forests, sometimes a major component of the vegetation, & on bunds of cultivated fields, to 1200 m, bidi wrappers (404)

AMARANTHACEAE

Achyranthus	*aspera*	herbs and weeds along roads, around cultivated fields, and near habitations in waste places (533)
Aerva	*javanica*	herbs along roads in waste places, on bunds in cultivated fields, along rivers and in open forests in poor soils (534)
A.	*lanata*	herbs along roads in waste places, edges of cultivated fields, & in open, cleared forests, often along watercourses to 1050 m (534)
A.	*monsoniae*	herbs as weeds in & around cultivated fields, along roads, & in open, sunny, grasses patches in forest areas to 800 m (535)
Allmania	*nodiflora*	herbs in & along cultivated fields and open areas to 900 m (536)
*Alternanthera	*pungens*	herbs. native of tropical America, weed of cultivated fields, along roads, and waste places at low elevations (537)
Amaranthus	*polygonoides*	herbs as weeds in & around cultivated fields, along roads, waste places & in open patches in scrub forests to 800 m (538)
Celosia	*argentea*	herb as weed of cultivated fields & along nullahs, in open forests to 850 m (540)
Digeria	*muricata*	herb as weed of cultivated field & along nullahs, in open forests to 850 m (540)
Pupalia	*lappaceae*	herbs along roads, in waste places & in forest undergrowth, mostly in deciduous forests to 1500 m (541)

ASCLEPIADACEAE

Calotropis	*gigantea*	shrubs as weeds along roads, near habitations, & on forest edges in open, disturbed habitats (408)
C.	*adscendens*	herbs in dry open situations at low elevations (409)
C.	*umbellata*	herbs among rocks to 1100 m (410)
Decalepis	*hamiltonii*	climbers atop trees & shrubs, often along streams (412)
Gymnema	*sylvestre*	climbing shrubs along roads, among hedges, & in forests (412)
Leptadenia	*reticulata*	twiners on bushes & small trees like *Acacia*, along roads & in scrub forests 500 to 750 m (413)
Oxystelma	*secamone*	twining herbs on bushes, partly submerged in wet situations along ponds, riverbanks, etc. (414)
Pentatropis	*capensis*	climbers along roads & in scrub forests, near water (415)
Pergularia	*daemia*	climbers on bushes & small trees, along roads, near habitations, in cultivated fields & open forests 400 to 900 m (415)

Sarcostemma	*acidum*	shrubs in scrub & deciduous forests in cleared patches, sometimes major component of vegetation (416)
Tylophora	*indica*	climbing undershrubs in scrub forests on forest edges & as a weed along roads 400 to 1000 m (418)
Wattakaka	*volubilis*	climbing shrubs covering bushes & tree tops along nullahs, in scrub or poor deciduous forests 400 to 750 m (419)

BIGNONIACEAE

Dolichandrone	*atrovirens*	trees in scrub & deciduous forests to 1000 m, sometimes major component of the vegetation (476)
D.	*falcata*	trees in open forests 400 to 600 m (477)
*Tecoma	*stans*	tall shrubs, native of South America, escape from cultivation, ornamental (478)

CAESALPINIA

Cassia	*auriculata*	shrubs in waste places, along roadsides & cultivated fields (274)
C.	*fistula*	trees in all situations in deciduous forests (275)
C.	*italica*	herbs among grasses along roadsides (276)
C.	*mimosoides*	herbs among grasses along roadsides & near moisture (276)
C.	*occidentalis*	herbs as a weed of waste places, along roadsides, & around cultivated fields (280)
C.	*senna*	undershrubs, escape from cultivation (dye plant) (278)
C.	*sophera*	undershrubs as weeds along roadsides, around cultivated fields (280)
C.	*surattensis*	shrubs or small trees in open forests along forest edges & around cultivated fields (280)

CAPPARIDACEAE

Cadaba	*fruticosa*	shrubs along hedges & in open thornscrub forests (137)
Capparis	*divaricata*	shrubs along roadsides & hedges in arid areas (138)
C.	*grandis*	shrubs along roadsides on black & yellow sandy soils (139)
C.	*zylanica*	shrubs along roads, in waste places, along rivulets & nullahs (140)
Maerua	*obligifolia*	climbing shrubs on bushes & trees in scrub forests (140)

CARYOPHYLLACEAE

Polycarpeae	*corymbosa*	herbs in sandy soils, cultivated fields, waste places, cleared forests (146)
P.	*aurea*	herbs found in rock crevices (146)

CASUARINACEAE

*Casuarina	*equisetifolia*	trees. introduced, often planted in large stands (590)

CHENOPODIACEAE

Spinacia	*oleraceae*	herbs, spinach
Beta	*vulgaris*	herbs, beets

COMPOSITAE (ASTERACEAE)

*Acanthospermum	hispidum	herbs, common weed, native of South America (360)
*Ageratum	conyzoides	herb, weed along roadsides, in waste places, cultivated fields, around villages, & in forests along nullahs & in forests along nullahs, native of tropical America (361)
Blainvillea	acmella	herb, weed in harvested cultivated fields, along roadsides & near habitations in waste places (363)
Blepharispermum	subsessile	herb among undershrubs & grasses on hilltops at 850 m (363)
Blumea	obliqua	herb in moist situations along roadsides & in open forests in the plains (365)
*Crassocephalum	crepidioides	herbs. African native, established since AD 1900 (367)
Dichoma	tomentosa	herbs in sandy soils on rocky surfaces, among grasses from plains to 1000 m (368)
Echinops	echinatus	herbs in waste places along roads, on forest edges in dry situations on gravelly soils (368)
Eclipta	alba	herbs in moist situations near or in water in nullahs, riverbeds & paddy fields (369)
Emilia	sonchifolia	herbs along roads, in cultivated fields, in open situations in forests (369-70)
Epaltes	divaricata	herbs in moist situations along roads, near nullahs & rivers (370)
*Flaveria	trinervia	herb in moist situations along roadsides, near nullahs, habitations, & cultivated fields. native of Peru (371)
Glossocardia	bosvallea	herbs in gravelly soils along roads & in open forest patches (372)
Goniocaulon	glabrum	herb, weed in cultivated fields (374)
*Lagascea	mollis	herb in waste places, along roads,in & around cultivated fields & forest edges. Central American native (375)
Laggera	alata	herb found under rocks in shady places (375)
L.	procumbens	herb, weed in jowar & cotton fields, along roads (376)
Oligochaeta	ramosa	herbs in sandy soils, riverbeds (377)
*Parthenium	hysterophorous	herb along roads, river courses, cultivated fields, forest edges. New World native introduced by AD 1810 (378)
Pluchea	tometosa	herbs in hedges bordering cultivated fields & near nullahs (378)
Pulicaria	angustifolia	herbs in sandy soil, along roads, near nullahs & in open forests among grasses in cultivated fields (379)
P.	wightiana	herbs among grasses in cultivated fields (379)
Senecio	tenifolius	herbs in dry & rocky surfaces or crevices among boulders on forest slopes (380)
Sphaeranthus	indicus	herbs near moisture or in dessicated fields (382)
Tricholepis	radicans	herbs near nullahs, open forests, & among grasses (382)
*Tridax	procumbens	herb, South American native (384)
Veronia	albicans	herbs on forest slopes & hilltops among boulders & grasses (384)
V.	cinerea	herb as weed in cultivated fields, in waste places, along roads, & in open forests on hilltops & slopes (384)
Vicoa	indica	herb on hilltops & slopes (385)

Xanthium   *strumarium*   herb in waste places, along roads, in cultivated fields, in & along nullahs, streams, & riverbeds. New World native (386)

EUPHORBIACEAE

Acalypha	alnifolia	undershrubs or shrubs among rocks & boulders in low elevations (557)
A.	indica	tall herbs found on the walls of forts (557)
*Croton	bonplandianum	herb along roads, in wastes, near habitations, & in cleared forest areas to 700 m. Native of South America (557)
Emblica	officialis	trees, confined to rich deciduous forests 450 to 1100 m "emblic myrobalan" (563)
Euphorbia	antiquorum	shrubs or small trees among rocks & boulders in waste land & scrub forests to 800 m (565)
E.	caducifolia	shrubs or small trees among rocks & boulders (581)
E.	cristata	herbs among grasses on rocky slopes in open patches in deciduous & scrub forests (566)
E.	hirta	herbs as weed in waste places, in forests, & along roads (567)
E.	thymifolia	herb in yellow soils (570)
Givotia	rottlerformis	trees in rich deciduous forests to 1000 m on bouldery hill slopes & tops (570-71)
Jatropha	glandulifera	shrub along roads, usually in black cotton soils (572)
J.	*gossypiifolia	herb along roads, nullahs, riverbeds. native of Brazil (572)
J.	heynei	herbs in rocky, open situations (572)
Kirganelia	reticulata	climbing shrubs along roads, cutivated fields, nullahs, ponds, & rivulets, in scrub & deciduous forests (may be same as *Phyllanthus*) (573)
Mallotus	philippensis	trees in deciduous forests on hillslopes to 1300 m (574)
Phyllanthus	maderspatensis	herbs as field weeds, & along roads, waste places, & open patches in forests (576)
Sebastiana	chamaelea	herb among grasses in rocky situations, in forests, along nullahs, & in harvested fields to 800 m. (577)
Securinega	leucopyrus	shrubs along rocky hilltops in scrub & deciduous forests (577)
Tragia	muelleriana	herbs or undershrubs among boulders, in cultivated fields, along roads, nullahs (578)
Ricinus	communis	herb, "castor oil plant" native of Africa (580)

MIMOSACEAE

Acacia	chundra	trees in poor soils in thorn scrub forests. May be major component of vegetation (287)
A.	eburnea	shrubs or trees on poor, rocky soils in scrub forests & near nullahs & rivers (287-88)
A.	latronum	tall shrubs or small trees in all soils in dry areas, major component of vegetation in scrub forests (288)
A.	leucoploea	trees in all situations along roads, in thorn scrub & dry deciduous forests (289)
A.	pennata	large climbers atop trees & shrubs in forests, in moist situations (290)
A.	polycantha	trees in deciduous forests (290)
A.	torta	large climbers in deciduous forests atop trees & shrubs (292)
Albizia	amara	trees in thorn scrub forests, often major component of the vegetation (293)

A.	*lathamii*	trees in scrub & deciduous forests & near nullahs at lower elevations (294)
A.	*mollis*	trees in deciduous forests (295)
Dichrostachys	*cinera*	shrubs or small trees in scrub forests on poor, rocky soils (296)
Mimosa	*prainiana*	shrubs or small trees in scrub forests & along roads at low elevations (297)
M.	*pudica*	woody herbs or underhrubs along roads in moist situations (298)
Prosopis	*cineraria*	trees in cultivated fields, along roads, & in dry scrub forests (299)
P.	**juliflora*	shrubs or trees, American native, recently introduced, widely planted (299)
*Pithecellobium	*dulce*	shrubs or trees, native of tropical America, cultivated as hedges (300)

MALVACEAE

Abutilon	*indicum*	woody herbs along roads, edges of cultivated fields, near nullahs (152)
A.	*pannosum*	undershrubs (152)
Hibiscus	*vitifolius*	herbs along roads and forest edges (155)
Kydia	*calycina*	trees on hilltops at 1000 m and above (155)
Pavonia	*patens*	herbs in riverbeds, along roads, & in cleared forests (158)
P.	*zeylanica*	herbs in cleared open forest areas (158)
Sida	*acuta*	herbs or undersrubs as weeds (159)
*Abelmoschus	*esculentus*	herb, bhindi or okra (161)
*Gossypium	*herbaceum*	herb, cotton (161)
*Hibiscus	*cannabinus*	herb, Deccan hemp, fiber plant (161)

MELIACEAE

Aglaia	*elaeagnoidea*	trees, evergreens (habitat now mostly destroyed) at ca. 650 m (189)
Chloroxylon	*swietenia*	trees in deciduous formations in scrub & mixed forests at low elevations (189)
Cipadessa	*baccifera*	tall shrubs in forest areas (190)
Soymida	*febrifugia*	trees in deciduous forests on dry, stony hills between 500 and 700 m (190)
Azadirachta	*indica*	trees, widely planted & escape from cultivation (190-191)

MENISPERMACEAE

Cocculus	*hirstutus*	small trees in drier locations, straggling or climbing on shrubs (129)

MORACEAE

Ficus	*arnottiana*	trees among boulders on rocky slopes & hilltops in deciduous forests to 1025 m (584-85)
F.	*benghalensis*	Banyan tree, widely planted (585)
F.	*drupcea*	trees in deciduous forests (585)
F.	*exasperata*	trees in deciduous forests (585)
F.	*heterophylla*	shrubs along banks of Tungabhadra, often in hedges along cultivated fields at low elevations (586)

F.	*hispida*	tall shrubs or small trees along nullahs & riverbanks, often among hedges of cultivated fields (586)
F.	*microcarpa*	trees in rocky-bouldery situations in deciduous forests to 1000 m (586)
F.	*tinctora*	trees along nullahs, in rock-crevices, & sometimes as epiphyte on mango trees 700-900 (587)
F.	**religiosa*	trees, sacred to Hindus (589), often cultivated

OLACEAE

Jasminum	*auriculatum*	scandent or climbing shrub atop bushes & trees in scrub forests, open patches in deciduous forests, in hedges, & along roads (396)

COMBRETACEAE

Anogeissus	*latifolia*	trees, mostly in deciduous forests, often major component of the vegetation (305)
Combretum	*ovalifolium*	large climber on trees & shrubs in dry deciduous forests & along roads & nullahs (305-306)
Terminalia	*alata*	trees among boulders in deciduous forests, often major component of vegetation (307)
T.	*arjuna*	trees along water courses, mostly in deciduous forests (307)
T.	*chebula*	trees on rocky slopes in deciduous forests (Myrobalan) (308)
T.	*crenulata*	trees on rocky hillslopes in deciduous forests (308)

FABACEAE (PAPILIONACEAE)

Abrus	*precatorius*	climbers in scrub forests & along roadsides (214)
Alysicarpus	*bupleurifolius*	herbs among grasses in rocky patches (215)
A.	*longifolius*	herbs as weeds of cultivated fields & waste places (205)
A.	*monilifer*	herbs in waste places & grassy open situations (216)
A.	*procumbens*	herbs as weeds of cultivated fields (216)
A.	*rugosus*	herbs along roadsides & as weeds of cultivated fields (216)
A.	*vaginalis*	herbs among grasses in open forests (217)
Butea	*monosperma*	trees in deciduous forests (219)
Canavalia	*gladiata*	climbers, escape from cultivation, pods used as vegetables (219)
C.	*virosa*	climbers atop shrubs & trees in open forests (220)
Clitoria	*ternatea*	climbing herbs along roadsides, near nullahs (221)
Crotalaria	*bifaria*	herbs in cultivated fields & open forests (224)
C.	*histuta*	herbs in rock crevices 600 to 700 m (224)
C.	*huillensis*	shrubs in cultivated fields, grassy patches, sandy soils (225)
C.	*juncea*	herbs cultivated for fiber, escape from cultivation (225)
C.	*medicaginea*	herbs among grasses 400 to 850 m in forest undergrowth & along roads (226)
C.	*mysorensis*	herbs in grassy patches 600 to 750 m (226)
C.	*orixensis*	herbs, weed of cultivated fields at ca. 500 m (226)
C.	*pusilla*	herbs among grasses in rocky situations 700 to 900 (228)
C.	*retusa*	undershrubs as weeds in cultivated fields & in river & nullah beds (228)

180 Fields of Victory

C.	sandoorensis	herb or undershrubs, among grasses in open patches in forests, endemic to Sandur Hills (228)
C.	verrucosa	herbs, weed of cultivated fields, along roads & in moist situations near nullahs & rivers (230)
Dalbergia	latifolia	trees in deciduous forests, major component of the vegetation in the Sandur Hills 900 to 1300 m (232)
D.	paniculata	trees in deciduous forests on slopes among boulders 500 to 1000 m (233)
Derris	indica	trees, often planted (oil-yielding seeds), runs wild near habitations & in forests near moisture (233)
D.	scandens	climbers atop trees & shrubs, near moisture (234)
Eliotis	trifoliolata	herb among grasses in open forests & in harvested *Elusine coracana* (*Ragi*) fields, endemic to Eastern Karnataka (237-39)
Goniogyna	hirta	herbs among grasses in open, rocky situations (240)
Indigofera	atragalina	herbs along roads, in cultivated fields, & in open forests among grasses or in rock crevices (241)
I.	coerulea	herbs in open situations on rocky-bouldery surfaces at 500 to 600 m (242)
I.	cassiodes	shrubs or small trees in deciduous forests among boulders, usually at 900 to 1100 (243)
I.	cordifolia	herbs along roads & in open forests among grasses in rocky-bouldery situations to 750 m (243)
I.	glandulosa	herbs as weeds in cultivated field & open forests (244)
I.	linifolia	herbs in cultivated fields, along roads, & in open forests among grasses, in sandy, gravelly, or rocky soils (244)
I.	linnaei	herbs as weeds along roads in waste places among grasses (245)
I.	oblongifolia	shrubs along roads in waste places in dry situations (246)
I.	tinctora	undershrubs growing among rocks, indigo, escape from cultivation (247)
I.	wightii	shrubs in cultivated fields, on rocky slopes & sandy soils in open situations from 400 to 1000 m (248)
Mundulea	sericea	shrubs in open forests on rocky hillocks, sometimes major component of vegetation (249-50)
Paracalyx	scariosa	large climbers in open forests & near cultivated fields (251)
Rhychosia	aurea	herbs in cultivated fields & waste places along roads (253)
R.	hirta	woody twiners in deciduous forests 850 to 1000 m (254)
R.	minima	twining herbs in & around cultivated fields, on hedges along roads, & in open forests among grasses (254)
R.	rothii	large climbers atop shrubs & trees along nullahs 400 to 1000 m (255)
R.	rufescens	herbs in open situations & on rocky slopes among grasses (255)
Taverniera	cuneifolia	herbs or undershrubs in waste places along roads, around cultivated fields, & in forest plantations in open areas (257)
Tephrosia	purpurea	herbs or undershrubs as weeds in waste places, along roads, on bunds in cultivated fields & open patches in rocky-bouldery situations (259-60)

Appendix 2   181

T.	*uniflora*	herbs among grasses near nullahs at 750 m (262)
Vigna	*trilobata*	herbs as weeds in cultivated fields & near nullahs along roads (263)
V.	**radiata*	herbs, mung bean (267-68)
*Cajanus	*cajan*	herb, pigeon pea, African origin (264-65)
*Cicer	*arietinum*	herb, chick pea, possibly from Asia Minor (265)

RUBIACEAE

Borreria	*articulatus*	herbs along roads, in open forests, near moisture (340)
Canthium	*parviflorum*	shrubs, sometimes a major component of the vegetation in thorn-scrub forests (342)
Gardenia	*resinifera*	shrubs or small trees in open deciduous forests (344)
Rubia	*cordifolia*	climbing herbs, now rare (357)
Haldina	*cordifolia*	trees on rocky slopes at low elevations (344)
Ixora	*arborea*	shrubs or small trees in hilly, rocky situations, mostly along watercourses (345)
Mitragyna	*parvifolia*	trees in forests, mostly along watercourses (349)
Morinda	*tomentosa*	trees or shrubs in deciduous forests, along roads & watercourses (347)
Oldenlandia	*offins*	herbs amid boulders in black soils (349)
O.	*aspera*	herbs in sandy soils near rivers & nullahs at 500 m (349)
O.	*umbellata*	herbs along roads in waste places, in sandy places along nullahs (351)
Wendlandia	*thyrsoidea*	shrubs or small trees in deciduous forests (355)
Xeromphis	*spinosa*	shrubs or trees in poor soils on hillslopes, along nullahs, in thorn scrub & deciduous forests (355)

SAPINDACEAE

Allophylus	*cobbe*	large shrubs or small trees (204)
Cardiospermum	*halicacabum*	climbing herbs in cultivated fields like cotton & jowar on bushes & trees in open scrub forests at elevations below 800 m (205)
Dodonea	*viscosa*	shrubs on boulders, often cultivated as hedges, dominant species in scrub forests (205)
Sapindus	*emarginatus*	trees in dry deciduous forests at 600 to 700 m (206)
Schleichera	*oleosa*	trees on hilltops at 1000 m in deciduous forests (206)

MONOCOTS

CYPERACEAE

Bulboylis	*barbata*	herbs in sandy yellow soils in open forests, plantations & in cultivated fields & along roads at low elevations (627)
Cyperus	*articulatus*	herbs in irrigated lands & near nullahs along roads 500 to 550 m (630)
C.	*laevigatus*	herbs in moist, marshy, or wet places along ponds, puddles, nullahs, & rivers, also in cultivated fields and waste places to 750 m (632)
C.	*rotundus*	herbs in moist places along nullahs, water channels, & in cultivated fields (633)
Fimbristylis	*cynosa*	herbs in river & nullah beds in marshy places (636)
F.	*ovata*	herbs in wet situations (637)

182 *Fields of Victory*

Fuirena	**trilobites**	herbs in moist situations along nullahs, water channels, gullies, ponds, & puddles, endemic to western peninsular India (639)
Lipocarpa	*sphacelata*	herbs in marshy places in forest areas along roads 700 to 1000 m (641)
PALMAE (ARECACEAE)		
Phoenix	**sylvestris**	trees in marshy places, along nullahs & ponds, wild date palm (620)
Areca	*catechu*	trees, cultivated, areca nut palm (620)
Borassus	*flabellifer*	tree, African native, often cultivated, sometimes self-grown, especially in swampy areas (620)
Cocos	**nucifera**	tree, coconut palm, cultivated (620)
Arenga	*pinnata*	tree, Gomuti palm, used for sugar & "sago" (Ambasta 1976:51)
A.	*wightii*	tree, grows on humid west coast (Saldanha 1984:16)
GRAMINEAE (POACEAE)		
63 genera	97 species	grasses
POTOMAGETONACEAE		
Potomageton	*nodosus*	fixed, submerged herbs with some upper leaves floating in shallow waters in puddles & ponds (623)
TYPHACEAE		
Typha	**angustata**	aquatic or marshy herbs in shallow water, both stagnant & flowing, along ponds & puddles (621)

All page numbers are from Singh 1988, unless otherwise indicated. Bold face text indicates taxa present in core 1KP; asterisk indicates New World introduction.

References Cited

Allchin, B.
    1959   The Indian Middle Stone Age: Some New Sites in Central and Southern India and their Implication. *Bulletin of the London University Institute of Archaeology* 11:1-36, London.
Allchin, B., and F. R. Allchin
    1982   *The Rise of Civilization in India and Pakistan.* Cambridge University Press, Cambridge.
Allchin, F. R.
    1960   *Piklihal Excavations.* Andhra Pradesh Government Archaeological Series, 1, Hyderabad
    1961   *Utnur Excavations.* Andhra Pradesh Government Archaeological Series 5, Hyderabad.
    1963   The Indian Stone Age Sequence. *Journal of the Royal Anthropological Institute of Great Britain and Ireland.* 93:210-34.
    1969   Early Domestic Plants in India and Pakistan. In *The Domestication and Exploitation of Plants and Animals*, edited by P. J. Ucko and G. W. Dimbleby, pp. 317-22. Duckworth, London.
Ambasta, S. P.
    1986   *The Useful Plants of India.* Council of Scientific and Industrial Research Publications and Information Directorate, New Delhi.
Ammerman, A. J.
    1985   Plow Zone Experiments in Calabria, Italy. *Journal of Field Archaeology* 12:33-41.
Ammerman, A. J., & M. W. Feldman
    1978   Replicated Collection of Site Surfaces. *American Antiquity* 43:734-40.
Ansari, Z. D.
    1985   Pebble Tools from Nittur (Mysore State). In *Studies in Indian Archaeology: Professor H. D. Sankalia Felicitation Volume*, edited by S. B. Deo and M. K. Dhavalikar, pp. 1-7. Popular Prakashan, Bombay.
Appadorai, A.
    1936   *Economic Conditions in Southern India, 1000-1500 A.D.* University of Madras, Madras.
Appadurai, A.
    1978   Kings, Sects, and Temples in South India, 1350-1800 AD. In *South Indian Temples: An Analytical Reconsideration*, edited by B. Stein, pp. 47-73. Vikas, New Delhi.
Archaeological Survey of India
    1904-38 *Annual Report on Epigraphy (ARE).* Archaeological Survey of India, Calcutta.
Barker, G., and C. Gamble
    1985   Beyond Domestication: Strategy for Investigating the Process and Consequence of Social Complexity. In *Beyond Domestication in Prehistoric Europe*, edited by G. Barker and C. Gamble, pp. 1-24. Academic Press, London.
Barker, G.
    1985   *Prehistoric Farming in Europe.* Cambridge University Press, Cambridge.
Barrett, S.
    1977   *Breeding Systems in Eichhornia and Pontederia, Tristylous Genera of the Pontederiaceae.* Unpublished Ph.D. dissertation, Department of Botany, University of California, Berkeley.
Bayliss-Smith, T. P.
    1978   Maximum Populations and Standard Populations: The Carrying Capacity Question. In *Social Organization and Settlement*, edited by D. C. Green, C. Haselgrove, and M. Spriggs, pp. 129-51. British Archaeological Reports Supplemental Series 47.

Begley, V.
> 1983 Arikamedu Reconsidered. *American Journal of Archaeology* 87:461-68.
> 1986 From Iron Age to Early Historical in South Indian Archaeology. In *Studies in the Archaeology of India and Pakistan*, edited by J. Jacobsen, pp. 297-319. Oxford and IBH, New Delhi.

Bender, B.
> 1978 Gatherer-Hunter to Farmer: A Social Perspective. *World Archaeology* 10:204-222.
> 1981 Gather-Hunter Intensification. In *Economic Archaeology: Towards an Integration of Ecological and Social Approaches*, edited by A. Sheridan and G. Bailey, pp. 149-58. British Archaeological Reports International Series 96.
> 1985 Emergent Tribal Formations in the American Midcontinent. *American Antiquity* 50:52-62.

Benninghof, W. S.
> 1962 Calculation of Pollen and Spores Density in Sediments by Addition of Exotic Pollen in Known Quantities. *Pollen et Spores* 4:332-33.

Binford, L. R.
> 1964 A Consideration of Archaeological Research Design. *American Antiquity* 29:425-41.
> 1968 Post Pleistocene Adaptations. In *New Perspectives in Archaeology*, edited by S. R. Binford and L. R. Binford, pp.313-41. Aldine, Chicago.
> 1983 *In Pursuit of the Past*. Thames and Hudson, New York.

Birks, H. J. B.
> 1986 Numerical Zonation, Comparison and Correlation of Quaternary Pollen-Stratigraphical Data. In *Handbook of Holocene Palaeoecology and Palaeohydrology*, edited by B. E. Berglund, pp. 743-74. Wiley, New York.

Birks, H. J. B., and H. H. Birks
> 1980 *Quaternary Palaeoecology*. Edward Arnold, London.

Birks, H. J. B., and A. D. Gordon
> 1985 *Numerical Methods in Quaternary Pollen Analysis*. Academic Press, London.

Birks, H. J. B., T. Webb III, and A. A. Berti
> 1955 Numerical Analysis of Pollen Samples from Central Canada: Comparison of Methods. *Review of Palaeobotany and Palynology* 20: 133-69.

Blake, S. P.
> 1979 The Patrimonial-Bureaucratic Empire of the Mughals. *Journal of Asian Studies* 39:77-94.

Blaike, P., and H. Brookfield
> 1987 Defining and Debating the Problem. In *Land Degradation and Society*, edited by P. Blaike and H. Brookfield, pp. 149-57. British Archaeological Reports International Series 96, Oxford.

Blanton, R. E.
> 1975 The Cybernetic Analysis of Human Population Growth. In *Population Studies in Archaeology and Physical Anthropology*, edited by A. C. Swedland, pp. 116-26. Society for American Archaeology Memoir 30, Washington D.C.

Blasco, F., and G. Thanikaimoni
> 1974 Late Quaternary Vegetational History of Southern Region. In *Aspects and Appraisal of Indian Palaeobotany*, edited by K. R. Surange, R. N. Lakhanpal, and D. C. Bharadwaj, pp. 632-43. Birbal Sahni Institute of Paleobotany, Lucknow.

Blurton, T. R.
> 1985 Palace Structures at Vijayanagara: The Archaeological Evidence. In *South Asian Archaeology 1985*, edited by K. Frifelt and P. Sorensen, pp. 426-40. Scandinavian Institute of Asian Studies Occasional Papers 4. Curzon Press, London.

Bohannon, P., and G. Dalton
> 1962 Introduction. In *Markets in Africa*, edited by P. Bohannon and G. Dalton, pp. 1-28. Northwestern University Press, Chicago.

Bonnefille, R.
> 1969 Analyse Pollinique d'un Sediment recent: Vases Actuelles de la Riviere Aouache (Ethiopie). *Spores* 11:7-16.

Bonny, A. P.
> 1976 Recruitment of Pollen to the Seston and Sediment of Some Lake District Lakes. *Journal of Ecology* 64:859-88.

Boon, J. A.
> 1982 *Other Tribes, Other Scribes: Symbolic Anthropology in the Comparative Study of Cultures, Histories, Religions, and Texts*. Cambridge University Press, Cambridge.

Boserup, E.
> 1965 *The Conditions of Agricultural Growth*. Aldine, Chicago.
> 1981 *Population and Technological Change: Study of Long-Term Trends*. University of Chicago Press, Chicago.
> 1983 The Impact of Scarcity and Plenty on Development. In *Hunger and History*, edited by R. I. Rothberg and T. K. Rabb, pp, 185-210. Cambridge University Press, Cambridge.
> 1990 *Economic and Demographic Relationships in Development*. Baltimore, Johns Hopkins University Press.

Bray, F.
> 1986 *The Rice Economies: Technology and Development in Asia*. Blackwell, New York.

Breckenridge, C. A.
> 1985 Social Storage and the Extension of Agriculture in South India 1350 to 1750. In *Vijayanagara: City and Empire*, edited by A. L. Dallapiccola, pp. 41-72. Franz Steiner Verlag, Wiesbaden.

Breckenridge, C. A., and P. van der Veer
    1993   Orientalism and the Postcolonial Predicament. In *Orientalism and the Postcolonial Predicament*, edited by C. A. Breckenridge and P. van der Veer, pp. 1-22. University of Pennsylvania Press, Philadelphia.

Bronson, B.
    1972   Farm Labor and the Evolution of Food Production. In *Population Growth: Anthropological Implications*, edited by B. Spooner, pp. 190-218. M.I.T. Press, Cambridge.
    1975   The Earliest Farming: Demography as Cause and Consequence. In *Population, Ecology, and Social Evolution*, edited by S. Polgar, pp. 53-78. Mouton, The Hague.
    1977   Exchange at the Upstream and Downstream Ends: Notes Toward a Functional Model of the Coastal State in Southeast Asia. In *Economic Exchange and Social Interaction in Southeast Asia: Perspectives from Prehistory, History, and Ethnography*, edited by K. L. Hutterer, pp. 39-54. Center for South and Southeast Asian Studies, University of Michigan Papers on South and Southeast Asia 13, Ann Arbor.

Brookfield, H. C.
    1972   Intensification and Disintensification in Pacific Agriculture: A Theoretical Approach. *Pacific Viewpoint* 13:211-38.
    1984   Intensification Revisited. *Pacific Viewpoint* 25:15-44.

Brookfield, H. C., and P. Brown
    1963   Struggle for Land: Agriculture and Group Territories among the Chimbu of the New Guinea Highlands. *Ethnology* 15:211-38.

Brookfield, H. C., and D. Hart
    1971   *Melanesia: A Geographical Interpretation of an Island World*. Methuen, London.

Brown, P., and A. Podolefsky
    1976   Population Density, Agricultural Intensity, and Group Size in the New Guinea Highlands. *Ethnology* 15:211-38.

Bradley, R.
    1978   Prehistoric Field Systems in Britain and North-West Europe - Review of Some Recent Work. *World Archaeology* 9:625-80.

Brubaker, R. P.
    in pr.   VMS-370: A Vijayanagara Period Fortification Wall and Reservoir Embankment in the Metropolitan Region. In *Vijayanagara: Progress of Research 1992*, edited by D. V. Devaraj and C. S. Patil. Directorate of Archaeology and Museums, Mysore.

Brumfiel, E., and T. K. Earle
    1987   Specialization and Exchange in Complex Societies, An Introduction. In *Specialization, Exchange and Complex Societies*, edited by E. Brumfiel and T. K. Earle, pp. 1-9. Cambridge University Press, Cambridge.

Brush, S. B., and B. L. Turner II
    1978   The Nature of Farming Systems and Views of Their Change. In *Comparative Farming Systems*, edited by B. L. Turner and S. B. Brush, pp. 11-48. The Guilford Press, New York.

Bryant, V. M., and R. C. Holloway
    1983   The Role of Palynology in Archaeology. In *Advances in Archaeological Method and Theory*, Vol. 6, edited by M. B. Schiffer, pp. 191-224. Academic Press, New York.

Bryant, V. M., and G. Williams-Dean
    1975   The Coprolites of Man. *Scientific American* 232(1):100-109.

Byers, T. J., and H. Mukhia (eds.)
    1985   Feudalism and Non-European Societies. *Journal of Peasant Studies* 12.

Butzer, K. W.
    1972   *Environment and Archaeology*. Methuen, London.
    1982   *Archaeology as Human Ecology*. Cambridge University Press, Cambridge.

Byrne, A. R., J. Michaelsen, and A. Soutar
    1977   Fossil Charcoal as a Measure of Wildfire Frequency in Southern California: A Preliminary Analysis. In *Proceedings of a Symposium on the Environmental Consequences of Fire and Fuel Management in Mediterranean Ecosystems*, edited by H. A. Mooney and C. E. Conrad, pp. 361-67. USDA Forest Service General Technical Report WO-3, Washington D.C.
    1979   Prehistoric Fire Frequencies in the Southern Las Padres National Forest: A Fossil Charcoal Record from the Santa Barbara Channel. Unpublished manuscript on file at the Department of Geography, University of California, Berkeley.

Byrne, A. R., and S. P. Horn
    1989   Prehistoric Agriculture and Forest Clearance in the Sierra de los Tuxtlas, Veracruz, Mexico. *Palynology* 13:181-93.

Carniero, R.
    1970   A Theory of the Origin of the State. *Science* 169:733-38.

Chakrabarti, D. K.
    1988   *A History of Indian Archaeology from the Beginning to 1947*. Munshiram Manoharlal, New Delhi.

Champakalakshmi, R.
    1981   Peasant State and Society in Medieval South India: A Review Article. *The Indian Economic and Social History Review* 18:411-26.

Champion, H. G.

       1936   A Preliminary Survey of Forest Types of India and Burma. *Indian Forest Record*, n.s. 1:1-286.

Chanda, S.
       1972   Potentiality and Problems of Quaternary Pollen Analysis in India. *Proceedings of the Seminar of Palaeopalynology and Indian Stratigraphy*, edited by A. K. Ghosh et al., pp. 336-34. Univ. Grants Commission and Dept. of Botany, University of Calcutta, Calcutta.

Charlesworth, B.
       1980   *Evolution in Age Structured Populations*. Cambridge University Press, Cambridge.

Chaudhuri, K. N.
       1985   *Trade and Civilisation in the Indian Ocean: An Economic History from the Rise of Islam to 1750*. Cambridge University Press, Cambridge.

Chisholm, M.
       1968   *Rural Settlement and Land Use*. Hutchinson University Library, London.

Chopra, P. N., T. K. Ravindran, and N. Subrahmanian
       1979   *History of South India*. S. Chand and Company, New Delhi.

Clary, K. H., and G. Dean
       1992   Pollen Analysis. In *Landscape Archaeology in the Southern Tularosa Basin, Volume 2: Testing, Excavation, and Analysis*, edited by W. H. Doleman, R. C. Chapman, J. A. Schutt, M. K. Swift, and K. D. Morrison, pp.359-86. Office of Contract Archaeology, University of New Mexico, Albuquerque.

Clarke, D. L.
       1972   Models and Paradigms in Contemporary Archaeology. In *Models in Archaeology*, edited by D. L. Clarke, pp. 1-60. Methuen, London.

Clark, J. S.
       1988a   Stratigraphic Charcoal Analysis on Petrographic Thin Sections: Application to Fire History in Northwestern Minnesota. *Quaternary Research* 30:81-91.
       1988b   Particle Motion and the Theory of Charcoal Analysis: Source Area, Transport, Deposition, and Sampling. *Quaternary Research* 30:67-800.

Clark, J. S., and W. A. Patterson III
       1984   Pollen, Pb-210, and Opaque Spherules: An Integrated Approach to Dating and Sedimentation in the Intertidal Environment. *Journal of Sedimentary Petrology* 54:1249-63.

Clark, R. L.
       1982   Point Count Estimation of Charcoal in Pollen Preparations and Thin Sections of Sediments. *Pollen et Spores* 24:523-35.

Clarke, W. C.
       1985   The Fabric of the World Farm. In *Prehistoric Intensive Agriculture in the Tropics*, edited by I. Farrington, pp. 865-81. British Archaeological Reports International Series 232, part ii, Oxford.

Classen, H. J. M., and P. Skalnik
       1978   The Early State: Theories and Hypotheses. In *The Early State*, edited by H. J. M. Classen and P. Skalnik, pp. 3-30. Mouton, The Hague.

Cohen, B. S.
       1990   *An Anthropologist among the Historians and Other Essays*. Oxford University Press, Delhi.

Colson, E.
       1979   In Good Years and Bad: Food Strategies of Self Reliant Societies. *Journal of Anthropological Research* 35:18-29.

Condimas, G.
       1986   Ritual Technology in Mon Gar Swidden Agriculture. In *Rice Societies: Asian Problems and Prospects*, edited by I. Norland, S. Cederroth, and I. Gerdin, pp. 28-48. Scandinavian Institute of Asian Studies, Studies on Asian Topics 10. Curzon Press, London.

Conelley, W. T.
       1992   Agricultural Intensification in a Philippine Frontier Community: Impact on Labor Efficiency and Farm Diversity. *Human Ecology* 20:203-223.

Conklin, H. C.
       1957   *Hanunoo Agriculture: A Report on an Integral System of Shifting Cultivation in the Philippines*. F.A.O. Forest Development Paper 12. Food and Agriculture Organization of the United Nations, Rome.

Costin, C. L.
       1991   Craft Specialization: Issues in Defining, Documenting, and Explaining the Organization of Production. In *Archaeological Method and Theory, Volume 3*, edited by M. B. Schiffer, pp. 1-56. University of Arizona Press, Tucson.

Covich, A. P.
       1978   Reassessment of Ecological Stability in the Maya Area: Evidence from Lake Studies of Early Agricultural Impacts on Biotic Communities. In *Pre-Hispanic Maya Agriculture*, edited by P. D. Harrison and B. L. Turner, pp. 145-56. University of New Mexico Press, Albuquerque.

Cowgill, G. L.
       1975a   On the Causes and Consequences of Ancient and Modern Population Changes. *American Anthropologist*, 77:505-525.
       1975b   A Selection of Samplers: Comments on Archaeo-Statistics. In *Sampling in Archaeology*, edited by J. Mueller, pp. 258-76. University of Arizona Press, Tucson.

  1990 Toward Refining Concepts of Full Coverage Survey. In *The Archaeology of Regions: The Case For Full Coverage Survey*, edited by S. K. Fish and S. A. Kowalewski, pp. 249-59. Smithsonian Institution Press, Washington D.C.

Cox, P. A.
  1993 Water-Pollinated Plants. *Scientific American* 269(4):68-75.

Cwynar, L. C.
  1978 Recent History of Fire and Vegetation from Laminated Sediment of Greenleaf Lake, Algonquin Park. *Canadian Journal of Botany* 56:10-21.

Dagans, B. (translator)
  1985 *Mayamata: An Indian Treatise on Housing, Architecture, and Iconography*. Sitaram Bhartia Institute of Scientific Research, New Delhi.

Dallapiccola, A. L. (editor)
  1985 *Vijayanagara City and Empire: New Currents of Research*. 2 vols. Franz Steiner Verlag, Wiesbaden.

Dallapiccola, A. L., J. M. Fritz, G. Michell, and S. Rajasekhara
  1992 *The Ramachandra Temple*. American Institute of Indian Studies and Manohar Press, New Delhi.

Dalton, G.
  1961 Economic Theory and Peasant Society. *American Anthropologist* 63:1-25.
  1969 Theoretical Issues in Economic Anthropology. *Current Anthropology* 10:63-101.

Dames, M. L. (editor and translator)
  1989 *The Book of Duarte Barbosa*. 2 vols. Asian Educational Services, New Delhi. Originally published 1919-1921, Hakluyt Society, London.

Das Gupta, A., and M. N. Pearson (editors)
  1987 *India and The Indian Ocean 1500-1800*. Oxford University Press, Calcutta.

Davies, C. C.
  1959 *An Historical Atlas of the Indian Peninsula*. 2d edition. Oxford University Press, Oxford.

Davis, M. B.
  1963 On the Theory of Pollen Analysis. *American Journal of Science* 261:897-912.
  1969 Palynology and Environmental History during the Quaternary Period. *American Scientist* 57:317-32.

Davis, M. B., and M. S. Ford
  1982 Sediment Focussing in Mirror Lake, New Hampshire. *Limnology and Oceanography* 27:137-50.

Davis, M. B., and J. C. Goodlett
  1960 Comparing Present Vegetation with Pollen Spectra in Surface Samples from Brownington Pond, Vermont. *Ecology* 41:356-57.

Davison-Jenkins, D. J.
  1988 *The Irrigation and Water Supply Systems of the City of Vijayanagara*. Unpublished Ph.D. dissertation, Department of Oriental Studies, University of Cambridge, Cambridge.

de Vries, J.
  1972 Labor/Leisure Tradeoff (Boserup as Economics and History). *Peasant Studies Newsletter* 1:45-50.
  1974 *The Dutch Rural Economy in the Golden Age, 1500-1700*. Yale University Press, New Haven.

Deloche, J.
  1984 *The Ancient Bridges of India*. Sitaram Bhartia Institute of Scientific Research, New Delhi.

Denevan, W. M.
  1980 Latin America. In *World Systems of Traditional Resource Management*, edited by G.A. Klee, pp. 217-44. John Wiley and Sons, New York.

Denevan, W. M., and B. L. Turner
  1974 Forms, Functions, and Associations of Raised Fields in the Old World Tropics. *The Journal of Tropical Geography* 39:24-33.

Deo, S. P.
  1973 *Problems of South Indian Megaliths*. Kannada Research Institute Research Lecture Series, 4. Karnatak University Press, Dharwar.

Desai, P. B., S. Ritti, and B. R. Gopal
  1981 *History of Karnataka*. Kannada Research Institute, Dharwad.

Devakunjari, D.
  1970 *Hampi*. Archaeological Survey of India, New Delhi.

Devaraj, D. V., and C. S. Patil (editors)
  1991a *Vijayanagara: Progress of Research 1984-87*. Directorate of Archaeology and Museums, Mysore.
  1991b *Vijayanagara: Progress of Research 1987-88*. Directorate of Archaeology and Museums, Mysore.

Digby, S.
  1982 The Maritime Trade of India. In *The Cambridge Economic History of India, Vol. I: c. 1200 - c. 1750*, edited by T. Rayachaudhuri and I. Habib, pp. 125-59. Cambridge University Press, Cambridge.

Dimbleby, G. W.
  1957 Pollen Analysis of Terrestrial Soils. *New Phytologist* 56:12-28.
  1985 *The Palynology of Archaeological Sites*. Academic Press, London.

Dirks, N. B.
  1987 *The Hollow Crown: Ethnohistory of an Indian Kingdom*. Cambridge University Press, Cambridge.
  1992 Introduction: Colonialism and Culture. In *Colonialism and Culture*, edited by N. B. Dirks, pp. 1-26. Univer-

Donkin, R. A.
    sity of Michgan Press, Ann Arbor.
    1979   *Agricultural Terracing in the New World*. Viking Fund Publications in Anthropology 56, Wenner-Gren Foundation for Anthropological Research, New York.

Donner, J. J.
    1962   On the Post-Glacial History of the Grampian Highlands of Scotland. *Society Scientifique Fennoscandia* 24:6.

Dumont, L.
    1980   *Homo Hierarchicus: The Caste System and Its Implications*. Translated by M. Sainsbury. University of Chicago Press, Chicago.

Dunnell, R. C., and W. S. Dancey
    1983   The Siteless Survey: A Regional Scale Data Collection Strategy. *Advances in Archaeological Method and Theory, Volume 6*, ed. M. B. Schiffer, pp. 267-83. Academic Press, New York.

Earle, T. K.
    1978   *Economic and Social Organization of a Complex Chiefdom: The Halilea District, Kauai, Hawaii*. Anthropological Papers of the Museum of Michigan 63, Ann Arbor.
    1980   A Model of Subsistence Change. In *Modeling Change in Prehistoric Subsistence Economies*, edited by T. K. Earle and A. L. Christiansen, pp. 1-29. Academic Press, New York.

Earle, T. K., and A. L. Christiansen (editors)
    1980   *Modeling Change in Prehistoric Subsistence Economies*. Academic Press, New York.

Ebert, J. I.
    1992   *Distributional Archaeology*. University of New Mexico Press, Albuquerque.

Edwards, K. J.
    1979   Palynological and Temporal Inference in the Context of Prehistory, with Special Reference to the Evidence from Lake and Peat Deposits. *Journal of Archaeological Science* 6:255-70.

Ehret, C.
    1984   Historical/Linguistic Evidence for Early African Food Production. In *From Hunter to Farmers*, edited by J. D. Clark and S. A. Brandt, pp. 26-36, University of California Press, Berkeley.

Erdtman, G.
    1969   *Palynology*. Hafner, New York.

Faegri, K., P. E. Kaland, and K. Krzywinski
    1989   *Textbook of Pollen Analysis, IV Edition*. John Wiley and Sons, Chichester.

Farrington, I. S., and C. C. Park
    1978   Hydraulic Engineering and Irrigation Agriculture in the Moche Valley, Peru c. A.D. 1250-1532. *Journal of Archaeological Science* 5:255-68.

Filliozat, P. S., and V. Filliozat
    1988   *Hampi-Vijayanagar: The Temple of Vithala*. Sitaram Bhartia Institute of Scientific Research, New Delhi.

Filliozat, V.
    1973   *Epigraphie de Vijayanagar de debut a 1377*. L'Eclole Francais d'Extreme-Orient 91, Paris.
    1984   The Vithala Temple at Hampi. In *South Asian Archaeology 1981*, edited by B. Allchin, pp. 305-307. Cambridge University Press, Cambridge.

Firth, R.
    1956   *Elements of Social Organization*. Watts, London.

Fish, S. K., and S. A. Kowalewski
    1990   Introduction. In *The Archaeology of Regions: A Case for Full Coverage Survey*, edited by S. K. Fish and S. A. Kowalewski, pp. 1-6. Smithsonian Institution Press, Washington D.C.

Fish, S. K., and S. A. Kowalewski (editors)
    1990   *The Archaeology of Regions: A Case for Full Coverage Survey*. Smithsonian Institution Press, Washington D.C.

Flannery, K. V.
    1969   Origins and Ecological Effects of Early Domestication in Iran and the Near East. In *The Domestication and Exploitation of Plants and Animals*, edited by P. J. Ucko and G. W. Dimbleby, pp. 73-100. Duckworth, London.

Foley, R.
    1981   *Off Site Archaeology and Human Adaptations in Eastern Kenya*. Cambridge Monographs in African Archaeology, British Archaeological Reports International Series 97, Oxford.

Foote, R. B.
    1887   Notes on Some Recent Neolithic and Palaeolithic Finds in South India. *Journal of the Royal Asiatic Society of Bengal* 56:259-82.
    1914   *Indian Prehistoric and Protohistoric Antiquities: Catalogue Raisonne*. Madras Government Museum, Madras.
    1916   *Indian Prehistoric and Protohistoric Antiquities: Notes on Their Ages and Distributions*. Madras Government Museum, Madras.

Forni, G.
    1984   From Pyrophytic to Domesticated Plants: The Palaeontological-Linguistic Evidence for a Unitary Theory on the Origin of Plant and Animal Domestication. In *Plants and Ancient Man*, edited by W. Van Zeist and W. A. Casparie, pp. 131-40. A. A. Balkema, Rotterdam.

Fowler, P. J., and J. G. Evans
    1967   Ploughmarks, Lynchets, and Early Fields. *Antiquity* 41:289-301.

Francis, W.
    1904   *Madras District Gazetteers: Bellary.* Government of India, Madras.

Fried, M. H.
    1967   *The Evolution of Political Society: an Essay in Political Anthropology.* Random House, New York.

Friedman, J.
    1979   *System Structure and Contradiction in the Evolution of Asiatic State Formations.* National Museum of Denmark Social Studies in Oceania and Southeast Asia 2.

Friedman, J., and M. J. Rowlands
    1978   Notes Toward an Epigenetic Model of the Evolution of 'Civilisation.' In *The Evolution of Social Systems*, edited by J. Friedman and M. J. Rowlands, pp. 201-278. University of Pittsburgh Press, Pittsburgh.

Fritz, J. M.
    1983   The Roads of Vijayanagara. In *Vijayanagara Progress of Research, 1979-83*, edited by M. S. Nagaraja Rao, pp. 51-56. Directorate of Archaeology and Museums, Mysore.
    1986   Vijayanagara: Authority and Meaning of a South Indian Imperial Capital. *American Anthropologist* 88:44-55.
    1987   Chaco Canyon and Vijayanagara: Postulating Spatial Meaning in Two Settlements. In *Mirror and Metaphor: Material and Social Constructions of Reality*, edited by D. Ingersoll and G. Bronitsky, pp. 314-49. University Press of America, Lanham.

Fritz, J. M., and G. Michell
    1985   Map Series on Cultural Remains at Vijayanagara. In *Vijayanagara Progress of Research 1983-84*, edited by M. S. Nagaraja Rao, pp. 164-98. Directorate of Archaeology and Museums, Mysore.
    1986   *Hampi: Splendours of the Vijayanagara Empire.* Lavanya Publishers, Bombay.

Fritz, J. M., G. Michell, and M. S. Nagaraja Rao
    1985   *Where Kings and Gods Meet: The Royal Centre at Vijayanagara.* University of Arizona Press, Tucson.

Fritz, J. M., and K. D. Morrison
    in pr.   *The Royal Centre at Vijayanagara: Enclosures I-IX and the West Alley.* Manohar Press, New Delhi.

Frykenberg, R. E.
    1979   Traditional Processes of Power in South India: An Historical Analysis of Local Influence. In *Land Control and Social Structure in Indian History*, edited by R. E. Frykenberg, pp. 217-36. Manohar, New Delhi.

Gallagher, J. P.
    1989   Agricultural Intensification and Ridged-Field Cultivation in the Prehistoric Upper Midwest of North America. In *Foraging and Farming: the Evolution of Plant Exploitation*, edited by D. R. Harris and G. C. Hillman, pp. 572-84. Unwin Hyman, London.

Gaussen, H., P. Legris, L. Labroue, V. M. Meher-Homji, and M. Viart
    1966   *Carte Inernationale Du Tapis Vegetal, Notice de la Feuille: Mysore.* Extrait des Travaux de la Section Scientifique et Technique de L'Institut Francais de Pondicherry, Hors Serie 7.

Geertz, C.
    1963   *Agricultural Involution.* University of California Press, Berkeley.
    1980   *Negara: The Theatre State in Nineteenth Century Bali.* Princeton University Press, Princeton.

Glassow, M. A.
    1978   The Concept of Carrying Capacity in the Study of Culture Process. In *Advances in Archaeological Method and Theory*, vol. 1, edited by M. B. Schiffer, pp. 32-48. Academic Press, New York.

Godelier, M.
    1978a   The Object and Method of Economic Anthropology. In *Relations of Production: Marxist Approaches to Economic Anthropology*, edited by D. Seddon, pp. 51-107. Frank Cass, London.
    1978b   The Concept of the Asiatic Mode of Production and Marxist Models of Social Evolution. In *Relations of Production: Marxist Approaches to Economic Anthropology*, edited by D. Seddon, pp. 209-257. Frank Cass, London.

Godwin, H.
    1944a   Neolithic Forest Clearance. *Nature* 153:511.
    1944b   Studies of the Postglacial History of British Vegetation. *Philosophical Transactions Bulletin* 233:275.
    1956   *The History of the British Flora.* Cambridge University Press, London and New York.

Gopal, B. H.
    1985a   *Vijayanagara Inscriptions.* Vol. 1. Directorate of Archaeology and Museums, Mysore.
    1985b   *Vijayanagara Inscriptions.* Vol. 2. Directorate of Archaeology and Museums, Mysore.
    1990   *Vijayanagara Inscriptions.* Vol. 3. Directorate of Archaeology and Museums, Mysore.

Government of India
    1887-   *Annual Report on Indian Epigraphy (ARIE).* Government Press, Madras.
    1887-   *Annual Report on South Indian Epigraphy (ARSIE).* Government Press, Madras.

Green, S. W.
    1980   Broadening Least-Cost Models for Expanding Agricultural Systems. In *Modeling Change in Prehistoric Subsistence Economies*, edited by T. K. Earle and A. L. Christiansen, pp. 209-242. Academic Press, New York.

Grigg, D. B.
    1982   *The Dynamics of Agricultural Change: The Historical Experience.* St. Martin's Press, New York.

Grist, D. H.
    1954   *Rice*. Longman, London.
Guinet, P.
    1966   What May Afford Palynology to Archaeology and Ancient History in India. *Journal of the M.S. University of Baroda* 51:195-201.
Hall, I.
    1983   Field Work and Field Books: Studies in Early Layout. In *Villages, Fields, and Frontiers: Studies in European Rural Settlement in the Medieval and Modern Periods*, edited by B. K. Roberts and R. E. Glasscock, pp. 115-31. BAR International Series 185, Oxford.
Hall, D. N.
    1982   *Medieval Fields*. Shire Publications, London.
Hanks, L. M.
    1972   *Rice and Man: Agricultural Ecology in Southeast Asia*. AHM Publishing Corp, Arlington Heights.
Harlan, J., and J. M. de Wet
    1964   Some Thoughts on Weeds. *Economic Botany* 18:16-24.
Hassig, R.
    1985   *Trade, Tribute, and Transportation: The Sixteenth Century Political Economy of the Valley of Mexico*. University of Oklahoma Press, Norman.
Heitzman, J.
    1987   Temple Urbanism in Medieval South India. *Journal of Asian Studies* 46:791-826.
Heras, H.
    1927   *The Arividu Dynasty of Vijayanagara*. B. G. Paul and Company, Madras.
Herskovits, M. J.
    1952   *Economic Anthropology*. Knopf, New York.
Higgs, E. S., and C. Vita-Finzi
    1972   Prehistoric Economies: Territorial Approach. In *Papers in Economic Prehistory*, edited by E. S. Higgs, pp. 27-36. Cambridge University Press, Cambridge.
Holloway, R. G., V. M. Bryant, and S. Valastro
    1981   16,000 Year Old Pollen Record From Central Alberta, Canada. *Palynology* 5:195-208.
Horn, S. P., R. D. Horn, and A. R. Byrne
    1992   An Automated Charcoal Scanner for Paleoecological Studies. *Palynology* 16:7-12.
Hunt, E., and R. C. Hunt
    1974   Irrigation Conflict and Politics: A Mexican Case. In *Irrigation's Impact on Society*, edited by T. E. Downing and M. Gibson, pp. 129-58. Anthropological Papers of the University of Arizona 23, Tucson.
Hunt, R. C.
    1988   Size and the Structure of Authority in Canal Irrigation Systems. *Journal of Anthropological Research* 44:335-56.
Hutchinson, G. F., and C. E. Goulden
    1966   The History of Laguna de Petenxil: The Plant Microfossils. *Memoirs of the Connecticut Academy of Arts and Sciences* 17:67-73.
Inden, R.
    1990   *Imagining India*. Basil Blackwell, Oxford.
Irwin, H., and E. Barghoorn
    1965   Identification of the Pollen of Maize, Teosinte, and Tripsacum by Phase Contrast Microscopy. *Botanical Museum Leaflets* 31: 7-56.
Ismail, K.
    1984   *Karnataka Temples: Their Role in Socio-Economic Life*. Sundeep Prakashan, Delhi.
Iverson, J.
    1941   Land Occupation in Denmark's Stone Age. *Danmarks Geologiske Undersolgelse* 2(66):1-68.
Jacobi, R. M., J. H. Tallis, and P. A. Mellars
    1976   The Southern Pennine Mesolithic and the Ecological Record. *Journal of Archaeological Science* 3:307-320.
Jarman, M. R.
    1972   European Deer Economies and the Advent of the Neolithic. In *Papers in Economic Prehistory*, edited by E. S. Higgs, 125-47. Cambridge University Press, Cambridge.
Johnson, A.
    1980   The Limits of Formalism in Agricultural Decision Research. In *Agricultural Decision Making: Anthropological Contributions to Rural Development*, edited by P. F. Barlett, pp. 19-44. Academic Press, New York.
Johnson, B. L. C.
    1969   *South Asia*. Heineman, London.
Judge, W. J., J. I. Ebert, and R. K. Hitchcock
    1975   Sampling in Regional Archaeological Survey. In *Sampling in Archaeology*, edited by J. Mueller, pp. 82-123. University of Arizona Press, Tucson.
Kaiser, T., and B. Voytek
    1983   Sedentism and Economic Change in the Balkan Neolithic. *Journal of Anthropological Research* 2:323-53.
Kanitkar, N. V.
    1960   *Dry Farming in India*. 2d edition. Indian Council of Agricultural Research, New Delhi.

Karashima, N.
    1984   *South Indian History and Society: Studies from Inscriptions, A.D. 850-1800*. Oxford University Press, Delhi.
    1992   *Toward a New Formation: South Indian Society Under Vijayanagar Rule*. Oxford and IBH, Delhi.

Keene, A. S.
    1983   Biology, Behavior, and Borrowing: A Critical examination of Optimal Foraging Theory in Archaeology. In *Archaeological Hammers and Theories*, edited by J. A. Moore and A. S. Keene, pp. 137-55. Academic Press, New York.

Kelley, W.
    1983   Concepts in the Anthropological Study of Irrigation. *American Anthropologist* 85:880-86.

Kelsall, J.
    1872   *Manual of the Bellary District: Compiled under the orders of Government*. Lawrence Asylum Press, Madras.

Killion, T. W.
    1992   The Archaeology of Settlement Agriculture. In *Gardens of Prehistory*, edited by T. W. Killion, pp. 1-13. University of Alabama Press, Tuscaloosa.

Kirch, P. V.
    1977   Valley Agricultural Systems in Prehistoric Hawaii: an Archaeological Consideration. *Asian Perspectives* 20:246-80.
    1984   *The Evolution of the Polynesian Chiefdoms*. Cambridge University Press, Cambridge.
    1985   Intensive Agriculture in Prehistoric Hawai'i: The Wet and the Dry. In *Prehistoric Intensive Agriculture in the Tropics, Part ii*, edited by I. S. Farrington, pp. 435-54. British Archaeological Reports International Series 232, Oxford.
    1992   *Anahulu: The Archaeology of History in the Kingdom of Hawaii*, Vol. Two. University of Chicago Press, Chicago.
    1994   *The Wet and The Dry: Irrigation and Agricultural Intensification in Polynesia*. University of Chicago Press, Chicago.

Kirkby, A. V. T.
    1973   *The Use of Land and Water Resources in the Past and Present Valley of Oaxaca*. University of Michigan Museum of Anthropology Memoir 5, Ann Arbor.

Kohl, P. L.
    1987   The Use and Abuse of World Systems Theory: The Case of the Pristine West Asian State. In *Advances in Archaeological Method and Theory*, vol. 11, edited by M. B. Schiffer, pp. 1-35. Academic Press, New York.

Kosambi, D. D.
    1956   *An Introduction to the Study of Indian History*. Popular Book Depot, Bombay.

Kotraiah, C. T. M.
    1959   Ancient Anicuts on the River Tungabhadra. *Indian Journal of Power and River Valley Development Tungabhadra Project Number* 1:49-53.
    1978   Boundary Stones: A Short Study With Special Reference to Those Available in the Hampi Museum. *Journal of The Andhra Historical Society* 37:129-46.
    1983   Hampi Before Founding of Vijayanagara. In *Shrinidhi: Perspectives in Indian Art and Archaeology*, edited by K. V. Raman, K.G. Krishnan, M. S. Ramaswami, N. Karashima, A. V. Narasimha Murty, P. Shanmugam, and S. Srinivasan, pp. 381-88. New Era Publications, Madras.

Kowalewski, S. A.
    1980   Population Resource Balances in Period I of Oaxaca, Mexico. *American Antiquity* 45:151-65.

Krader, L.
    1975   *The Asiatic Mode of Production: Sources, Development, and Critique in the Writings of Karl Marx*. Van Gorcum and Company, Assen.

Krishnaswami Ayyangar, S. (editor)
    1919   *Sources of Vijayanagara History*. University of Madras, Madras.

Krishnaswami Ayyangar, S.
    1921   *South India and Her Muhammedan Invaders*. University of Madras, Madras.

Krishnaswami Pillai, A.
    1964   *The Tamil Country Under Vijayanagara*. Annamalai Historical Series, 20. Annamalai University, Annamalainagar.

Krisnamurthy, M.
    1978   *Geology and Mineral Resources of the Bellary District, Karnataka (Mysore) State*. Memoirs of the Geological Survey of India 108, New Delhi.

Kulke, H.
    1985   Maharajas, Mahants, and Historians: Reflections on the Historiography of Early Vijayanagara and Sringeri. In *Vijayanagara City and Empire: New Currents of Research*, Vol. 1, edited by A. L. Dallapiccola, pp. 120-43. Franz Steiner Verlag, Wiesbaden.

Kulke, H., and D. Rothermund
    1986   *A History of India*. Dorsett Press, New York.

Lansing, J. S.
    1991   *Priests and Programmers: Technologies of Power in the Engineered Landscape of Bali*. Princeton University Press, Princeton.

Leach, E. R.
- 1971 *Pul Eliya, A Village in Ceylon: A Study in Land Tenure and Kinship.* Cambridge University Press, Cambridge.
- 1990 Aryan Invasions Over Four Millennia. In *Culture Through Time: Anthropological Approaches*, edited by E. Ohnuki-Tierney, pp. 227-45. Stanford University Press, Palo Alto.

Leshnik, L.
- 1974 *South Indian "Megalithic" Burials: The Pandukal Complex.* Franz Steiner Verlag, Wiesbaden.

Lewarch, D. E., & O'Brien M. J.
- 1981 The Expanding Role of Surface Assemblages in Archaeological Research. *Advances in Archaeological Method and Theory, Volume 4*, ed. M. B. Schiffer, pp. 297-342. Academic Press, New York.

Livingstone, D. A.
- 1984 Interactions of Food Production and Changing Vegetation in Africa. In *From Hunter to Farmers*, edited by J. D. Clark and S. A. Brandt, pp. 22-25. University of California Press, Berkeley.

Longhurst, A. H.
- 1916 The Cinder Mound at Kudatini in the Bellary District. *Annual Report of the Archeological Survey of India 1912-1913*, New Delhi.
- 1917 *Hampi Ruins Described and Illustrated.* Government Press, Madras.

Loschorn, E.
- 1985 Vijayanagara—as seen by European Visitors. In *Vijayanagara: City and Empire*, edited by A. L. Dallapiccola, pp. 344-53. Franz Steiner Verlag, Wiesbaden.

Ludden, D.
- 1985 *Peasant History in South India.* Princeton University Press, Princeton.

Lycett, M. T.
- 1991a Chipped Stone Tools of the Vijayanagara Metropolitan Region. In *Vijayanagara: Progress of Research 1987-88*, edited by D. V. Devaraj and C. S. Patil, pp. 85-94. Directorate of Archaeology and Museums, Mysore.
- 1991b Limited Activities and Continuous Distributions: Toward an Archaeology of Anasazi Landscapes. Paper presented at the 56th Annual Meeting of the Society of American Archaeology. New Orleans.
- 1994 Searching for Patterns in Ambiguous Categories: Nonarchitectural Sites of the Vijayanagara Metropolitan Region. In *South Asian Archaeology 1993*, edited by Asko Parpola and Petteri Koskikallio, Annales Academiae Scientiarum Fennicae, Series B, Vol. 271, pp. 412-23. Helsinki, Suomalainen Tiedeakatemia, 1994.

MacDonald, G. M., C. P. S. Larsen, J. M. Szeicz, and K. A. Moser
- 1991 The Reconstruction of Boreal Forest Fire History from Lake Sediments: A Comparison of Charcoal, Pollen, Sedimentological, and Geochemical Indices. *Quaternary Science Reviews* 10:53-71.

MacLean, C. D.
- 1877 *Standing Information Regarding the Official Administration of the Madras Presidency.* Government Press, Madras.

Mahalingam, T. V.
- 1940 *Administration and Social Life Under Vijayanagara.* University of Madras, Madras.
- 1951 *Economic Life in the Vijayanagar Empire.* University of Madras Press, Madras.

Major, R. H.
- 1857 *India in the Fifteenth Century.* Hakluyt Society, London.

Majumdar, G. G., and S. R. Rajguru
- 1966 *Ashmound Excavations at Kupgal.* Deccan College Postgraduate and Research Institute, Pune.

Malthus, T. R.
- 1872 *An Essay on the Principle of Population*, 7th edition. Reeves and Turner, London.

Martin, M. F.
- 1983 Optimal Foraging Theory: A Review of Some Models and Their Applications. *American Anthropologist* 85: 612-29.

Martin, P. S.
- 1963 *The Last Thousand Years, Fossil Pollen of the American Southwest.* University of Arizona Press, Tucson.

Marx, K.
- 1969 *Karl Marx on Colonialism and Modernization*, edited by S. Avineri. Anchor Books, New York.

Matheney, R. T.
- 1978 Northern Maya Lowland Water-Control Systems. In *Pre-Hispanic Maya Agriculture*, edited by P. D. Harrison and B. L. Turner, pp. 185-210. University of New Mexico Press, Albuquerque.

Mathew, K. S.
- 1983 *Portuguese Trade with India in the Sixteenth Century.* Manohar, New Delhi.

Maxwell, T. D., and K. F. Anschuetz
- 1992 The Southwestern Ethnographic Record and Prehistoric Agricultural Diversity. In *Gardens of Prehistory*, edited by T. W. Killion, pp. 35-68. University of Alabama Press, Tuscaloosa.

McAndrews, J. H.
- 1976 Fossil History of Maize Impact on the Canadian Flora: An Example from Southern Ontario. *Canadian Botanical Association Bulletin, Supplement* 9: 1-6.

McAnany, P. A.
- 1992 Agricultural Tasks and Tools: Patterns of Stone Tool Discard Near Prehistoric Maya Residences Bordering

Pulltrouser Swamp, Belize. In *Gardens of Prehistory*, edited by T. W. Killion, pp. 184-214. University of Alabama Press, Tuscaloosa.

Means, B. K.
   1991   A Small Settlement Near the City of Vijayanagara. In *Vijayanagara: Progress of Research 1987-88*, edited by D. V. Devaraj and C. S. Patil, pp. 154-64. Directorate of Archaeology and Museums, Mysore.

Meister, M. W., and M. A. Dhaky (editors)
   1986   *Encyclopedia of Indian Temple Architecture: South India, Upper Dravidadesa Early Phase, A.D. 500-1075*. American Institute of Indian Studies and University of Pennsylvania Press, Philadelphia.

Mellars, P.
   1976   Fire Ecology, Animal Populations, and Man: Study of Some Ecological Relationships in Prehistory. *Proceedings of the Prehistoric Society* 42:15-45.

Mencher, J. P.
   1978   *Agriculture and Social Structure in Tamil Nadu*. Carolina Academic Press, Durham.

Michell, G. A.
   1985a   Architecture of the Muslim Quarters at Vijayanagara. In *Vijayanagara Progress of Research 1983-84*, edited by M. S. Nagaraja Rao, pp. 101-118. Directorate of Archaeology and Museums, Mysore.
   1985b   A Never Forgotten City. In *Vijayanagara City and Empire: New Currents of Research*, Vol. 1, edited by A. Dallapiccola, pp. 196-207. Franz Steiner Verlag, Wiesbaden.
   1990   *Architectural Inventory of Vijayanagara*, 2 vols. Directorate of Archaeology and Museums, Mysore.
   1991   Architectural Documentation at Vijayanagar in 1987 and 1988: Hemakuta Hill and the Virupaksha Temple Complex at Hampi. In *Vijayanagara Progress of Research 1987-1988*, edited by D. V. Devaraj and C. S. Patil, pp. 35-43. Directorate of Archaeology and Museums, Mysore.

Michell, G. A., and V. Filliozat
   1981   *Splendours of The Vijayanagara Empire - Hampi*. Marg Publications, Bombay.

Michels, J. W.
   1973   *Dating Methods in Archaeology*. Seminar Press, New York.

Mitchell, G. F.
   1951   Studies in Irish Quaternary Deposits No. 7. *Proceedings of the Royal Irish Academy* 53:14.

Mookerji, R. K.
   1960   *Chandragupta Maurya and His Times*. Motilal Banarsidass, Delhi.

Moore, P. D., and J. A. Webb
   1978   *An Illustrated Guide to Pollen Analysis*. Wiley, New York.

Moreland, W. H.
   1920   *India at the Death of Akbar: An Economic Study*. Macmillan, London.

Mores, G. M.
   1931   *The Kadamba Kula: A History of Ancient and Medieval Karnataka*. Studies in Indian History of the Indian Historical Research Institute 5. St Xavier's College, Bombay.

Morris, B.
   1982   *Hill Traders: Socioeconomic Study of the Hill Pandaram*. The Athalone Press, New Jersey.

Morrison, K. D.
   1989   Urban Agricultural Production in South India: Agricultural Intensification at Vijayanagara. Paper presented at the 54th Annual Meeting of the Society for American Archaeology, Atlanta.
   1990   Patterns of Urban Occupation: Surface Collections at Vijayanagara. In *South Asian Archaeology 1987*, edited by M. Taddei. Instituto Italiano per il Medio ed Estremo Oriente, Rome.
   1991a   The Vijayanagara Metropolitan Survey: Preliminary Season. In *Vijayanagara: Progress of Research 1984-1987*, edited by D. V. Devaraj and C. S. Patil, pp. 136-41. Directorate of Archaeology and Museums, Mysore.
   1991b   Small-Scale Agricultural Features: Three Vijayanagara Embankments. In *Vijayanagara: Progress of Research 1987-88*, edited by D. V. Devaraj and C. S. Patil, pp. 81-84. Directorate of Archaeology and Museums, Mysore.
   1993   Supplying the City: the Role of Reservoir Irrigation in an Indian Urban Landscape. *Asian Perspectives* 32:133-51.
   1994a   Intensification of Production: Archaeological Approaches. *Journal of Archaeological Method and Theory* 1:111-59.
   1994b   Monitoring Regional Fire History through Size-Specific Analysis of Microscopic Charcoal: The Last 600 Years in South India. *Journal of Archaeological Science* 21:675-85.
   1994c   Power, *Prasad*, and the Marketplace: Food Grains in Southern India. Paper presented at the 93rd Annual Meeting of the American Anthropological Association, Atlanta.
   in pr.   Pollen Analysis from the Kamalapuram Kere, to appear in *Vijayanagara: Progress of Research 1989-92*, edited by D. V. Devaraj and C. S. Patil. Directorate of Archaeology and Museums, Mysore.

Morrison, K. D., and M. T. Lycett
   1989   Persistent Lithics: Post Iron Age Chipped Stone Technology in South India. Paper presented at the Annual Meeting of the Association of South Asian Studies, Madison.
   1994   Centralized Power, Centralized Authority? Ideological Claims and Archaeological Patterns. *Asian Perspectives* 32:327-50

Morrison, K. D., and Sinopoli, C. M.
   1992   Economic Diversity and Integration in a Precolonial Indian Empire. *World Archaeology* 23:335-52.

    in pr. a   Archaeological Survey in the Vijayanagara Metropolitan Region: 1990. In *Vijayanagara: Progress of Research 1989-92*, edited by D. V. Devaraj and C. S. Patil. Directorate of Archaeology and Museums, Mysore.

    in pr. b   The Vijayanagara Metropolitan Survey: 1994. In *Vijayanagara: Progress of Research 1993-94*, ed. D. V. Devaraj and C. S. Patil. Directorate of Archaeology and Museums, Mysore.

Morrison, M. E. S.
    1959   Evidence and Interpretation of Landnam in the Southeast of Ireland. *Sar Tryk Ur Postaniska Notiser* 112: Fax. 2.

Mosley, M. E., and E. E. Deeds
    1982   The Land in Front of Chan Chan: Agrarian Expansion and Collapse in the Moche Valley. In *Chan Chan: Andean Desert City*, edited by M. E. Mosley and K. C. Day, pp. 25-53. University of New Mexico Press, Albuquerque.

Muller, J.
    1984   Mississippian Specialization and Salt. *American Antiquity* 49:489-507.

Nagaraja Rao, M. S. (editor)
    1983   *Vijayanagara: Progress of Research 1979-83*. Directorate of Archaeology and Museums, Mysore.
    1985   *Vijayanagara: Progress of Research 1983-84*. Directorate of Archaeology and Museums, Mysore.
    1988   *Vijayanagara Through the Eyes of Alexander J. Greenlaw, 1856, and John Gollings, 1983*. Directorate of Archaeology and Museums, Mysore.

Nagaraja Rao, M. S.
    1983   Nomenclature of a Royal Road of Vijayanagara. In *Vijayanagara: Progress of Research 1979-1983*, edited by M. S. Nagaraja Rao, pp. 57-60. Directorate of Archaeology and Museums, Mysore.

Nagaraja Rao, M. S., and C. S. Patil
    1985   Epigraphical Studies. In *Vijayanagara Progress of Research 1983-84*, edited by M. S. Nagaraja Rao, pp. 21-53. Directorate of Archaeology and Museums, Mysore.

Nagaraju, H. M.
    1991   *Devaraya II and His Times: History of Vijayanagara*. Prasaranga University of Mysore, Mysore.

Nagaswamy, R.
    1965   South Indian Temples as an Employer. *Indian Economic and Social History Review* 2:367-72.

Nakana, A. K.
    1980   An Ecological View of Subsistence Economy Based Mainly on the Production of Rice in Swidden and in Irrigated Fields in a Hilly Region of Northern Thailand. *Tongan Ajia Kenkyu (Southeast Asian Studies)* 18:40-67.

Naqvi, S. M., and J. J. W. Rogers
    1987   *Precambrian Geology of India*. Oxford Monographs on Geology and Geophysics 6. Clarendon Press, New York.

Narian, A.
    1974   Castor. In *Evolutionary Studies in World Crops: Diversity and Change in the Indian Subcontinent*, edited by J. H. Hutchinson, pp. 71-78. Cambridge University Press, Cambridge.

Neale, W. C.
    1979   Land is to Rule. In *Land Control and Social Structure in Indian History*, edited by R. E. Frykenberg, pp. 3-16. Manohar, New Delhi.

Netting, R. McC.
    1974   Agrarian Ecology. *Annual Review of Anthropology* 3:21-56.
    1977   *Cultural Ecology*. Cummings, Menlo Park.
    1993   *Smallholders, Householders: Farm Families and the Ecology of Intensive, Sustainable Agriculture*. Stanford University Press, Stanford.

Netting, R. McC., R. R. Wilk, and E. J. Arnould (editors)
    1984   *Households: Comparative and Historical Studies of the Domestic Group*. University of California Press, Berkeley.

Newell, A. R.
    1984   On the Mesolithic Contribution to the Social Evolution of Western European Society. In *Social Evolution*, edited by J. Bintliff, pp. 69-82. University of Bradford, Bradford.

Nilakanta Sastri, K. A.
    1966   *A History of South India*, 3d edition. Oxford University Press, London.

Nilakanta Sastri, K. A., and M. A. Venkataramanayya (editors)
    1946   *Further Sources of Vijayanagara History*. University of Madras, Madras.

O'Brien, M. J., & D. E. Lewarch (editors)
    1981   *Plowzone Archaeology*. Vanderbilt University Publications in Anthropology 27, Nashville.

O'Connell, M.
    1986   Reconstruction of Local Landscape Development in the Post-Atlantic Based on Palaeoecological Investigations at Carrownaglogh Prehistoric Field System, County Mayo, Ireland. *Review of Paleobotany and Palynology* 49:117-76.

O'Leary, B.
    1989   *The Asiatic Mode of Production*. Basil Blackwell, London.

O'Sullivan, P. E., and D. H. Riley
    1974   Multivariate Numerical Analysis of Surface Pollen Spectra from Native Scots Pine Forest. *Pollen et Spores* 16:239-64.

Paddayya, K.
    1973   *Investigations into the Neolithic Culture of the Shorapur Doab, South India.* Brill, Leiden.
    1982   *The Achulean Culture of the Hungsi Valley (Peninsular India): A Settlement System Perspective.* Deccan College Postgraduate and Research Institute, Pune.
    1985   The Achulean Culture of the Hungsi Valley, South India: Settlement and Subsistence Patterns. In *Recent Advances in Indo-Pacific Prehistory*, edited by V. N. Misra and P. Bellwood, pp. 59-64. Oxford and IBH, New Delhi.
    1993   Ashmound Investigations at Budihal, Gulbarga District, Karnataka. *Man and Environment* 18(1):57-88.

Palat, R.
    1987   The Vijayanagara Empire: Re-integration of the Agrarian Order of Medieval South India. In *Early State Dynamics*, edited by H. J. M. Claessen and P. van der Velde, pp. 170-86. E. J. Brill, Leiden.

Pachamukhi, V. R. S.
    1953   *Virupaksha Vasantotsava Champu.* Kannada Research Institute, Dharwar.

Parsons, R. W., and I. C. Prentice
    1981   Statistical Approaches to R-Values and the Pollen Vegetation relationship. *Review of Paleobotany and Palynology*, 32:127-52.

Pascher, B.
    1987   *The Pattabhirama Temple: A Description and Iconographic Analysis.* Unpublished M.A. thesis, Department of Art History, Vermont College of Norwich University.

Patil, C. S.
    1991a   Epigraphical Studies. In *Vijayanagara Progress of Research 1987-88*, edited by D. V. Devaraj and C. S. Patil, pp. 15-34. Directorate of Archaeology and Museums, Mysore.
    1991b   Mummadi Singa, Kampila and Kumara Rama. In *Vijayanagara Progress of Research 1987-88*, edited by D. V. Devaraj and C. S. Patil, pp. 179-98. Directorate of Archaeology and Museums, Mysore.
    1991c   Kummata. In *Vijayanagara Progress of Research 1987-88*, edited by D. V. Devaraj and C. S. Patil, pp. 199-216. Directorate of Archaeology and Museums, Mysore.

Patil, C. S., and Balasubramanya
    1991   Epigraphical Studies. In *Vijayanagara Progress of Research 1984-87*, edited by D. V. Devaraj and C. S. Patil, pp. 19-70. Directorate of Archaeology and Museums, Mysore.

Patir, L.
    1987   Agricultural Intensification in Two Migrant Communities of Arunachal Pradesh, Northeast India. *Research in Economic Anthropology* 9:223-50.

Patterson, W. A., K. J. Edwards, and D. J. Maguire
    1987   Microscopic Charcoal as a Fossil Indicator of Fire. *Quaternary Science Reviews* 6:3-23.

Pearson, M. N.
    1981   *Coastal Western India: Studies from the Portuguese Records.* XCHR Studies Series No. 2. Concept Publishing, New Delhi.

Peck, R.
    1973   Pollen Budget Studies in a Small Yorkshire Catchment. In *Quaternary Plant Ecology*, edited by H. J. B. Birks and R. G. West, pp. 43-60. Wiley, New York.

Perlin, F.
    1983   Proto-Industrialization and Pre-Colonial South Asia. *Past and Present* 98:30-95.

Plog, S.
    1976   Relative Efficiencies of Sampling Techniques for Archaeological Surveys. *The Early Mesoamerican Village*, edited by K. V. Flannery, pp. 136-58. Academic Press, New York.

Polanyi, K.
    1957   The Economy as an Instituted Process. In *Trade and Market in the Early Empires: Economies in History and Theory*, edited by K. Polanyi, C. M. Arensberg, and H. W. Pearson, pp. 243-69. The Free Press, Glencoe.

Possehl, G. L.
    1986   African Millets in South Asian Prehistory. In *Studies in the Archaeology of India and Pakistan*, edited by J. Jacobsen, pp. 237-56. Oxford and IBH, New Delhi.

Postgate, J. N.
    1992   *Early Mesopotamia: Society and Economy at the Dawn of History.* Routledge, London and New York.

Pratt, M. L.
    1986   Fieldwork in Common Places. In *Writing Culture: The Poetics and Politics of Ethnography*, edited by J. Clifford and G. E. Marcus, pp. 27-50. University of California, Berkeley.

Prentice, I. C., and R. W. Parsons
    1983   Maximum Likelihood Linear Calibration of Pollen Spectra in Terms of Forest Composition. *Biometrics* 39:1051-1057.

Purandare, S.
    1986   *The History and Archaeology of Anegondi.* Unpublished Ph.D. dissertation, Department of Archaeology, Deccan College Postgraduate and Research Institute, University of Poona.

Rajasekhara, S.
    1985a   Inscriptions at Vijayanagara. In *Vijayanagara: City and Empire: New Currents of Research*, Vol.1, edited by A. L. Dallapiccola, pp. 101-119. Franz Steiner Verlag, Wiesbaden.
    1985b   Vijayanagara Studies: A Bibliography. In *Vijayanagara: City and Empire: New Currents of Research*, Vol. 2, edited by A. L. Dallapiccola, pp. 9-65. Franz Steiner Verlag, Wiesbaden.

Ramaswamy, V.
    1985a   Artisans in Vijayanagar Society. *Indian Economic and Social History Review*. 22:417-44.
    1985b   The Genesis and Historical Role of the Masterweavers in South Indian Textile Production. *Journal of the Economic and Social History of the Orient*. 28:294-325.
    1985c   *Textiles and Weavers in Medieval South India*. Oxford University Press, New Delhi.

Ramesan, N.
    1979   *A Catalogue of Vijayanagara Coins of the Andhra Pradesh Government Museum*. Archaeological Series 4, Government of Andhra Pradesh, Hyderabad.

Randhawa, M. S.
    1980   *A History of Agriculture in India*. Indian Council of Agricultural Research, New Delhi.

Rawski, E. S.
    1972   *Agricultural Change and the Peasant Economy of South China*. Harvard University Press, Cambridge.

Rawson, R. R.
    1963   *The Monsoon Lands of Asia*. Aldine, Chicago.

Ray, H. P.
    1986   *Monastery and Guild: Commerce under the Satavahanas*. Oxford University Press, Delhi.

Rea, A.
    1886   Vijayanagara. *Christian College Magazine* December:426-28.
    1887   Vijayanagara. *Christian College Magazine* January:502-509.

Renberg, I., and M. Wilk
    1985   Soot Particle Counting in Recent Lake Sediments: An Indirect Dating Method. *Ecological Bulletins* 37:57-67.

Renfrew, C.
    1982   Polity and Power: Interaction, Intensification and Exploitation. In *An Island Polity: The Archaeology of Exploitation in Melos*, edited by C. Renfrew and M. Wagstaff, pp. 264-89. Cambridge University Press, Cambridge.

Roberts, N.
    1989   *The Holocene: An Environmental History*. Basil Blackwell, Oxford.

Rowly-Conwy, P.
    1984a   The Laziness of the Short-Distance Hunter: The Origins of Agriculture in Western Denmark. *Journal of Anthropological Archaeology* 3:300-324.
    1984b   Slash and Burn in the Temperate European Neolithic. In *Farming Practice in British Prehistory*, edited by R. Mercer, pp. 85-96. Edinburgh University Press, Edinburgh.

Rubin, J.
    1972   Expulsion From the Garden (Boserup and Malthus). *Peasant Studies Newsletter* 1:35-38.

Ruyle, E. E.
    1987   Rethinking Marxist Anthropology. In *Perspectives in U.S. Marxist Anthropology*, edited by D. Hakken and H. Lessinger, pp. 24-56. Westview Press, Boulder.

Sachs, I.
    1966   La Notion de Surplus et son Application aux Economies Primitives. *L'homme* 6:5-18.

Sahlins, M.
    1972   *Stone Age Economics*. Aldine, Chicago.

Said, E. W.
    1978   *Orientalism*. Random House, New York.

Saletore, B. A.
    1934   *Social and Political Life in the Vijayanagara Empire (A.D. 1346- A.D. 1646)*. Paul and Company, Madras.
    1973   *Early Indian Economic History*. N. M. Tripathi Ltd., Bombay.
    1982   *Vijayanagara Art*. Sundeep, Delhi.

Saldanha, C. J.
    1984   *The Flora of Karnataka* Vol. 1. Oxford and IBH, New Delhi.

Sanders, W. T.
    1972   Population, Agricultural History, and Societal Evolution in Mesoamerica. In *Population Growth: Anthropological Implications*, edited by B. Spooner, pp. 101-153. M.I.T. Press, Cambridge.

Sanders, W. T., J. R. Parsons, & Santley, R. S.
    1979   *The Basin of Mexico*. Academic Press, New York.

Sanders, W. T., and R. Santley
    1983   A Tale of Three Cities: Energetics and Urbanization in Pre-Hispanic Central Mexico. In *Prehistoric Settlement Patterns: Essays in Honor of Gordon R. Willey*, edited by E. Z. Vogt, pp. 243-92. University of New Mexico Press and the Peabody Museum, Albuquerque.

Sankalia, H. D.
    1962   *Indian Archaeology Today*. Asia Publishing House, Bombay.

Saraswati, M. L.
   1984   *Irrigation in the Vijayanagara Empire.* Unpublished Ph.D. dissertation, Department of History, Mysore University, Mysore.
Sarmaja-Koronen, K.
   1992   Fine-Interval Pollen and Charcoal Analyses as Tracers of Early Clearance Periods in S Finland. *Acta Botanica Fennica* 146:1-75.
Schiffer, M. B.
   1972   Archaeological Context and Systemic Context. *American Antiquity* 37:156-65.
Schwartzberg, J. E.
   1992   *A Historical Atlas of South Asia.* Second Impression, Oxford University Press, New York.
Seneviratne, A.
   1989   *The Springs of Sinhala Civilization: An Illustrated Survey of Ancient Irrigation Systems of Sri Lanka.* Navrang, New Delhi.
Service, E.
   1962   *Primitive Social Organization: An Evolutionary Perspective.* Random House, New York.
Sewell, R.
   1900   *A Forgotten Empire (Vijayanagar): A Contribution to the History of India.* S. Sonnenschein and Company, London.
Sharma, R. S.
   1965   *Indian Feudalism: c. 300-1200.* University of Calcutta, Calcutta.
Sharma, R. K., and T. K. Sharma
   1990   *Textbook of Irrigation Engineering, Volume I: Irrigation and Drainage.* Oxford and IBH, New Delhi.
Sherratt, A. G.
   1973   The Interpretation of Change in European Prehistory. In *The Explanation of Culture Change*, edited by C. Renfrew, pp. 419-28. University of Pittsburgh Press, Pittsburgh.
   1981   Plough and Pastoralism: Aspects of the Secondary Products Revolution. In *Pattern of the Past*, edited by I. Hodder, G. Isaac, and N. Hammond, pp. 261-305. Cambridge University Press, Cambridge.
Siemens, A. H., and D. E. Puleston
   1972   Raised Fields and Associated Features in Southern Campeche: New Perspectives on the Lowland Maya. *American Antiquity* 37:228-39.
Simmons, I. G.
   1969a Evidence for Vegetation Changes Associated with Mesolithic Man in Britain. In *The Domestication and Exploitation of Plants and Animals*, edited by P. J. Ucko and G. W. Dimbleby, pp. 111-19. Duckworth, London.
   1969b Environment and Early Man on Dartmoor, Devon, England. *Proceedings of the Prehistoric Society* 42:203-219.
Singh, G., A. P. Kershaw, and R. Clark
   1981   Quaternary Vegetation History and Fire in Australia. In *Fire and The Australian Biota*, edited by A. M. Gill, pp. 23-54. Australian Academy of Science, Canberra.
Singh, R. L., K. N. Singh, K. N. Singh, M. S. Vishwanath, and S. N. Singh
   1971   Karnataka Plateau. In *India: A Regional Geography*, edited by R. L. Singh, pp. 791-820. National Geographic Society of India, Varanasi.
Singh, N. P.
   1988   *The Flora of Eastern Karnataka.* 2 vols. Mittal, New Delhi.
Sinopoli, C. M.
   1983   The Earthenware Pottery of Vijayanagara: Some Observations. In *Vijayanagara: Progress of Research 1979-83*, edited by M. S. Nagararaja Rao, pp. 68-74. Directorate of Archaeology and Museums, Mysore.
   1985   The Earthenware Pottery of Vijayanagara: Documentation and Interpretation. In *Vijayanagara City and Empire: New Currents of Research*, Vol. 1, edited by A. L. Dallapiccola, pp. 216-28. Franz Steiner Verlag, Wiesbaden.
   1986   *Material Patterning and Social Organization: A Study of Ceramics From Vijayanagara.* Ph.D. dissertation, Department of Anthropology, University of Michigan, Ann Arbor.
   1988   The Organization of Craft Production at Vijayanagara, South India. *American Anthropologist* 90:580-97.
   1989   Standardization and Specialization: Ceramic Production at Vijayanagara, South India. In *Old Problems, New Perspectives in the Archaeology of South Asia*, edited by J. M. Kenoyer. Wisconsin Archaeological Reports 2, Madison.
   1991a Vijayanagara Ceramics: the 1986 Field Season. In *Vijayanagara: Progress of Research 1987-88*, edited by D. V. Devaraj and C. S. Patil, pp. 97-104. Directorate of Archaeology and Museums, Mysore.
   1991b A Vijayanagara Period Road System: VMS-42, VMS-47, VMS-50. In *Vijayanagara: Progress of Research 1987-88*, edited by D. V. Devaraj and C. S. Patil, pp.70-80. Directorate of Archaeology and Museums, Mysore.
   1993   Defining a Sacred Landscape: Temple Architecture and Divine Images in the Vijayanagara Suburbs. In *South Asian Archaeology 1991*, edited by A. J. Gail and G. V. R. Mevissen, pp. 625-36. Franz Steiner Verlag, Stuttgardt.

1994 Political Choices and Economic Strategies in the Vijayanagara Empire. In *The Economic Anthropology of the State*, edited by E. M. Brumfiel, pp. 223-43. Monographs in Economic Anthropology, Vol. 11. University Press of America, Lanham, MD.

Sinopoli, C. M., and T. R. Blurton
1986 Modern Pottery Production in Rural Karnataka. In *Dimensions of Indian Art: Pupul Jayakar Seventy*, edited by L. Chandra and J. Jain, pp. 439-56. Agam Kala Prakashan, New Delhi.

Sinopoli, C. M., and K. D. Morrison
1991 The Vijayanagara Metropolitan Survey: The 1988 Season. In *Vijayanagara: Progress of Research 1987-88*, edited by D. V. Devaraj and C. S. Patil, pp.55-69. Directorate of Archaeology and Museums, Mysore.
1992 Archaeological Survey at Vijayanagara. *Research and Exploration* 8(2):237-39.
1995 Dimensions of Imperial Control: The Vijayanagara Capital. *American Anthropologist* 97:83-96.
in pr. The Vijayanagara Metropolitan Survey: the 1992 Season. In *Vijayanagara: Progress of Research*. Directorate of Archaeology and Museums, Mysore.

Sircar, D. C.
1966a *Indian Epigraphical Glossary*. Motilal Banarsidass, Delhi.
1966b *Land System and Feudalism in Ancient India*. Calcutta University Press, Calcutta.
1969 *Landlordism and Tenancy in Ancient and Medieval India as Revealed by Epigraphical Records*. Dr. Radha Kumud Mookerji Endowment Lectures. University of Lucknow, Lucknow.
1975 *Inscriptions of Asoka*. Government of India Ministry of Information and Broadcasting Publication Division, New Delhi.

Sivamohan, M. V. K.
1991 Vijayanagar Channels: A Traditional Agricultural System in Transition. In *Farmers in the Management of Irrigation Systems*, edited by K. K. Singh, pp. 53-72. Sterling, New Delhi.

Slicher Van Bath, B. H.
1963 *The Agrarian History of Western Europe A.D. 500-1850*. Arnold, London.

Smith, C. A. (editor)
1976 *Regional Analysis*. 2 Vols. Academic Press, New York.

Smith, E. A., and B. Winterhalder (editors)
1992 *Evolutionary Ecology and Human Behavior*. Aldine de Gruyter, New York.

Southall, A. W.
1956 *Alur Society*. W. Heffer, Cambridge.

Spate, O. H. K.
1954 *India and Pakistan: A General and Regional Geography*. Methuen, London.

Spencer, J. E., and G. A. Hall
1961 The Origin, Nature, and Distribution of Agricultural Terracing. *Pacific Viewpoint* 2:1-40.

Stahl, A. B.
1984 History and Critique of Investigations into Early African Agriculture. In *From Hunter to Farmers*, edited by J. D. Clark and S. A. Brandt, pp. 9-21. University of California Press, Berkeley.

Stanley, H. E. J.
1867 *A Description of the Coasts of East Africa and Malabar in the Beginning of the Sixteenth Century, by Duarte Barbosa, a Portuguese*. Translated, with notes and a preface by H. E. J. Stanley. Hakluyt Society, London.

Stein, B.
1978 Temples in Tamil Country, 1350-1750 A.D. In *South Indian Temples*, edited by B. Stein, pp. 11-45. Vikas, New Delhi.
1979 Integration of the Agrarian System of South India. In *Land Control and Social Structure in Indian History*, edited by R. E. Frykenberg, pp. 175-216. Manohar, New Delhi.
1980 *Peasant State and Society in Medieval South India*. Oxford University Press, Delhi.
1982 South India: Some General Considerations of the Region and its Early History. In *The Cambridge Economic History of India*, Vol. 1: c. 1200 - c. 1750, edited by T. Rayachaudhuri and I. Habib, pp. 14-42. Orient Longman, New Delhi.
1985 Vijayanagara and the Transition to Patrimonial Systems. In *Vijayanagara: City and Empire*, edited by A. L. Dallapiccola, pp. 73-87. Franz Steiner Verlag, Wiesbaden.
1989 *Vijayanagara*. The New Cambridge History of India, vol. 1, part 2. Cambridge University Press, Cambridge.

Stewart, O. C.
1956 Fire as the First Force Employed by Man. In *Man's Role in Changing the Face of the Earth*, edited by W. L. Thomas, pp.115-33. University of Chicago Press, Chicago.

Stockmarr, J.
1972 Tablets with Spores used in Absolute Pollen Analysis. *Pollen et Spores* 13:615-21.

Stone, G. D.
1993a Agrarian Settlement and the Spatial Disposition of Labor. In *Spatial Boundaries and Social Dynamics*, edited by A. Holl and T. Levy, pp. 25-38. International Monographs in Prehistory, Ann Arbor.
1993b Agricultural Abandonment: A Comparative Study in Historical Ecology. In *The Abandonment of Settlements and Regions: Ethnoarchaeological and Archaeological Approaches*, edited by C. Cameron and S. Tomkato, pp. 74-81. Cambridge University Press, Cambridge.

Stone, G. D., R. McC. Netting, and M. P. Stone

    1990   Seasonality, Labor Scheduling, and Agricultural Intensification in the Nigerian Savanna. *American Anthropologist* 92:7-23.

Subrahmanyam, S.
    1984   The Portuguese, the Port of Basrur, and the Rice Trade, 1600-50. *Indian Economic and Social History Review* 21:433-62.
    1990   *The Political Economy of Commerce: Southern India, 1500-1650.* Cambridge University Press, Cambridge.

Swain, A. M.
    1973   A History of Fire and Vegetation in Northeastern Minnesota as Recorded in Lake Sediments. *Quaternary Research* 3:386-96.

Tadulingam, C., and C. Venkatanaranyana
    1932   *A Handbbok of Some South Indian Weeds.* Government Press, Madras.

Tauber, H.
    1965   Differential Pollen Dispersion and the Interpretation of Pollen Diagrams. *Geologiske Undersogelse* 89:1-70.

Temple, R. C. (editor)
    1928   *The Itinerary of Ludovico de Varthema of Bologna from 1502 to 1508, as translated from the Original Italian Edition of 1510 by John Winter Jones in 1863 for the Hakluyt Society.* Hakluyt Society, London.

Thackston, W. M.
    1989   Kamaluddin Abdul-Razzaq Samargandi Mission to Calicut and Vijayanagara. In *A Century of Princes: Sources on Timurid History and Art*, edited and translated by W. M. Thackston, pp. 299-322. Aga Khan Library for Islamic Architecture, Cambridge.

Thapar, R.
    1961   *Asoka and the Decline of the Mauryas.* Oxford University Press.

Thomas, D. H.
    1975   Nonsite Sampling in Archaeology: Up the Creek Without a Site? In *Sampling in Archaeology*, edited J. W. Mueller, pp. 61-81. University of Arizona Press, Tucson.

Tilak, S. T.
    1989   *Airborne Pollen and Fungal Spores.* Vajayanti Prakashan, Aurangabad.

Tolonen, K.
    1986   Charred Particle Analysis. In *The Handbook of Holocene Paleoecology and Paleohydrology*, edited by B.E. Berglund, pp. 485-96. John Wiley and Sons, New York.

Tringham, R. E., and D. Kristic
    1989   Conclusion: Selevac in the Wider Context of European Prehistory. In *Selevac: A Neolithic Village in Yugoslavia*, edited by R. E. Tringham and D. Krstic, pp. 567-616. Monumenta Archaeologica 15. UCLA Institute of Archaeology, Los Angeles.

Tripathi, R. C. (editor)
    1987   *Indian Archaeology 1984-85 —A Review.* Archaeological Survey of India, New Delhi.

Tskuda, M., and E. S. Deevey
    1967   Pollen Analysis from Four Lakes in the Southern Maya Area of Guatemala and El Salvador. In *Quaternary Paleoecology*, edited by E. J. Cushing and H. E. Wright, Jr., pp. 303-332. Yale University Press, New Haven.

Tschudy, R. H.
    1969   Relationships of Palynomorphs to Sedimentation. In *Aspects of Palynology*, edited by R. H. Tschudy and R. A. Scott, pp. 79-96. Wiley, New York.

Turner, B. L. II
    1974   Prehistoric Intensive Agriculture in the Maya Lowlands. *Science* 185:118-24.
    1992   Comments, In *Gardens of Prehistory*, edited by T.W. Killion, pp. 263-73. University of Alabama Press, Tuscaloosa.

Turner, B. L., R. Q. Hanham, and A. V. Portararo
    1977   Population Pressure and Agricultural Intensity. *Annals of the Association of American Geographers* 67:384-96.

Venkata Ramanayya, N.
    1929   *Kampli and Vijayanagar.* Christian Literature Society, Madras.
    1933   *Vijayanagara: Origin of the City and Empire.* University of Madras, Madras.
    1935   *Studies in the History of the Third Dynasty of Vijayanagara.* University of Madras, Madras.

Verghese, A.
    1989   *Religious Traditions in the City of Vijayanagara prior to 1565 A.D. (Based on a Study of Monuments).* Unpublished Ph.D. dissertation, Department of History, University of Bombay.

Vivian, R. G.
    1974   Conservation and Diversion: Water Control Systems in the Anasazi Southwest. In *Irrigation's Impact on Society*, edited by T. E. Downing and McG. Gibson, pp. 95-112. Anthropological Papers of the University of Arizona 23, Tucson.

Vishnu-Mittre
    1972   Problems and Prospects of Quaternary Palynology in India. In *Proceedings of the Seminar of Paleopalynology and Indian Stratigraphy, Calcutta 1971*, edited by A. K. Ghosh et al., pp. 348-56. Univ. Grants Commission and Dept. of Botany, University of Calcutta, Calcutta.
    1985   The Uses of Wild Plants and the Process of Domestication in the Indian Subcontinent. In *Advances in*

Indo-Pacific Prehistory, edited by V. N. Misra and P. Bellwood, pp. 281-92. Oxford and IBH, New Delhi.

Vishwanath, K.
    1985   *The Agrarian System Under the Vijayanagara Empire*. Unpublished Ph.D. dissertation, Department of History, Mysore University, Mysore.

Von Thunen, J. H.
    1966   *The Isolated State*. Pergamon Press, Oxford.

Waddell, E.
    1972   *The Mound Builders: Agricultural Practices, Environment, and Society in the Central Highlands of New Guinea*. University of Washington Press, Seattle.

Waddington, J. C. B.
    1969   A Stratigraphic Record of the Pollen Influx to a Lake in the Big Woods of Minnesota. *Geological Society of America Special Paper* 123:263-82.

Wagoner, P. B.
    1991   Architecture and Mythic Space at Hemakuta Hill: A Preliminary Report. In *Vijayanagara Progress of Research 1984-1987*, edited by D. V. Devaraj and C. S. Patil, pp. 142-48. Directorate of Archaeology and Museums, Mysore.
    1993   *Tidings of the King: A Translation and Ethnohistorical Analysis of the Rayavacakamu*. University of Hawaii Press, Honolulu.

Wallerstein, I.
    1974   *The Modern World System*. Vol. 1. Academic Press, New York.

Wandsnider, L.
    1989   *Long Term Land Use, Formation Processes, and the Structure of the Archaeological Landscape: A Case Study from Southwestern Wyoming*. Unpublished Ph.D. dissertation, Department of Anthropology, University of New Mexico.

Webb, T. III, S. Howe, R. H. W. Bradshaw, and K. Heide
    1981   Estimating Plant Abundances from Pollen Percentages: the Use of Regression Analysis. *Review of Palaeobotany and Palynology* 34: 269-300.

Webb, T. III, R. A. Laseski, and J. C. Bernabo
    1978   Sensing Vegetational Patterns with Pollen Data: Choosing the Data. *Ecology* 59:1151-63.

Webster, C. C., and P. N. Wilson
    1966   *Agriculture in the Tropics*. Longman, London.

Wheatley, P.
    1965   Agricultural Terracing: Discursive Scolia on Recent Papers on Agricultural Terracing and Related Matters Pertaining to Northern Indochina and Neighboring Areas. *Pacific Viewpoint* 6:123-44.

Wheeler, J. T.
    1974   *Early Travels in India, 16th and 17th Centuries: Reprints of Rare and Curious Narratives of Old Travellers in India in the Sixteenth and Seventeenth Centuries*. Deep Publications, Delhi. Originally Published 1864, Englishman Press, Calcutta.

Wilk, R. R. (editor)
    1989   *The Household Economy: Reconsidering the Domestic Mode of Production*. Westview Press, Boulder.

Wilk, R. R., and R. McC. Netting
    1984   Households: Changing Forms and Functions. In *Households: Comparative and Historical Studies of the Domestic Group*, edited by R. McC. Netting, R. Wilk, and E. J. Arnould, pp. 1-18. University of California Press, Berkeley.

Wilkinson, T. J.
    1982   The Definition of Ancient Manured Zones by Means of Extensive Sherd-Sampling Techniques. *Journal of Field Archaeology* 9:321-33.
    1989   Extensive Sherd Scatters and Land-Use Intensity: Some Recent Results. *Journal of Field Archaeology* 16:31-46.

Williams, B. J.
    1989   Contact Period Rural Overpopulation in the Basin of Mexico: Carrying-Capacity Models Tested with Documentary Data. *American Antiquity* 54:715-32.

Winkler, M. J.
    1985   Charcoal Analysis for Paleoenvironmental Interpretation: A Chemical Assay. *Quaternary Research* 23:313-26.

Winterhalder, B., and E. A. Smith (editors)
    1981   *Hunter-Gatherer Foraging Strategies: Ethnographic and Archaeological Analyses*. University of Chicago Press, Chicago.

Wiseman, F. M.
    1978   Agricultural and Historical Ecology of the Maya Lowlands. In *Pre-Hispanic Maya Agriculture*, edited by P. D. Harrison and B. L. Turner, pp. 63-116. University of New Mexico Press, Albuquerque.

Wittfogel, K.
    1955   Developmental Aspects of Hydraulic Societies. In *Irrigation Civilizations: A Comparative Study*, edited by J.

H. Steward. Organization of the American States, Washington D.C.
1957 *Oriental Despotism.* Yale University Press, New Haven.

Wobst, H. M.
1974 Boundary Conditions for Paleolithic Social Systems: A Simulation Approach. *American Antiquity* 39:147-78.
1978 The Archaeo-Ethnology of Hunter-Gatherers or the Tyranny of the Ethnographic Record in Archaeology. *American Antiquity* 43:303-309.

Wolf, E. R.
1982 *Europe and the People Without History.* University of California Press, Berkeley.

Wolpert, S. A.
1989 *A New History of India.* 3rd edition. Oxford University Press, Delhi.

Wood, W. R., and D. L. Johnson
1978 A Survey of Disturbance Processes in Archaeological Site Formation. In *Advances in Archaeological Method and Theory, Volume 1*, edited by M. B. Schiffer, pp.315-81. Academic Press, New York.

Wright, H. E.
1967 The Use of Surface Samples in Quaternary Pollen Analysis. *Review of Palaeobotany and Palynology* 2:321-330.

Yegna Narayan Aiyer, A. K.
1980 *Field Crops of India.* Bappco Publications, Bangalore.

Zeuner, F. E.
1960 On the Origins of the Cinder Mounds of the Bellary District, India. *Bulletin of the London University Institute of Archaeology* 2:37-44.

Zipf, G. K.
1949 *Human Behavior and the Principle of Least Effort: An Introduction to Human Ecology.* Addison-Wesley Press, Cambridge.

Zvelebil, M.
1986 Mesolithic Prelude and Neolithic Revolution. In *Hunters in Transition*, edited by M. Zvelibil, pp. 5-16. Cambridge University Press, Cambridge.

THE ARCHAEOLOGICAL RESEARCH FACILITY

UNIVERSITY OF CALIFORNIA AT BERKELEY

The Archaeological Research Facility was founded as the California Archaeological Survey in 1948 by Professor Robert Heizer. The present name was adopted in 1961 as the University of California at Berkeley's research took on a more international scope. Today the Archaeological Research Facility is an organized research unit of the University reporting to the office of the Vice Chancellor for Research. The Facility serves the needs of twenty-six faculty and associates from the departments of Anthropology, Art History, Classics, Geography, Near Eastern Studies, and the Graduate Group in Ancient and Mediterranean Archaeology, as well as the needs of allied specialists in the physical and biological sciences. Current fieldwork by associates of the Facility includes projects in North America, Mesoamerica, Europe, the Mediterranean, and Oceania. In addition to sponsoring and facilitating archaeological field and laboratory research, the Facility publishes the results of such work in the **Contributions** and other series. Priority is given to publication of research carried out by Facility associates, although manuscripts from other scholars may be considered.

For a complete listing of the Archaeological Research Facility's publications, please write to the University of California, Administrator, Archaeological Research Facility, 232 Kroeber Hall, Berkeley, CA 94720.

DIRECTOR Margaret Conkey   ADMINISTRATOR Hillari Allen   EDITOR Tanya Smith